China's Asia

Triangular Dynamics since the Cold War

Lowell Dittmer
University of California, Berkeley

ROWMAN & LITTLEFIELD
Lanham • Boulder • New York • London

Published by Rowman & Littlefield
An imprint of The Rowman & Littlefield Publishing Group, Inc.
4501 Forbes Boulevard, Suite 200, Lanham, Maryland 20706
www.rowman.com

Unit A, Whitacre Mews, 26-34 Stannary Street, London SE11 4AB, United Kingdom

British Library Cataloguing in Publication Information Available

Library of Congress Cataloging-in-Publication Data
Names: Dittmer, Lowell, author.
Title: China's Asia : triangular dynamics since the Cold War / Lowell Dittmer.
Description: Lanham : Rowman & Littlefield, [2018] | Series: Asia in world politics | Includes bibliographical references and index.
Identifiers: LCCN 2017047120 (print) | LCCN 2017047573 (ebook) | ISBN 9781442237575 (ebook) | ISBN 9781442237551 | ISBN 9781442237551(cloth ; alk. paper) | ISBN 9781442237568 (pbk. ; alk. paper)
Subjects: LCSH: China—Foreign relations—Asia. | Asia—Foreign relations—China. | China—Foreign relations—1976–
Classification: LCC DS33.4.C5 (ebook) | LCC DS33.4.C5 D58 2018 (print) | DDC 327.5105—dc23
LC record available at https://lccn.loc.gov/2017047120

∞ ™ The paper used in this publication meets the minimum requirements of American National Standard for Information Sciences Permanence of Paper for Printed Library Materials, ANSI/NISO Z39.48-1992.

Printed in the United States of America

To Helen
love of my life

Contents

Acknowledgments

I first became interested in the logic of the strategic triangle in the 1970s, following the American opening to China, and used it to reconceptualize the shifting relationships between the United States, China, and the Soviet Union. I owe much to Professor Wu Yu-Shan in helping me work out the implications of triangular logic, particularly in shifting the model to the pivotal US relationships with Taiwan and China at the end of the Cold War. Many others have also found the triangular schema useful—I have learned from Tom Gottlieb, Ilpyang Kim, James Hsiung, Tom Robinson, and Gerald Segal, inter alia. The ambitious notion of applying the schema to the relationship between the United States and the Asia-Pacific region as a whole I owe to an offhand comment by Professor David Zweig. Of course, none of these scholars bears the slightest responsibility for what I have done with the idea. Taking on such a broad swath presents numerous complications given the wide diversity of Asian nation-states involved and their relationships to the two dominant powers of the region. Whether or to what extent I have succeeded in meeting these challenges is for you, dear reader, to decide.

I am indebted to the East Asian Institute of the National University of Singapore for two stints there as a visiting research professor in the fall of 2011 and the summer of 2016. I benefited from my exchange of information and views with Wang Gungwu, Zheng Yongnian, Lance Gore, Chen Kang, and many others. The first vague preview of the plan for the book was presented at the Academia Sinica in Taipei in the spring of 2014 amid the Sunflower Movement's occupation of the legislature. I wish to thank the academy and its chair, Wu Yu-Shan, for hosting me as a visiting research professor and for the fruitful conversations I had with the very distinguished scholars assembled there, including especially Wu Yu-Shan, Chu Yun-Han, Dalton Lin, Leng Tse-Kang, Tsai Chung-min, and Chang Liao Nien-Cheng.

On the Korean chapter, I benefited from conversations with Sohn Yul and Steven Denney at Seoul's Yonsei University in spring 2012. I wish to thank George Breslauer, Vitaly Kozyrev, and Jim McAdams for reading and offering astute suggestions on chapter 3. I am profoundly indebted to the outside reader in the world who made copious subtle, perceptive, and detailed comments throughout. It is a great honor to me to be part of the publication series of my old friend and esteemed colleague Samuel S. Kim. And I was fortunate to have the legendary Susan McEachern as editor; I appreciate her tireless encouragement and advice. Finally, I am indebted to the Center for Chinese Studies at the University of California at Berkeley for financial support.

The title, "China's Asia," may be a bit jarring—or perhaps not jarring at all. He Yafei, ex–vice foreign minister of the PRC, announced in September 2017 that "we have entered a post–American Era," meaning that the so-called Pax Americana and American century is over, and China stands prepared to accept the chimeric wreath of global leadership. Is Asia ready to follow? Asia's fate has shifted momentously with decolonization and modernization and will continue to change with China's amazing rise. "If a doctor predicts that his patient will die presently," wrote Joseph Schumpeter, "this does not mean that he desires it." But my title is meant neither as celebration of a new status quo nor a jeremiad at the passing of the old one. The point is merely to describe and analyze as clearly as possible, *sine ira et studio*, the thrust of the prevailing trends as they appear to me at the time. Criticism is welcome: Dittmer@berkeley.edu.

Abbreviations

ABM	antiballistic missile
ACFTA	ASEAN-China Free Trade Agreement
ADB	Asian Development Bank
ADIZ	air defense identification zone
ADMM Plus	ASEAN Defense Ministers Meeting plus defense ministers from the ARF countries
AEC	ASEAN Economic Community
AFC	Asian financial crisis (1997–1998)
AIIB	Asian Infrastructure Investment Bank
ANZUS	Australia, New Zealand, United States Security Treaty
APEC	Asia-Pacific Economic Cooperation (forum)
APT	ASEAN Plus Three
ARF	ASEAN Regional Forum (the ten ASEAN members plus representatives from relevant other Asian countries)
ASEAN	Association of Southeast Asian Nations
BRICS	Brazil, Russia, India, China, and South Africa (an association of major emerging nations)
CAFTA	China-ASEAN Free Trade Agreement
CAR	Central Asian republic
CCP	Chinese Communist Party
CCTV	China Central Television

CDB	China Development Bank
CIS	Commonwealth of Independent States
COC	Code of Conduct (for the conduct of nations in the South China Sea)
Comecon	Council for Mutual Economic Assistance
CPEC	China-Pakistan Economic Corridor
CPPCC	Chinese People's Political Consultative Conference
CPSU	Communist Party of the Soviet Union
CSTO	Collective Security Treaty Organization
DOC	Declaration on the Conduct of Parties in the South China Sea
DPRK	Democratic People's Republic of Korea
DTTI	Defense Technology and Trade Initiative
EAS	East Asia Summit (meeting)
EEU	Eurasian Economic Union (headquarters Moscow)
EEZ	exclusive economic zone
EU	European Union (headquarters Brussels)
FDI	foreign direct investment
FIE	foreign-invested enterprise
FONOP	freedom of navigation operation
FTAAP	Free Trade Area of the Asia-Pacific
GDP	gross domestic product
GFC	global financial crisis (2008)
IAEA	International Atomic Energy Agency
ICBM	intercontinental ballistic missile
IGO	international governmental organization
IMF	International Monetary Fund
JASA	Japan-America Security Alliance
JASDF	Japan Air Self-Defense Force
JDZ	joint development zone
JMSDF	Japan Maritime Self-Defense Force
KMT	Kuomintang (ruling party in mainland China from 1928 to its retreat to Taiwan in 1949, and thereafter in Taiwan)

MFN	most-favored nation
MIRVs	multiple independently targetable reentry vehicles
MNC	multinational corporation
MOU	memorandum of understanding
MSR	Maritime Silk Road
NDB	New Development Bank
NGO	nongovernmental organization
NIC	newly industrialized country (refers to Taiwan, Hong Kong, Singapore, and South Korea, though not all are countries)
NPC	National People's Congress
NPT	Non-Proliferation Treaty
NSG	Nuclear Suppliers' Group
OBOR	One Belt, One Road (project); also referred to as BRI (Belt and Road Initiative)
ODA	official developmental aid
PBC	People's Bank of China
PCA	Permanent Court of Arbitration (an arbitral tribunal established at The Hague under UNCLOS to resolve disputes among members)
PLA	People's Liberation Army
PLAN	People's Liberation Army Navy
PPP	purchasing power parity
PRC	People's Republic of China
RCEP	Regional Comprehensive Economic Partnership (multilateral FTA initiated by ASEAN and being negotiated among sixteen potential Asian member nations)
ROA	the rest of Asia (i.e., all but China and the United States)
ROC	Republic of China (on Taiwan)
ROK	Republic of Korea
SAARC	South Asian Association for Regional Cooperation
SALT	Strategic Arms Limitation Talks
SCO	Shanghai Cooperation Organization
SDF	Self-Defense Forces (Japan)

SDR	Special Drawing Rights
SLBM	submarine-launched ballistic missile
SOE	state-owned enterprise
SREB	Silk Road Economic Belt
TAC	Treaty of Amity and Cooperation (among ASEAN and ARF members)
THAAD	terminal high-altitude area defense (missile system)
TMD	theater missile defense
TPP	Trans-Pacific Partnership (multilateral FTA negotiated among twelve Pacific Rim nations)
UNCLOS	United Nations Convention on the Law of the Sea (UN agreement finalized in 1994 on the rules of the game in deciding maritime rights)
UNSC	United Nations Security Council
WTO	World Trade Organization

Chapter One

China's Asia?

Why "China's Asia"?[1] If the South China Sea is China's "since ancient times," surely so is Asia. Is China not Asia's dominant nation-state? Does it not boast its largest economy and most powerful military? It is the largest manufacturer and trading state in the world, the largest economy as well, by purchasing power parity (PPP)—and soon enough, by widely accepted extrapolations, in nominal gross domestic product (GDP). It still has the largest population in the world, though India's is growing faster and may soon overtake it. Aside from its high historical level of civilization, China's brilliant scientific and technological contributions have been amply documented.[2] It has historically been dominant in Asia, receiving (and reciprocating) tribute from many neighbors, sometimes punishing them in its absence, as the history of Vietnam, Burma, Korea, even Russia attests. True, it is not the largest Asian country: Russia, even limited to Asian Russia, remains the largest country in the world. But most Russians do not live in Asia and are not ethnically or culturally Asian. And it is not the first Asian great power: Japan was first to industrialize, to China's bitter rue, first to use its modernity to try forcibly to integrate the rest of Asia into its sway. But Japan has had its day.

Today, China is once again the "central kingdom" with land borders abutting fourteen Asian countries and maritime boundaries adjoining six others. Beginning in the middle of the nineteenth century, China suffered a "century of humiliation" (*bainian guochi*) during which its domestic political system decayed and its sovereignty fell prey to Western (and Japanese) imperialism. China was poor and weak, unable to defend itself in the post-Westphalian world of predatory nation-states. Still, unlike most of its neighbors, China was never colonized, though it was the victim of what Sun Yat-sen called "semi-colonialism," ceding territory and power via a series of unequal

1

treaties and tacitly recognized spheres of influence. The sense of having overcome this embarrassing setback has lent a sense of vindication to China's current "rejuvenation." Now it is back, and it expects, and demands, due deference. And it usually gets it. The Association of Southeast Asian Nations (ASEAN) has been so deferential it dare not take public issue with many of China's assertions lest China be offended.

China is well on its way to the realization of the old China Dream—but wait! It is not quite there yet. Even after finally having stood up from the ruins of a protracted, seesaw revolution–cum–liberation–civil war followed by an uncharted journey from socialism to state-guided market socialism, China finds its way to its prized Asian leadership role frustrated. It is blocked, in Chinese eyes, above all by the United States, in what has become a new pattern in Asia. The United States is, after all, a newcomer from the historical perspective. Most challenges to China had come from the west or the north historically: the Mongols, the Manchu, the Xiongnu, the Toba Turks. After subjugating indigenous tribes and penetrating to the west coast of the North American continent, the United States occupied Hawaii, Guam, and the Philippines, and (among other imperialist powers) imposed unequal treaties on China, enjoyed opium profits, and engaged in lucrative galleon trade. But what most deeply engaged the Americans in Asia was war: world war with Japan, followed by limited wars in Korea and Vietnam. Excluded after the Korean War by a US blockade and sincerely convinced of the exclusive international validity of a Marxist-Leninist developmental pattern, China's first-generation leadership leaned to one side, fought alongside North Korea in its war against South Korea and the United Nations, actively supported insurgent movements (wars of national liberation) throughout Asia, and provided support for revolutionary movements throughout the Third World.[3]

US opposition to this crusade was anticipated, but not the opposition of many of China's postcolonial neighbors, nor the self-destructive ideological cleavage within the communist camp itself. Despite China's continuing ideological attachment to Marxism-Leninism, the ideological dispute with the Soviet Union over the correct interpretation of that doctrine suffused China's foreign policy, not only bilaterally but also internationally. In Asia the two engaged in "proxy" contests arousing China's dread of being encircled by enemies—thus while the Soviet Union supported Vietnam after its reunification, China supported Cambodia against Vietnam, the mujahideen against the Soviet-supported regime in Afghanistan, and Pakistan against India. The United States proved a resilient and skillful coordinator of the international counterrevolutionary coalition, however, exacerbating the Sino-Soviet split by favoring one against the other, surviving several eagerly awaited political-economic declines. At the end of the day, China's attempt during the Cold War to lead Asia to a bright communist future via violent revolutionary liberation could boast few success stories and polarized much of the region against it. The end of the Cold War emancipated China from this self-abnegating export of revolution.

In Asia, the Cold War really had two endings. The first was in 1971–72, when China's triumphant entry into the United Nations and the Nixon visit to China ended the Sino-American confrontation. Though it was narrowly limited to the strategic dimension while proxy wars and the contest with the Soviet "evil empire" continued, now complicated by Chinese interests, it ended the US economic blockade and laid the basis for strategic coordination. The Cold War's second and more definitive ending was in 1989–91, when a series of mass uprisings beginning at Tiananmen in May 1989 ricocheted through Eastern Europe, bringing about the extinction of Leninist dictatorships in all but four countries in the world and an apparent end of global bipolarity. Both endings had a profound impact on China and its relationship with Asia. The first ending coincided with the Nixon Doctrine, first enunciated in 1969 to justify Vietnamization but then applied more broadly to US military commitments in Asia. Hoping to avoid being trapped in further unaffordable proxy wars, the United States called on Asian countries to defend themselves, promising to sell them whatever weaponry they needed (US weapons sales boomed). The United States withdrew from Vietnam after negotiating a peace agreement in 1973 (fecklessly watching it fall two years later) and cut 20,000 troops in Korea, reducing its Asian forces from 130,000 to 100,000 troops. This withdrawal was based on an informal understanding that China would not take advantage of the US drawdown, as negotiated in 1972 in Beijing. Indeed, while continuing to uphold its ideology of international revolution, China was too convulsed in its own Cultural Revolution at the time to pursue new revolutionary initiatives abroad. Although Chinese support of the Khmer Rouge in Cambodia and White Flag guerrillas in Burma and the Philippine insurgency continued at a modest level until at least 2016, no more dominoes would fall to communism after Vietnam (which promptly turned against Beijing, deeming the Nixon-Mao rapprochement a betrayal). Still, the long-term implication of the Nixon Doctrine was to create a power vacuum in Asia for others to fill. The terrorist attacks in New York and Washington in 2001 prolonged that, transfixing Washington in the global war on terror in the Middle East for the next decade and beyond.

The second ending of the Cold War in 1989–91 eliminated China's foremost national security threat, the Soviet Union, from its power balance, facilitating postcommunist Sino-Russian détente and allowing Beijing to redeploy military forces from its northern frontier to the east coast fronting Taiwan, Japan, and Southeast Asia. At the same time the collapse of the communist bloc left China ideologically almost alone in the world, while the use of armed force to quell a protracted but unarmed protest movement before international television at Tiananmen had a distinct—if temporary—chilling effect on China's relations with the United States and other economically advanced countries that, at the time, composed China's major export market and source of high-tech imports and technology. It was under these circumstances that China rediscovered the strategic and economic value of Asia.

During the Cold War, China had been strategically preoccupied with the great powers that alone had the capability to threaten China's national security (particularly the two superpowers). China's post-Mao shift of foreign policy priorities from permanent revolution to economic modernization gave Asia greater relevance. While the industrialized West imposed trade sanctions after Tiananmen, China's Asian neighbors proved more understanding of China's growing concern with domestic stability and responded avidly to Beijing's introduction of liberalized trade and foreign investment rules. In 1994, China devalued its currency, becoming an export-oriented growth economy like Japan and the Asian newly industrialized countries (NICs) before it, and geographic proximity made Asia economically very useful. Beginning with the Plaza Accord in 1985 when Japan revalued the yen, Japan's corporate sector began to relocate entire value-added production chains to South Korea, China, and Southeast Asia. But in the 1990s, while Japan slipped into prolonged economic stagnation after its asset bubble burst, China became the ideal haven for foreign direct investment (FDI) and transshipment to developed consumer markets. Taiwan, the Philippines, Thailand, South Korea, Singapore, and Malaysia became major suppliers of China's industrial juggernaut, relegating Japan, the traditional regional trading hub, to secondary status. Importing raw materials from the less developed countries and intermediate components from Japan and the NICs, China flooded Western markets with inexpensive finished products. Between 1992 and 2006, Chinese exports of finished products to East Asian countries fell from 55 percent to 26.5 percent of its total exports as China shifted exports to the United States and Europe. Although processing trade now accounts for a declining share of China's total trade, declining from 49 percent (55 percent of all exports and 42 percent of all imports) in 2000 to 39 percent in 2010 (47 percent of all exports and 30 percent of all imports), it still remains significant. Since 2005, China has become Asia's most important trade hub, both in terms of exports and imports, and with the realization of the ASEAN-China Free Trade Agreement (ACFTA) in 2010, it was the largest trade partner of Korea, Japan, and most of ASEAN, as well as the second-largest investor in ASEAN (after the United States).

The Cold War's end emancipated China in two ways. The collapse of the Soviet Union and reconciliation with the chronic Soviet (now Russian) threat facilitated a redeployment of military forces and, more important, strategic imagination from the northern frontier to new openings on its southeastern coast. Meanwhile, the end of the Cultural Revolution with the death of Mao Zedong, its instigator and champion, allowed Deng Xiaoping to alleviate the CCP's ideological dogmatism and take a more flexible approach to Asia. In the early 1990s, China countered a potentially dangerous wave of disinvestment by the advanced democracies on human rights grounds with a liberalization of its rules on incoming FDI, resulting in a big influx of investments from Japan, Korea, Taiwan, and Southeast Asia. And China took an increasingly constructive approach to multilateral institution building in the 1990s by joining the ASEAN Regional Forum (ARF), the Asia-Pacific Economic Cooperation (APEC) forum, the Asian Development Bank (ADB), and the East Asian Summit (EAS); setting up the Shanghai Cooperation Organization (SCO); and helping construct ASEAN Plus Three (APT). The breakthrough in the region was achieved during the Asian financial crisis (AFC, 1997–99) when China gave desperately needed financial aid to crisis-stricken Southeast Asian neighbors and refrained from devaluing the yuan again. Based on Deng Xiaoping's "24-character expression" exemplified by the phrase *tao guang yang hui* (hide your light, nourish obscurity), in the 2000s China focused on burnishing its "soft power" or *huayu quan* with rhetoric emphasizing "peaceful rise/development" and a "harmonious world," and launching Confucius Institutes throughout the region amid a diplomatic charm campaign. Despite the impact of the global financial crisis (GFC) on China's export markets in 2009, the first decade of the 2000s boasted the highest GDP growth in China's modern history.

But beginning around 2008 a shift in China's Asia policy became perceptible. China seemed to have decided that the conciliatory peaceful rise/peaceful development approach pursued the previous decade had outlived its utility and embarked on a more assertive campaign to gain actual control of the sizable portions of the East and South China Seas over which it had long claimed sovereignty.[4] The reasons for this shift are complex and myriad. In 2008 the first Chinese Olympics were held in Beijing, in 2009 the sixty-year anniversary of liberation was celebrated with a full military parade through the streets of Beijing, and in 2010 the International Shanghai Expo showcased China's economic achievements.[5] At the elite level, at the Seventeenth Party Congress in November 2007 Communist Party veteran and strong reform advocate Zeng Qinghong retired.[6] Perhaps even more significant, two new members were elevated to the Politburo Standing Committee in October 2007: Li Keqiang and Xi Jinping. As Xi unexpectedly ranked above Li in the elite balloting, he was designated heir apparent to Hu Jintao. Xi also gained the top-ranking membership of the Communist Party's Central Secretariat, and at the Eleventh National People's Congress (NPC) in March 2008 he was elected vice president of the People's Republic of China (PRC). He also became president of the Central Party School in Beijing and, most important, in 2010 was appointed vice chair of the Central Military Commission

(CMC). Xi, vaunting his military experience as former secretary for then CMC secretary-general Geng Biao plus his wife's background as People's Liberation Army (PLA) entertainer (and major-general), placed top priority on leadership of the military as the ultimate base of political power, as Deng Xiaoping had done before him; hence, he was inclined to appeal to the PLA's more hawkish strategic proclivities. Though he did not initiate China's assertive stance, he reinforced it upon his accession, convinced that the Soviet Union had collapsed because (as he put it in December 2012) "nobody was man enough to stand up and resist."

China's foreign policy behavior had been up to this point in time deferential (sometimes grudgingly) to what Americans like to call the "rules-based international order," but when that order began to exhibit signs of decline, Beijing began to reassess its position. The GFC that began with the bursting of the US housing bubble in 2008 inflicted a deep and protracted recession on the advanced capitalist democracies, puncturing faith in the "Washington consensus." Beijing survived the crisis with a US$586 billion stimulus package of loans to state-owned enterprises (SOEs), salvaging the Chinese economy from all but a one-year dip in growth. This had a major differentiating impact on the two economies and concomitantly on the world power balance. In 2007, before the crash, US GDP was US$14.48 trillion, compared to China's $3.49 trillion; in 2014 US GDP was $16.77 trillion while China's was $9.24 trillion. In other words, China's GDP rose from a mere 24 percent of US GDP to 55 percent in a mere seven years. China surpassed Japan in GDP in 2010 and, by 2015, was more than twice as large (China: $10.4 trillion; Japan: $4.12 trillion). China's GDP was now also ten times the size of Russia's, nearly five times larger than India's (4.66 times richer in nominal terms, 2.20 times in purchasing power parity [PPP], as of 2015), and more than four times larger than the combined GDP of the ten ASEAN countries. Doubling its GDP every seven years or so, the country's share of global GDP rose from just under 4 percent in 1978 to 18 percent in 2015 (while its share of world population declined slightly, falling from 22 percent to 19 percent). The PRC's military spending, less than $10 billion in 1990, grew to more than $129.4 billion by 2014, second only to that of the United States and accounting for 9.8 percent of total global military expenditures.[7] It was certainly plausible to infer from such figures that the old Western order (led by the United States) was in terminal decline while China's rise was inexorable.

This confidence first became visible when high-ranking Chinese military officers toward the end of the decade began expounding their indignant (and not yet officially endorsed) views of the international situation to the media. When the United Nations Commission on the Limits of the Continental Shelf set a 2009 deadline for submitting claims for extended continental shelves beyond the two-hundred-nautical-mile exclusive economic zone (EEZ) limit,

Malaysia and Vietnam were first to submit a joint claim. China immediately submitted its own sweeping counterclaim, based on a map first outlined by the Chinese Nationalist government in 1947. That claim was not new, but China was now much stronger than its rival claimants and displayed greater determination to enforce its claim. This upset neighboring states, particularly those with which China's territorial claims overlapped. It also disturbed the United States, which in 2010 announced that it had a national interest in freedom of navigation and urged that the conflict be settled peaceably among disputants. Great power intervention complicated the dispute from China's perspective and was most unwelcome. China's frontline rivals (Vietnam and the Philippines) preferred multilateral negotiation of the dispute via ASEAN to reduce China's asymmetrical bilateral advantage; but China refused, pointing out that ASEAN per se had no territorial claims at all, and concerted to block any multilateral consensus impeding its claims. Bilateral talks failed to bridge the sovereignty issue or negotiate workable arrangements for joint development. This is not the first time the issue had surfaced, but in previous cases, it would have been shelved at this point without resolution. But China persisted undeterred, thanks to Xi's strong leadership. Avoiding for the most part the use of lethal violence, China's coast guard and fisheries police showed both skill and muscle in moving China's de facto control incrementally forward, unilaterally proclaiming an air defense identification zone (ADIZ) over the East China Sea in 2013, detaining fishing boats, cutting oil exploration cables, placing their deep-sea drilling platform in Vietnam's EEZ, pushing the Philippines out of Scarborough Shoal, and finally dredging sand from the adjoining seabed to expand the seven South China Sea islets it occupies by some 2,300 acres to accommodate ports, lighthouses, and air strips—sometimes anti-aircraft batteries as well.

Thus, China's rise has offered not only lucrative economic opportunities but also the threat of an ambitious maritime territorial expansion thrusting its neighbors into a subordinate and economically dependent position. Both opportunity and threat are likewise evident in China's One Belt, One Road initiative first introduced in 2013, which has been compared to a super Marshall Plan in its vast economic and political scope. In sum, China's vigorous expansionist thrust offered both profitable economic opportunities to its neighbors and the potential intrusion of foreign fishing boat fleets, oil derricks, and powerful air and naval assets off their shores.

The response of various Asian neighbors to China's two-pronged thrust outward has varied depending on their jeopardized stakes and perceived opportunities but has been generally characterized as "hedging." To define it first in terms of what it is not, "hedging" is a policy that is neither "balancing" nor "bandwagoning." "Bandwagoning," or complying with rather than resisting the *force majeure*, takes advantage of the rewards offered by the rising hegemon at the risk of sacrificing more concessions than it might otherwise prefer (in this case, access to the natural resources in respective near seas). "Balancing" entails resisting the larger power's encroachments, either with larger military budgets (internal balancing) or by forming offsetting coalitions with other threatened states (external balancing). There has been some evidence of both: Cambodia and Laos have tended to bandwagon, while Vietnam and the Philippines (until 2016) have been more inclined to balance. But a recent comparison of budgets indicates that China is clearly winning any Asian arms race. Given China's heavily asymmetric endowments of population and aggregate GDP, balancing seems heroically unrealistic. Moreover, most Asian states have become deeply enmeshed in economic relations with China; the latter has lately demonstrated a willingness to suspend trade for political reasons, and they would rather not antagonize a major trade partner. Russia, having at long last settled its border dispute with China and enjoying cross-cutting ties with China rivals India and Vietnam, opted to avoid involvement in maritime territorial disputes until recently. But in the September 2016 meeting of the Group of 20 in Hangzhou, where Putin was given a red carpet welcome as the host's guest of honor, he joined China in repudiating the Permanent Court of Arbitration's decision on the South China Sea. Japan's response to China's claim to the Diaoyu islets and surrounding waters has been a refusal to admit even the existence of a dispute with its largest trade partner; meanwhile, Japan's military budget has gone up for the first time in several years (though it remains less than 1 percent of GDP). Taiwan's East China Sea and South China Sea claims duplicate and legitimize China's claims, and 40 percent of its exports go to the PRC, yet Taipei has avoided joining China's efforts to make good its claims and eschews any interest in reunification with the motherland. Laos and Cambodia, both recipients of generous Chinese aid and investment and having no maritime territorial claims that overlap China's, have supported China's opposition to multilateralization of the dispute. All these rather disparate policies are conflated together as forms of hedging. Common to all is an asymmetrical confrontation between powerful and less powerful actors ("China is a big country and you are just small countries," as Yang Jiechi pointed out at a 2010 ARF meeting), in which the former makes demands the latter prefers not to accept but surely does not wish to fight.

But what exactly does "hedging" mean? The provenance of the term is found in three fields: gardening, rhetoric, and finance. In gardening, the first origin of the term, it means "to surround by a hedge," referring to foliage designed to screen off a dwelling or piece of property from public scrutiny. In rhetoric, it consists of the use of words that qualify, soften, or otherwise attenuate the full illocutionary force or value that the utterance would have in its absence, often in order to avoid answering embarrassing questions or committing oneself to an unpleasant or risky action or decision. Thus, a diplomat might use such phrases as "as it were," "in a manner of speaking," and "if you will" or adjectives ("weasel words") such as "somewhat" or "essentially." In financial transactions, a hedge is an investment position intended to insure against potential loss by a companion investment in the opposite direction. Thus, one buys a stock but at the same time buys a future stock at a lower price to redeem if the stock goes down. Common to all three is a wish to conceal; common to the latter two is a desire to pursue gains with protection against risks.

What, then, does the term tell China's neighbors about how to cope with a rising China? In its rhetorical sense, it tells them to be polite and avoid giving unnecessary offense. This is not too informative, as it would normally be implicit in diplomatic intercourse in any event. It tells them to make due provision to offset possible loss, always prudent advice but probably obvious when facing a more powerful threat. Beyond such bromides, what can it tell us? What should Vietnam do when China emplaces an oil rig in its EEZ? Fight? Talk? Permit mass protest movements? Form an alliance with the Philippines? What should Japan have done when the mayor of Tokyo started a fund-raising drive to purchase the Senkaku/Diaoyu islets and a hundred Chinese cities erupted in protest movements? Or, to take an example from China-Taiwan relations, in the early 1990s both China and Taiwan were engaged in rapprochement, but both remained highly suspicious of each other, so what did they do? Hedge—but in quite different ways. Taiwan hedged by linking each step toward entente with the mainland with a step toward integration with the international community, relaxing its foregoing "one China" policy in favor of "flexible diplomacy." China hedged as well, by pairing its slight relaxation of the "one China principle" vis-à-vis Taiwan with the emplacement in the early 1990s of hundreds of short-range missiles along the Fujian coast.

Just as there are different hedges, they have different results. Empirically, most hedging is practiced by a weaker power against a stronger one because the weaker cannot hope to fight and win yet does not wish to capitulate. Certainly this is the case in Asia, given the large and growing asymmetry between China and its neighbors. Speaking of asymmetry, the historical record of underdog hedgers has not been reassuring. The classic historical case is that of the Melians in the Peloponnesian War, who tried to dissuade the Athenians from sacking their town not by bandwagoning with them but by promising benign neutrality. The Athenians, confident of their overweening superiority, demanded a zero-sum choice, and crushed the city when it refused.[8] Rome finally destroyed Carthage after the Third Punic War. The September 1938 Munich Agreement among Germany, England, France, and Italy is one of the most infamous modern cases of hedging, in which the allies sought both to appease Germany with limited concessions to national self-determination and to elicit Hitler's promise that he sought no further territorial encroachments (which he gave but then quickly broke).

Although the term came into being because of the semantic gap between "bandwagoning" and "balancing," it does not really fill that gap—that is, it fills it not with too little but too much. Hedging turns out not to be a coherent strategy but a wide array of options. How is one to distinguish among hedges? Limiting ourselves for the moment to asymmetric hedging, the type most common in Asia, surely one relevant practical distinction would be between successful and unsuccessful outcomes. By success, we mean the weak hedger avoids either war or unacceptable concessions to the stronger demander. As in a call option, the hedger bets to accept the strong nation's demand but wants insurance in case things go south. According to Evelyn Goh, the weaker Southeast Asian nations have hedged by enmeshing all relevant countries in ASEAN or its many "Plus" affiliates (ASEAN Plus Three, ASEAN Defense Ministers Plus, the ARF, etc.) and by encouraging the involvement of the great powers in regional affairs.[9] The Philippines, under recently elected Rodrigo Duterte, apparently seeks to hedge by tactfully refraining from publicly mentioning the Permanent Court of Arbitration (PCA) award won by his predecessor and by canceling joint exercises in an effort to distance his country from the United States in pursuit of a better deal with China, including big infrastructure projects—without, however, canceling the US-Philippine mutual defense treaty, or even the Enhanced Defense Cooperation Agreement (EDCA), a key defense agreement with the United States that his country signed in 2014 (and noting that he is constitutionally prohibited from ceding national territory). Both these hedges seem to have been successful (so far): no war, no unacceptably costly concessions. But both are still very much in play.

If we compare successful and unsuccessful hedges, surely among the most decisive criteria distinguishing success from failure is simple: can the hedger enlist a third party? If it can, and if the enlistment is decisive (that is, strong enough to provide the necessary insurance if the situation becomes untenable), the hedge succeeds. This is a tactic we shall refer to hereafter as *triangulation*. If that support is unreliable, as in the case of Milos, which vainly hoped Sparta would come to its rescue, or Czechoslovakia, which believed the promise Chamberlain elicited from Hitler (and that Britain would otherwise intercede), triangulation fails. Formation of a triangle is not exactly the same as external balancing, for the weaker state does not necessarily oppose and may even continue to need the stronger. Moreover, the weaker state, state B, while fearing state A, may not fully trust the third party (state C), and may derive advantages from sustained relations with state A (or fear the consequences of breaking that relationship). The relationship between B and C may also vary from close embrace to very tenuous collaboration. Russia and China have long formed a triangular relationship with North Korea (Democratic People's Republic of Korea [DPRK]), in which three generations of Kims have quite skillfully exploited competition between the two to enhance DPRK leverage. To take another example, the Central Asian republics Kyrgyzstan, Kazakhstan, Tajikistan, and Uzbekistan were suddenly and involuntarily emancipated upon Yeltsin's dissolution of the Soviet Union in December 1991. All welcomed China's blossoming political and economic interest and proceeded to negotiate border agreements and then join the Shanghai Cooperation Organization, but they did not abruptly spurn Russian patronage. By befriending both powers they could take advantage of the competition between them and avoid excessive dependence on either.

We can map out this relationship. A strategic triangle may be said to exist if three conditions are met: (1) all three participants are sovereign (i.e., free to decide their foreign policies based on perceived national interests), rational actors (i.e., not overly inhibited from expedient maneuver by alliance commitments or ideological dogmatism); (2) each actor in its bilateral moves must take into account the interests and possible reactions of a third actor; and (3) each must be deemed essential to the game insofar as its defection from one side to the other would critically shift the strategic balance.

The most renowned previous application of triangular logic has been to the relationship among China, the Soviet Union, and the United States during the last two decades of the Cold War, when the Nixon administration succeeded in taking advantage of the growing alienation of China from the Sino-Soviet alliance in order to form a triangular relationship in which Washington's relationship to Beijing and Moscow was better than either had with the other. This created a "romantic" triangle permitting Washington to head off imminent war between wings and extract more concessions from each wing than might otherwise have been feasible. But that is only one of four possible configurations, and this particular triangle was to evolve through several. If we assume that relations among players may be classified as either positive or negative (a simplification, but a necessary one routinely made by national security planners, insurance agencies, budget chiefs, international banks, etc.), there are only four logically possible configurations of the triangle. These are the unit veto, consisting of negative relationships between each player and both others; the "marriage," consisting of a positive relationship between the two spouses each of whom have negative relationships with a third "pariah"; a "romantic triangle," consisting of positive relationships between one "pivot" player and two "wing" players, who in turn have better relations with the pivot than they have with each other; and finally, the "ménage à trois," consisting of positive relationships among all three players (see figure 1.1).[10]

The rules of the game are to maximize national interests by having as many positive and as few negative relationships as possible, for positive relationships are economically and politically advantageous while negative ones are expensive and risky. The implication is that, first, each player will

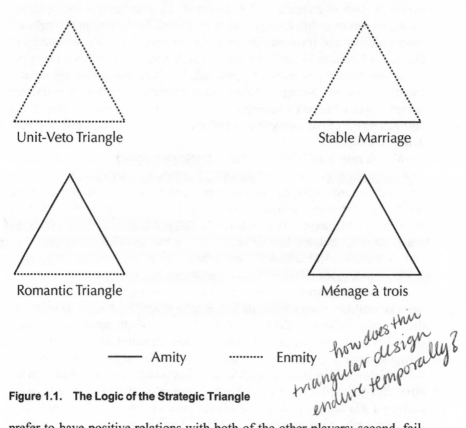

Unit-Veto Triangle   Stable Marriage

Romantic Triangle   Ménage à trois

———— Amity   ·········· Enmity   *how does this triangular design endure temporally?*

Figure 1.1.   The Logic of the Strategic Triangle

prefer to have positive relations with both of the other players; second, failing that, each player will wish to have positive relations with at least one other player; and third, that in any event each player will try to avoid incurring negative relations with both of the other players. This would imply a simple rank order of triangular configurations, with a ménage being the optimal configuration, followed by a romantic triangle, followed by a marriage, with unit veto least preferable. Yet the rank order of options for individual actors is not the same: the most advantageous role is that of pivot in a romantic triangle, second most advantageous would be partner in a marriage, third would be partner in a ménage à trois, and fourth and least desirable would be a pariah facing a marriage.

Why? Each actor's level of satisfaction is measured in part by the relative dissatisfaction of the other actors. Envy for positional advantage is one of the factors driving the game. If the two wing players are envious or competing for the pivot's favor, it reduces the risk that they will collude against the pivot. The pivot also enjoys better communication with the two wings than they have with each other. Some configurations (and some roles) are inherently more stable than others: a marriage tends to be relatively stable (contingent on the level of trust between spouses), while a ménage is typically a relatively unstable and transient configuration given maximal opportunity for collusion. Given that the payoffs for each player vary based on one's position within the triangle, it is logical to assume that any nation finding itself at a positional disadvantage will seek to elevate its position in the game.[11] But the power and attraction of an actor will vary not only based on one's triangular position but according to a more conventional calculus of relative power, including such indices as GDP, population, military force projection capability, and geography. To some extent, it is possible to mask weakness temporarily, as Saddam Hussein did from 2001 until his execution in 2006. In any case, positive relations with a strong actor will be valued more than positive relations with a weak actor, which is also true for negative relations, mutatis mutandis.

This book is based throughout on a triangular model: it presumes that China's relations with the rest of Asia may be best understood as a triangular relationship in which the United States is the third actor.[12] Behind its bilateral and multilateral relations with its Asian neighbors China always sees the United States scheming, manipulating, and impeding its road to the China Dream.[13] Of course there are many smaller powers as well, and China must take their interests into account, but in its current scheme of things they are less important and sometimes even implicitly relegated as mere puppets of the great powers. China tends to assume that there are two sides to any disagreement, its own and that of the United States, and so smaller powers are warned "do not take sides." That is to say, China sees the rest of Asia much as it sees Chinese domestic politics: some are ranked in higher positions than others, and those below are expected to defer to those above them. Granted, China articulates its official Asia policy ("peripheral/neighborhood diplomacy") in more euphemistic language. At this relatively abstract level, Beijing's more euphemistic rhetoric is formulated in terms of "win-win cooperation," "harmonious world," and "international democracy." This language is, however, considerably less useful for understanding or reconciling conflicts of interest. For these, Beijing skillfully intermixes an openness to multilateral diplomacy such as the ASEAN forums, the SCO, or various multilateral free trade agreements (FTAs) with a willingness to paralyze them when necessary. When China's "core interests" are at stake it will veto or tie up or endlessly delay multilateral discussion forums and demand bilateral negotiations. But in many cases, China finds it impossible to formulate strictly bilateral or even multilateral policies as it wishes, finding that the United States already has a presence on the scene or anticipating that the US hegemon will find it expedient to intrude. Whether building pipelines through Central Asia, setting up the Asian Infrastructure Investment Bank (AIIB), or putting together even such domestic policies as SOE reform or dealing with human rights dissidents or ethnic minorities, China sees the United States ineluctably as a factor. And although the United States, for its part, has profusely denied this conspiratorial malevolence, both sides acknowledge a lack of "strategic trust."[14]

Though there is a general sense of resentment about it, this is a diplomatic fact of life that has burned ever more brightly even as what Chinese call the "comprehensive national power" gap between China and the United States has narrowed. That is not to say that the relationship is zero-sum or necessarily headed for war. US spokespersons stoutly deny any intention to surround or encircle China or stymie its rise, pointing out that the United States has contributed in numerous ways to China's success, for example, by tolerating a huge trade deficit for several decades, and by investing billions in China's industrial modernization. The United States and China have many shared interests, and elite forums and other exchanges have been set up to clear up misunderstandings and coordinate joint solutions to shared problems. Although China does not really believe US professions of best intentions, China has also found the United States to be in many cases highly useful, even after the Cold War when its hitherto primary nemesis, the Union of Soviet Socialist Republics (USSR), was no longer a threat necessitating outside support. The United States remains China's largest export market (temporarily replaced by the EU, before Brexit) and fastest growing source of imports. China and the United States now basically agree on such fundamental priorities as the need to prevent nuclear proliferation and global terrorism. The United States finds China an indispensable partner on certain issues, such as the North Korean nuclear issue or the Taiwan Strait imbroglio. The trade relationship is complementary, if rather lopsided. There is no bilateral border dispute, few direct conflicts of interest, and albeit culturally antipodal there is a certain reciprocal respect and fascination. Yet the rivalry between the two is increasingly obvious. It is not a zero-sum rivalry in which each hates and wants to destroy the other, but a rivalry about something else, the control of Asia. To put it plainly, America fears that America's Asia is becoming China's Asia.

The study begins, then, with China's relations with the United States, focusing on the world's most important bilateral relationship. We then move from north to south to cover the region. Chapter 3 deals with China's relations with the Russian Federation, once China's bitter adversary but currently viewed in Beijing as a "strategic partnership" and model of successful "great power relations." This chapter also includes the former Soviet republics on China's western frontier now in play between them. Chapter 4 covers China's relations with Japan, one of China's largest trade partners but otherwise the absolute antithesis of a positive great power relationship. Chapter 5 follows with a discussion of Asia's two divided nations, China-Taiwan and Korea, which have in common the dilemma of being divided and depending on China to resolve their national division. The sixth chapter concentrates on China's increasingly ambivalent and fractious relationship with the ten Southeast Asian countries that make up ASEAN. Chapter 7 focuses on China and India, a former friend, now a rival and border disputant since the late 1950s, and on the neighboring South Asian countries China has courted in this rivalry. Chapter 8 focuses on China's relations with Australia. Australia is technically not part of Asia but the broader Asia-Pacific region, yet it is closest to Asia and has become increasingly engaged with the region since the 1960s as trade and investment patterns have shifted and Australian security concerns have adjusted accordingly. These substantive chapters are then followed by a brief concluding chapter.

NOTES

1. Asia, the world's largest continent, is distinguished by a remarkable diversity of characteristics in all respects: geography, culture, weather, ethnicity, languages, religion, politics, economics, and technological development. According to UN statistics, as of 2017 there were forty-eight nations and five subregions in Asia: Eastern Asia (five countries), South Asia (nine), Southeast Asia (twelve), Western Asia or the Middle East (eighteen), and Central Asia. This study omits the Middle East, which has its own distinctive issues, and includes Oceania, which has become increasingly integrated with Asia.

2. See Joseph Needham's *Science and Civilisation in China* (Cambridge: Cambridge University Press, 2015). To date there have been seven volumes and twenty-seven books, but the project continues.

3. "Third World" is a Cold War term first introduced by the French anthropologist Alfred Sauvy to refer to nonaligned nations, later used by Mao Zedong to refer to developing nations, which he considered apt adherents to the global communist revolution.

4. This has been disputed; see Alastair Iain Johnston, "How New and Assertive Is China's New Assertiveness?" *International Security* 37, no. 4 (Spring 2013): 7–48; Dingding Chen and Xiaoyu Pu, "Correspondence: Debating China's Assertiveness," *International Security* 38, no. 3 (Winter 2013/14): 176–83; different but related cf. Alastair Iain Johnston's "Is Chinese Nationalism Rising? Evidence from Beijing," *International Security* 41, no. 3 (Winter 2016/17): 7–43. While conventional wisdom (or "discursive bandwagoning") should never be uncritically accepted, this study contends that there was indeed a rise in Chinese assertiveness in 2009–10 that is distinguished from previous assertive episodes (e.g., the 1995–96 Taiwan missile crisis, the 1999 Belgrade bombing, the 2001 EP-3 incident) or clashes over China's maritime sovereignty claims by its more sustained duration, proactive rather than reactive quality, seemingly coherent strategic planning rather than spontaneous improvisation, and greater willingness to risk conflict in the face of resistance.

5. China's first world's fair and the largest in history by size, attendance, and international participants, Expo 2010 also saw the largest world's fair attendance in a single day: over one million on October 16, 2010.

6. See David Shambaugh, *China's Future* (Cambridge, MA: Polity Press, 2016), 112–13.

7. Keith Crane et al., *Modernizing China's Military: Opportunities and Constraints* (Santa Monica, CA: RAND, 2005), 134; and the International Institute for Strategic Studies, *The Military Balance 2015* (New York: Routledge, 2015), 21–22.

8. See Thucydides, *The History of the Peloponnesian War*, trans. Richard Crawley (Gutenberg Project, 2009), chap. 17, http://www.gutenberg.org/files/7142/7142-h/7142-h.htm.

9. Evelyn Goh, "Great Powers and Hierarchical Order in Southeast Asia: Analyzing Regional Security Strategies," *International Security* 32, no. 3 (Winter 2007/8): 113–57.

10. See Lowell Dittmer, "The Strategic Triangle: An Elementary Game-Theoretical Analysis," *World Politics* 33, no. 4 (July 1981): 485–516; "The Strategic Triangle: A Critical Review," in *The Strategic Triangle: China the United States, and the Soviet Union*, ed. Ilpyong Kim (New York: Praeger, 1987); "China and the Two Koreas: A Triangular Perspective," *Korean Journal of Security Affairs* 17, no. 2 (December 2012): 23–39; and "Washington between Beijing and Taipei: A Triangular Analysis," in *The Changing Dynamics of Relations among China, Taiwan, and the United States*, ed. Cal Clark (Newcastle upon Tyne, UK: Cambridge Scholars, 2011), 10–30.

11. See Yu-Shan Wu, "Power Shift, Strategic Triangle, and Alliances in East Asia," *Issues & Studies* 47, no. 4 (December 2011): 1–42.

12. I owe this seminal insight to Professor David Zweig of the Hong Kong University of Science and Technology.

13. See Mathieu Duchâtel, "La politique étrangère de la Chine sous Xi Jinping," *Hérodote* 3, no. 150 (2013): 172–90, http://www.cairn.info/revue-herodote-2013-3-page-172.htm.

14. Kenneth Lieberthal and Jisi Wang, *Addressing U.S.-China Strategic Distrust* (Washington, DC: Brookings Institution Monograph Series, 2012).

Chapter Two

Contesting Hegemony

We begin with China's interactions with the most important, most powerful, and most frustrating power on China's horizon: the United States. Its size and power have made it both a facilitator and an impediment to China's rise. As Odd Arne Westad puts it, "Throughout the 20th century, Chinese have had a complicated but almost obsessive relationship with the United States . . . endless fascination with things American, with American wealth, and with American ideas."[1] The relationship has been frustrating to Beijing not only because of this duality but because in Chinese eyes the United States is not properly an Asian power at all, but the leading representative of Western developed countries and an exogenous intruder. This is implicitly conveyed in occasional Chinese references to US Asian policies as "interference" or "intervention" by a "country outside the region." Thus President Xi Jinping at an international conference in 2014 declared that Asian powers could take care of their own security without outside help. But of course, the United States has never agreed with this characterization. For better or worse, the United States first asserted its presence in Asia in its "liberation" of the Philippines in the Spanish-American War at the dawn of the twentieth century, and not only retained its presence but fought three major wars in Asia: against imperial Japan in 1941–45, the Korean War in 1950–53, and the Vietnam War in 1965–75. The United States also played a major economic and strategic role in Asia during the Cold War, instigating land reform and economic reconstruction in client states and opening the vast US consumer market to Asian exports, also forming a network of economic and security ties with the Asian rimland during the Cold War.

Of course, it is understandable that China might think otherwise, for many of these arrangements were made not in concert with but counter to the China threat. Even after the Cold War, while China gained profitable entry to international markets, its inclusion in the US-dominated regional security community has been hesitant and partial, spawning neologisms like "congagement." Not until the new millennium, particularly after the Beijing Olympics in 2008 and actualization of the ASEAN-China Free Trade Agreement (ACFTA) in 2010, did China begin to feel itself to be a fully accredited member of the Asian community. Yet China's sense of having clawed back its wonted central place in Asia also precipitated the pivot or rebalance of the United States, which China interpreted (despite US denials) as clearly designed to encircle and contain its rise. Although it is some seven thousand miles away, the US presence in Asia remains resilient and ubiquitous. It is China's most significant interlocutor, its sugarcoated adversary and implicit hegemonic role model, something to be overcome and surpassed, still stubbornly resisting the inevitable passing of the torch, vainly hatching tricks and snares and stage-managing futile resistance by smaller countries. China's Asia policy is thus not a series of bilateral and multilateral relationships but in all cases a triangular one, overshadowed by the presence of a still powerful third power.

This chapter consists of four parts. The first compares the national identities of the two countries, which, though not immutable or overpowering, are assumed to have certain lasting essential features, to see to what extent they are compatible. The second part adumbrates in brief the modern history of the relationship. The third focuses on the various dimensions of the period since 2008 when the relationship, hitherto characterized by constructive engagement, became increasingly competitive. The final section analyzes the basis for this mistrust and some of its possible policy implications.

NATIONAL IDENTITIES

The national identity of a country refers to the qualities that distinguish it from other countries, making it "exceptional." A national identity profile is hence a natural basis for patriotism or nationalism, which can in certain circumstances be carried to chauvinistic extremes, as in the case of the fascist dictatorships of the World War II era, but in moderate form provides a basis for morale, loyalty, and collective purpose, all of which are integral to the successful functioning of a nation-state. National identity can lead a nation into coalition or alliance with another nation or category of nations with which that nation identifies, or into opposition to a nation or nations with whom an identity gap is perceived.[2] Like everything in human affairs, this is no "iron law" but a propensity *caeteris paribus* that can be counteracted by other factors, including leadership will or defeat in major war. National identity can change, as people change, to reflect their ambitions and fears. Yet identity must have sufficient thematic continuity to retain credibility and commitment.

The quintessential American identity has been individualistic, democratic, and voluntarist, based on the conviction that the country is rich and free, a land of boundless opportunity to which anyone in the world of whatever ethnic creed or class background can come and, with the requisite skill and determination, succeed. As James Truslow Adams defined it, the American Dream is "that dream of a land in which life should be better and richer and fuller for everyone, with opportunity for each according to ability or achievement."[3] People are born equal in opportunities and rights but not in outcomes, as the high Gini coefficient attests. Political authority is expected to be reasonably competent if not necessarily brilliant with little tolerance for scandal; embarrassing leaders are electorally replaceable. The political culture is vaguely pious but open textured, pluralistic, casually brutal, and competitive to the point of anarchy, only loosely knit together by consensus on a constitutional/legal framework. Economically the country is a leading practitioner of laissez-faire capitalism. However formless and protean, Americans deem their national identity to be exemplary to the point that they have attempted to encourage (at times perhaps too insistently) other countries to emulate the American model of democratic capitalism. In the wake of the American rise during World War II, this has led it to assume the role of world policeman, exercised rather erratically (the "cowboy") and despite an obvious conflict of interest between disinterested judge and interested stakeholder.

Chinese national identity consists of a mixture of Confucianism, Leninism, and eclectic modernism, and has been in constant turmoil since the fall of the Qing. Individualism is discouraged—the nail that sticks up must be hammered down—on behalf of group solidarity; self-interest is deemed selfish and must be sacrificed to the collective interest. The orientation to authority is highly respectful, contingent, however, on the moral rectitude of the leader; legitimacy is still based on virtue more than law. The political culture is hierarchical and age deferential, although the hierarchy can be overthrown if stained by perceived corruption or tyranny. Historically the normative emphasis has been on harmony, though there is also a narrative of rebellion, anarchy, and martial heroism dating from Sun Tzu and the classic novels, as recently displayed in the 2009 and 2015 military parades.[4] In the reform era, stability (*wending*) has replaced revolutionary ardor in the value hierarchy while chaos (*luan*) must be suppressed and driven underground (and dissent is believed to lead to chaos). This intolerance of disorder unwittingly engenders an underground subculture of violence, iconoclasm, and radical egalitarianism that during crises arises to compete with the regnant official identity. The communist party rose by fully embracing this revolutionary subculture, only to spurn it later for an attempted fusion with traditional conservative morality. There is similar ambivalence vis-à-vis the international arena between fitting into the dominant paradigm and quietly swallowing grievances, only to erupt in indignation over seemingly minor symbolic slights. China's embrace of Leninism has given it license to attack global imperialism, and it has never been an imperialist power in the classic sense, but its rise has fueled episodic attempts (like the Americans) to impose a transformative vision on the world, as in Mao Zedong's Three Worlds schema of world revolution or Xi Jinping's New Asian Security Order.

There is obviously a considerable "gap" between the American and Chinese identities: between authoritarian stability, collective self-sacrifice, filial piety, and hierarchical conformity on the one hand and libertarian individualism, egalitarianism, and a high tolerance for disorder on the other.[5] Yet there are also points of similarity and convergence. Both nations imbue foreign policy with idealism in the sense that they view some nations as better than others and their own as best of all. This is exceptionalism, albeit about different exceptional qualities: the American dream is one of boundless individual opportunity, while the Chinese believe they have assembled a just political order that is the natural envy of all. Both have shown little compunction in defying international convention, partly due to this sense of exceptionalism. For example, although China signed on to the UN Convention on the Law of the Sea (UNCLOS), it refused to honor the UNCLOS verdict when Manila challenged China's claims; although the United States is not even a member of UNCLOS, it has not hesitated to criticize China's legal position. Both have had the occasional ambition and requisite power to proselytize their own governmental preferences internationally. While none of these similarities has been conducive to convergence, both nations have endeavored to modulate national identity dissonance with informal circumlocutions skirting divisive issues. And despite identity divergence, there has been reciprocal admiration of some of these differences: Chinese admire American egalitarianism, informality, and openness; Americans admire Chinese collective self-discipline, pragmatic intelligence, civic spirit, and tenacious purposiveness.

Since the rise of Xi Jinping, China's emphasis on its own distinct national identity has taken a certain edge. In his efforts to leave his own mark on Chinese politics, Xi has boldly called for national "rejuvenation" (*fuxing*) to realize the "China Dream" (*zhongguo meng*), a vague but highly popular formulation that seems so far to be primarily focused on foreign policy, particularly "great power relations" (*da guo guanxi*).[6] The arrival of a new great power tends to make the existing ones nervous. The idea of catching up and surpassing the existing great powers seems to have first been articulated by Mao Zedong at a communist international convocation held in November 1957 to celebrate the fortieth anniversary of the October revolution: "Comrade Khrushchev has told us, the Soviet Union 15 years later will surpass the

United States of America," Mao observed. "I can also say, 15 years later, we may catch up with or exceed the UK." On December 2, 1957, Liu Shaoqi reiterated and extended this goal at the Eighth National Congress of Chinese Trade Unions, and the slogan of "surpassing Britain and catching up with the United States" then gained wide currency during the Great Leap Forward.[7] The Great Leap failed resoundingly, yet Mao's frequently repeated words have been internalized as the ultimate goal of China's developmental trajectory, particularly since the advent of "reform and opening" at the Third Plenum of the Eleventh Congress when so much of the rest of the Maoist package was quietly pared away. In the cultural tradition of filial piety the People's Republic of China (PRC) reluctantly inherited and has since rehabilitated, the son is expected eventually to surpass the father and the student to surpass the teacher, and the latter is expected to graciously retire to a position of honored impotence. And though some recommend this course to the United States, in the dog-eat-dog jungle of world politics Washington has declined retirement, giving rise to tension.

National identity changes, usually more slowly than its causes, either autonomously as driven by political and economic events or as a result of deliberate symbol manipulation by political elites seeking to steer the nation in a preconceived direction. The Chinese Communist Party (CCP) has consistently placed high priority on molding national identity to sustain its own monopoly on power and mobilize support for whatever policy line it happens to be pushing at the time. Since the 1989 protest and crackdown and the downfall of communist regimes in Eastern Europe and the Soviet Union, the CCP leadership has attempted to reprise China's historical (prerevolutionary) identity while de-emphasizing (without directly impugning) its revolutionary heritage and trying to keep Western influence at bay. Marxist-Leninist-Maoist thought remains authoritative within the ruling party but is no longer a basis for economic development or international identity except in a vague and discretionary sense. Looking forward are the two "centenary goals" (*liang ge yibainian mubiao*) of 2021, the anniversary of the founding of the CCP, and 2049, of the founding of the PRC, by which time the nation will have become "moderately well-off" (*xiaokang shehui*), and a "rich and powerful socialist nation" (*fuqiang de shehuizhuyi guojia*), respectively. The revival of prerevolutionary traditional identity reinforces the Chinese "central kingdom" (*zhong guo zhong xin*) meme as benign host of a throng of admiring tributary states, while blaming Western and Japanese imperialism for the "one hundred years of shame" (*bainian guochi*) that temporarily derailed its historical trajectory. Japan has fallen under particular onus in museum and memorial construction, and Japan is in Chinese eyes distinguished mainly by its past war crimes but also for "leaving Asia and joining the West" (as Fukuzawa once put it).

Yet China itself recognized its Asian identity only recently. After marching into Beijing in 1949, the PRC identified wholly with the communist bloc and the Third World in the global communist revolutionary project. This failed policy was diffused in the turn to all-azimuth charm diplomacy on behalf of "reform and opening" in the post-Mao era, when China identified with the newly industrialized countries (NICs), an identity that was, however, then jeopardized by international sanctions and Western foreign direct investment (FDI) flight in the aftermath of 1989. In the context of post-Tiananmen reform resurgence, Chinese identity returned to Asia, conflating Chinese nationalism with Asian values and joining the ASEAN Regional Forum, Asia-Pacific Economic Corporation (APEC), ASEAN Plus Three (APT), the East Asia Summit (EAS), and a host of other regional associations. By the late 2000s, China, having triumphantly survived the 2008–10 global financial crisis (GFC) and emerged as Asia's and even (by some measures) the world's largest economy, began to see its identity not only as Asian but as the economic locomotive and natural political leader of the region. China would become the Asian "pole" in a new multipolar global order.

China's emergent identity as Asia's natural leader and international representative is manifest in three dimensions. First, China's comprehensive national power has been steadily enhanced while holding down relative mass consumption for prolonged periods, chiefly via financial repression (formerly known as "primitive socialist accumulation"). Already economically and militarily peerless in Asia after thirty years of hypergrowth, arms budgets have since 1989 consistently outpaced gross domestic product (GDP) growth.[8] Second, China has vigorously laid claim to its long asserted but hitherto unenforced territorial claims to its near seas, gradually asserting proprietary rights via local naval superiority. Third, China has begun to exercise leadership of the regional commons with policy innovations, boosting multilateral trade agreements such as the ACFTA, the Regional Cooperative Economic Partnership (RCEP), and the Free Trade Area of the Asia-Pacific (FTAAP), and introducing new financial institutions (e.g., the Asian Infrastructure Investment Bank and the BRICS New Development Bank), and pledging funding for ambitious infrastructure projects on China's periphery. The funds promised for these massive projects presumably can be covered by China's vast (over US$3 trillion in 2017) cache of foreign exchange. ASEAN centrality in the region is hence eclipsed by China's visionary "One Belt, One Road" (*yi dai yi lu*) initiative (a "Silk Road Economic Belt" across Central Asia linking China to Europe, and a "Twenty-First-Century Maritime Silk Road" stretching from south China through a series of ports in Southeast and South Asia to the Middle East and the Mediterranean). Though some have compared China's emerging role to the ancient tributary system, there are significant differences. While tributary relations were merely a form of diplomatic etiquette to facilitate trade and mutual amity, China's current claims include sovereignty over vast swathes of open sea, and are functionally integrated into its own vaulting, resource-hungry industrial revolution.

SINO-AMERICAN HISTORY IN A NUTSHELL

The United States participated in the international expeditionary force to suppress the so-called Boxer Rebellion in 1900 (later donating their share of reparations to Chinese charities) but otherwise did not participate in the imperialist depredations that humiliated China in the century from the First Opium War to the communist revolutionary victory. Although US merchants also participated in the opium trade, they did not openly challenge Lin Zexu's embargo like the British and refrained from what Sun Yat-sen called carving up China like a melon. Indeed, the United States in 1899 under Secretary of State John Hay declared an open door policy renouncing such tactics and admonishing Western imperialist powers to refrain from colonialism and leave China open to economic commercial ties with all. The victory of Japan in the Sino-Japanese War (1894–95) precipitated a scramble for colonies from which the United States did not want to be shut out; but rather than enter into the imperialist competition they declared it immoral. Although Americans like to believe that this puts China in its debt, it is discounted by most Chinese historians and with good reason: the open door policy was only a declaration of principle, never enforced—any moderation of Western imperialism was likely due more to a balance of power among imperialist powers.[9] The Treaty of Wangxia establishing diplomatic relations between the two nations was clearly unequal, though the United States (unlike the United Kingdom) did illegalize opium trade and promise to remand offenders to the Chinese authorities. But from the Chinese perspective most objectionable was American behavior not in China but in the United States: the Chinese Exclusion Act of 1882 barred Chinese workers from entering the country for more than sixty years.

In sum, as imperialists go, the US record was not great but better than most, no land grabbing or imperialist wars, but rather low risk, opportunistic, and hypocritical. Thus although the United States did not fight the Opium Wars, it was glad to free ride on imperialist victories. For example, the 1860 Treaty of Tientsin ending the Second Opium War also gave France and the United States the right to establish administrative offices in Beijing; although the United States protested the Japanese invasion of Manchuria in 1931, it did nothing about it. Sino-American relations throughout the first half of the twentieth century remained cordial; commerce and investment flourished, culminating in inconsequential military assistance to the nascent republic after the Japanese invasion in 1937, vastly increasing after the December

1941 attack on Pearl Harbor. Despite complaints of corruption and incompetence, the United States loyally supported Chiang Kai-shek's Nationalist regime before and after its defeat on the mainland in 1949 and subsequent exile in Taiwan.

Whether the United States "lost" China remains controversial. The initial interpretation of the loss was by Republicans who accused the Democratic administration of having failed to render sufficient support for the Nationalist incumbents to prevent their defeat by the Red Army, then using this as grist for congressional inquiries and election campaigns. Subsequent historians interpreted the loss as a missed chance in 1949–50 for the newborn People's Republic of China (PRC) and the United States to reach an accommodation and avoid future confrontations. But did the CCP leadership really want to normalize relations with the United States? CCP leaders made early diplomatic overtures at the end of the war to investigate the possibility of reconciliation, but after Beijing's public endorsement of Zhdanov's "two camps theory" in 1947, the collapse of Czechoslovakia, and announcement of the Truman Doctrine, the international system polarized. As Chen Jian has pointed out, the CCP leadership by 1949 was far too committed to consolidating the new regime and "continuing the revolution" to have much interest in establishing relations with what they regarded as the leading imperialist and class enemy.[10] Britain's early attempt to establish diplomatic relations was not welcomed.[11] With Mao's announcement that China would "lean to one side" in 1949 and its entry into the Korean War the following year, the die was cast.[12] As Gordon Chang has noted, although the Soviet Union posed the greatest security threat to the United States during the ensuing years, quickly catching up in nuclear and thermonuclear capability and launching the world's first intercontinental ballistic missile (ICBM) and satellite in 1957, Washington was perceptibly tougher on China than on the Union of Soviet Socialist Republics (USSR).[13]

The following two decades was the era of high Cold War, when the United States confronted both the Soviet Union and China simultaneously. This geopolitically daunting imbalance was somewhat extenuated by the fact that while the United States, undamaged by the war, produced about 50 percent of global GDP in 1945, both China and the Soviet Union lay in ruins. And while during the Korean War the two communist giants were able to cooperate smoothly, in their subsequent pursuit of world revolution they agreed to a division of labor that ultimately satisfied neither. China, with the first communist revolution to succeed in the developing world, would be the appropriate leader among the postcolonial new nations in Africa and Asia, Stalin advised Mao, while the Soviet Union would lead revolution in the industrialized West. But Germany and Japan were held in thrall by Western occupation forces, and while European communism learned to play parliamentary politics (the Italian Communist Party could command about a third of the vote and the French Communist Party crested at 16.2 percent in 1981), neither could ever garner the necessary plurality to form a cabinet. Meanwhile, prospects for revolution in the Third World appeared much more promising. The Indonesian Communist Party was the largest in the free world by the early 1960s, and National Liberation Wars were launched in Vietnam, Burma, Malaysia, the Philippines, India, Nepal, Algeria, Cuba, and elsewhere. China deemed this the cusp of the coming world revolution and denigrated Soviet support for the "parliamentary road" as "revisionist," viewing violent class struggle as a necessary prerequisite for true revolution (though Beijing was not rigorously consistent on this point, also supporting the Five Principles of Peaceful Coexistence).

Mao's dauntless critique of tepid Soviet revolutionary leadership in Cuba, India, the Taiwan Strait, and elsewhere marked the public commencement of the Sino-Soviet rift. In positive response to Chinese criticism, the Soviet Union rescinded the original division of labor agreed by Stalin and Mao and became actively reengaged in support for revolutionary movements in the Third World as well. With a more advanced economy and more ample fiscal resources than China (particularly after the resounding failure of the Great Leap Forward), the Soviet Union proved able to outbid the PRC in what became a global competition for the allegiance of revolutionary movements. Revolutionary competition enhanced support for nascent leftist movements in Asia and sub-Saharan Africa and improved the bargaining position of aid recipients like North Korea or Vietnam, who played the two sponsors against each other. From the US foreign policy perspective, this engendered a dual adversary "worse than a monolith."[14] But from the perspective of world revolution it was almost certainly self-destructive, splitting communist parties in some countries (e.g., India and the United States), transforming international meetings from celebrations of solidarity and effective coordinating sessions into bitterly polemicized debates, and finally even giving rise to "proxy" wars between clients of rival communist sponsors (as in Cambodia-Vietnam, or Afghanistan). Even more than the sustained and often effective counterrevolutionary efforts of the United States, competition between the PRC and the USSR contributed to the meager cumulative results of what was once a vibrant international movement. Of course, even more decisive was China's abandonment of the export of revolution after 1980 and the collapse of the communist bloc a decade later, orphaning ongoing insurgencies in Nepal, northeastern India, the Philippines, and elsewhere. At the end of the Cold War, nation-states still professing allegiance to Marxism-Leninism numbered only five in the world: China, North Korea, Vietnam, Laos, and Cuba. The experience left the CCP with a suspicion of multilateral projects abiding some ten years thereafter and decreased the impact of ideology on foreign policy in favor of a calculating mercantilism and nationalist realism.

But ideological deradicalization for the first time made China's relations with the two superpowers amenable to pragmatic compromise.

The period from the early 1970s to 1980 represented a transitional period, shifting from a stridently acrimonious but still legally valid alliance with the Soviet Union to an ideologically awkward but strategically necessary realignment with the leading capitalist power. While the 1971 entry to the United Nations (UN) opened the way to cost-free exploration of free world multilateral affiliations, hosting the 1972 Nixon visit represented a step away from "continuing revolution" to realism. Foreign policy rhetoric remained radical, consistent with Deng Xiaoping's proclamation of "Three Worlds" to the UN General Assembly in 1974, yet China quietly accepted US extended nuclear deterrence against preemptive Soviet attack and cooperated in monitoring Soviet nuclear tests in Xinjiang and by supplying arms to the Khmer Rouge in Cambodia and to the mujahideen resisting the Soviet occupation of Afghanistan. Bilateral rapprochement was dramatic but limited to the strategic plane, where both shared concern with a perceived growing Soviet threat. This was the era of the Great Strategic Triangle, during which the United States nurtured strategic relations with China while preserving détente with the Soviet Union, at first balancing the two commitments but in the course of the decade moving closer to the former as Soviet-American strategic arms limitation talks stalled. The strategic triangle finally collapsed with the disintegration of the USSR into fifteen sovereign republics in 1991, removing the strategic rationale for Sino-US rapprochement for both sides. Although political relations were normalized in 1979, the Tiananmen crackdown a decade later reawakened abiding Sino-American ideological and identity differences. Bilateral economic relations strongly recovered with the revival of reform momentum following Deng's 1992 voyage to the south, but the national identity gap was reawakened after 2010 by maritime sovereignty disputes. Meanwhile, the foundation of the relationship shifted from mutual strategic necessity to shared economic interests, though even these have grown frayed with the Chinese economic slowdown and rebalancing.

Tiananmen and its repercussions mark a turning point in the relationship. After protracted inner-party debate in the aftermath of the post-Tiananmen economic recession and the dissolution of the Soviet Union, the Chinese leadership built a post–Cold War foreign policy on two canonic texts: the Five Principles of Peaceful Coexistence (and various reformulations of these such as the New Security Concept introduced in 2005),[15] and Deng's "24-character expression."[16] The PRC in the aftermath of Tiananmen ignored Western sanctions and capital flight while cultivating closer relations with developing countries, particularly in Asia (what Beijing termed *zhoubian waijiao*, or "neighborhood diplomacy"), liberalizing domestic markets and FDI regulations to invite foreign direct investment. Strategically the focus during the decade was on forming strategic partnerships and reassuring the powers (preeminently the United States) that China would peacefully develop and posed no threat to the regional status quo (while at the same time lambasting them for implementing a strategy of peaceful evolution). The ringleaders of the spontaneous Tiananmen demonstrations were rounded up and imprisoned, and the Chinese people were encouraged to stay out of politics and "plunge into the sea" (*xia hai*) of commerce. Western and US capital responded eagerly to Beijing's liberalized investment climate, cementing bilateral relations with ample profit chances on both sides. So long as the boom lasted, Chinese and US trajectories seemed to converge. China's entry after hard bargaining into the World Trade Organization (WTO) in late 2001 anchored reform in international law and effectively removed the threat of trade discrimination based on most-favored-nation status. This facilitated the massive expansion of China's export sector in the 2000s, financed by FDI and embedded technology and sustained by Western consumer demand, resulting in double-digit GDP growth and a swiftly mounting foreign exchange surplus.

A CURRENT APPRAISAL

Sino-American relations have been on a downward spiral since 2008. It is somewhat puzzling why this should be so in view of their relatively friendly bilateral history. According to Kenneth Lieberthal and Wang Jisi, the problem is one of a lack of "strategic trust."[17] Yet this merely begs the question: Why? Is strategic distrust subjective, based on misinterpretations of each other's international behavior and objectives? Or is it objective, based on national interests? This is not an easy question to answer, for as we have seen the relationship throughout its history has been ambiguous and shifting. Whether distrust is subjective or objective is itself in a way subjective. From the beginning of the reform and opening policy in 1978 until recently (with a brief lapse of confidence in the wake of 1989), the prevailing interpretation on both sides has been that strategic distrust is essentially subjective, and that the two sides share sufficient strategic, cultural, and even identity interests to forge mutually beneficial bonds. Contrariwise, inasmuch as distrust is subjective, critical thinking might translate into hostile action (what Graham Allison calls the "Thucydides trap"). This interpretation has been favored by vested economic interests, diplomats, and other relationship maintenance specialists on both sides, as well as by public opinion given that war between nuclear powers would be mutually ruinous. Based on this interpretation great effort has been devoted to resolving subjective mistrust. There are more than sixty regular government-to-government dialogues plus myriad scholarly and cultural exchanges. President Obama met personally with his Chinese counterpart on an average of once a quarter during his eight-year tenure.

China has invested heavily in Confucius Institutes, CCTV (China Central Television) networks, and other instruments of soft power in the United States. The Sino-US trade and investment nexus is one of the largest in the world, and tourism has thrived. Yet mistrust persists. Both sides build two of the world's biggest military machines for the prospect of war with each other and suspect each other of subverting their political and value systems and of encircling them with enemies.

Despite Thucydides, strategic trust has both subjective and objective dimensions: it is not a purely subjective mind-set that can be wished away. In this section, we review both dimensions of mistrust, followed by an inquiry into its underlying causes. Based on our overall framework, we divide the bases of distrust into two forms: bilateral (concerning relations strictly between the two sides) and triangular (relations also involving third parties). The three bilateral issues between the two powers are ideological dissonance, economic friction, and the security dilemma. The triangular dimension concerns both nations' competitive courtship and pressure on the other Asian powers in competitive pursuit of regional primacy.

Bilateral Issues

Ideal Interests

The ideological difficulty has to do with allegedly conflicting conceptions of human rights. Interestingly, this never became a major issue from the opening to China in 1972 to 1989, as the relationship was so clearly based on strategic balance-of-power considerations that ideological convergence was never expected. But when the Cold War ended and world communism was no longer seen as a viable threat, human rights replaced anticommunism as the ideological rationale of American foreign policy.[18] This was facilitated in China's case by the highly visible CCP crackdown at Tiananmen, which aroused moral indignation in the West and the imposition of economic sanctions. The Chinese view of human rights differs somewhat from that of the United States, notably, in assigning greater weight to economic and collective rights and less to political, civil, and religious rights. Yet the PRC has signed the International Covenant on Economic, Social and Cultural Rights (ICESCR) and the International Covenant on Civil and Political Rights (ICCPR) in 1997 and 1998, respectively (though it has formally ratified only the former), and had (by 2014) signed more than twenty international treaties on human rights. Thus, it follows that in principle China agrees with these universalistic definitions. And it has made progress in fulfilling its commitments. Since 2012, China abolished reeducation through labor camps, for example, and although it still executes more people than the rest of the world combined, capital punishment has been substantially reduced since its high point in the 1980s, particularly since the Supreme People's Court regained the authority to review all death penalty cases in 2007.

The real crux has to do with China's enforcement priorities. Here, human rights have a lower priority than the accomplishment of collective goals, for which preservation of the CCP's monopoly on power is deemed an essential prerequisite, whether in terms of the "four cardinal principles" or the consistent preamble to PRC constitutions asserting the leading role of the CCP. That role, however, from the leadership's perspective, can be destabilized by overzealous exercise of certain rights (notably rights to speech, assembly, and the press). Thus, US encouragement of human rights is interpreted as a malevolent plot to instigate "peaceful evolution," ultimately leading to regime change from socialism to bourgeois democracy. Because the leadership's sense of the state's fragility is acutely sensitive, the enforcement of human rights has varied over time and circumstance, typically undergoing a "freeze-thaw" cycle (*yi jiao, jiu fang; yi fang, jiu luan; yi luan, jiu shou*: "people complain, so there is a thaw; once there is thaw, there is chaos; once there is chaos, there is a freeze"). Despite such cyclical variations, the aggrieved Western consensus is that repression of human rights has intensified rather than easing with economic modernization. In 2015, the Pew Research Center conducted a public opinion poll in forty-nine countries in which a majority opined that since 2013 the human rights situation in the PRC has been bad and getting worse.[19] The CCP, aware of its soft power deficit, has expended billions to improve its image abroad and suppress any manifestation of domestic discontent, establishing a CCTV broadcast facility in Washington, D.C., covering the whole Western hemisphere, and circulating *China Daily* en masse.[20] But image softening is hard to do having given foreign reporters entrée to the country and then arousing their suspicions by placing tight constraints on their investigations.

One popular defense of China's human rights record has been the pseudo-Marxist idea that economic development will necessarily eventuate in democratization. Although China is now one of the largest economies on earth, per capita income has lagged investment (US$8,069 in 2016, according to the World Bank), but when it reaches $10,000 or some other transformative threshold, democratization is inevitable. A related idea is that human rights are technologically determined, particularly via communications technology. "In the new century, liberty will spread by cell phone and cable modem," President Bill Clinton theorized in a 2010 speech defending China's admission to the WTO. "We know how much the Internet has changed America, and we are already an open society. Imagine how much it could change China."[21] Interpersonal contact is also believed to have some impact: in the 2014–15 academic year, according to the Institute for International Education (IIE), over 304,000 Chinese were studying at American colleges, almost one-third of the total international student population.[22]

James Mann was among the first Westerners to challenge this assumption in his 2008 book *The China Fantasy.*[23] The Chinese leadership itself also has challenged and fiercely resisted any signs of identity convergence. Even as China's Internet population has become the world's largest, the Chinese leadership has created a vast and sophisticated "stability maintenance" (*wei wen*) apparatus dedicated to the elimination of politically unacceptable ideas at every stage of the Internet evolution, from chat rooms to bulletin boards to microblogs. Since 2010, the government has spent more on internal than on external security, and Xi Jinping's signature crackdown on corruption has been accompanied by a dragnet on human rights lawyers, public intellectuals, and media outlets, and greater emphasis on doctrinal orthodoxy in educational and judicial institutions.[24] The infiltration of Western political ideas was denounced by then National People's Congress (NPC) chair Wu Bangguo in a 2011 speech to the NPC in which he denounced the "five noes" or *wu bu gao*; in the spring of 2013, the attempt to shut out Western liberalism was intensified by the issuance of Document no. 9 to universities proscribing "seven unmentionables" (*qi bu jian*).[25] Denial of the relevance to China of Western political ideas is part of a general identity divergence that has widened since 2008, in part through the technological reinforcement of China's "Great Firewall" against non-Chinese Internet access. There are two conceivable interpretations of this prolonged freeze: one is that the failure of liberal capitalism in the GFC reinforced convictions of the decline of the West and confidence in the inexorable triumph of Chinese socialism; the other is a contrary assumption of growing insecurity about the decline of faith in the CCP.[26]

The pursuit of global human rights as the new ideological foundation of US foreign policy began in the Carter era and has continued under his successors of both parties. The usual vehicle for this pursuit has been the exercise of soft power, supported by such government propaganda agencies as the US Information Agency, Voice of America, Radio Free Asia, or, with specific regard to human rights, the Bureau of Democracy, Human Rights, and Labor, which publishes annual Country Human Rights Reports documenting abuses. But while anticommunism could tap economic and military constituencies (in the name of free markets, extended deterrence, etc.), human rights has an ambiguous or even indifferent relationship to established US economic and military interests. Governmental support for the pursuit of international human rights has consequently been relatively weak and episodic, and the issue can arouse a consequential popular constituency only after headline-setting abuses (such as Tiananmen). Hence much of the institutional support comes from the private sector, principally a congeries of nongovernmental organizations (NGOs). These, however, segment the human rights market by issue area, each NGO mobilizing a particular constituency of ideal interests (e.g., pro–underground churches, anti–death penalty, antiabortion, environmentalist) whenever an issue relevant to that NGO is raised. Rarely is an issue joined that is flagrantly violent enough to arouse a crosscutting mass constituency, and even more rarely is human rights a potential casus belli.[27] In China's case, the gradual tightening of the screws under Hu Jintao and Xi Jinping cannot compare in dramatic public impact to a televised massacre, and meanwhile, other aspects of the relationship—mutual economic benefits, high-level leadership summits, social and cultural exchanges—have had an offsetting effect, not to mention the deterrent impact of war between two increasingly evenly matched adversaries. There is little question that CCP repression incurs an abrasion of China's soft power, but the current regime seems to believe hard power is more important than soft power if forced to choose, preferring, however, to brandish both at once (and quite deftly).[28] In sum, the issue of human rights is apt to abrade US support in the long run but is unlikely in itself to precipitate confrontation.

Material Interests

The second aspect of bilateral relations is economic: although a cautious, top-down political rapprochement began in 1972, the economic relationship between the United States and China did not begin to blossom until the early 1980s, gaining a second wind after a post-Tiananmen pause. As China liberalized investment requirements in the 1990s to gain access to embodied technology, Western FDI began to flood in, creating investment and supply chains and contributing to a high-tech export sector. The bilateral economic relationship displaced the lost strategic rationale and remains the mainstay of the relationship since the end of the Cold War. Total trade between China and the United States has grown from $2 billion in 1979 to $601.1 billion in 2015. China is currently the third-largest export market for US goods (after Canada and Mexico), largest trading partner (displacing Canada in 2015), and by far the largest source of imports. From 2000 to the first quarter of 2017, the Chinese have invested almost $120 billion in the United States, nearly half of which came since early 2016.[29] In 2016, incoming Chinese FDI for the first time exceeded US investment in China (though in terms of accumulated stock, US investment in China is still several times larger than the Chinese footprint in the United States). Many US firms view participation in China's market as critical to staying globally competitive. General Motors (GM), for example, which has invested heavily in China, sold more cars in China than in the United States each year from 2010 to 2014, and the Greater China region in 2015 became Apple's largest market, exceeding even the Americas. US imports of low-cost goods from China benefit US consumers, holding down price inflation, and US firms that use China as the final point of assembly for their products or use Chinese-made inputs for production in the United States are thereby able to lower production costs.

China is the second-largest foreign holder of US Treasury securities ($1 trillion as of November 2016, down from $1.24 trillion in December 2014), helping keep US interest rates low. In the 2015–16 academic year, a total of 328,547 Chinese students studied at US universities and vocational schools, generating $11.43 billion in revenue. Additionally, an estimated fifty thousand Chinese students attended US secondary schools during this period. In 2014, Chinese tourists spent an impressive $24 billion in the United States, making up 10 percent of the $200 billion Chinese tourist market. In addition to Chinese students and tourists there are more than two million Chinese-born immigrants in the United States.

Of course there are also problems with the economic relationship. But then there have always been problems, so it may be useful to distinguish chronic problems from emergent problems. The biggest single chronic or structural problem is that of a consistently ballooning imbalance of trade and current accounts. There has been a slight imbalance in China's favor ever since China opened up, but this increased more rapidly after China entered the WTO in December 2001, thereby gaining immunity from unilateral US revocation of MFN (most-favored-nation) status to limit imports. In the fifteen years since it joined, China has consistently enjoyed extremely large trade surpluses with the United States even after its overall trade surplus declined, exporting about $4 worth of goods for every $1 of American goods that it imports. From 2006 to 2016, China's total exports fell 35 percent while imports rose, yet the US trade deficit with China (in goods) rose from $83.0 billion in 2001 to $367.2 billion in 2015, an increase of $284.1 billion. US exports to China rose at a rapid rate from 2001 to 2015, but from a much smaller base, from $19.2 billion in 2001 to $116.1 billion in 2015. China's trade surplus declined during the global financial crisis (GFC) but has grown rapidly since the crisis and, as of 2015, represents 60 percent of the US current account deficit. Economists and politicians have sometimes attributed the consistent imbalance to currency manipulation (i.e., holding down the value of the yuan in order to gain a price advantage for Chinese exports).[30] This was true for many years, but in response to US pressure on this issue (e.g., the then pending Schumer-Graham Bill, which threatened a 27.5 percent tariff on all Chinese imports unless China revalued its currency) China in 2005 instituted a "crawling peg," allowing the currency value to appreciate incrementally within a narrow band. From 2005 to 2014, the yuan thus appreciated vis-à-vis the US dollar by about 20 percent, temporarily interrupted by a People's Bank of China (PBC) peg during the GFC. In May 2015, the International Monetary Fund (IMF) estimated that the currency was fairly valued. We may infer that trade deficits are no longer driven by currency manipulation but by policies that distort domestic savings rates by subsidizing production at the expense of households.[31] Still the trade imbalance has risen every year since 1985 and continues to rise, reaching

US$367.17 billion in 2015 ($531 billion or 83 percent of the US deficit, compared to 33 percent in 2008).[32] Between 2008 and 2015, the US goods trade deficit with China increased $100.8 billion despite the GFC and subsequent decline of the overall US trade deficit. Trump promised in his 2016 campaign to reduce the trade deficit, and at the April 2017 Florida summit with Xi Jinping, the two agreed to a one-hundred-day plan for trade talks aimed at boosting US exports and reducing China's trade surplus; however, since that time, the trade deficit has continued to increase.

There are three likely suspects for the persistently burgeoning imbalance. China has protected industrial strategic sectors (such as IT) from competition, not only from foreign but domestic firms.[33] Second, the Chinese savings rate rose steeply in the early 2000s to one of the highest in the world (52.34 percent of GDP in 2009) and has remained high since (47.92 in January 2015) despite efforts to rebalance, outstripping investment. The average savings rate is 32 percent for developing economies and 21 percent for advanced economies. Third is Beijing's political will to preserve a positive trade balance in order to reach its planned goals of doubling 2010 GDP by 2020 and finance its Belt and Road Initiative. The US trade surplus amounts to more than 3 percent of China's GDP. As Xi's leading economic advisor Liu He put it in 2013, China "cannot shoulder excessive responsibility" for reducing its trade deficits with other economies.[34]

At the Third Plenum of the Eighteenth Congress in 2013, the Xi leadership unveiled a series of economic reforms aimed at rebalancing the economy from excessive reliance on export growth to domestic consumer demand, which would, all things being equal, facilitate more imports and less exports, thereby stimulating the global economy. Domestic consumer demand has, however, remained anemic, with the result that rather than allowing a flailing rebalance to drive growth rates still lower Beijing in 2015 liberalized loan terms and relaxed monetary constraints on investment in order to revive growth. In terms of the trade imbalance, the net effect was to further aggravate it. Despite frequent US complaints of this problem, which they claim has resulted in the loss of some 2.4 million jobs to China from 1990 to 2010 while running the largest bilateral trade deficits ever,[35] countermeasures have been weak and ineffective and are likely to remain so for at least three reasons. First, the long-standing US commitment to free trade, aside from the WTO rules the United States helped draft, invalidates any resort to explicit protectionism. Second, US FDI has made China a platform for exports into the American market from US-based multinational corporations (MNCs), creating a powerful domestic lobby against any restraint on Chinese imports (as the critical reaction to Bill Clinton's 1993 attempt to link imports to human rights demonstrated). These foreign-invested enterprises (FIEs) have grown to dominate China's export economy, particularly in the high-tech sector. Third, though only a fraction of Chinese imports, American exports to China are large and growing, creating their own protective domestic lobby.

Piling onto this chronic issue is a number of newly emerging ones. Under a debt load of some 250 percent of GDP (mostly corporate and local government debt), China's economic growth rate has slackened in recent years: real GDP growth fell from 10.4 percent in 2010 to 7.8 percent in 2012 to 6.9 percent in 2015 to 6.7 percent in 2016. The IMF projects that, over 2015–21, China's real annual GDP growth will average 5.9 percent. Economic uncertainty was compounded by the gyrations in stock market prices from January to September 2015 and by attendant flight capital.[36] Overall FDI entering China has declined, while outgoing Chinese investment has increased.

Amid the economic slowdown there has emerged on both sides a growing disenchantment with the business relationship. Among the outcomes that have cooled US enthusiasm are intellectual property violations estimated in the hundreds of billions of dollars, vast disparities in openness to foreign investment, state subsidies that distort markets and competition, and periodic manipulation of the renminbi to benefit China's export sector. According to various Western chambers of commerce (e.g., American and European), the investment climate has cooled as domestic industry has become more competitive.[37] Foreign investors are daunted by prosecutions based on a recently enacted antimonopoly law (from which Chinese SOEs are exempt), the continuing anticorruption campaign, and implementation of an indigenous innovation policy that privileges domestic firms and commits foreign competitors to share intellectual property.[38] Unnerved by former NSA contractor Edward Snowden's 2013 disclosures of NSA cyberintrusions in China, China passed a new national security law in July 2015, which was followed the next year by a cybersecurity law designed to ensure "secure and controllable" (*anquan kekong*) technology without a back door open to foreign espionage. This legislation obliges foreign firms that want access to the Chinese market to relocate their production, research and development, and data storage to the mainland and to hand over their computer source codes and other technological assets. Since 2006, China has been passing legislation protecting a growing list of strategic ("pillar") SOEs from either foreign or domestic competition (e.g., petrochemicals, electronics, aerospace), even as the SOEs in these sectors aggressively pursue their own acquisitions abroad.[39] Without relinquishing export markets, China's industrial policy is shifting to a kind of technological import substitution. Disappointed with its share of the profits and division of labor in joint ventures with foreign-invested firms, China has set about in its thirteenth five-year plan to scale the value-added ladder, bringing it into direct competition with the FIEs whose help it once welcomed.[40] This worries the FIE sector, leading the EU Chamber of Commerce to quip in 2015 that China was undergoing "reform and closing up."[41]

Meanwhile, China's birth-control policies have reduced population growth and labor has become more expensive ($8,986 per capita income in 2015); although wage rates are still well below those in the United States, they have risen more rapidly and are now higher than those in the Philippines, Thailand, Indonesia, and Vietnam (over five times the average manufacturing wage in India). The Chinese dependency ratio (the proportion of the populace less than fifteen and more than sixty years of age) has become demographically burdensome.

Yet the Chinese side has been unreceptive to such plaints. Rebutting attribution of the GFC to a global financial imbalance caused by China's huge capital account surplus (Bernanke's "savings glut"), China has argued that US fiscal profligacy precipitated the GFC and that subsequent US monetary policy fueled asset price bubbles around the world. The forcefulness with which Chinese leaders have put forward these narratives reflects their conviction that the balance in the bilateral relationship has shifted decisively in their favor. China no longer needs the United States as much as it once did: US investment in China is well below potential.[42] Still holding the world's largest cache of foreign exchange reserves, China has begun to draw down its unremunerative holdings of US treasuries, diversifying trade and outgoing FDI from the stagnant developed to the developing world (long heralded as the global proletariat).[43] The latest and most ambitious vehicle aiming to recycle China's capital surplus is the One Belt, One Road initiative, which proposes to loan up to US$2 trillion (not all of it Chinese) to client states on China's periphery to facilitate vast infrastructure projects crisscrossing Eurasia (and hire Chinese construction SOEs to build them). Meanwhile, Washington concentrated its political energy on the ambitious Trans-Pacific Partnership (TPP), covering everything from tariffs, state-owned enterprises, and intellectual property protection to investment rights and labor and environmental standards, only to finally give up on this effort with the change of administrations in 2016. Though the future is unclear, the outlook for the near future is a somewhat more economically detached and possibly competitive bilateral relationship, as the two turn in different foreign political economic directions.

Security Interests

The Sino-US security dilemma is in a bilateral sense illusory: neither China nor the United States has the slightest intention of invading, occupying, or declaring war on the other. This is not nineteenth-century Germany versus France, Cold War Europe, or a geopolitical confrontation in which one side's territorial gain is the other side's loss. "The broad Pacific Ocean is vast enough to embrace both China and the United States," Xi Jinping told John Kerry in May 2015.[44] Both are nuclear weapon states with assured second-strike capabilities; however, the balance of terror is asymmetric but stable, and there seems to be no quantitative strategic arms race.[45] Yet, at the same time, the two have the world's biggest arms budgets; the United States has the largest, and China's is the fastest growing. From 2006 to 2015, the US military budget shrank by 4 percent, from $768 billion in 2010 to $595 billion in 2015 in constant dollars, while China's grew by 132 percent, to fund the constant innovation of new weaponry conceived with each other in mind.[46] Still boasting the world's largest standing army, the People's Liberation Army (PLA) in the last decade has invested increasingly in its air force and navy: by 2030, the People's Liberation Army Navy (PLAN) intends to have 430 major surface combatants and a hundred submarines, and soon will have the world's largest merchant marine and coast guard (partly to protect the world's largest fishing fleet). Since the Gulf War, there is a competitive relationship in advanced conventional arms acquisition as well, accelerated on the Chinese side by the purchase of advanced Russian hardware and cybertheft of US weapons technology.[47] The recent Chinese introduction of SLBMs (submarine-launched ballistic missiles), stealth fighters, hypersonic glide vehicles, and antisatellite weaponry indicates that China is closing the strategic gap. Over the last several years, we have seen the testing of a new rail-mobile intercontinental ballistic missile (ICBM), the deployment of multiple independently targetable reentry vehicles (MIRVs) on some of its silo-based ICBMs, a new medium-range ballistic missile that is nuclear capable, and the first ever deterrence patrols of Chinese SSBNs (nuclear-powered ballistic missile submarines). China is also beginning to challenge US dominance in cyber and space warfare.

For the present, the problem is not the global strategic balance of power as in the US-Soviet Cold War but military preeminence in the economically dynamic Asia-Pacific region. The focus of China's ongoing military modernization is the air force and navy, two vehicles of force projection that will threaten US extended nuclear deterrence and ability to protect its Asian allies. China is not close to catching up to the United States in terms of aggregate capabilities, but it does not need to catch up globally to challenge the United States on its periphery.[48] China's efforts since the Cold War have been focused on what US military analysts call "A2/AD" (anti-access/area denial) weaponry to take Taiwan and prevent US intrusion into its territorial waters (the Yellow, East, and South China Seas). Beyond that, the PLAN aims to break through three island chains and project force into the Pacific and Indian Oceans; in the longer term, Chinese strategic ambitions extend to the far seas as well.[49] For now, China asserts the right to regulate foreign military activities within its exclusive economic zone (EEZ), which the United States disputes, resulting in incidents between Chinese and US ships and aircraft in 2001, 2002, 2009, 2013, 2014, and 2016. China also insists on its right to curtail the sale of arms to Taiwan and has become increasingly critical of the five US bilateral security alliances in Asia. But these issues are triangular rather than bilateral as they involve third parties.

Triangular Issues

While the bilateral relationship has hence diverged in its many dimensions with the rise of China, the triangular aspect emerged relatively suddenly to transform an ambivalent but sustainable socioeconomic nexus into a potentially dangerous geostrategic rivalry. The triangular dimension refers to China's relations with the other actors in the Asia-Pacific region, which serve as both audience and constituency to the bilateral dynamic.[50] Of course, grouping them all together as one point of a triangle involves enormous oversimplification, as China's relations with each actor are specific and unique. However, they all have certain basic things in common. In foreign as in domestic politics, Chinese tend to think hierarchically and to believe hierarchy reflects the rules of the game. Thus it is relevant that all are now smaller than China, both individually and collectively, while China is smaller than the United States.[51] China's bilateral relationship to each of its Asian neighbors is thus dominant but contingent on each country's relationship to a third power that can potentially trump it—in other words, it is triangular. This asymmetrically triangular dimension complicates Chinese foreign policy with fears of encirclement, collusion, and other contingencies. At the same time, it encumbers US policy with weighty issues of relative decline and power transition. It is more dangerous than the bilateral relationship because the third-party countries are autonomous and at greater risk, and that risk leads to unpredictable defensive measures hence escalating uncertainty. Yet triangular goals are highly prioritized on China's aspirational agenda and cannot easily be detached and bilateralized (though Beijing has tried to do so) because they all fit into a common strategy.

China has had a propensity for strategizing in implicitly triangular terms since the days of the United Front, when the CCP faced two adversaries at once: a "class enemy" with whom it had a zero-sum, or antagonistic contradiction, and a coalition partner with whom it had only nonantagonistic contradictions that could be temporarily compromised. During the latter phase of the Cold War, a strategic triangle was formed with the USSR in the former role and the United States in the latter, generalizing this conception in the Three Worlds theory of 1994. But throughout the Maoist period, China's strategic thinking was focused on global revolution and on great power politics.[52] As noted above, only after Tiananmen and the fall of European communism did China begin to envisage the Asia-Pacific region as a potential junior partner against the overweening power of a unipolar capitalist hegemon. But its image of its own position vis-à-vis Asia since the fall of the Iron Curtain has evolved over time from "hiding and biding" in the aftermath of its post-Tiananmen ostracism into "being able to accomplish something." Throughout the Deng Xiaoping period, China insisted that it was a developing country, refusing to join Group of 7 meetings because all the others were developed countries, for example. In 1996 (further elaborated in a July 1998 white paper), China introduced the New Security Concept calling for mutual trust, mutual benefit, equality, and coordination.[53] This innocuous document (very similar in content to the Five Principles of Peaceful Coexistence) appeared, however, in the context of a critique of existing security architecture as "outdated," "militaristic," and characterized by a "Cold War mentality."[54] The implicit target of these critiques was of course the US pentagonal alliance structure including Japan, South Korea, the Philippines, Thailand, and Australia, which from the Chinese perspective was designed to encircle and contain China's rise. This outdated framework should not be replaced by new security alliances but by nonbinding partnerships and informal win-win cooperation without need for anxiety-fraught formal blocks or alliances. To reinforce its charm campaign, China joined in signing the nonbinding Declaration on Conduct of parties to the South China Sea controversy in 2002 and the following year became the first non–Southeast Asian nation to sign ASEAN's Treaty of Amity and Cooperation (TAC), which pledged all signatories to settle disputes peaceably. The emphasis on reassurance continued with the peaceful rise/development and harmonious world rhetoric of the 2000s.

While the peace and harmony refrain has been repeated at the Eighteenth Party Congress in 2008 and beyond, subtle rhetorical changes have emerged. In May 2014, Xi Jinping gave the keynote speech at the Conference on Interaction and Confidence Building Measures in Asia (CICA), where he presented the New Asian Security Concept. Otherwise similar to the 1996 New Security Concept, this was accompanied by two slight but significant adjustments: First, the New Security Concept was now the "New *Asian* Security Concept," conceived to be regionally self-contained: "Asian problems should be solved by Asian people," as Xi put it in his CICA keynote.[55] Second, the core of national security is *economic* development. Implicit is the assumption that as the PRC becomes the leading trade partner of an ever increasing number of Asian countries their developmental prospects will depend on their economic relations with China. As Senior Counselor Yang Jiechi pointed out in June 2014, "By being the largest trading partner, the largest export market and a major source of investment for many Asian countries, China has accounted for 50 percent of Asia's total economic growth."[56] Indeed, since 2000 Sino-ASEAN trade rose from $32 billion to $350 billion in 2014, with estimates for 2015 reaching as high as $500 billion. Given the relative size of the two respective sides (not to mention the distribution of the trade imbalance), this will be an asymmetric interdependency in which the PRC can expect to wield predominant political influence.

Although most countries in the Asia-Pacific region are spending more on defense, China's defense spending far outpaces that of its neighbors. China now spends around three times as much as India on defense, and more than Japan, South Korea, Taiwan, and Vietnam combined.[57] The picture emerges of a classic bilateral security dilemma in which each side's defensive efforts are interpreted as menacing, precipitating defensive countermeasures that are similarly misinterpreted by the other side creating a spiral effect. The situation is complicated by the fact that this is not a bilateral but a triangular security dilemma. China's goal seems to be to catch up with the United States, while the other East Asian states for various reasons have shown no particular interest in keeping pace with China's arms spending. This gives China an increasingly formidable military overcapacity vis-à-vis its Asian neighbors, which China has flaunted since 2008 in frequent military exercises and hard-line rhetoric in defense of expansive territorial claims. This strategic asymmetry is not only regionally specific but relatively recent: Concerned about the "China threat" outcry after the 1995–96 Taiwan missile crisis, Chinese rhetoric had been reassuring ("harmonious world," "peaceful development") in the 1998–2008 period. But at the 2014 work conference on foreign policy, Xi emphasized specifically that Chinese diplomacy should be conducted "with a salient Chinese feature and a Chinese vision" in defending China's core national interests, while developing "a distinctive diplomatic approach befitting its role of a major country."[58]

Since around 2010, the rest of the region responded to Chinese increasing assertiveness in different ways. Japan, Vietnam, and India increased military spending and readiness. ASEAN's strategy, on the other hand, was to pursue a Code of Conduct and try to socialize China into the ASEAN Way of peaceful dispute resolution via engagement in the ASEAN Plus network. More than this it proved unable to do, as its ranks split between those with conflicting territorial claims and those without. As the third actor in this triangle, the United States, having no formal territorial claim at stake and yet increasingly upset by China's perceived territorial and power grab, announced a pivot or rebalance strategy, in which it alternately sought to encourage Asian resistance and to find some way to intervene directly without precipitating conflict with China. Since August 2013, the United States thus conducted six freedom of navigation operations (FONOPs) by sailing near Chinese-occupied islands despite Chinese warnings. But no other Asian nation joined these FONOPs, and aside from eliciting Chinese protests, they had no discernible impact on China's reclamation and militarization of the islands it occupied. China has tried (quite successfully) to keep the issue strictly bilateral, not just between China and ASEAN but between China and each national disputant, thereby maximizing its leverage. The threat of resistance from rival claimants or US intervention China met with threats of war.[59]

The Underlying Dynamic

What may we conclude from this review of the fraying bonds between the United States and the PRC? Clearly the relationship has become increasingly competitive and mistrustful despite strong trade ties and numerous institutionalized regimes and forums designed to alleviate misunderstandings and resolve difficulties. The question is, why? After all, many other littoral countries in Southeast Asia, particularly Vietnam and the Philippines, have been exploiting the fishing grounds and the subsurface hydrocarbon deposits of the South China Sea for decades, and some have expanded the islets they control. The territorial dispute is not a new one, having precipitated chronic altercations, including violent clashes in 1974 and in 1988, when more than seventy Vietnamese were killed. But the United States always maintained a strictly neutral position in previous skirmishes, pointing out that it had no sovereignty claim to any of the territory in question and urging disputants to resolve the issue peaceably. When Mischief Reef was occupied and gradually transformed into a military listening post housing more than a hundred Chinese soldiers in 1995, the United States did nothing and said little. Yet since 2010, the United States has repeatedly protested actions by the PRC that have not escalated to that level of violence. In April 2014, Obama was the first US president to include publicly the defense of Japan's administration of the Senkaku/Diaoyu islets in the Japanese-American treaty alliance. Still taking no official position on conflicting sovereignty claims in the South China Sea, the United States justified its intervention in terms of protecting the freedom of the seas and halting any unilateral change in the status quo. In a more militarized response, the United States in 2011 initiated a pivot or rebalancing of military forces to East Asia, including an air-sea battle concept that included new deployments or rotations of troops and equipment to Australia and Singapore.

The bilateral escalatory impetus has not been one-sided. While the PRC typically plays down Southeast Asian protests, describing its tactics as routine policing, American interventions have provoked vociferous Chinese protests, warning littoral states against inviting outside interference or meddling in local disputes. Why this disproportionate response—on both sides? The reason is that, although the United States admittedly has no skin in the game, the United States is the only participant with the military power to stop China's advance if it so chooses. Thus China is very sensitive to any US signal of opposition to China's salami-slicing tactics. While there is no indication the United States has any plan or strategy to do so, its statements of solidarity with contending claimants, freedom of navigation patrols, military exercises, arms sales, and strengthening of military ties with existing allies and courtship of new ones (such as Vietnam and India) have raised the level of tension, strengthened Chinese hard-liners, and contributed to regional polarization.

If heightened US defensiveness cannot be explained by the nature or magnitude of the threat, might the bilateral and triangular irritants discussed in this chapter more fully account for it? It is true that bilateral relations have deteriorated perceptibly over the past decade. On the ideological front, China has underscored its divergent national identity, seeking to ground this in a reconstruction of an Asian political culture and drawing a sharp distinction with Western liberal democratic values. Sensitive to being out of step with trends elsewhere in Asia, the CCP has applied an "internally tight, externally loose" (*nei jin wai song*) policy, lauding international democracy and arguing in favor of normative relativism in bilateral and multilateral human rights forums while cracking down ruthlessly on any domestic movement in that direction. Sino-US trade has become increasingly imbalanced in both good economic times and bad, regardless of the value of the yuan. As China closes the technological gap in the development of advanced and "smart" weaponry and its military budget escalates apace, security relations have also become increasingly fraught. All these trends are indeed troubling, but they have all long been extant. Yet bilateral relations, though uneven, were generally deemed reasonably manageable from 1978 to 2008. Thus the level of strictly bilateral tension is not sufficient to account for the emerging "Cool War."[60]

The argument here is that the current deterioration of relations can be attributed to a perceived power transition, which has emerged in both bilateral and triangular arenas. Though the bilateral and triangular dimensions feed into each other, the latter has been both more intense and difficult to resolve. Bilaterally, the preeminent challenge is the economic rise of China, an event whose geopolitical implications have only recently seized the American imagination. In 2008, China held the first Beijing (summer) Olympics, following a worldwide torch run and a four-hour video introduction by Zhang Yimou that displayed to the world China's historic achievements, whereupon China, like Germany in 1936, won more gold medals than any other contender. This was the first of a number of portentous symbols of China's achievements that clustered at the end of the decade, including the Shanghai Expo and the sixtieth anniversary of the revolution military parade in 2009.[61] The timing of China's rise was all the more impressive in contrast with a challenging global financial context. Lehman Brothers filed the largest bankruptcy filing in US history in September 2008, plunging much of the Western capitalist world into deep and prolonged recession. Although China's currency remained unconvertible at the capital account and the PRC had little exposure to collateralized debt obligations and other toxic US assets, China's developmental strategy had relied heavily on export-oriented growth and the sudden decline in export demand in developed country markets threatened an overall decline in its rate of growth as well. To prevent that, the Hu Jin-

tao–Wen Jiabao leadership in late 2009 implemented a four trillion yuan
(around US$640 billion) stimulus package, largely in the form of loans from
the banking sector to large SOEs. The stimulus focused on areas such as
housing, rural infrastructure, transportation, health and education, environment, industry, disaster rebuilding, income building, tax cuts, and finance.
The short-term impact was to enable the Chinese economy to offset falling
exports with domestic investment, sparing China from any single year of
negative growth throughout the crisis period. This bold fiscal rescue package
was to prove problematic in the long run as debts continued to mount, out-
pacing GDP growth, but that is another story. At the time the prevailing
view, both in China and abroad, was that through its bold and timely intercession China alone adroitly sidestepped the financial tsunami that the United States had unleashed upon the world. The United States also introduced a
stimulus package that was smaller and less effectively targeted, so the Chinese rebound was more impressive. As US indebtedness to China mounted,
its relationship to China was increasingly considered its most important ("G-
2"). Perhaps the United States was at last in terminal decline relative to a
demonstrably superior "socialism with Chinese characteristics"?[62] By the
time Hu Jintao and Wen Jiabao stepped down in 2012, China's growth rate
had slowed to 7.8 percent and another, smaller fiscal stimulus was deemed
necessary. Still they had achieved a GDP growth record exceeding 10 percent despite a worldwide economic downturn, the highest ten-year growth
rate China had yet achieved.

This meant that quite suddenly, much sooner than expected, China began
to regard itself as a "great power" (*da guo*). Whereas during the Maoist
period China's estimate of its international import outpaced its economic and
strategic capabilities (as did its estimate of the potential for the world revolution it aspired to lead), in the reform era (specifically the Deng Xiaoping era)
self-estimates tended to lag capabilities. As China joined regional and international organizations but did not actively participate in proceedings, its
undue modesty sometimes even occasioned accusations of being a "free
rider," taking what the institution had to offer while stinting its own contributions. China under Deng called itself (the largest and most successful) "developing country," and its voting record (and dues payments) in the UN
reflected that. But consciousness of greatness gradually dawned, and China
acknowledged its long-awaited arrival at great power status. Beginning in the
early 1990s, China dubbed itself a "responsible great power," anticipating
Zoellick's 2005 admonition to be a "responsible stakeholder."[63] When Libya
became embroiled in the Arab Spring in 2011, jeopardizing local Chinese
business interests, the Chinese navy was deployed to evacuate 35,800 Chinese workers; in March 2015, the PLAN again evacuated endangered Chinese workers from Yemen. China has become more willing to use its UN
Security Council veto in recent years.[64] And it has successfully pressed to

increase its voting rights in the World Bank and IMF, where it also suggested replacement of the dollar as international reserve currency and, in October 2015, successfully applied to have the renminbi included in the IMF's Special Drawing Rights (SDR) basket, even though the renminbi alone among SDR currencies has a politically fixed exchange rate.[65] With the rise of Xi Jinping in 2012, China publicly acknowledged its arrival as a great power of a new type. Thus, during Xi's June 2013 summit with US president Barack Obama at the Sunnylands Retreat in Southern California, he introduced "China's new model for great power relations," meaning (as was later explained) "no conflict, no confrontation, mutual respect, and win-win results."[66] By 2017, China's "great power" or "strong power" was evoked some twenty-six times in Xi Jinping's speech to the 19th Party Congress.

Even as it has pushed to boost its influence in existing international governmental organizations, China has also begun sponsoring its own alternative globalist hierarchy. In 2001, China founded the Shanghai Cooperation Organization (SCO) with Russia and four (later five) former Soviet Central Asian republics and a growing number of observers, two of which (India and Pakistan) have since become full members.[67] China took an active part in the Group of 20, particularly since it began to meet semiannually in 2008, and helped found the BRICS forum in 2010 (Brazil, Russia, India, China, and South Africa) partly to serve as a steering committee for the G20. China took the leading role in forming the ASEAN Plus Three (APT) forum in 1997, and the ACFTA in 2010. In 2013–14, China created two new development banks: the BRICS New Development Bank (NDB) and the Asian Infrastructure Investment Bank (AIIB) to supplement the existing Asian Development Bank and the World Bank. Likely clients of these banks will almost certainly include China's SOEs, which have aggressively pursued natural resource assets abroad (including infrastructure construction and farming), particularly in Africa and Latin America, with loans, joint ventures, and wholly owned investments. They will also very likely play major roles in the ambitious regional infrastructure projects China has recently launched.

This change of national identity and status has obviously had wide-ranging implications. China has come to view the ongoing power transition as inevitable, and has begun to comport itself as the natural leader of the smaller Asian states and a global pole rivaling the United States and the EU in world affairs. Indeed, with the collapse of the TPP and US withdrawal from the Paris climate agreement, China has volunteered for global leadership. Other countries, particularly in East Asia, have come to accept this self-concept and future trajectory and accord Beijing greater deference. While the United States has reasserted its primacy, a growing number of nations have ignored US warnings—for example, in the case of the AIIB, now including sixty-four nations but not the United States. These developments beg at least three questions about the ongoing power transition. First, is it subjectively real? Second, it is objectively true? Third, will it lead to war?

The question of subjective reality—in other words, whether there is a subjective will on the part of the rising power to overtake and surpass the hegemon—is crucial because in the absence of this subjective dimension the objective transition (in terms of GDP, military capabilities, etc.) becomes politically irrelevant. Thus as late as 1800, according to Angus Maddison, China's GDP in both per capita and aggregate terms was greater than that of the United States, Japan, or the leading European powers, yet there was no sense of rivalry or power transition between China and the West at that point simply because the two remained isolated and posed no perceived threat to each other.[68] Yet since the Chinese revolution, the core Chinese ambition to rise has always been in oblique reference to the United States, its model and rival. In 1978, Deng Xiaoping broached the "revival of China" (*zhenxing zhonghua*) slogan. In 1989, Jiang Zemin called for the "great rejuvenation of the Chinese nation" (*da fuxing*) to achieve a "prosperous, strong, democratic, culturally advanced, and harmonious modern socialist state" by the centenary of the founding of the PRC in 1949. The first two decades of the twenty-first century were conceived to be a "period of strategic opportunity,"[69] with an interim goal, incorporated into the Sixteenth Party Congress Work Report in 2002, to quadruple China's 2000 GDP by 2020. This will require an annual average growth rate of 7 percent (providing a better rationale than the need to avoid unemployment for the obsession with maintaining high growth). All this is encapsulated in Xi's China Dream, a vague but evocative vision of a great future, modern and traditional, great yet humble, and egalitarian but hierarchical.[70] In sum, the subjective will to overtake and surpass the United States has been sustained with almost obsessive intensity for the past fifty years. The US response, in contrast to the alarm about the Soviet and Japanese challenges, has thus far been relatively nonchalant, partly because China, until quite recently, played down its ambitions.[71]

There is also empirical evidence of the objective reality of power transition, though it is not undisputed. China has quintupled its GDP since 1990, surpassing US GDP in purchasing power parity (PPP) terms in 2014, and aims to double it again by 2020. In terms of nominal GDP, the conventional basis for national growth comparisons, China's GDP is now about 60 percent that of the United States. In the five years from 2010 to 2015, even as China was slowing down, China's GDP growth rate averaged 8.52 percent, while that of the United States, in supposed recovery from the GFC, was 2.21 percent. If we extrapolate from these or any other set of recent comparison years into the future China will soon overtake and surpass the United States in nominal GDP as well—according to the IMF, by 2020–25.[72] To be sure, as private investors are often prudently advised, past performance does not indicate future results. The American eclipse has been prematurely anticipated before: the Soviet Union boasted a much higher growth rate in the 1950s when Khrushchev threatened to "bury" the United States economically. Japan, during its era of high-speed growth, threatened to overtake the United States as well, and as Wang Jisi has pointed out, China itself has previously anticipated the American demise more than once only to see hopes fade.[73]

Could the Chinese juggernaut also "choke"? Although China has achieved record-breaking growth for over three decades, the huge stimulus package that saved China from the GFC resulted in massive overcapacity and a debt burden that has continued to rise faster than the rate of GDP growth. The incremental capital output ratio has increased, meaning a given amount of investment achieves progressively lower productivity as much of it is used to service existing debt. Wage rates have been rising quite steeply since 2011 for demographic reasons;[74] export-oriented growth faces declining external demand in stagnant developed economies. The stock market fails to obey CCP dictates, and there has been serious capital flight to escape the campaign against corruption.[75] China has been trying to shift from the investment-driven growth model that propelled its rise to greater reliance on domestic consumption, but the reforms introduced to do so at the Third Plenum of the Eighteenth Congress in December 2013 have not yet been successfully implemented. China has been quite successful in its efforts to shift the industrial structure from manufacturing to services, but it has made far less progress in boosting private consumption. Particularly disappointing in the eyes of many economists has been the limited progress in letting the market play a decisive role in resource allocation. The high priority placed on the anticorruption campaign, though sorely needed and highly popular, seems to have stifled cadre initiative. Thus, China may find itself stuck in a middle-income trap.[76] Lant Pritchett and Lawrence Summers predict a "regression to the mean," meaning China's growth rate will drop from its current velocity to the global average of around 2 percent, simply because that is what high-growth economies typically do.[77]

The future is unknown; different assumptions lead to different trajectories. Nonetheless the premise of this book is that, all things being equal, China will indeed probably overtake the United States in nominal GDP in the near if not precisely foreseeable future. Any such forecast is a leap in the dark, but it may be heuristically useful to pursue it as far as it will go, given that it is realistically plausible and has thus far received surprisingly little serious consideration.[78] Our premise is based on the following considerations. Predictions based on "regression to the mean" or "middle-income trap" are derived from general propositions about developing economies and then extrapolated to China, but is it not conceivable that China is exceptional, not like other developing economies? Indeed it might be deemed distinctive in at least three ways. First, the subjective will remains very strong: Chinese Leninism is a goal-rational system in which regime legitimacy is premised largely on collective performance, for which catching up with the developed nations has long been the ultimate touchstone. This determination no doubt has been rekindled by the rise of Xi, who by barring any prospect of political reform or freedom of discourse leaves the economy as the only field open to the Chinese people to realize their China Dream. And with a relatively modest standard of living, the Chinese people are still highly motivated (per capita GDP is still only 25 percent that in the United States). Second, the Chinese economic leadership has heretofore been highly competent at managing their economy, focusing narrowly on growth while relegating environmental damage, human rights abuses, and other externalities to lower priority. Thus, they have successfully negotiated financial crises that derailed many of their peers (such as Brazil or Russia). Though China's total indebtedness is dangerously high, resulting in real estate and stock market bubbles, the debt is internally financed, there is high domestic savings, and a closed capital account and hence is not vulnerable to the sudden departure of foreign investments that precipitated the collapse of Thailand in the Asian financial crisis (AFC). In China, there is no firm distinction between monetary and fiscal policy, between banking and monetary policy, or really between the private and the public sector. Despite extensive market reform, it is still essentially a command economy, and so Chinese leaders have more resources at their disposal than bourgeois politicians. Third, even though China's GDP growth has slowed considerably and may slow still further, it is even in decline growing around three times the pace of the United States in alleged recovery. These exceptional Chinese characteristics are likely to sustain Chinese growth well beyond the normal range of developing nation growth sprints.

Assuming a power transition is then occurring, will it lead to war? Graham Allison has pointed out that in twelve of sixteen cases in the past five hundred years when a rising power challenged a ruling power, the outcome was war.[79] Yet this is no iron law; at best it is a probable but avoidable outcome. According to classical realism, a symmetrical distribution of capabilities leads to a balance of power, which is deemed relatively stable. And the advent of nuclear weapons increases the mutual incentive to achieve a peaceful power transition. Historical experience suggests that to have a successful (peaceful) transition, three preconditions are necessary: First, the challenger must not infringe on the incumbent's core interests. Second, the incumbent hegemon must be willing to yield gracefully to the challenger's reasonable demands. Third, both must share a determination not to let their differences become kinetic (i.e., go to war).

Both sides have expressed their preference to avoid war, reasonably enough: war would ruin the China Dream even if it survived, and the United States has some very unhappy memories of wars in Asia, not to mention general war fatigue. This was the first point in Xi Jinping's "new type of great power relations" outlined at Sunnylands, with which Obama agreed. But meanwhile, China has also made clear its intention to push the United States out of the region, as Mearsheimer puts it, and to reassert its remembered historical hegemony over the maritime commons.[80] And China is in a relatively strong position to do so, given its size, population, growth rate, and large and increasingly sophisticated security apparatus. On the other hand, the US economy is now about twice as trade dependent on the Pacific as on the Atlantic and sees its economic future in enhancing that linkage.[81] Thus despite the agreement to avoid war, there has been little agreement on either the specific preconditions or consequences of power transition. The United States insists that it welcomes China's rise, to which it has contributed by opening the US market and helping modernize the Chinese economy (and inadvertently, the military), but at the same time, it refuses to countenance any catching up and surpassing scenario. In terms of national identity and ideology, the two have been on diverging tracks since at least 2012. In terms of core interests, China's are empirically clear while US interests are often not, and those that are (e.g., the pentagonal alliance network, the Taiwan Relations Act) are orthogonal to some of China's core interests.[82] Both seem to prefer multilateral organizations that exclude the other (e.g., the RCEP, the TPP). The United States asked China to act as a "responsible stakeholder" but failed to implement reforms of the IMF it promised in 2009 to allow China to hold commensurate financial stakes, so Beijing proceeded to set up the NDB and the AIIB, which Washington vainly attempted to block. The US rebalance to Asia announced in 2011 consists of a military component and an economic component. The PRC was included in neither, and it is hard to find grounds to confute the Chinese suspicion that both are designed to encircle and contain it. In short, the only one of the three preconditions for a smooth power transition that has been upheld with any consistency is the mutual commitment to avoid war. Both approach the "America passing" scenario with self-protective hypocrisy: while the United States pretends it welcomes China's rise it does all it can to forestall it; while China insists it has no intention of pushing the United States out of the Western Pacific, its actions belie its words. This is not mere vainglorious hypocrisy, for to surrender a hegemonic position even in order to preserve the peace would have momentous long-term consequences for the losing nation and for the form of life of everyone in it.

The approaching power transition seems likely to resemble neither the forced transition from Spain to England following the defeat of the Spanish Armada in 1588 nor the smooth transition from England to the United States in the early twentieth century. A major hegemonic war seems unlikely, as both are aware of the costs and well equipped with nuclear deterrents. Yet conflicting ambitions and a widening political cultural trajectory gap as China seeks to establish a more distinctly Chinese identity make peaceful power transition increasingly difficult. At the same time, the United States deems any hint of power transition incompatible with its own identity. Both have attempted to quarantine still relatively intact zones of cooperation, such as trade and more recently climate control, from issue linkage to the more contentious zones, but this is becoming increasingly difficult as suspicion spreads. Chinese nationalism is certainly part of the reason, but this can also be seen in the rise of Trump in the United States. Both agree on the need to avoid war but find their core interests to be mutually incompatible and diplomatically intractable. So what lies ahead? If not a new cold war a rather fragile peace, full of elevated discourse above the diplomatic table and kicking beneath it.

CONCLUSIONS

Despite a long and, for the most part, amicable relationship, Sino-US relations have recently cooled. This can be ascribed to a mixture of plausible subjective and objective irritants that had previously been deemed annoying but negotiable. The puzzle of why previously tolerable frictions have become less tolerable, we have argued, lies in the dynamic factor of power transition. As the two near the tipping point in China's rise and America's relative decline, the underlying dynamic becomes impossible to ignore. The United States becomes increasingly sensitive about signs of decline and China becomes anticipatorily assertive. US attempts to co-opt the PRC to its preferred rules-based international order run athwart Chinese resistance to "peaceful evolution" and quest for a distinctive nationalist cultural identity. As political cultural trajectories diverge, soft power imaginations on both sides run riot over the nightmare of life under opposing hegemonic auspices. These problems are manifest in both bilateral and triangular relations, but the latter has become the hostage and trigger for bilateral mistrust. There are at least three reasons for this: First, rivalries involving third parties tend to be dismissed from bilateral talks on jurisdictional grounds. China generally insists in principle on talks only with the countries concerned, avoiding internationalization or multilateralization of the issue. Second, the third parties involved in these disputes, though smaller and weaker, all have decision-making autonomy that must be taken into account, multiplying possible scenarios. Finally, while the United States cannot very well order China not to overtake it when it has been insisting all along that it welcomes China's rise, if it views China's assertive turn as a form of aggression, there is ample precedent in the international normative framework to assemble an international coalition to block that; and to some extent, it has indeed been doing so.

The United States has been saying that it welcomed China's rise and has urged it to become a responsible stakeholder in the international order for years, and now that it has done so the United States has had second thoughts. While in Chinese eyes this bespeaks rank hypocrisy, to the United States China's rise looked much more innocuous at an earlier stage when the developmental gap between the two was wider and when China was more deferential to US leadership. Beijing's irenic rhetoric has continued, but its actions in defense of its perceived interests have become more forcible. Still, China insists that its headline policy remains "peace and development" and that it has no current intention of challenging US core interests. China's view that there are no intractable differences tends, however, to focus on bilateral issues. Thus the September 2015 Washington summit could claim progress toward a bilateral investment treaty, regulation of cyberespionage, peaceful resolution of air-sea encounters, and policies to stem global warming, but discussion of maritime disputes in China's near seas went nowhere. These China insists on settling bilaterally with the countries concerned. Yet bilateral negotiations for joint development have also gone nowhere, as China stipulates that joint development is contingent on recognition of Chinese sovereignty. And on sovereignty claims China is unyielding: "national sovereignty and territorial integrity are not bargaining chips," as Cui Tiankai put it.[83] To reinforce its claims China bolsters its air and naval assets, already regionally dominant. For ASEAN, hopes of internally balancing a nation of nearly 1.4 billion with the world's largest army and second-largest arms budget are not high.[84] So states with the most to lose turn to external balancing, and the United States welcomed their embrace. Meanwhile, the decline of strategic trust between the two giants means that the doubletalk employed by each side to reassure the other loses credibility. China does not believe US assurances that the rebalancing is not aimed at containment nor does the United States believe Chinese assurances that it will not fortify the islets it has constructed in the South China Sea. While China's response to Southeast Asian protests has been relatively low key, to the prospect of US intervention the response has been high decibel, presumably because while the former represents no serious threat to its claims the latter does. Thus, although the United States has no territorial claims to any of China's near seas, the maritime dispute has become increasingly bipolar.

If the difference between the outspoken but ineffectual US response to China's current assertiveness in contrast to its more discreet response to earlier PRC advances is attributable to power transition, does it follow that the issue has been blown out of proportion? Is the crisis all just a paranoid phantasm of "America passing"? True, the United States has no countervailing claim to these waters, or the resources beneath them. While the Seventh Fleet routinely patrols them to safeguard the maritime commons it has not interdicted Chinese commercial or naval vessels, even when they intrude in the territorial waters of Guam, Hawaii, or the Aleutians. The United States is in that sense already "sharing" the South China Sea, the East China Sea, and so forth. It is China that has challenged the US naval presence. Still China complains of "containment." Should the United States then "give" China the seas it claims to own by not actively contesting Chinese sovereignty claims with FON patrols? It is probably fair to say that US "loss" of all these small islets and reefs would not critically damage US national interests. Most of the vast maritime traffic in these waters is Asian, not American, as is the bounteous fishing. Regardless of the size of subsurface hydrocarbon deposits these are not owned by the United States. Even if China makes good all its sovereignty claims, declaring an air defense identification zone (ADIZ) over the South China Sea to defend them and then subsuming Japan, Korea, and Southeast Asia in the Chinese economic and security orbit, mutually profitable trans-Pacific economic relations can still continue for as long as there is complementary supply and demand for capital, technology, and commodities. In material terms, the biggest losses would be to China's East Asian neighbors, not the United States. For the United States, the short-term significance of the loss would be chiefly reputational, discrediting US leadership and commitments to its allies—why should I follow you if you cannot protect me?

This line of argument is brought to a point by Hugh White, who finds the underlying cause of the standoff in the inability of the United States to yield graciously to China's rise.[85] The United States has treated China like the nemesis it hopes to avoid, surrounding it with bases, filling its airwaves with capitalist propaganda, and bolstering mutual defense alliances and quasi alliances all along its periphery, vainly trying to prolong its own doddering regional primacy. Instead of trying to keep China down the United States should construct a concert of powers similar to the post-Napoleonic Holy Alliance. For a successful power transition, surely it is necessary for the hegemon to yield gracefully to otherwise reasonable requests by the challenger. This the United States has failed to do. Refusal to yield raises the risk that China wins anyhow, as in the AIIB debacle, with even greater damage to its reputation.

But is a concert of powers not what already exists? China is a member in good standing of APEC, the ASEAN Regional Forum, EAC, the UN Security Council, and most other important regional and international forums. China wants more, insisting on its own institutional architecture—the AIIB, SCO, and the belt and road megaproject. How much more will China want as it rises? Beijing may not yet know (and will certainly not tell us). Its demands may well be elastic, dependent on opportunities. US-Asia policy is still the main impediment to those opportunities. If the United States yields, will the PRC be satisfied, or will it take it as a sign of weakness and press its advantage? Which interests should the United States be ready to yield in order to orchestrate a more harmonious concert of powers? Taiwan? The Philippines?

The practice of trading off other people's sovereignty claims has a long inglorious history.

Yet the struggle is not over who controls East Asia, or even whether China will eventually surpass the United States in GDP, for based on population size and relative GDP growth rates both outcomes have good odds in the long run. If a peaceful transition is all that is desired, Beijing would be only too glad to oblige. The more troubling underlying question is, a transition to what? Ironically, China's near-term vision of its future domestic and international identity has diverged increasingly from the Western paradigm even as it has narrowed the modernization gap with the West. China is aware of the risks of being a political cultural outlier and has tried to mask this divergence with a dualistic rhetoric—international democracy, value relativism, and economic globalism in the international arena and dogmatic uniformity enforced by a massive security apparatus and Great China Firewall at home. It is as yet unclear whether this is a path-dependent institutional pattern or merely a short-term reaction to its recent growth slowdown. Can a two-dimensional solution be sustained? There is risk of a sort of discourse arbitrage in which values intended for export leak back home, as at Tiananmen.

In any case, the more China's trajectory diverges from the West the more the latter is likely to resist power transition, because life under an anathematic hegemon could be unpleasant. And the more it resists, the greater the risk that power transition will not be harmonious. As the power gap closes and capabilities are more equally distributed between the two, Chinese confidence grows and its willingness to compromise declines: China can say no. At the same time, the outcome of war, should it come to that, becomes more unpredictable and destructive with the acquisition of advanced weaponry. Differing growth rates (assuming the PRC growth continues to outpace that of the United States) may contribute to miscalculation: for example, the rising power may overestimate its chances by anticipating its future advances, and the incumbent power may perceive a need to strike first as it sees its marginal advantage slipping away. Still, if both sides act rationally a bilateral strategic standoff may be prolonged and reasonably stable, for each still has the power to inflict unacceptable devastation on the other, and is likely to retain that even after loss of a precise balance. Though economic ties have deteriorated somewhat, they are still sufficiently attractive that absolute gains trump relative loss. The situation may come to resemble the thirty-year Cold War between the United States and the USSR—with the crucial difference that the United States may well lose this match.

NOTES

1. Odd Arne Westad, *Restless Empire: China and the World since 1750* (New York: Barnes & Noble, 2015), 365.

2. See Gilbert Rozman, ed., *East Asian National Identities: Common Roots and Chinese Exceptionalism* (Stanford, CA: Stanford University Press, 2012)

3. Cf. James Truslow Adams, *The Epic of America* (Boston: Little, Brown, 1931).

4. In his speech commemorating the latter occasion, Xi Jinping referred to China as "the major battlefield of World War II in the East," and celebrated the defeat of Japan as "the first occasion when China won a war completely against a foreign enemy" (ignoring the Pacific theater). Quoted in Rana Mitter, "Beijing's History Narrative," *Japan Times*, September 7, 2015, https://www.japantimes.co.jp/opinion/2015/09/07/commentary/world-commentary/beijings-history-narrative/#.WfULG0HaZkg.

5. Gilbert Rozman, *National Identities and Bilateral Relations: Widening Gaps in East Asia and Chinese Demonization of the United States* (Washington, DC: Woodrow Wilson Center Press, 2013).

6. By mid-2014, 8,249 articles with "*zhongguo meng*" in the title had been published in China according to the China National Knowledge Infrastructure (CNKI; China academic journals database); cf. Camilla T. N. Sorenson, "The Significance of Xi Jinping's 'Chinese Dream' for Chinese Foreign Policy: From 'Tao Guang Yang Hui' to 'Fen Fa You Wei,'" *Journal of Chinese International Relations* 3, no. 1 (2015): 55.

7. Nikita Khrushchev, *Khrushchev's Memoirs* (New York: Little, Brown), 250–57. Bo Yibo, *In Reflection of Certain Critical Decisions and Events* (Beijing: Central Party School Press), 692, as cited in Shen Zhihua, "The Great Leap Forward, the People's Communes and the Rupture of the Sino-Soviet Alliance," *Parallel History Project on NATO and the Warsaw Pact: The Cold War History of Sino-Soviet Relations*, June 2005.

8. Between 2000 and 2011, PRC defense expenditures increased at an average annual rate of 13.4 percent, making China the biggest defense spender in East Asia. David Isenberg, "Shifting Defense Expenditures in East Asia," *Time*, October 26, 2012. GDP growth averaged around 10 percent during this period. In 2014, the Chinese military budget rose more than 12 percent while GDP growth stood at 7.4 percent.

9. As in the tripartite intervention by Russia, Germany, and France in 1895 over the terms of the Treaty of Shimonoseki signed between Japan and Qing Dynasty China that ended the First Sino-Japanese War, in which Japan was forced to return the Liaodong Peninsula to China.

10. Chen Jian, "The Myth of America's 'Lost Chance' in China: A Chinese Perspective in Light of New Evidence," *Diplomatic History* 21, no. 1 (December 1997): 77–86.

11. Z. P. Feng, *The British Government's China Policy, 1945–1950* (Keele: Ryburn Publishing, 1994).

12. "In the light of the experiences in these 40 years and these 28 years, all Chinese without exception must lean either to the side of imperialism or to the side of socialism," Mao said in 1949. "Sitting on the fence will not do, nor is there a third road" (2:21–22), as quoted in J. Chester Cheng, *Documents of Dissent: Chinese Political Thought since Mao* (Stanford, CA: Hoover Institution Press, 1980), 8.

13. Gordon H. Chang, *Friends and Enemies: The United States, China, and the Soviet Union, 1948–1972* (Stanford, CA: Stanford University Press, 1990). Although Chang attributes this differential to a deliberate US strategy to split the two, there were also reasons to consider China a more radical and dangerous adversary.

14. Thomas Christensen, *Worse than a Monolith: Alliance Politics and Problems of Coercive Diplomacy in Asia* (Princeton, NJ: Princeton University Press, 2011).

15. The Five Principles of Peaceful Coexistence, first formulated in an agreement with Nehru as early as 1954 and frequently reaffirmed since, are "mutual respect for sovereignty and territorial integrity, mutual non-aggression, noninterference in each other's internal affairs, equality and mutual benefit, and peaceful coexistence." The 2005 New Security Concept is "mutual trust, mutual benefit, equality and coordination." Xi Jinping articulated his New Asian Security Concept in May 2014 as "common, comprehensive, cooperative and sustainable" and "development is the greatest form of security." Xi Jinping, "New Asian Security Concept for New Progress in Security Cooperation," Remarks at the 4th Summit of the Conference on Interaction and Security-Building Measures in Asia, Ministry of Foreign Affairs of the People's Republic of China, May 21, 2014.

16. Deng Xiaoping, *Selected Works of Deng Xiaoping*, vol. 3, *1982–1992* (Beijing: Foreign Language Press, 1994), 350.

17. Kenneth Lieberthal and Wang Jisi, *Addressing U.S.-China Strategic Distrust*, John L. Thornton China Center Monograph Series no. 4 (Washington, DC: Brookings, March 2012).

18. L. Dittmer, "Chinese Human Rights and American Foreign Policy: A Realist Approach," *Review of Politics* 63, no. 3 (Summer 2001): 421–61.

19. Richard Wike, Bruce Stokes, and Jacob Poushter, "Views of China and the Global Balance of Power," Pew Research Center, June 23, 2015, http://www.pewglobal.org/2015/06/23/2-views-of-china-and-the-global-balance-of-power/.

20. See David Shambaugh, "China's Soft-Power Push: The Search for Respect," *Foreign Affairs*, July–August 2015. While exploiting democratic latitude to propagate Chinese viewpoints, China blocks or restricts the intrusion of Western soft power (civic NGOs, think tanks, Internet companies, and media outlets) into China.

21. "Full Text of Clinton's Speech on China Trade Bill," *New York Times*, March 9, 2000, https://partners.nytimes.com/library/world/asia/030900clinton-china-text.html.

22. Tea Leaf Nation Staff, "The Most Chinese Students in America," *Foreign Policy*, January 4, 2016, http://foreignpolicy.com/2016/01/04/the-most-chinese-schools-in-america-rankings-data-education-china-u/.

23. James Mann, *The China Fantasy: Why Capitalism Will Not Bring Democracy to China* (New York: Penguin, 2008).

24. In the so-called 709 Crackdown, on July 9, 2015, some three hundred Chinese rights lawyers and activists were detained, interrogated, or threatened in what some observers have called the harshest crackdown on human rights and civil society in decades.

25. Wu Bangguo's "five noes" were "no to multiparty politics; no to diversification of [the party's] guiding thought; no to the separation of powers; no to a federal model; and no to privatization." Cary Huang, "Outgoing NPC Standing Committee Chief Rejects Western Political Models," *South China Morning Post*, March 9, 2013, http://www.scmp.com/news/china/article/1186652/outgoing-npc-standing-committee-chief-rejects-western-political-models. Xi Jinping's "seven unmentionables" (*qige buyaojiang*) are universal values; press freedom; the civil society; citizens' rights; the party's historical aberrations; the "privileged capitalistic class" (*quangui zichan jieji*) (i.e., senior party cadres); and an independent judiciary. "Document 9: A China File Translation" *ChinaFile*, November 8, 2013.

26. See Wang Huning, *Meiguo fandui Meiguo* (Shanghai: Wenyi chubanshe, 1992); also Zheng Yongnian, *Zhongguo moshi: jingyan yu kunju* (Beijing: Yangzhi wenhua, 2011).

27. True, human rights was used by the G. W. Bush administration to justify the US invasion of Iraq in 2002, but only post hoc after no weapons of mass destruction (WMDs) could be found.

28. Xi Jinping's visit to India in September 2014 was immediately preceded by PLA border incursions into the disputed border area of Ladakh, attributed by many commentators at the time to lack of coordination or even military insubordination. But the officers in charge of the units deployed were promoted in August 2015.

29. According to the Rhodium Group, as cited by Noam Scheiber and Keith Bradsher, "China-US Culture Clash," *New York Times*, International Edition, June 13, 2017, 7.

30. The currency was not "manipulated," exactly, but pegged at a fixed rate while productivity increased, pushing prices down while product quantity and quality increased. Nonetheless it had a major impact on American manufacturing at the time: "New research shows that currency manipulation by China and other countries was the main cause of historically high trade imbalances in the 2000s, widening the US trade deficit by $200 billion or more starting in 2003." Joseph E. Gagnon and Melina Kolb, "Currency Manipulation Was the Leading Cause of Record Trade Imbalances in 2000s," Peterson Institute of International Economics, June 15, 2017, https://piie.com/research/piie-charts/currency-manipulation-was-leading-cause-record-trade-imbalances-2000s.

31. The US Treasury Department disagreed, stating in October 2014 that the yuan remains "significantly undervalued." Ian Talley, "U.S. Trade Gap with China, 80% of Trade Deficit, Hits Historic High," *Wall Street Journal*, November 4, 2014, http://blogs.wsj.com/economics/2014/11/04/u-s-trade-gap-with-china-80-of-trade-deficit-hits-historic-high/.

32. Furthermore, the IMF in 2016 projected that at current exchange rates, the China-US current account imbalance will increase substantially in the medium term and that China's surplus will double in size as a share of global GDP in five years.

33. China has tried since the late 1990s to move past catch-up industrial strategies and push techno-industrial policy into global innovation and high-tech industries, resulting in the selection of large "pillar" or "strategic" industries favored by state subsidies and protected from competition. Thus seven new "emerging strategic industries" were selected in 2010, and ten were designated in "China 2025."

34. Liu, He, "中国发展成功的原因及未来发展趋势" [The reasons for China's success and future developments], *China Trade Magazine*, May 17, 2013.

35. Economists generally agree that China trade (among other things) has had negative effects on US manufacturing employment, which declined from seventeen million in 2000 to eleven million in 2010, though they differ over exactly how much. Some have estimated that the China factor explains 25 percent of the decline in American manufacturing jobs between 1991 and 2007 and 40 percent of the loss after 2000. David H. Autor, David Dorn, and Gordon H. Hanson, "The China Shock: Learning from Labor Market Adjustment to Large Changes in Trade," National Bureau of Economic Research Working Paper 21906, 2016, http://www.nber.org/papers/w21906.

36. According to Goldman Sachs, $500 billion left the country in the first nine months of 2016 (as much as $2 trillion over the past two years), driving down the price of the yuan.

37. According to an American Chamber of Commerce in China report published in 2016, of nearly five hundred member companies surveyed, 80 percent felt less welcome in China, one in four have already moved their capacity out of China in the last three years, or were planning to move. Half of those companies moved or were planning to move to other Asian countries, while 38 percent chose to move back to North America.

38. For example, in June 2014, Beijing rolled out a new semiconductor strategy that entailed investing up to RMB1 trillion (US$156 billion) over five to ten years, to cut a reliance on imports for more than 90 percent of national supply. China spent $241 billion buying semiconductors in 2014—more than on any other import, including oil. Simon Mundy, "Taiwan's Chipmakers Push for Chinese Thaw," *Financial Times*, December 6, 2015, https://www.ft.com/content/e2554560-98cf-11e5-9228-87e603d47bdc?mhq5j=e7.

39. Take the automobile sector, for example. When US automakers sell in China, they are met with import tariffs of 25 percent. That's why 96 percent of the 27.5 million vehicles sold in China in 2016 were built there. When US automakers like GM build in China, they are required by law to form joint ventures with Chinese companies, allocating them 50 percent or more of the shares. The United States, by contrast, imposes tariffs of just 2.5 percent and lets foreign car companies own their entire US-based operations. Jonathan Swan, "Car Wars: Trump Plans Auto Fight with China," *AXIOS*, March 19, 2017, https://www.axios.com/trump-preparing-to-confront-china-over-cars-2320999602.html.

40. China's "Made in China 2025" plan calls for Chinese companies to produce 40 percent of core components and materials in China's manufacturing chain by 2020, and 70 percent by 2025. Thus, between January 2014 and August 2016, out of 991 mergers and acquisitions in the global chip sector, almost one-third involved China. Chinese state media has reported that as much as $160 billion will be aimed at funding China's domestic semiconductor industry in the next decade.

41. According to an Organisation for Economic Co-operation and Development (OECD) measure for investment effectiveness, as cited by David Dollar, "China as a Global Investor," Brookings Institution, May 18, 2016.

42. See David Dollar, "United States–China Two-Way Direct Investment: Opportunities and Challenges," Discussion Paper, John L. Thornton China Center, Brookings, January 2015. As the Chinese have become increasingly restrictive about foreign investment in their high-growth service sectors, by the end of 2014 the United States had about $1 trillion invested in its prospective TPP partners but only $67 billion invested in China. This may to some extent be attributed to China's attempt to climb the global value-added ladder: when manufacture was king, China's annual FDI inflow averaged around 6 percent per annum, but this has dropped to 1 percent as China shifts to the tertiary sector.

43. China has engaged in two major recent sell-offs of US debt, in August 2015 and January 2016. As of October 2016, China had liquidated US$413 billion, leaving it with $1.12 trillion, compared to Japan's $1.13 trillion.

44. David Brunnstrom, "Despite Tension, Xi Says US-China Relations Are Stable," Reuters, May 16, 2015, https://www.reuters.com/article/us-usa-kerry-china/despite-tension-xi-says-u-s-china-relations-are-stable-idUSKBN0O203J20150517.

45. All countries keep these numbers classified, China especially, but best estimate as of 2014 is that while the United States has around 2,000 active nuclear warheads China has around 250.

46. "Military Expenditure," Stockholm International Peace Research Institute, April 1, 2016, https://www.sipri.org/research/armament-and-disarmament/arms-transfers-and-military-spending/military-expenditure. China's defense budget grew by roughly 640 percent (adjusted for inflation) between 1996 and 2014, and Beijing raised spending by another 10 percent (before inflation) in 2015. For an excellent up-to-date overview, see Eric Heginbotham et al., *The U.S.-China Military Scorecard: Forces, Geography, and the Evolving Balance of Power, 1996–2017* (Santa Monica, CA: RAND Corp., 2015).

47. China has improved its technological sophistication faster than anticipated, having developed (or cloned) two stealth jets, multiple independently targeted intercontinental ballistic missiles (MIRVs), sub-launched ballistic missiles, anti-ship ballistic missiles, and hypersonic glide bombers. China has more medium- and short-range missiles than any other nation, many of them deployed against Taiwan.

48. Eric Heginbotham, Michael Nixon, Forrest E. Morgan, Jacob Heim, Jeff Hagen, Sheng Li, Jeffrey G. Engstrom, Martin C. Libicki, Paul DeLuca, David A. Shlapak, David R. Frelinger, Burgess Laird, Kyle Brady, and Lyle J. Morris, *The U.S.-China Military Scorecard: Forces, Geography, and the Evolving Balance of Power, 1996–2017* (Santa Monica, CA: RAND Corp., 2015), http://www.rand.org/pubs/research_reports/RR392: "Over the next five to 15 years, if U.S. and PLA forces remain on roughly current trajectories, Asia will witness a progressively receding frontier of U.S. dominance. . . . PLA forces will become more capable of establishing temporary local air and naval superiority at the outset of a conflict. In certain regional contingencies, this temporal or local superiority might enable the PLA to achieve limited objectives without 'defeating' U.S. forces. Perhaps even more worrisome from a military-political perspective, the ability to contest dominance might lead Chinese leaders to believe that they could deter U.S. intervention in a conflict between it and one or more of its neighbors. This, in turn, would undermine U.S. deterrence and could, in a crisis, tip the balance of debate in Beijing as to the advisability of using force."

49. China's *Defence White Paper 2014*, released on May 26, 2015, signals a shift in the PLA Navy's focus from "offshore waters defence" to "open seas protection" of China's "overseas interests." State Council Information Office of the People's Republic of China, "China's Military Strategy," May 2015, Beijing, http://eng.mod.gov.cn/Database/WhitePapers/. On July 1, 2015, China's National People's Congress passed a new domestic law that confers upon the PLA Navy the duty to defend these overseas interests, through military action if necessary.

50. See L. Dittmer, "The Strategic Triangle: An Elementary Game-Theoretical Analysis," *World Politics* 33, no. 4 (July 1981): 485–516; also anthologized in Klaus Knorr, ed., *Power, Strategy, and Security: A World Politics Reader* (Princeton, NJ: Princeton University Press, 1983), 37–68; also published in Philip M. Chen, ed., *Faces and Phases of Triadic/Triangular Relationships* (Taipei: Asia and the World Institute, 1987).

51. The hierarchical dimension is to China ambiguous and protean: China is a great power but only recently, and it still defers to Russia, for instance, which is now much smaller in population and GDP. China surpassed the United States in 2014 as measured in purchasing power parity (PPP) but is only around 60 percent in nominal GDP; yet it is growing faster than the United States and looks forward to surpassing it.

52. Apparently uneasy with the hegemonic connotations of "great power," Beijing prefers to translate *da guo* as "large country." That is, in my view, a form of persuasive translation. See C. L. Stevenson, "Persuasive Definitions," *Mind* 47 no. 187 (1938): 187–331.

53. "Each country has the right to choose its own social system, development strategy, and way of life and no other country should interfere in the internal affairs of any other country in

any way or under any pretext, much less resort to military threats or aggression." See David M. Finkelstein, *China Reconsiders Its National Security: The Great "Peace & Development Debate" of 1999* (Alexandria, VA: CNA Corporation, 2000).

54. Chinese commentators complain of Asia's frustrating inability to be "self-reliant," pushing it into the US embrace (*Renmin ribao* [*People's Daily*], May 24, 2014). And the US alliance system creates "tension and antagonism" *People's Daily*, May 1, 2013.

55. Xi Jinping, "New Asian Security Concept for New Progress in Security Cooperation," Remarks at the 4th Summit of the Conference on Interaction and Confidence Building Measures in Asia, http://www.fmprc.gov.cn/mfa_eng/zxxx_662805/t1159951.shtml.

56. Ministry of Foreign Affairs of the People's Republic of China, "Join Hands in Working for Peace and Security in Asia and the World," June 21, 2014; as cited in Bonnie S. Glaser and Deep Pal, "Is China's Charm Offensive Dead?" *China Brief* 14, no. 15 (July 31, 2014), accessed August 15, 2014, http://www.jamestown.org/single/?tx_ttnews%5Btt_news%5D=42691&no_cache=1#.U_POkX7q5v8.

57. Institute of International Strategic Studies, "Military Balance 2014 Press Statement," http://www.iiss.org/en/about%20us/press%20room/press%20releases/press%20releases/archive/2014-dd03/february-0abc/military-balance-2014-press-statement-52d7.

58. As quoted in Angela Poh and Mingjiang Li, "China in Transition: The Rhetoric and Substance of Chinese Foreign Policy under Xi Jinping," *Asian Security* 13 (2017), http://www.tandfonline.com/doi/abs/10.1080/14799855.2017.1286163?src=recsys&journalCode=fasi20.

59. After the fifth FONOP in July 2016 (coinciding with the UNCLOS arbitral ruling), Chinese defense minister Chang Wanquan warned of maritime security threats and called for increased preparations for what he termed a "people's war at sea" to "safeguard sovereignty." In May 2017, President Rodrigo Duterte of the Philippines reported on a recent exchange with Xi Jinping: "We intend to drill oil there, if it's yours, well, that's your view, but my view is, I can drill the oil, if there is some inside the bowels of the earth because it is ours," Duterte said. "His response to me, 'we're friends, we don't want to quarrel with you, we want to maintain the presence of warm relationship, but if you force the issue, we'll go to war.'" Manuel Mogato, "Duterte Says China's Xi Threatened War If Philippines Drills for Oil," Reuters, May 19, 2017, http://www.reuters.com/article/us-southchinasea-philippines-china-idUSKCN18F1DJ.

60. Noah Feldman, *Cool War: The Future of Global Competition* (New York: Random House, 2013).

61. In the last twenty years, China's GDP surpassed that of Canada in 1993, Italy in 2000, France in 2005, the United Kingdom in 2006, Germany in 2008, and Japan in 2010. In 2012, it surpassed the United States as the world's biggest trading nation, ending long US dominance of world trade. At the advent of reform and opening, China's total trade value was only $20.6 billion, ranking thirty-second among all trading nations; by 2014, it was $4.3 trillion—number one in the world. In three decades, China's economy has grown more than a hundredfold, at an average annual rate of around 10 percent. By 2016, China's foreign exchange reserves reached US$3.1 trillion, down from 2014 but still the largest such cache ever amassed. And, as China's economy grew, its military prowess has increased correspondingly. From the mid-1990s to the late 2000s, China's share of global wealth doubled while its military budget grew around sixfold. According to the Stockholm International Peace Research Institute (SIPRI), a Swedish research institute, annual defense spending rose from over $30 billion in 2000 to almost $120 billion in 2010, second only to the United States. The United States still spends about four times as much on defense, but if spending trends continue, China will achieve military parity within fifteen to twenty years. The speed of China's development of technologically advanced weapons has continued to surprise intelligence analysts, with the development of anti-ship ballistic missiles and fourth-generation stealth fighter jets, and recent experiments with hypersonic glide missiles. Politically, as one of five officially acknowledged nuclear weapon states and permanent member of the UN Security Council (UNSC), China has also become more willing to use its UNSC veto in recent years, usually in concert with Russia.

62. See Wu Xinbo, 'Understanding the Geopolitical Implications of the Global Financial Crisis," *Washington Quarterly* 33, no. 4 (2010): 155–63.

63. Robert B. Zoellick, Deputy Secretary of State, "Remarks to National Committee on U.S.-China Relations, New York City, September 21, 2005," US Department of State Archives, https://2001-2009.state.gov/s/d/former/zoellick/rem/53682.htm.

64. From the time China joined the UN in 1971 until 2007, China used its UNSC veto only three times, in connection with the Taiwan issue. Since 2007, it has used the veto six times, all in concert with Russia.

65. In 2010, China succeeded in having its voting rights and those of developing countries increased at the World Bank so that China is now third after the United States and Japan. A similar arrangement was also made at the IMF, but it came to naught due to the failure of the US Congress to ratify the agreement.

66. China's core interests were defined in the Three-Point Proposal as a new formula for the US-China relationship in particular and for other great powers in general. The Three-Point Proposal received little coverage in the US media but ample coverage in Chinese media: "(1) No clash or confrontation. This means that the two nations will objectively and reasonably look at each other's strategic intent, insist on becoming partners not opponents, and handle conflicts and differences through dialogue and nonconfrontational means. (2) Mutual respect. The countries will respect the choice the other side has made on its sociopolitical system and path of development, mutually respect each other's core interests and major national concerns, seek harmony and bury hatchets, be forgiving, learn from each other, and make progress together. (3) Seeking cooperation and win-win. The two sides should abandon a zero-sum mindset, be considerate of the other's interests, promote common development while pursuing its own, and deepen integration of interests." *China Daily*, "Visit to Lift New Type of Ties," February 13, 2015, www.chinadaily.com.cn/opinion/2015-02/13/content_19575693.htm.

67. In the summer of 2015, the SCO decided to admit India as the sixth full member.

68. Angus Maddison, *Contours of the World Economy, 1–2030 AD; Essays in Macroeconomic History* (Oxford: Oxford University Press, 2007); see also his *Chinese Economic Performance in the Long Run* (Paris: Development Centre, Organisation for Economic Co-operation and Development, 1998).

69. In his 2002 report to the Sixteenth Party Congress, Jiang Zemin foresaw a "20-year period of strategic opportunity" during which China could focus on building its domestic economy. "Full Text of Jiang Zemin's Report at 16th Party Congress on November 8, 2002 (17/11/2002)," Permanent Mission of the People's Republic of China to the United Nations Office at Geneva and Other International Organizations in Switzerland, http://www.china-un.ch/eng/ljzg/smwx/t85795.htm.

70. "*Xi Jinping: chengqian qihou jiwang kailai jixu chaozhe Zhonghua minzu weida fuxing mubiao fenyong qianjin*" [Xi Jinping: From past to future carry forward and courageously advance toward the goal of the great rejuvenation of the Chinese nation], Xinhua Net, November 29, 2012, http://news.xinhuanet.com/politics/2012-11/219/c_113852724.htm.

71. Cf. Michael Pillsbury, *The Hundred-Year Marathon: China's Secret Strategy to Replace America as the Global Superpower* (New York: Henry Holt, 2015), passim.

72. See also Dwight Perkins et al., "Forecasting China's Growth to 2025," in *China's Great Transformation*, ed. Loren Brandt and Thomas G. Rawski (Cambridge: Cambridge University Press, 2008).

73. "The theory of the decline of the United States is not something that has just appeared in the past few years. In 1946, Mao Zedong said that the American imperialists were a paper tiger. At the time a series of events occurred, such as the launch of a satellite by the Soviet Union in 1957 and, in the 1970s, the defeat of the United States in the Vietnam War and the de-linking of the dollar from gold, there were invariably people around the world who predicted the decline of the United States. There was the rapid development of the Japanese and West German economies at the end of the 1980s and in 1991 the United States asked its allies for money to fight the Gulf War, and at those times theories about the decline of the United States also abounded. Following the Iraq war, there has been an abrupt decline in the soft power of the United States, and at present there is also the sub-prime mortgage crisis, so there is really nothing strange about some people being pessimistic about the United States." Wang Jisi, "US Power/US Decline and US-China Relations," *Asia-Pacific Journal-Japan Focus* 6, no. 11 (November 1, 2008), http://apjjf.org/-Wang-Jisi/2950/article.html.

74. China's "demographic dividend" has expired. The labor force continues to decline and its aging population continues to expand. According to data that China's National Bureau of Statistics released in January 2017, at the end of 2016, the number of working-age Chinese who were between the ages of sixteen and sixty was about 33.25 million lower than in 2011. At the same time, China's population aged sixty years and over at the end of 2016 increased by 45.87 million compared with 2011. *Caixin*, February 27, 2017, http://datanews.caixin.com/2017-02-27/101059600.html.

75. The rate of working-age population growth has fallen from 2.5 percent in 1979 to less than 1 percent in 2011, and is expected to turn negative before 2020. Jane Hallmaier, "Challenges for the Future of Chinese Economic Growth," Board of Governors of the Federal Reserve System International Finance Discussion Papers No. 1072, January 2013, http://www.federalreserve.gov/pubs/ifdp/2013/1072/ifdp1072.pdf.

76. See Wing Thye Woo, "China Meets the Middle-Income Trap: The Large Potholes in the Road to Catching Up," *Journal of Chinese Economic and Business Studies*, 4, no. 4 (November 2012): 313–36.

77. Lant Pritchett and Lawrence H. Summers, "Asiaphoria Meets Regression to the Mean," NBER Working Paper No. 20573, October 2014, http://www.nber.org/papers/w20573.

78. For an exception, see Martin Jacques, *When China Rules the World: The End of the Western World and the Birth of a New Global Order* (London: Penguin Press, 2012).

79. Graham Allison, *Destined for War: Can America and China Escape Thucydides's Trap?* (Boston: Houghton Mifflin, 2017).

80. John Mearsheimer, "Can China Rise Peacefrully?" *The National Interest*, October 25, 2014, accessed at http://nationalinterest.org/commentary/can-china-rise-peacefully-10204.

81. "The United States has been, and always will be a Pacific nation," as Barack Obama put it in his November 2011 address to the Australian parliament. "As the world's fastest growing region—and home to more than half the global economy—the Asia-Pacific is critical to achieving my highest priority, and that's creating jobs and opportunity for the American people. With most of the world's nuclear power and some half of humanity, Asia will largely define whether the century ahead will be marked by conflict or cooperation." "Remarks by President Obama to the Australian Parliament," The White House—Office of the Press Secretary (November 17, 2011), http://www.whitehouse.gov/the-press-office/2011/11/17/remarks-president-obama-australian-parliament.

82. The United States generally prefers to define its foreign policy interests in terms of adherence to general rules, rather than spheres of interest. On the question of reunification of Taiwan, for example, American policy has been neither to support nor oppose reunification outright but to stipulate that it take place peacefully and with the democratic consent of the citizenry of Taiwan.

83. As quoted in "'Sovereignty Not a Bargaining Chip': China's Ambassador," Reuters, December 15, 2016, http://www.atimes.com/article/chinese-ambassador-u-s-sovereignty-not-bargaining-chip/?utm_source=The+Daily+Brief&utm_campaign=ac8fc584a4-2016_12_15&utm_medium=email&utm_term=0_1f8bca137f-ac8fc584a4-16240211.

84. See David C. Kang, "A Looming Arms Race in East Asia?" *National Interest*, May 14, 2014, http://nationalinterest.org/feature/looming-arms-race-east-asia-10461. Only Vietnam has made serious efforts to keep pace.

85. See Hugh White, *The China Choice: Why America Should Share Power* (New York: Oxford University Press, 2013).

Chapter Three

The "Great" Strategic Triangle

The relationship between these two vast autocracies confronting each other astride the Eurasian heartland was recently lauded by Xi Jinping as a model of great power relations. But historically it has been more ambivalent. Russia, though its expansionist thrust was toward the east and the south, was culturally acclimated to the West, where it felt like a cultural outlier; as Dostoyevsky put it, "In Europe we are too Asiatic, whereas in Asia we are too European."[1] China's historical self-image, in contrast, was that of the self-sufficient "central kingdom," with little need for international reference groups. The relationship between the two has been in constant flux, bewildering observers with diametrical shifts from friendship to rivalry and back again. The premodern relationship was initially distant, with growing proximity in the nineteenth century leading to a predatory turn. This was seemingly overcome in the first half of the twentieth century by Soviet adoption of a revolutionary foreign policy and its nurturance of Chinese revolutionary efforts, only to lapse once again into fierce ideological and limited physical violence during the second half of the century. The relationship currently finds itself in full flower of postideological collaboration. Despite the current painstakingly institutionalized "constructive and strategic partnership," the overwhelming emphasis in the analytical literature has been on the more disputatious periods, leaving little basis for understanding the nature and dynamics of the periodic shifts between harmony and antagonism.[2] These shifts seem to have been determined by three factors: geography (still one of the longest land borders in the world), relative power, and triangulation (to what extent are the two jointly threatened by a third power). The most decisive of these factors is the third, the only one of the three susceptible to strategic choice.

59

We begin with a discussion of Sino-Russian history and the accommodation of national identities. We then move to an analysis of bilateral issues,
including ideal and material aspects, which is followed by consideration of
the relevance of power asymmetry in the relationship. We then move to
triangular issues, of which there are two: the shared relationship to the former
Soviet republics of Central Asia, many of which border China, Russia, or
both, and the United States, with which both have had a rather mixed experience. This is followed by a brief conclusion.

HISTORICAL AMBIVALENCE

Until the rise of the Mongols, the Chinese empire was largely oblivious to the
less developed Slavic principalities to the west, only recently brought to a
semblance of unity under Kievan Rus' (ca. 882–1240). In 1223–40, Batu
Khan, grandson of Genghis (Temujin) and leader of the Golden Horde that
fell heir to the northern realms of the sprawling Mongol empire, accompanied by his principal strategist Subutai, invaded Kievan Rus' and other Russian principalities, sacking and burning Moscow, Kiev, and twelve other
cities, sparing only Smolensk and Novgorod when the latter agreed to pay
tribute. This was no mere raid; the Golden Horde built themselves a capital
called Sarai on the lower Volga, where they continued to collect tribute and
exercise dominion for nearly three centuries, by far outlasting the reign of the
Mongol Yuan dynasty in China. The impact of what became known as the
Tatar yoke has been mythologized as one of grievous suffering, the source of
Oriental despotism (as subsequently practiced by Ivan the Terrible), the
death penalty, long-term imprisonment and torture, even Russia's being left
out of the Western European Renaissance, Reformation, and Enlightenment.
But the Mongols also contributed to the development of a postal road network, census, fiscal system, and more efficient military organization. And
they did not really interfere much in social life; as Shamanists (at the time)
they were quite broad-minded about other religions and permitted subject
populations to retain their own customs and culture, letting Russian princes
collect taxes on their behalf.[3] Though the descendants of the Golden Horde
were swept aside in imperial Russia's penetration into Siberia in the sixteenth and seventeenth centuries, the Mongol heritage is still visible in that
some 15 percent of the families of the boyars, or Russian nobility, claimed
Mongol descent (e.g., Boris Godunov, Nikolai Bakhmetev).

   If the Mongols profoundly affected Russian civilizational development,
Russia's reciprocal impact on imperial China was relatively minor. Russia
would lag China developmentally for the next several centuries, with a population that did not reach thirteen million until 1725 (compared to China's
brilliant civilization of some 150 million people). Imperial Russia's expan-

sion was gradual, motivated at first largely by overcoming the Mongol or Tatar occupation. After pushing back the Teutonic Knights and the Swedes in the west, the thrust was eastward, sweeping aside the last remnants of the Mongol khanates in the sixteenth and seventeenth centuries in a drive to the Siberian Pacific that extended to Alaska and even Northern California. Initial contacts with the Qing were deferential (mid-seventeenth-century Russian visitors to Beijing were obliged to *koutou* [prostrate themselves] before the emperor). But the decline of the Qing coincided with the Russian industrial revolution following the defeat of Napoleon, and Russian appetites for trade, natural resources, and territory led to increasing infringements on imperial China. Moving down the Amur basin they founded a fortified township named Nerchinsk on its headwaters, building forts and fur-trading posts on both the Amur/Heilongjiang and Ussuri/Wussuli Rivers. In response to growing Chinese concern, in 1685 the Russians proposed negotiations to delimit a boundary, and the two sides met in August 1689 outside Nerchinsk. The Chinese delegation brought a retinue numbering in the thousands, with cannon-armed junks on the river in support, heavily outnumbering the Russian side. When the two sides could not agree, the Chinese threatened to destroy Nerchinsk, whereupon the Russians returned to the table and at length acquiesced to most of the Chinese claims. The treaty provided for the destruction of the Russian forts and settlements in the Amur basin, and its overall effect was to preserve imperial China's territory from Russian encroachment for the next century and a half.

By the mid-nineteenth century, the Chinese empire had fallen on harder times, weakened by the Taiping Rebellion and by defeat in the Opium Wars and other imperialist depredations. From 1730 to 1900, imperial Russia swallowed up most of Central Asia as well as all of the Transcaucasus. In the Far East, Russia participated in China's "century of humiliation," seizing the 350,000-square-mile Primorsky and Khabarovsk regions (including the future city of Vladivostok) to add to its empire. (These are the only territories taken from China by Europeans that still remain unreturned.) With the Treaty of Nerchinsk in effect defected, the Russians demanded a new boundary settlement. By the Treaties of Aigun (1858) and Peking (1860),[4] negotiated amid the Taiping Rebellion, China was cut off from the Pacific north of its erstwhile tributary Korea and from the entire Amur River below its confluence with the Ussuri (because a clever Russian diplomat named Kozakevich drew the boundary along the Chinese bank of the channel, China was barred from navigating the two rivers). Construction of the Trans-Siberian Railway (1891–1916) and the decline of the Qing offered further opportunity for territorial gains, and in 1898, Russia elevated Port Arthur and Dalian to treaty port status, occupied Manchuria in the wake of the Boxer Rebellion, and further extended its sphere of influence over China's northeast in 1905 (though the Japanese evicted them from Manchuria after the Russo-Japanese

War in 1904–5). After encouraging the Mongols to rebel in 1910, Russia established a protectorate over Outer Mongolia in the course of the 1911 Xinhai Revolution. By the end of the Tsarist Era, Russia had seized some 1.65 million square kilometers of Chinese territory (by Chinese estimate).

The Bolshevik Revolution marked another dramatic shift, as the new Soviet regime unilaterally renounced its share of the Boxer reparations as well as all the tsars' territorial acquisitions in China in the Karakhan Manifesto (1919). Basking in Chinese gratitude, Moscow quickly established diplomatic relations with the warlord-dominated Peking Republic (1924), while also advising and helping organize the Chinese Communist Party (CCP), and simultaneously directing the reorganization of the Nationalist Party (Kuomintang, or KMT) along Leninist lines. As it happens, much of the area that the newborn Union of Soviet Socialist Republics (USSR) promised to relinquish was out of its control, held by counterrevolutionary White forces, and as soon as that problem was solved, Moscow quietly abandoned much of the Karakhan declaration and set about reconsolidating tsarist boundaries. Despite this, and despite the quite fallible advice the CCP got from their Comintern advisors on how to wage revolution, Russia managed to maintain cordial, often influential, relations with both KMT and CCP, avoiding duplicity by consistently urging cooperation between the two.[5] Moscow divided its commitments, signing a nonaggression pact in 1937 and a "treaty of friendship and alliance" in 1945 with the Nanking regime, promising not to support the CCP (while supporting the CCP), in return for which China agreed to Mongolian "independence."[6] After some three decades of turmoil, during which two KMT-CCP united fronts were formed (to protect Moscow's eastern flank from Japan) and then dissolved, the two antagonists were brought together in 1945 for a year's fruitless negotiations. When civil war resumed at the end of 1946, CCP forces, with crucial Soviet assistance,[7] prevailed surprisingly swiftly over an apparently superior but corrupt and exhausted KMT regime. The KMT was driven across the Yangtze, then from Hainan, finally taking refuge in tiny Taiwan (where against all odds, it eventually succeeded in building a successful capitalist democracy), while the CCP turned to the Communist Party of the Soviet Union (CPSU) for help in consolidating its revolution.

The two risks in any security alliance are abandonment and entrapment, and beginning in the late 1950s, Nikita Khrushchev became increasingly leery of being entrapped by what he perceived as Mao Zedong's "adventurist" proclivities, leading Mao to accuse Khrushchev of abandonment. The context of this dynamic was the rise of China in the 1950s and the even more conspicuous rise of the Soviet Union, which averaged 7.2 percent gross domestic product (GDP) growth and became the second-largest economy in the world,[8] culminating in the launching of *Sputnik I* and *II* and the first intercontinental ballistic missile in 1957, to international astonishment. Mao was mightily impressed by this achievement, leaping to the conclusion that, as he said in Moscow later the same year, "the east wind is prevailing over the west wind. That is to say, the forces of socialism are overwhelmingly superior to forces of imperialism. . . . We have left the west behind." In itself this expression of confidence in the socialist future was not inconsistent with the views of Khrushchev ("Whether you like it or not, we will bury you," as he put it in 1956) or any other communist leader. But later in the same speech, he expostulated his views of nuclear warfare:

> Let us imagine, how many people will die if war should break out? Out of the world's population of 2,700 million, one-third—or if more, half—may be lost. It is they and not we who want to fight; when a fight starts, atomic and hydrogen bombs may be dropped. I debated this question with a foreign states-man. He believed that if an atomic war was fought, the whole of mankind would be annihilated. I said that if the worst came to the worst and half of mankind died, the other half would remain while imperialism would be razed to the ground and the whole world would become socialist.[9]

The Soviet leadership was appalled. Khrushchev, in his secret speech denouncing Stalin at the Twentieth Congress of the CPSU in 1956, had proclaimed a new era of "peaceful coexistence and peaceful competition" with capitalism. When the United States cultivated the "spirit of Camp David" with Khrushchev in 1959 (keeping Beijing at arms' length), this seems to have had an additional radicalizing impact on Beijing's foreign policy, as the CCP denounced Khrushchev's peaceful coexistence (forgetting their own Five Principles of Peaceful Coexistence) and began fomenting criticism of Soviet revisionism throughout the communist bloc. And the dispute was not merely rhetorical: China started shelling Jinmen and Matsu after Taipei fortified these small islands off China's coast in 1954 and continued to do so until the Eisenhower administration threatened a nuclear strike; in the summer of 1958, Beijing launched an even fiercer artillery bombardment. Moscow maintained public support for China against US threats but quietly sent Gromyko to Beijing to urge caution. China started the first border clash with India in 1959 (in the Julong and Kongka incidents) by ambushing Indian border patrols that were investigating the road across the contested Aksai plain from Xinjiang to Tibet, which the Chinese had been clandestinely constructing since 1957. Moscow took a neutral public stance on the issue while criticizing Beijing internally, both of which Mao rebuked as a betrayal of socialist solidarity. On June 20, 1959, just before talks between the Soviet Union, the United States, and Britain on stopping nuclear tests and the summit between American and Soviet leaders, the Soviet Union unilaterally halted transfer of the atomic bomb model and design technology to China. In 1960, the Soviets completely withdrew their military advisors and abolished large portions of arrangements for economic and military cooperation. China would build its own bomb, Mao promptly decided, and within five years, China did.

Thus the period of "friendship" segued into three decades of fratricidal polemics, geopolitical encirclement and counterencirclement, arms race, and border violence that obsessed both sides at the time and has puzzled them since. Deng Xiaoping retrospectively summed up the roots of Chinese discontent by calling the alliance "unequal." But of course that was the whole point: the Soviet Union was developmentally superior, a "big brother" or model for China's socialist future, ideally suited to help China grow and develop. Besides, the relationship became far more equal after the death of Stalin, as Khrushchev needed Chinese support. The complaints voiced by the CCP at the time of the rift began with Khrushchev's "secret speech" denouncing Stalin at the Twentieth CPSU Congress in November 1956, which had a democratizing but unsettling effect on party leaderships in all communist party-states and on Mao's leadership position in particular. Mao's Great Leap Forward initiative raised Soviet objections, because of its intrinsic flaws and because it hubristically challenged the ideological leadership of the CPSU. This and cumulative other grievances (including Mao's unconcealed personal contempt for the younger man) prompted Khrushchev to withdraw all Soviet advisors in 1960, thereby curtailing many joint industrial projects, with ruinous impact on a Chinese economy already reeling from a Leap failure that China refused to admit publicly.

But the dispute also spread beyond the bloc to the Third World, where two now diverging models of communist revolution began to compete for sponsorship of national liberation wars. National identity eclipsed ideological consensus as each sought to demonstrate the unique relevance of its own revolutionary and subsequent nation-building experience to other developing countries. Ideological competition pressured Third World countries and parties to make irrelevant choices on fine points of Marxist Doctrine. The dispute thus escalated from speeches at internal forums of the communist international in Moscow to public polemics in the early 1960s and finally to a protracted Red Guard siege of the enormous Soviet embassy in Beijing during the Cultural Revolution. In 1962, Beijing accused Khrushchev of both adventurism and then capitulationism in the 1962 Cuba missile crisis; Khrushchev retorted by accusing China of capitulationism in allowing Britain to retain Hong Kong. Beijing then finally brought the border issue into contention, calling the Treaty of Peking an "unequal treaty" and saying in effect: "You taunt us that we should have broken a treaty and used force to seize back Hong Kong: but how would you like us to break the Treaty of Peking and seize back the lands the tsars stole?" Moscow took that rhetorical rejoinder as unveiling a serious threat of Chinese irredentist aggression.

From Beijing's perspective, the most sensitive phase of the rivalry was touched off by the Soviet invasion of Czechoslovakia in August 1968, exciting Chinese apprehensions of analogous application of the Brezhnev Doctrine to the People's Republic of China (PRC). Mutual suspicion and escalating polemics resulted in the mutual fortification of border forces, culminating in a Chinese-initiated "warning" clash at Zhenbao (Damansky) Island on the Chinese side of the main channel of the Wusuli (Ussuri) River on March 2, 1969. The Russians not only retaliated savagely (resulting, according to recent revelations, in thousands of casualties in an apparently indecisive outcome) but also subjected the Chinese to a sustained siege of coercive diplomacy.[10] For the next half year, they provoked a series of clashes along the entire length of the border (including Xinjiang), augmented by both veiled and public warnings to the effect that the USSR was considering a preemptive nuclear strike against the nascent Chinese nuclear first-strike force. Meanwhile, the Vietnam War was still at a delicate stage, where US strategic bombing of Hanoi and Haiphong and the US incursion into Cambodia made the possibility of Chinese fraternal intervention quite real. The PRC, finding itself on the brink of confrontation with both superpowers at once (in the context of which Moscow was suggesting to Washington the option of Soviet-US collusion), was obliged to calculate its national security carefully. The Soviets did succeed in driving the Chinese to the negotiating table— border talks convened in Moscow in October 1969, alternating between capitals on a semiannual schedule for the next decade. But they won few concessions there. The Americans achieved a much more meaningful breakthrough, signaled by the February 1972 Nixon visit and the opening of trade, defense consultations, and implied US protection from Soviet nuclear blackmail—in return for which China would scale down its support for the Vietnam War.

Although Washington had helped aggravate the rift, it did not begin to exploit it strategically until the concept of a "strategic triangle" was introduced during the Nixon administration in the early 1970s. In the context of increasing polarization between China and the Soviet Union, a highly asymmetrical confrontation in which further hostilities between nuclear weapon states was on the horizon, American intervention on behalf of the weaker side was only logical in terms of the balance of power. What was novel was Washington's attempt to shield the weaker power while still maintaining détente with the stronger. Thus the birth of the triangle first took the form of a romantic triangle in which the United States in the pivot role cultivated better relations with the two wings than they had with each other. Although China was the immediate beneficiary (now under the US nuclear umbrella) the United States was now in the structurally optimal position, able to enjoy cooperation with each "wing" (SALT talks with the USSR, US withdrawal from Vietnam and East Asia under the Nixon Doctrine) with minimal commitment to either. For Chinese foreign policy, the opening to the outside world represented by the Nixon visit and China's foregoing entrée into the United Nations Security Council marked the advent of "reform and opening," a more ideologically flexible approach to policy that would be more generally applied following the Third Plenum of the Eleventh Congress in 1978. After facing a series of foreign policy excesses with serious threat to regime survival, the leadership responded by allowing strategic power-political expedience to override ideological reservations. In the wake of this deradicalization, China would chart its course according to a more conventional national interest calculus, compromising with capitalist countries to gain entrée into the international market system, for example. To be sure, the opening was initially limited by ideological commitments—in April 1974, Deng Xiaoping announced Mao's Three Worlds worldview to the UN General Assembly, declaiming,

> The two superpowers are the biggest international exploiters and oppressors of today. They are the source of a new world war. . . . They carry on a keenly contested arms race, station massive forces abroad and set up military bases everywhere, threatening the independence and security of all nations. They both keep subjecting other countries to their control, subversion, interference or aggression. They both exploit other countries economically, plundering their wealth and grabbing their resources. [11]

The overweening Soviet threat perceived by both nonetheless facilitated growing strategic cooperation (e.g., US access to radar sites in Xinjiang to eavesdrop on Soviet nuclear tests, collaboration in opposing Soviet "proxy" gains in Vietnam and Afghanistan). By 1976, this had pushed the triangle from a "romantic" or balanced configuration toward an ideologically antipodal strategic "marriage" between the United States and China against the "polar bear."

After Mao's death in August 1976, the ideological resistance to Sino-Soviet reconciliation began to dissipate. Beginning in 1980 Ronald Reagan's crusade against the "evil empire" led to a revived Cold War and an arms race over the innovation of cruise missiles and Star Wars antiballistic missile (ABM) systems. Beijing seized the opportunity of the two superpowers' growing preoccupation with each other to relieve its own security burden. The military was relegated last among the "four modernizations," and after a temporary spike in the wake of the February 1979 border war with Vietnam, PRC defense spending was cut by some 7 percent per annum as a proportion of GDP from 1979 to 1989. While allowing the thirty-year Sino-Soviet treaty to lapse upon its expiry in 1981, the Chinese agreed to discuss outstanding bilateral contradictions. Thus beginning in 1982, after transacting Sino-US normalization and the Third Communiqué, Beijing and Moscow launched a series of Sino-Soviet normalization talks, alternating semiannually between the two capitals in the spring and fall of each year, involving roughly the same team of officials on each side. Progress was initially glacial due to Soviet intransigence over what Beijing called the "three fundamental obstacles": heavy fortification of the Sino-Soviet and Outer Mongolian borders, Soviet troops in Afghanistan, and CPSU support for the Vietnamese threat to China's southeastern flank (and to China's proxy, Cambodia). Talks nevertheless continued on schedule, accompanied by gradually increasing trade and cultural exchanges, helping to contain the dispute during the post-Mao and post-Brezhnev successions.

When Mikhail Gorbachev in his focus on domestic reform decided to rationalize Soviet foreign policy in the late 1980s, he decided, while retrenching ill-conceived ventures in the Third World, to try to revive post-alliance Sino-Soviet relations, in hopes of at least cutting defense costs, perhaps fostering a turn to the rising East. In speeches at Vladivostok (July 1986) and Krasnoyarsk (September 1988), he proposed a freeze on deployment of nuclear weapons in the Asia-Pacific region, Soviet withdrawal from the Cam Ranh Bay in Vietnam, and unilateral reduction of the Soviet military by five hundred thousand troops within two years, nearly half (two hundred thousand) of which would come from the region east of the Urals. This Soviet "new thinking" (*novo myshlenie*), according to which Brezhnev's vaunted achievement of strategic parity, had redounded in few substantive gains at immense cost, eventually satisfied all three Chinese obstacles. Meanwhile, inasmuch as both countries' economies were running aground on the limits of extensive development under command planning—the Soviet Union after years of stagnation under Brezhnev, China after radical Maoism exhausted itself in the Cultural Revolution—fresh leadership teams in both capitals turned to socialist reform, an attempt at revitalization referred to as "perestroika" and *gaige kaifang*, respectively. For a brief moment, there was a sense that both countries, with symmetrically structured and ideologically inspired economies, might learn from one another. Because China had been first to experiment with reform, much of the initial learning was by the Soviet Union. But China also paid close attention to Soviet experiments; in fact, the liberalization that culminated in the fall 1986 protest movement that led to the fall of Hu Yaobang had been initially stimulated by Gorbachev's prior call for Soviet political reform (as well as Deng Xiaoping's Delphic encouragement earlier that spring). Whereas such learning was to be sure selective and ultimately led in somewhat divergent directions, the fact that both countries were engaged in analogous socioeconomic experiments and interested in each other's experience helped to orchestrate their détente. Based then on both foreign policy and domestic policy convergence, it had become possible by the end of the 1980s to convene a summit meeting sealing the normalization of party-to-party relations.

This summit, held in May 1989 amid student demonstrations at Tiananmen Square that necessitated moving all ceremonies indoors, quite unexpectedly marked both climax and terminus to this process of convergence on socialist reform. The sanguinary Chinese solution to spontaneous student protests, executed within a fortnight of Gorbachev's departure, led to international sanctions and to a quiet Soviet determination to avoid any analogous crackdown, either domestically or among fellow Warsaw Pact Organization signatories. But without resort to outside force the European socialist regimes could not stand, and by the end of 1990 all but China, North Korea, Laos, Vietnam, Cuba, and the Soviet Union had succumbed to a wave of anticommunist protest movements. Throughout this period, the Chinese leadership, still defending both Marxism-Leninism and its own brutal solution to mass protest, deplored this turn of events, criticizing the Gorbachev leadership for deviating from the path of socialism and contributing to the collapse of the bloc. In early 1990, Deng Liqun and the more ideologically orthodox (leftist) wing of the CCP even advocated public criticism of Soviet errors, which Deng Xiaoping vetoed. No sooner had Beijing become grudgingly reconciled to cooperation with Gorbachev—after the Gulf War (January–February 1991), some joint socialist rejoinder to a triumphalist American new world order was deemed advisable—than was Gorbachev's own survival threatened by the August 1991 coup attempt. Though Beijing came perilously close to endorsing the coup publicly before its consolidation, it recovered in time to reaffirm its commitment to noninterference, only to witness (with mounting horror) the ensuing dissolution of the Soviet Union into fifteen republics under the abominated Boris Yeltsin in December 1991. Twelve of these newly independent states later agreed to join the loose-knit Commonwealth of Independent States (CIS).

Part of the reason for the PRC's quick recognition of this new political reality was that had it not, many alternatives seemed open to Russia and its fourteen lost republics. At the time, there seemed every likelihood of reconciling the old Russo-Japanese territorial dispute (involving three small islands and a tiny archipelago north of Hokkaido) and signing a peace treaty with Japan; South Korea had just granted Moscow a $3 billion concessionary loan in appreciation for its diplomatic recognition of Seoul. Taiwan, alert to new diplomatic opportunities, briefly established consular relations with Latvia and very nearly exchanged ambassadors with Ukraine and Outer Mongolia before being warned off by Beijing. The new line in the Kremlin under Yeltsin and Kozyrev, the CCP's bête noires (who not unreasonably suspected the CCP of supporting the August 1991 coup conspirators), was anticommunist and pro-American. Indeed, the world's first bilateral "strategic partnership" to be proclaimed (in 1992) was between the United States and the fledgling Russian Federation. Chinese strategic analysts were concerned lest successful democratic reform lure foreign direct investment (FDI) from China to Russia, undermining the CCP's performance-based legitimacy.

Yet Moscow's rosy international prospects as a postcommunist liberal democracy proved greatly exaggerated. The decisive domestic factor is that the Russian "double bang" of marketization and privatization failed utterly to revive the economy, which went into free fall: real GDP declined 13 percent in 1991, 19 percent in 1992, 12 percent in 1993, and 15 percent in 1994; from 1991 to 1998, the cumulative GDP loss was 43 percent. Privatization ushered in a two-tiered market, consisting of oligarchs at the top, largely former managers of state-owned enterprises (SOEs) who grabbed the country's major industrial assets in management buyouts (MBOs), and a geographically balkanized patchwork of small and medium enterprises at lower levels, as the country's distribution network essentially collapsed. Under the circumstances, leading Western industrial powers, still overburdened with debt in the wake of the arms race and a worldwide recession following the second oil price hike, were far less munificent with financial support than had been expected. Only Germany, now reunified thanks to Gorbachev's refusal to invoke the Brezhnev Doctrine, made substantial subventions to Russian economic development (ca. US$50 billion in aid, loans, and credits in 1989–91 alone).[12] In the West, after Russian arms were discredited and a former ally defeated in the 1991 Gulf War (in which Russia, despite voting in support of the enabling Security Council resolution, was not involved), Russia was in effect demoted from bipolar nemesis to diplomatic nonentity. Excluded from any role in resolving the Yugoslav imbroglio, Moscow was finally invited to the Group of 7 but only as an observer. Yeltsin's emergent political rivals, both on the left (Zyuganov and the surviving communist party, the Communist Party of the Russian Federation [CPRF]) and the right (e.g., Lebed) challenged his nationalist bona fides and urged a shift from West to East, arguing on geostrategic grounds in favor of a more balanced international posture between East and West.

Even in the East, hopes of new openings were quickly dispelled. Negotiations with Japan premised on a territorial compromise realizing Khrushchev's (never implemented) 1958 agreement (provisionally splitting the four, then phasing in a more comprehensive settlement later) aroused unexpectedly passionate military and local opposition at home, prompting Yeltsin to postpone his visit twice and not even table a proposal when he finally arrived in Tokyo in October 1993. With regard to South Korea, the initial euphoria elicited by Gorbachev's 1988 Krasnoyarsk speech and by the September 1990 establishment of diplomatic relations (to Pyongyang's outrage) did not survive the shock at the collapse of the Soviet Union, though bilateral-trade-revived Russia has not lured much South Korean investment.

But the most bitter setback was in Europe, where Gorbachev elicited an oral agreement that Germany's reunification was contingent on no movement of the North Atlantic Treaty Organization (NATO) eastward, only to see the deal vanish after the fact.[13] Thus the 1993 admission of six former satellites to the Council of Europe, and the 1994 proposal to enlarge NATO to include three former Eastern European satellites, finalized by Washington in 1997 in apparent response to US election-year constituency concerns more than any realistically perceived security threat, was but the latest in a series of diplomatic setbacks. Having dissolved the Warsaw Pact upon the collapse of the Iron Curtain, Moscow could see no further point to NATO's expansion but to push Russia out of Europe, and it protested but in vain. Russia began to move eastward, conceiving a new geopolitical role for itself as Eurasian land bridge.

Thus ironically, two nations who had never been able to agree in their interpretations of a shared ideology now found it possible in the absence of shared ideological assumptions but under straitened international circumstances (post-Tiananmen Chinese ostracism, the Russian economic meltdown) and a mutually lowered ideological fervor to converge on a "strategic cooperative partnership" (*zhanlue xiezuo huoban guanxi*). First proposed in the form of a "constructive partnership" by Yeltsin in September 1994 (at the inaugural presidential summit in Moscow), then elevated to a "strategic partnership for the twenty-first century" during Yeltsin's April 1996 summit in Beijing (a month after China's confrontation with the United States over Taiwan and in the context of Clinton's reaffirmation of a strengthened Japanese-American Security Alliance), the partnership has since become a fungible form of semiformal cooperation in the diplomatic repertoire of both powers. China has since formed partnerships with Pakistan, France, Germany, the European Union, Japan, Korea, and the Association of Southeast Asian Nations (ASEAN), among others, while Russia claimed partnerships with Japan, Iran, and India, as well as the United States. The implication is to vaguely privilege a relationship without making (or demanding) any commitments—and one can have an indefinite number of "partners" at once. Yet for both, the first partnership has remained pivotal, an entry ticket back to what Jiang Zemin called "great power strategy" (*da guo zhanlue*), precisely because this is the only relationship with sufficient leverage to pose a credible counterweight to the lone superpower. The partnership explicitly disavows any threat to a third party, more specifically the United States, from which each still hopes to gain. The United States has long been China's most important trade partner, for example, with some ten times as much trade as with Russia (though this is not true for Russia).

RELATIVE POWER

As both nations emerged from autocratic traditions one would expect power to play a role in their relationship and so it has, though not always as one might expect. In the centuries after the Mongol conquests, the Chinese empire remained superior not only in hard but soft power for several centuries. Prior to the 1600s, China and Russia faced each other on opposite ends of Siberia, which was sparsely populated by independent nomads. By about

1640, Russian settlers had conquered most of Siberia and founded settlements in the Amur River basin. Official contacts between China and Russia began with border clashes in the 1680s that, however, were settled in 1689 by the Treaty of Nerchinsk, which delineated what was then the common border. At this time, Beijing had no political or diplomatic links with any other European state save the Vatican. Albeit weaker, the Russian empire was an ambitious rising power, while the Chinese Qing empire was, after its initial conquests, dedicated to consolidating the status quo, walling itself off as much as possible from outside influence. By the late 1700s, the Chinese state was experiencing internal strains—particularly, an expanding population that taxed food supply and government control—and these strains led to rebellions, corruption, and a weakening of the central government. By the mid-nineteenth century, the balance of power had tilted to Russia, which took advantage of the Taiping Rebellion (1850–64) and the Opium Wars to annex large tracts of territory: The 1860 Convention of Peking awarded Russia full rights to Outer Manchuria, and the Treaty of Aigun (1858) gave some six hundred thousand square kilometers of land along the Amur to Russia. In the process of conquering Central Asia, Russia also occupied Xinjiang, though in 1881 it sold it back to China. In 1891, Russia pushed forward the construction of the Trans-Siberian Railway. Russia's annexations excited intense resentment in China. During the Boxer Rebellion, rebels damaged the Siberian railway, prompting Russia to deploy one hundred thousand troops in Manchuria and to annex more territory (Port Arthur in 1898).

This fits the familiar Melian pattern of "the strong do what they can while the weak suffer what they must" recounted by Thucydides. This pattern, however, was to some extent reversed by the force of ideology during the first half of the twentieth century. The revolutionary Bolshevik regime, inspired by Lenin's diagnosis of imperialism as an intrinsic excrescence of late capitalism and weakened by war with Western-affiliated White armies from 1917 to 1922 (which the Beiyang government joined, incidentally, sending troops to fight the Reds), quickly recognized the revolutionary prospects in China, in turmoil since overthrowing dynastic rule. And on July 25, 1919, Lev Karakhan, deputy commissioner for foreign affairs for the revolutionary Soviet regime, issued a manifesto offering to relinquish various concessions Russia had obtained by unequal treaty with China, including extraterritoriality and Russia's share of the Boxer indemnity. In contrast with the Treaty of Versailles the same year, which awarded Shandong to Japan, this created a most favorable impression in China, inspiring the founding of the Chinese Communist Party in 1921. The Beiyang government, closer to Japan, did not accept the offer, but the Kuomintang, since being shut out since 1913 in extraparliamentary opposition, was more receptive. The Soviet government supported both the Kuomintang and the 1921 organization of the Chinese Communist Party (CCP) and urged the latter to form a united front with the

former. It continued to support both parties even after the united front violently split in 1927 and throughout the Second Sino-Japanese War.

The point is that the stronger and more advanced power supported a
weaker and more backward one, not honoring the generous Karakhan offer
but making no further territorial encroachments on a vulnerable neighbor and
working to advance the jointly held ideal of world revolution. True, the
Soviet Union also had material interests at stake, such as fending off the
territorial ambitions of a rising Japan. And the subtext of benevolent socialist
nurturance of the weak by the strong was a hierarchical patron-client model:
the Comintern deputed advisors to China, who attended CCP politburo sessions and cultivated "returned students" to assume command of the younger
party. Comintern leadership led to many costly mistakes, eventually leading
to the rise of Mao Zedong, who purged returned students and quietly ignored
Comintern advice when he deemed it expedient. The relationship was asymmetric and formally hierarchical within the communist international movement, but informally loosely symmetrical in the sense that the CCP remained
autonomous.

Upon the unexpectedly swift CCP victory in October 1949, a formal
alliance was formed that explicitly acknowledged the asymmetrical, hierarchical nature of the relationship: the Soviet Union was a big brother that
would place its more advanced economic capabilities at China's disposal: the
Soviet today would be China's tomorrow. Despite Soviet devastation in the
wake of the Nazi invasion, Moscow provided subsidized loans and sent
thousands of advisors to help build Chinese socialism. The Chinese leadership enthusiastically accepted this asymmetrical patron-client arrangement
initially, but soon came to resent Soviet tutelage, above all (according to
Deng Xiaoping's later reflections) the unequal nature of the relationship.
While this was undeniably a factor underlying all the myriad divergences
that arose between the two powers (and explaining their inability to resolve
them), it is still somewhat controversial to both Chinese and non-Chinese
observers why a relationship whose inequality was once gladly accepted with
all it entailed had become intolerable. The implicit premise in China's initial
acceptance of inequality was presumably that we can accept subordination
while exploiting our unequal position to become truly equal, whereupon we
can reclaim our sovereign equality. In that case the Sino-Soviet dispute,
precipitated by a China that could no longer accept subordination, was developmentally premature and even dangerous, exposing China to attack from
counterrevolutionary forces and to abandonment by a powerful spurned patron. This split would necessitate a drastic strategic and identity shift. But
from China's perspective the original model of instrumental inequality broke
down because the patron was no longer willing to underwrite the client's rise
to full equality (as symbolized most poignantly by unilateral Russian discontinuation of the nuclear technology transfer deal).

After China adopted reform and opening and the disintegration of the Soviet Union, bilateral asymmetry was in many respects upended: China's GDP is now larger, its military budget bigger, its growth rate faster. The Russian leadership recognizes this with a subtle mixture of admiration, envy, and foreboding. So far Russia has not elected to balance but to bandwagon the faster rising power, hoping to "catch the Chinese economic wind in our sail," as Putin put it in 2013. The Chinese attitude toward Russia now bears a sotto voce undertone of contempt, as in the many Chinese references to a "resource appendage." But this undertone is kept well below the surface officially, where the attitude has always been one of elaborate respect. Xi Jinping has met with Putin more than twenty times, more than with any other foreign counterpart. In April 2017, Putin boasted that Russia-China relations had reached "unprecedented heights." And prior to the G20 meeting in Hamburg in July 2017, the two men held a summit in Moscow at which they affirmed their common position on a broad range of issues, including North Korea, where both called for removal of terminal high-altitude area defense (THAAD) in the South. At the Belt and Road Forum in Beijing in May 2017, Putin was given the honor of being second speaker after President Xi. Xi's warm personal regard for Putin is echoed in the latter's status as the most admired foreign leader in Chinese public opinion. And on the world stage, as in UN Security Council vetoes, for example, it is China that usually follows the Russian lead. Although China's GDP is now more than seven times Russia's and China is spending more than three times as much on defense, China still buys its most advanced weaponry from Russia, and in China's own rankings of "comprehensive national power" Russia still ranks above the PRC.[14]

In sum, the impact of asymmetry in defining the bilateral relationship has been less than one might expect.[15] The Sino-Russian relationship has always been asymmetrical, though the balance has obviously shifted. When Russia was asymmetrically powerful, its official purport (as informed by the ideology both professed) was to support and nurture its fraternal socialist party-state; as China became asymmetrically powerful in the twenty-first century, it took great pains to express continuing respect for a Russia that though falling behind has sought international relevance by taking ever bolder foreign policy initiatives. The role of asymmetry in the first case remained tacit and below the surface, manifest in the stronger power's tacit patronization of the weaker and in the silent conviction of the weaker that the stronger power was taking advantage of it, all protestations to the contrary notwithstanding. Now that the tables have turned and China is taking the lead, it has been careful to avoid public smugness. Even repressed, asymmetry and the resentment it breeds can have a corrosive impact on the relationship; but both sides have been alert to this risk, mitigating it by evoking the shared threat of

democratic subversion of the authoritarian order to which both remain committed.

CURRENT BILATERAL RELATIONS

Without mutually agreed strategic objectives or adversaries, just how meaningful is this vaguely formulated "partnership"? This has been constantly
debated, with several hypotheses still in play. The first and most widespread
is that the enhanced amity of the past decade is artificial and lacks firm
economic foundations. Despite the increase of trade, Russia's largest trade
partner remains Europe while China's is the United States; Sino-Russian
trade lacks complementarity, and its imbalance will generate growing resentment, as will China's economic drive into Central Asia, which Russia still
considers in its sphere of interest. Despite a comprehensive border settlement, suspicions of revanchist Chinese territorial ambitions, steep demographic imbalance, and growing economic asymmetry still haunt the relationship. Finally, the two have foreign policy interests and ambitions leading
in different directions, and are unlikely to sacrifice their own respective core
interests on behalf of some joint military adventure.

The other perspective, while conceding many of these points, would
argue as follows. First, shifting established trade patterns would entail costs,
but the existing patterns may well be played out. Both European and US
economies have experienced secular stagnation since the global financial
crisis (GFC) with declining demand, while Russia and China see one another
as emerging economies with complementary market potential and a bright
future. True, trade is somewhat artificial, arranged from the top rather than
the market, but this is a pattern familiar to *dirigiste* economies with entrepre-
neurial political elites. And those elites have devoted scrupulous care to
cultivating mutually beneficial ties. From 1996 to 2012, there were more
than sixteen premier meetings, resulting in hundreds of agreements. [16]
Among the most important were the 1991 agreement to initiate border demarcation (completed in 1997), the 1992 summit agreement gradually to
demilitarize the border, the September 1994 agreement to de-target strategic
weaponry, mutual nonaggression and non–first use of nuclear force; and the
1997 agreements on trade, oil, and gas development and cultural cooperation.
The year 2006 was declared the Year of Russia in China, and in 2007, the
Russians christened the year of China in Russia, prompting a medley of
exhibitions and friendship rituals. The year 2014 was an important wa-
tershed, as Putin turned from an angry EU after his Crimean annexation to
seek better economic and political opportunities in the East. The masses have
been slow to follow, especially in the Russian Far East, but since 2010 public
opinion has become more favorable as views of the United States have dark-

ened. [17] Second, while it is true that the two are situated on opposite ends of the Eurasian landmass and have different security interests, both see those interests threatened by a common opponent—the United States. Against a shared opponent moves in service of different national interests can be supported insofar as they weaken that common foe. Third, along with common opposition to the same adversary the two see eye to eye on the political values they are defending. Even after Russia's repudiation of Marxism-Leninism and China's turn to the market, both have evolved into strongman governments dedicated to defense against Western interference in regimes upheld by repression at home and nationalistic self-assertion abroad.

Certainly one important dimension of the partnership has been the 2,265-mile land border, still among the world's longest bilateral land boundaries, which has undergone a transition from a formidable concentration of troops, tanks, and land mines into an economic thoroughfare. From a legal perspective, the territorial issue has been fully resolved. The border issue was solved in principle once Gorbachev agreed to the thalweg principle (i.e., the boundary is the deepest channel of the river) in his Vladivostok speech. Yeltsin and Jiang Zemin agreed on this basis to begin boundary demarcation in 1991. Following disintegration of the Soviet Union, negotiations with the four new border states (Russia, Kazakhstan, Kyrgyzstan, and Tajikistan) acting in tandem with Russia culminated in the Treaty on Deepening Military Trust in Border Regions in April 1996 and the subsequent Treaty on Reduction of Military Forces in Border Regions in April 1997. By the beginning of the next century, the western boundary had been agreed and confirmed in three treaties, while the entirety of the Sino-Russian boundaries was also covered by treaty, setting aside two unresolved disputes: Black Bear (Heixia) Island near Khabarovsk and another small island on the Argun River. In 2004, the two sides suddenly announced that continued negotiations had produced solutions to these last two problems as well. The comprehensive agreement was formalized in a new treaty in Vladivostok in 2005. Russia transferred to China a part of Abagaitu Islet, the entire Yinlong (Tarabarov) Island, about a half of Bolshoy Ussuriysky (Heixiazi) Island, and some adjacent river islets. The boundary was shifted from the Chinese side of the channel to the thalweg, which meant that both rivers were for the first time opened to Chinese commercial navigation; China, then, also gained sixty-four square miles of Amur riverine islands.

Meanwhile, mutual border demilitarization reducing the number of troops required for peaceful border patrolling (formerly numbering some two hundred thousand troops) has permitted both sides to shift strategic priorities, as China transferred forces to its southeast coast facing Taiwan and the South China Sea and Russia addressed the security threat represented by the expansion of NATO in the West. But as Bobo Lo puts it, the paradox is that while the territorial issue is now formally resolved, it has not fully relieved Russian anxieties—the Russians, amid declining demographics, continue to fear mass Chinese immigration, Chinese exploitation of natural resources, land purchases, a Chinese takeover of domestic retail trade, and so forth.[18] Some Chinese, still aware that Russia continues to occupy some six hundred thousand square miles of once-Chinese territory (the only colonial legacy not requited), continue to harbor the hope that mutual participation in each other's economies would transform Dongbei-RFE (i.e., the Chinese northeast, formerly known as Manchuria, plus the Russian Far East) into a single geo-economic space that would contribute to an industrial revitalization on both sides. What makes the RFE so attractive to the Chinese is its abundant natural resources. The area holds almost all Russia's diamonds, a third of its gold, and major oil, natural gas, and zinc deposits. This has spurred Chinese mining expeditions into Russian territory. Economic integration, however, is a vision that makes Moscow uneasy, as Russians are vastly outnumbered, especially locally: as of 2015, the population of the Amur Oblast, Primorski Krai, Jewish Autonomous Oblast, and Khabarovsk Krai numbered altogether a mere 4.3 million, while the populations of adjoining Heilongjiang, Jilin, and Liaoning provinces totaled 109,520,844. Beijing reasons that because China is now Russia's most important economic partner in the Asia-Pacific and the RFE is in a weak developmental position it is only natural that the RFE would remain a net exporter of raw materials with little choice but to cooperate with China.[19]

Bilateral trade has vacillated widely, due only partly to market vicissitudes. Trade has remained largely state managed on both sides, and both are neo-mercantilist states intent upon managing economic relations in their national interest. The Russians have been most nervous about losing control of the relationship, and the Chinese have superficially accommodated their concerns. Thus, shuttle trade was subjected to strict regulation in 1993, in effect consigning trade to SOEs and giant trading companies on each side, which trade according to plans agreed at the top. Migration flows (flowing mostly from China to Russia) have also been policed, albeit not entirely successfully. Trade first took off in the early 1990s, amid the early thaw of the thirty-year Sino-Soviet cold war, to fill the vacuum caused by the Tiananmen sanctions (the value of all Western investment in China plunged 22 percent during the first half of 1990). Meanwhile, the collapse of the centralized Russian distribution system and disappearance of state subsidies upon the collapse of the USSR made China an obvious economic alternative. While total Soviet foreign trade dropped 6.4 percent in 1990, Sino-Soviet trade volume increased to US$5.3 billion, a quarter of which was border trade. Several Special Economic Regions were established in emulation of China's thriving Special Economic Zones in the southeast, more than two hundred cooperative projects were initiated between localities of the two countries, and China dispatched some fifteen thousand citizens to the Soviet Far East for temporary labor service. But these steep early rates of commercial growth could not be sustained, despite Yeltsin's announced goal of raising it to US$20 billion by the millennium; the 1991–92 economic crisis in the Russian Far East left Russians unable to repay Chinese exporters, and the Russians complained of shabby product quality and disruption of local retail networks. Visa-regime negotiation in 1993 (designed to control shuttle trade, a source of smuggling and illegal immigration) and Moscow's subsequent imposition of border duties, cuts on transport subsidies, and restrictions on organizations entitled to engage in foreign trade caused trade to plunge by nearly 40 percent in the first half of 1994. In 1995, it began to recover, reaching US$5.1 billion that year and $6.85 billion in 1996, only to fall again in 1997, to $6.12 billion, dropping still further in 1998, particularly after the November devaluation of the ruble.

Trade began to grow more vigorously after 2000, as the Russian economy under Putin recovered as an energy exporter. Official data from Russia's Federal State Statistics Service shows that from 2000 Russia's trade with China rose more than with all other trade partners. From 2000 to 2012, the value of Russian foreign exchange rose 6.1 times and Sino-Russian exchanges rose 14.1 times, whereas Russian purchases abroad rose 9.2 times and imports from China rose 52 times. Trade growth stalled in 2007–8 and dropped in 2009, due in part to China's abrupt discontinuation of weapons purchases and in part to the GFC. It then rebounded the following year, to reach $59.3 billion in 2010, $83.5 billion in 2011, $87.5 billion in 2012, and $95.28 billion in 2014. But then it plunged to $64 billion in 2015 and $66 billion in 2016, accounting for 12 percent of Russia's trade. Both, however, are still aiming for $200 billion by 2020. In 2011, the two sides also agreed to allow bilateral trade to be conducted in renminbi or rubles, in accord with China's ambition to make the renminbi a reserve currency. In the June 2012 summit between Hu Jintao and Vladimir Putin, President Hu emphasized four areas of cooperative development:

> (1) Expansion of cooperation in joint investments, especially energy, including oil exploration, drilling, and refining. (2) Expansion of cooperation in high-technology research. The two sides should also work together in bringing new inventions to market, including through more joint ventures. (3) Development of new venues for strategic cooperation ideally with both governments providing policy direction and provision of capital. (4) Joint construction of basic infrastructure to facilitate cross-border joint development at the local level. [20]

The most recent developments, spurred by a Russian determination to pivot to Asia in the teeth of the Ukraine crisis and subsequent Western sanctions, have stimulated ambitious goals for cooperative achievements despite a global economic slowdown. The East Siberian Pacific Ocean pipeline (ESPO) from Angarsk to Daqing, though long in negotiation (since 2001) was completed in December 2010 (thanks to a US$25 billion Chinese loan in 2009) with a spur to Daqing (activated in 2011) that will provide China with oil supplies for twenty-five years in a deal valued at $270 billion. As of May 2017, the volume of oil shipped to China through ESPO had reached one hundred million tons.

In 2012, Gazprom announced another proposal to supply gas to northeast China through the Power of Siberia pipeline (Yakutsk-Khabarovsk-Vladivostok) from Chayanda gas field in east Siberia. The two agreed to share the $77 billion cost of building the pipeline—Russia would build it up to the Sino-Russian border, and a Chinese company would build China's section. This $400 billion deal was signed (after nearly fifteen years of haggling over price) by the two sides during Putin's May 2014 trip to Shanghai, acclaimed (by Putin) as "the biggest contract in the gas sector in the history of the former USSR."[21] Russia herewith agrees to supply thirty-eight billion cubic meters (bcm) of gas to China for thirty years beginning as soon as the pipeline is completed (originally 2018, since postponed to 2019–20, reaching full capacity by 2023–25).[22]

Yet another gas pipeline, the Altai, linking western Siberia to the western provinces of the PRC, was initialed by the two leaders in November 2016 in Beijing, but a formal contract remains in abeyance due to pending Chinese reassessment of fiscal circumstances. The price for the deal was never publicly revealed, and according to past practice the Chinese will insist on renegotiating it even after a contract is signed in view of the fluctuating world price of oil.

Why has Moscow suddenly agreed after endless haggling and complaints about becoming a "resource appendage" on energy deals relatively favorable to the PRC? Russian interest in a pivot to the East seems to have begun with Putin's return to the presidency and the simultaneous rise of Xi Jinping in 2012. Putin's first trip abroad after assuming the Russian presidency again in 2012 was China, and Xi Jinping visited Russia as part of his inaugural tour as president in 2013. Xi has expressed his personal admiration for Putin, which has come to be shared by the Chinese public—the two met no less than twelve times in two and half years in bilateral settings and in the expanding number of multilateral venues in which their countries have membership. Both share an aversion to the US unipolar order and an interest in revising that system in their favor, as expressed in Russian initiatives to recover a sphere of influence in former Soviet republics in Eastern Europe and Chinese maritime claims in the East and South China Seas. As expressed in almost simultaneous military parades in the summer of 2015 (which both attended), they also share a faith that the threat and skillful use of force will help achieve these goals. This coincidence of strategic interests has coincided with falling global energy prices and a Russian hope to replace a stagnating Europe with dynamic markets to the East, closer to its energy sources. Russia's ambition under Putin has been consistently focused on expanded commodity exports, while China as workshop of the world has become the leading commodity importer and has a horde of foreign exchange reserves to afford them. In 2016, Russia overtook Saudi Arabia to become the largest crude oil exporter to China, though it only supplies 20 percent of China's imports.

Yet the Russian rebalance eastward has been limited in three ways. First, Russia's Asian turn has remained Sinocentric—Sino-Russian trade in 2016 was three times that with Japan (US$20 billion) and four times that with South Korea ($16 billion). An additional spur to the ESPO to Nakhodka/Kozmino on the Pacific coast was inaugurated on December 25, 2012, for transshipment to Japan and Korea, but China has been buying an increasing proportion of this oil as well: 70 percent in 2016, compared to 51 percent in 2015. Japan under Abe showed avid interest in developing the relationship, but Russia has balked on the territorial issue and economic cooperation remains limited to the LNG facility in Sakhalin, where Japan holds stakes and is the biggest buyer of gas. Second, the balance of trade has shifted from Russia to China, and the trade deficit has deepened steadily since 2007 (2009 being the sole exception). Given heavy state involvement in the economy and the neo-mercantilist bias on both sides, this remains a sensitive issue. Third, the trade composition is also increasingly neocolonial. Russian complaints of being derogated to the position of resource appendage are statistically warranted: the proportion of raw materials rose from 10 percent of Russian exports to 20 percent in 2003, to 30 percent in 2004, up to 73 percent in 2012, thanks in part to timely recent Chinese "loans" to hard-pressed Russian energy suppliers. But this is true for the Russian economy overall, whose recovery under Putin was based largely on commodity (especially petroleum) exports, neglecting the transition to the more balanced economy he once promised.

A further complication is Russia's inability to pay for the pipelines, and the question of whether China needs the Russian gas badly enough to finance their construction. Russia's hope that China would finance a lifeline to sustain Russia through the sanctions and the falling oil prices may have been ill timed given China's ongoing economic slowdown and the availability of other energy sources. The Russian government also agreed in 2014 to sell Chinese companies minority stakes in the country's most lucrative oil field and the world's third-largest copper field, both located in Eastern Siberia. The agreement for China to build a high-speed rail line to Moscow is apparently also stalled for now over an apparent disagreement about who pays. The potential is there, but it may take a while for the Putin-Xi nexus to become economically sustainable. In 2009, Russia's share of China's oil imports was 7.5 percent. China is since 2011 Russia's largest national trade partner, but even after a year of sanctions precipitating a 40 percent drop since 2014 Russian trade with the EU in 2015 was 44.8 percent of its total trade and nearly four times that with China (US$344.26 billion versus $95 billion). While Chinese investment in Russia increased 250 percent in 2014, that amounted to only $8 billion versus the EU's $186.2 billion, making China Russia's fourth-largest foreign investor.

Aside from raw materials, China's major import from the early 1990s through 2006 was advanced Russian military technology and equipment. Deprived by sanctions of US and European arms sales since the 1989 Tiananmen massacre, the Chinese returned to Russian arms merchants, who supplied much of their original hardware, which offered advantages in terms of compatibility of parts. Soviet global arms sales dropped precipitously in the wake of the Gulf War, where Soviet equipment was visibly eclipsed by "smart" US weaponry. Due to budget difficulties during the long 1990s recession, the Russian military was unable to afford Russian weapons, while China's military budget surpassed Russia's throughout the 2000s and doubled it by 2010. As military equipment was the second-largest item in the Soviet export repertory (after petroleum products), continued Chinese interest was particularly welcome at this point, and Russian strategic monitoring of arms exports relaxed to accommodate the demand.[23] Negotiations for the purchase of Sukhoi SU-27 fighters, under way since early 1990, culminated in the purchase of twenty-six at a "friendship" price of more than US$1 billion each (about 35 percent of which China could pay in hard currency, the rest in barter goods), with an option to buy an additional forty-eight. In March 1992, China also took delivery of the sophisticated S-300 anti-aircraft missile system and SA-10 anti-tactical ballistic missiles. The first contingent of Chinese pilots was sent to Moscow in June 1992 to undergo an eighteen-month training course, and by 1993, more than one thousand Russian experts were based in China by private contractual arrangement, helping to modernize Chinese nuclear and missile capabilities.[24] China's humiliation by US aircraft carriers in the 1995–96 Taiwan Strait confrontation whetted PRC appetites for further acquisitions. In November 1996, the two sides thus signed a bilateral defense cooperation pact resulting in China's purchase of thirty to fifty SU-30 multipurpose fighters, four diesel-powered (Kilo-class) submarines, and two Sovremenniy-class destroyers with accompanying Sunburn antiship missiles designed to counter US Aegis-equipped ships. The Chinese J-11, J-15, and J-17 are all modifications of Russian designs. Arms trade reached a peak in 2005 at almost $4 billion, rivaled only by India. Between 1992 and 2006, the total value of Russian arms exports to China amounted to approximately $26 billion, or almost half of all the weapons sold abroad by Russian firms.[25]

By 2006, the arms sales dimension of the relationship, however, suddenly cooled. China had by then modernized its own military-industrial complex and was less dependent on the purchase of Russian military equipment.[26]

China hence insisted on purchasing only the most advanced Russian systems, also demanding technology transfer as a condition for purchase. Russia may have also had reservations. China's growing power was hard to ignore. Questions began to be raised about the wisdom of arming a once and possibly future security risk.[27] Russia began trying to shift Chinese interest to the purchase of nonlethal technology; thus some 25 percent of the Chinese commercial aircraft pool is now Russian.[28] Russia also complained about China's persistent reverse engineering of Russian systems. For example, in 2005 the Chinese obtained a fifteen-year licensing agreement contract to produce two hundred Russian SU-27SK fighters as J-11As. After a few years, China claimed that the fighter no longer met their needs and canceled the contract. The Russians then discovered that the Chinese had illegally copied the design to produce the same aircraft indigenously as the J11B. Not only that, China was seen as a cost-cutting competitor on global arms markets (now ranking third in the world, after the United States and Russia), often selling cloned weapons. Thus Russia became increasingly reluctant to provide China with additional military equipment, especially advanced weapons that it had yet to provide to its own military. In particular, Russia began to reject Chinese requests to purchase single examples of their most advanced systems on a trial basis. The year 2006 proved to be the final year for large-scale arms transfers, total volume reaching US$2.5 billion. In 2007 and 2008, sales declined to $1.5 billion and $1.4 billion, respectively. Sales fell even more sharply in 2009 and 2010, to well below $1 billion per year.

Since the reelection of Putin in 2012, there have been indications that selective sales of weapons to China may resume. China still struggles to produce certain kinds of military equipment, such as jet engines, quiet submarine technology, integrated air defense systems, and advanced radar systems, and alternative sources of supply remain limited. In 2011, for example, China purchased 123 AL-31FN aircraft engines from Russia valued at $500 million.[29] In April 2015, China negotiated the purchase of a regiment of the highly advanced Russian Triumf S-400 surface-to-air missile system for US$3 billion as well as twenty-four of Russia's advanced Su-35 fighters. The most likely deployment for People's Liberation Army (PLA) S-400s is against Taiwan, where the system can detect and engage high-altitude targets not only off the Fujian coast but over the island itself; it could also potentially be used against Japan or northern India. The YJ-12 and YJ-18 supersonic antiship ballistic missiles currently being deployed in China are both spinoffs from Russian designs. Russia also continues to provide China with components and spare parts.[30] Moreover, direct military cooperation has increased. The most significant development has been the increasing level of joint military exercises: Since 2005, the two have held several "Peace Mission" exercises under the auspices of the Shanghai Cooperation Organization (SCO). But they have also conducted ever larger bilateral exercises outside the SCO context, including the joint drills held in the Sea of Japan (2012), Mediterranean Sea (2013), East China Sea (2015), Black Sea (2015), South China Sea (2016), and the Baltic Sea (2017). Many of these combined exercises were held in areas contested by either China or Russia (e.g., East and South China Sea, Black Sea), sending a signal to the United States that the two countries are prepared to support one another's strategic core interests.

Ironically the most immediate beneficiary of expanded trade is the region that has complained most vociferously about the relationship, the Russian Far East (RFE). The Far Eastern Federal District established in 2000 is the largest of Russia's eight federal districts (with an area of 6,215,900 square kilometers), while being also the least populated one. Most live along a narrow beltway just north of the border—facing over one hundred million Chinese on the other side of the border. The RFE grew in the late nineteenth century when it was on the frontier, and subsequently thrived as the base of defense installations, but has languished since the collapse of the Soviet Union. The region experienced its first population contraction of 250,000 in 1992 and it has continued to shrink through out-migration amid reduced central subsidies, massive unemployment in the military-industrial sector in the wake of Russia's economic disarray, and the collapse of the Soviet infrastructure network in the 1990s. Against this background, the influx of Chinese workers or traders (allegedly including criminals, prostitutes, and other undesirables) was functionally useful but incited populist resentment. According to Chinese statistics, border crossings amounted to 1.38 million in 1992 and 1.76 million at their peak in 1993.

But for the Russians, the central issue was not how many legal crossings but how many are illegal and how many stay: unofficial Russian estimates of Chinese illegal residents run as high as one million in the Far East and six million nationally, versus a Chinese official estimate of 250,000. In light of these trends, the future seems apt to consist of a dialectic between a growing Russian need for supplemental labor to unlock the economic potential of the Far East in the wake of continuing national population decline and Russian fears of Chinese demographic inundation. Since 2007, Russia has prohibited "all foreigners" from engaging in retail trade in Russia, also proscribing "Chinatowns," forcing a million Chinese businesspeople to emigrate. Beijing has cooperated by enforcing tough visa requirements on Chinese shuttle traders, resulting in a sharp decline in such traders (also in Russian consumer shortages and barren markets). China is the dominant trading partner of the RFE border provinces and represents a vital market for the RFE's most important products such as metals, coal, and timber; China is also an essential supplier of foodstuffs, clothing, and electronic products to the RFE's inhabitants. Although FDI lags trade in both countries, China is reportedly a bigger investor in the RFE than Russia, mostly concentrated in resource extraction. Russia has agreed in principle to open its Far East to more comprehensive cooperation with China; in September 2009, the two sides settled on a program for regional cooperation envisioning almost two hundred joint projects in the RFE. The details of particular joint ventures remain unclear, but the overall pattern suggests that China is attempting to monopolize resource processing in the country and to limit Russia to the role of resource supplier.

TRIANGULAR RELATIONS

In addition to bilateral relations Russia and China are engaged in triangular relations of two types: one with Central Asia, and the other with the United States. The first is asymmetrical and primarily political economic, as both sides essentially agree on security relations. The second is a "great power" relationship, both strategic and economic (but primarily the former), still vitally important to both.

Central Asia

At China's behest, the partnership, since the fall of the USSR, has been expanded to include the now independent republics in Central Asia: Kazakhstan, Kyrgyzstan, and Tajikistan, which border China, and (more recently) to Uzbekistan and Turkmenistan, which do not. Moscow agreed to chaperone a somewhat unusual negotiating team following the disintegration of the Soviet Union, facilitating border agreements between the PRC and all three bordering Central Asian republics (hereinafter CARs). This amounted to a disaggregation of the Sino-Soviet border talks that had been conducted since the early 1990s, the newly independent republics operating initially out of the cavernous Russian embassy building in Beijing. A set of five-power agreements between China and Russia and the three bordering Central Asian republics was signed in Beijing in April 1996 and Moscow in April 1997. In the former, both sides agreed on mutual force reduction and military confidence-building measures on their respective borders, while the latter established a zone of stability restricting military activity to a depth of one hundred kilometers along the frontier and making border security exercises more transparent. This negotiating exercise was regularized in annual meetings and, in the summer of 2001, expanded to include Uzbekistan and formalized as the Shanghai Cooperation Organization (SCO), thereby forming the largest security-related international organization in the world of which the United States is not a member. With the addition of India and Pakistan in 2015, the SCO accounts for about 23 percent of the planet's landmass, 45 percent of its population, and 25 percent of global GDP.

China's three main concerns from the outset have been borders, terrorism, and energy. While China's overall security situation was immensely improved by the fragmentation of one powerful border state into five weaker ones (including a newly independent Mongolia), some of these new states, notably Kyrgyzstan, include overlapping national minorities in China's Xinjiang Uyghur Autonomous Region (XUAR; e.g., the Uyghurs). Contagious nationalist enthusiasm for their sudden independence has thus stimulated ethnic support for an autonomous "Eastern Turkestan" to replace the XUAR. But these independent new states all retained holdover Soviet regional leaderships who had no more interest in ethnoreligious emancipation than the CCP. They quickly agreed with the Chinese emphasis on fighting the "three evils" (*san gu e shili*): terrorism, separatism, and religious extremism. A joint antiterrorist center was established at Bishkek, Kyrgyzstan (subsequently moved to Uzbekistan).

There is a certain amount of subsurface tension between the two major powers, not over security exactly but over the primary function of the SCO. Moscow continues to regard the region as in its own sphere of interest and to view the SCO as a vehicle through which China attempts to cultivate economic ties with the CARs and build oil and gas pipelines eastward, thereby cultivating an economic relationship over which Moscow once held a monopoly. In the power vacuum of the 1990s when Moscow was preoccupied with a very difficult economic and political transition, China indeed came to see considerable potential in importing Central Asian natural resources in return for Chinese capital, consumer goods, and services. And Russia had no objection, seeing that this would reduce the motivation for the CARs to seek routes to Europe bypassing Russia. In 2013, China overtook Russia as Central Asia's major trading partner (China–Central Asia trade around $50 billion, Russia–Central Asia trade $30 billion); Sino–Central Asian trade is up one-hundred-fold since 1992. Chinese companies now control nearly a quarter of Kazakhstan's oil industry and more than half of Turkmenistan's gas exports. The trade relationship is complementary, in a neocolonial way—80–90 percent of Chinese exports to Central Asia consist of finished, diversified goods, while about three-quarters of Central Asian exports to China comprise raw materials, petrol, and ferrous and nonferrous metals. China is transforming these local economies into raw material support bases and is destroying, through mechanisms of competition, the already fragile post-Soviet industries. China has also (in 2015) overtaken the Russians in FDI into the region. Notable recent achievements include completion of two Chinese-financed infrastructure projects to bring in oil and gas from Kazakhstan and Turkmenistan, respectively. Beijing agreed in 1997 to invest US$9.7 billion in Kazakhstan (the equivalent of half the country's GNP) to build oil and gas pipelines from the Caspian oil fields to the Xinjiang region and ultimately on to Shanghai. The Kazakhstan-China pipeline, running from Kazakhstan's Caspian shore to Xinjiang in China, was completed in 2003; two new sections were added in 2005 and 2009.[31] Some 28 percent of Kazakhstan's total trade volume is now with China. From Turkmenistan, a pipeline carrying natural gas to China via Uzbekistan and Kazakhstan was opened in late 2009, reaching full capacity in 2013; this promises to provide sixty-eight billion cubic meters over the next thirty years. The new pipeline connects with the Chinese West-East Gas Pipeline, the world's longest, running from Xinjiang to China's east coast, taking Turkmen gas to Pacific coastal cities such as Shanghai and Hong Kong. In March 2014, China agreed to build another gas pipeline running through Tajikistan and Kyrgyzstan. In 2013, the Sino-Burman gas pipeline was also completed.

But the bonanza is the Silk Road Economic Belt (SREB) launched by Xi Jinping in a speech in Astana, Kazakhstan, in 2013, promising US$1 trillion in investment capital to build roads, high-speed rail, airports, and other mega-projects. By May 2015, Beijing had signed partnership agreements on the SREB with national infrastructure development programs in Kazakhstan, Kyrgyzstan, and Tajikistan, culminating on May 8 in a declaration signed by Vladimir Putin and Xi Jinping on coordination between the SREB and the Russian-backed European Economic Union (EEU). The first direct freight train drew into London from Xinjiang in early 2017, cutting the trip from forty-five days by sea to sixteen days (of course only one day by air, but air costs four times as much; sea costs half as much but takes three times the time). The trip could be faster, but only after additional investment, as Soviet tracks are wider than Chinese—at present, freight must be reloaded twice en route. The SREB has turned out to be much more useful for promoting Beijing's geoeconomic interests than the SCO, in which all decisions are made strictly by consensus. How much functional integration between the EEU and the SREB will actually be achieved remains to be seen—the China-Pakistan Economic Corridor linking the port of Gwadar to Xinjiang could be merged with the EEU.

The strategic import of an independent cluster of Central Asian states is complex and evolving. The CARs, initially unaccustomed to independence, lack a common regional identity, trade less with each other than with outside partners, and have quite diverse interests, resources, and aspirations. Only two (Turkmenistan and Kazakhstan) are well endowed with hydrocarbon resources, though the mountainous terrain of Kyrgyzstan and Tajikistan has hydropower potential. Kazakhstan is the most bountifully endowed with natural resources; Uzbekistan is the most populous and economically developed. The only state with democratic pretentions, Kyrgyzstan has also been the most unstable, having experienced a "flower (tulip) revolution" in March 2005 followed by repeated government turnovers and new constitutions.[32] The SCO was organized to protect the group's mutual interests: antiterrorism, preventing color/flower revolutions attributed to the West, and facilitating intraregional economic transactions. The first two interests have been met, but the third has excited competition as well as cooperation. China has consistently advocated turning SCO into a common market, a goal that Russia resists, pointing out that the Eurasian Union (which it hopes to expand) already has a common market. Given their economic interests, the Chinese since 2010 have pushed for the establishment of an SCO development bank and an SCO free trade zone. Almost all of SCO member countries were uneasy about the idea of a trade zone, wary of seeing domestic infant industries destroyed by Chinese economies of scale without tariff protection. In the wake of the GFC desperately in need of cash, the CARs liked the idea of an SCO bank. But Moscow liked neither the free trade zone nor bank, pointing out that the EEU already has a common market and a bank (which Russia controls), encouraging China to join these instead. China dropped the proposal, but then proceeded to sign a free trade agreement (FTA) with the SCO (at the SCO summit in November 2016) and to enter into bilateral financial arrangements with each CAR.

The SCO is an anarchic organization (one actor's veto can block action by a majority). That said, the two dominant SCO members, China and Russia, provide a kind of dual leadership of the group. Albeit the SCO's initiator, China is a latecomer to the region, moving into the vacuum left by the Soviet Union's collapse and accepted by the Central Asian states as a useful counterweight to Moscow. But this duopoly presupposes they agree and are willing to share the power that either alone might more easily wield over the smaller states. In the "great game" for leadership, China's strategy has been to claim economic leadership by providing needed public goods. China has contracted to build not only oil and gas pipelines leading to China but also roads and high-speed rail, the extension of power lines (e.g., to link the northern and southern electric grids through the mountains of Kyrgyzstan), construction of the Shar-Shar tunnel and power stations in Tajikistan, and other such public works. Xi Jinping's ten-day September 2013 tour of all five states concluded with extended aid sums reminiscent of the Marshall Plan: all told, Xi signed an estimated US$48 billion worth of investment and loan agreements, with a focus on the energy, trade, and infrastructure sectors. Xi also proposed in 2013 that China and Kazakhstan work together in building China's grand vision of a China-to-Europe commercial corridor running westward from Xi'an through Central Asia and then on to Europe via Turkey. The Russians counter Chinese economic penetration by using their continuing military superiority to monopolize weapon sales, base building, antiterrorist activity, and other security arrangements, and the Chinese have not (yet) challenged this.

The competition also plays out multilaterally. As the Chinese have an edge in the SCO (headquartered in Beijing, despite the name), the Russians prefer to work through other multinational organizations of which China is not a member. These include not only the CIS but two later offshoots (both headquartered in Moscow): the Collective Security Treaty Organization or

CSTO (founded in 1992), which commands its own Collective Rapid Reaction Force and holds annual joint military command exercises, and the Eurasian Economic Union (2015 successor to the Eurasian Economic Community founded in 2000 and the 2012 Eurasian Economic Customs Union), now consisting of Belarus, Kazakhstan, and Russia.[33] But regional leadership implies willing followers: Russian efforts have been plagued by defections— Uzbekistan from CSTO in 2012, Ukraine more cataclysmically from the EEU in 2014. The Chinese were initially greeted by the CARs as a welcome alternative to the Russians, but Central Asians have since grown a bit more apprehensive about Chinese commercial and/or demographic penetration (e.g., price undercutting indigenous retail networks, monopolizing natural resource extraction, purchasing large swathes of farmland, importing all-Chinese work crews). While China was initially quite generous in its border settlements with these governments it has subsequently begun to revise borders with Kazakhstan, Kyrgyzstan, and Tajikistan in far less benign ways than it did in 1991–96, wielding asymmetrical financial power to smother resistance.[34] Thus the Central Asians increasingly see wisdom in maintaining a balance among suitors, valuing the SCO above other regional organizations precisely because it includes both major powers, enabling the smaller states to play one against the other.

Only a perceived outside threat to all members can crystallize a common strategic purpose, and the US involvement in the region as the bearer of alien values (human rights, democracy) has to the autocratic leaderships of member states come to serve that unifying function. The Americans were originally welcomed by Putin and respective host governments (more reluctantly by the PRC) to establish bases in Uzbekistan and Kyrgyzstan in 2002 pursuant to the global war on terror in nearby Afghanistan, viewed as a useful antidote to the Islamist threat faced by all these regimes. This calculation proved correct initially. The Islamic Movement of Uzbekistan (IMU) was decimated in northern Afghanistan in 2001 and its remnants retreated to northwest Pakistan. The leader of the East Turkestan Islamic Party (ETIM) was reported killed in Waziristan in autumn 2003 in a US-Pakistan operation. In 2002, the United States and the UN agreed to put ETIM on their lists of terrorist organizations. By 2004, Uyghurs were the fourth-largest nationality in Guantánamo.

But when the Bush administration in 2004 shifted its rationale from the fruitless search for weapons of mass destruction in Iraq to the promotion of democracy as the ultimate rationale of this "global war on terror," the US presence was deemed more problematic. The color revolutions in Ukraine, Georgia, and Kyrgyzstan in 2003–5 and the unsuccessful Andijan protest in Uzbekistan were all tied to the American presence and the activities of Western nongovernmental organizations (NGOs). Moscow noticed that in every dispute between Russia and other former Soviet states, even with authoritarian and repressive Belarus, the United States and the European Union sided with Moscow's opponents. China (quite plausibly) suspected the Manas base in Kyrgyzstan, among others, of being used to monitor Chinese security arrangements.[35] Thus with SCO blessing, Uzbekistan evicted the Americans from their air base in Karshi-Khanabad in 2005 and improved ties with China and Russia; the Manas base in Kyrgyzstan remained open until 2014 only because of the unsettled domestic situation (and because the United States agreed to pay a tripled rent).[36] The SCO has subsequently been expanded to include Mongolia, India, Pakistan, Iran, and Afghanistan as observers, and, more recently, Turkey, Sri Lanka, and Belarus as dialogue partners, but the US application for observer status in 2008 was demurred. In the summer of 2017, both India and Pakistan became full members, thus maintaining a balance between Chinese and Russian clients, making the SCO a truly massive intergovernmental organization (IGO). Both China and Russia are also members of the BRICS (Brazil, Russia, India, China, and South Africa), another non-Western IGO, where the addition of South Africa ensures them a three-fifths majority.

The United States

Mao's decision to "lean to one side," although following path-dependently from long prior Soviet sponsorship of the CCP when it lacked any other outside support, has occasioned subsequent controversy over a possible "lost chance" for the United States to normalize relations with the PRC. This possibility, based on Huang Hua's overtures to Leighton Stuart in the late 1940s when the CCP was still vulnerable to US intervention in the civil war, faded quickly upon seizure of power. This can be understood in triangular terms: When the United States and the USSR were still allies the CCP had an interest and saw no drawback to befriending both, but as relations polarized at the onset of the Cold War around 1947, Beijing had to choose between two camps. As a revolutionary Mao had little interest in preserving relations with the leading capitalist state, which was at the time preoccupied with saving expatriate US capitalists from incipient asset expropriation during China's collectivization campaigns. Shared ideological worldviews were decisive.[37]

Even so, negotiations leading to the thirty-year Sino-Soviet Treaty of Friendship, Alliance and Mutual Assistance (signed by Stalin and Mao on February 14, 1950) were long and difficult. Stalin, initially disinclined to negotiate a treaty with China, preferring to retain the 1945 treaty with Chiang, finally agreed to sign a treaty after two months of equivocation. The agreement was quite generous under the circumstances (the Soviet Union had been devastated by the Nazi invasion) providing a loan of US$300 million over five years at a subsidized rate of interest (1 percent), plus construction aid and plans for building fifty (eventually three times that) massive industrial projects. Moscow also gave back some of the concessions it had gained in 1945 negotiations with the KMT regime. But not until Beijing sent "volunteers" into the Korean War (where it lost some half a million men) to rescue the Kim Il Sung regime after McArthur's Inchon landing, while at the same time underwriting the first Indochina War (particularly at Dienbienphu), was Stalin fully convinced of Chinese commitment to the cause. Although the massive exercise launched in the 1950s to transplant modern (socialist) industrial culture to a developing country was to end badly, the period of cooperation made a seminal and lasting contribution to Chinese political and economic development. The Soviet model—a monocratic, hierarchically organized Leninist party-state focused on growth and designed to provide comprehensive welfare and security to all at the expense of personal liberty—would remain definitive for the PRC, despite inconclusive organizational experimentation in the Great Leap Forward and the Cultural Revolution.

The assumption in much of the Western literature has been that the end of the Cold War sounded the death knell of the Sino-Soviet-US Great Strategic Triangle. After all, the end of the Cold War not only saw the disintegration of the Soviet Union into fifteen sovereign republics but unleashed a sweeping new globalization, eliminating the Iron Curtain and other ideological impediments to transnational capital and labor markets. In their wake came the World Trade Organization (WTO) and various international and regional organizations (the EU, the Asia-Pacific Economic Cooperation forum [APEC]) dedicated to the elimination of tariff barriers. Commercially and economically it was now one "flat" world. It also seemed at first blush to be one world ideologically: the Soviet Union had disavowed Marxism-Leninism, which China continues to embrace, but in an extensively revised, "socialist market" form that includes many market components. Despite lingering suspicion and the collapse of ideological bonds, the two neighbors overcame territorial disputes and constructed a viable partnership based on shared interests. Both disavowed the export of revolution or percussive challenges to the international status quo. To US "triumphalists," this new world seemed to cohere around a liberal Washington consensus economically and a respect for international law and universal human rights politically. Surely triangular machinations were no longer relevant, and economic globalization would drive political cooperation as well.

But this optimistic early take has proved premature. It was premised on a genuine reconciliation between the United States and Russia after the latter disavowed communism, but the Western response to the birth of Russian democracy proved half-hearted. While the Warsaw Pact Organization and Comecon (Council for Mutual Economic Assistance) all collapsed, NATO remained a staunch barrier to Russian integration into Europe. Unlike the reunification of Austria (which accepted neutrality as the price of unity), Germany remained a key member of NATO, with thirty-five thousand US troops still on its soil in 2017.[38] Disregarding oral (never written) promises at the time of the collapse that NATO would not expand, NATO expanded ever farther into Eastern Europe, in three stages: in 1999, Poland, Hungary, and the Czech Republic joined; in 2003, Lithuania, Latvia, Estonia, Bulgaria, Romania, Slovakia, and Slovenia joined; and in 2009, Albania and Croatia joined. Russia objected at each point but became most perturbed when NATO in 2011 began considering the candidacies of former historical constituents of Russia (not merely the USSR) such as Georgia and Ukraine. In 1994, Russia joined the Partnership for Peace program with NATO, and in 2002, the Russia-NATO Council was established to handle security issues and joint projects, but neither gave Moscow any say over the enlargement of NATO and the EU.

The major issue for the former Soviet satellites was security. Russia offered to provide this with its Collective Security Treaty Organization (CSTO), plus a variety of bilateral security agreements. But the underlying reason for the insecurity of these former satellites was a lack of trust in the giant on which they remained asymmetrically dependent economically.[39] Thus trade arrangements became securitized. The 2008 NATO summit in Budapest declared that Ukraine and Georgia will become NATO members, and in 2009, the EU launched its Eastern Partnership Program, offering them Association Agreements or enhanced FTAs preparatory to full membership. Russia expressed concerns over the Eastern Partnership, seeing it as an attempt to expand the European Union's sphere of influence. Unsatisfied with the response, Russia started building its own set of multilateral institutions. In 2015, Russia agreed with Belarus and Kazakhstan to launch a competing Eurasian Customs Union and converted the CSTO into a military alliance. NATO refused to establish ties with the CSTO, forcing its members to make a binary choice.[40] Some CIS members opted for the CSTO, including Ukraine, but when President Viktor Yanukovych was forced from power by popular demonstrations at Euromaidan and the EU rushed to endorse a new government consisting of his opponents, this incited Russian suspicions of Western motives. Russia already had a naval base housing its Black Sea Fleet in the Crimea, and Putin moved quickly to secure it, staging an impromptu election in legitimation.[41] Crimea's population is around 58.5 percent ethnic Russian according to the last census (2001).

The lingering suspicion that led these former Soviet tributaries to seek membership in a Western defense organization and inclined that organization to accept them was no longer based on ideology. In retrospect, it seems the role of ideology in the Cold War was perhaps exaggerated, leading to the naive assumption that once ideology was repudiated the basis for conflict disappeared. There are at least two problems with this view. First, ideology was repudiated in Russia but not in China and not in the United States. The US ideology was in fact reinforced, inspiring an ambition to roll back the

Iron Curtain and other market barriers and promote a globalized rules-based Washington consensus. China has indeed sullied the purity of revolutionary Maoism with elements of market capitalism for the sake of efficiency and dropped the export of revolution as bad for business, but it continues to profess confidence in the superiority and eventual international victory of socialism. While China no longer espouses Mao's Three Worlds, China also continues to demand redistributive justice on behalf of the developing world, or south, and to oppose hegemony. This eclectic potpourri has assumed gradual coherence as a Beijing consensus fit to challenge the capitalist world order that failed in the Wall Street crash. And while Russia has indeed repudiated Leninism, it soon became apparent how much of that ideology had seeped into the national identity of the country, into the "great Russian soul." This has manifested itself both organizationally and politically. Yeltsin's attempt at economic privatization in the 1990s facilitated massive corruption (*katastroika*) and the creation of a class of oligarchs via management buyouts, which Putin reversed in a process of reverting to SOEs; thus as of 2015, the state owns about 30 percent of total production, second only to China.[42] While the 1993 Federal Constitution awarded local self-government, since 2000 Putin introduced federal districts to recentralize both appointment and fiscal power. Under what Putin calls a "vertical of power," the state retook the economic commanding heights of large-scale upstream industry (electricity generation, heavy manufacturing, resource extraction, and transportation) and sought to dominate the media and the life of the mind as well. Second, foreign policies and linkages once ascribed to ideological motives have in many cases outlived the demise of their ideological rationale. As many of Russia's new capitalist friends (the EU, the United States) proved fickle, many old friends, such as India, Syria, Cuba, and Vietnam, remain loyal. This invites the notion (encouraged by both Beijing and Moscow) that their foreign policies, though no longer based on ideology per se, bespeak an underlying strategic consensus. One pivotal common feature is opposition to US unipolarity, which has often frustrated their respective ambitions.

Strategic ambition is after all based not solely on ideology but on geography, history, national identity, and capabilities. Since the millennium, both China and Russia, two ancient empires now revitalized as emerging nations, have both outperformed the United States economically.[43] The triangle was always asymmetrical, and since the rise of China, it is asymmetrical in a different way. But in terms of capabilities, it is perhaps more symmetrical than ever before: while China's GDP now exceeds Russia's in aggregate terms by about four times, Russia's strategic force-projection capabilities still exceed China's, making it the only peer competitor of the United States in the current international arena. And since the GFC, the dominant US economic position has declined relative to the rise of both (spectacularly

China, but also Russia). In the immediate aftermath of the Cold War, the United States could disregard triangular logic because its power exceeded the combined power of both Russia and China, as when the United States launched an attack on Iraq in 2003 despite public opposition not only from China and Russia but from Germany and France. But contrast this with August 2012, when after drawing a red line against chemical weapons positing US intervention in the Syrian civil war, the combined opposition of China and Russia, who four times cast joint UN Security Council vetoes against any such unilateral intervention, sufficed to inhibit the US use of force in favor of a compromise solution. Sino-Russian relations, lauded by Xi Jinping in 2013 as the epitome of a "new type of great power relations," have never been closer.[44]

Naturally they also have their limits. China quietly underwrote the SCO's refusal to support Russia's invasion of Georgia in August 2008 on behalf of ethnic Russian minority separatists in South Ossetia and Abkhazia, which violated China's long-standing principle of nonintervention in internal affairs. Even in 2014, the Russian takeover of Crimea and subsequent military support for ethnic Russian separatists in eastern Ukraine was never explicitly endorsed by the PRC, which abstained on UN Security Council sanctions rather than joining Russia's veto. But Chinese opposition has always been understated, while Chinese media railed against the pro-NATO coup by the self-selected new Georgian government and hectored the United States for imposing sanctions.[45] Although Russia has not endorsed China's controversial territorial claims in the East and South China Seas, Putin on several occasions declared that outside powers should not interfere in the dispute and, at the 2016 meeting of the Group of 20 in Nanjing, supported China's defiance of the 2016 Permanent Court of Arbitration (PCA) award. The two navies held a joint exercise in the South China Sea shortly after the arbitral ruling in the summer of 2016, though not in contested regions.

We may infer from this not only the renewed relevance of the triangle but also that the current configuration is structurally disadvantageous to the United States, just as was the postwar Sino-Russian marriage against an American pariah. Of course there are conflicts of interest, but the relationship has successfully negotiated each of them and grown ever closer. For us to wonder how the United States could have allowed itself to be maneuvered into such a disadvantageous position is not necessarily to imply that it could quickly or easily be shifted to a more advantageous one. Although triangular position is a vitally important criterion for rational strategy it is not the only one, and more to the point it is not necessarily uppermost in the minds of foreign policy decision makers. Foreign policy positioning evolves based on geographic, ideological, and sociocultural criteria and is, to some extent, historically path dependent. The fact that the United States has managed to antagonize both of these major powers at once came about because of irritants specific to each bilateral relationship. Partly due to an effluence of American self-confidence after the global collapse of the communist bloc, US foreign policy makers became more idealistic, more insistent on conformity to democratic values than they had been during the Cold War and less concerned with considerations of power-political balance. Despite its repudiation of communism and adoption of parliamentary democracy, under Putin Russia has become increasingly authoritarian, as has Chinese communism under Xi Jinping. This has forged a bond for joint resistance to American unipolarity. Any American attempt to reconfigure the triangle more advantageously would need to compromise its highest political ideals.

This has been done before, usually by imagining the eventual prevalence of democratic evolutionary trends. The advent of the Trump presidency in 2016 makes such a shift once again realistically possible. In this case, however, the main impediment is not conflicting ideologies or conceptions of human rights but extratriangular foreign policy ambitions. China wants to regain possession of maritime territory it has convinced itself it had in the distant past, while Russia is determined to regain at least informally the sphere of influence it had during the Soviet era. Both countries have become bolder in their claims since the GFC in 2008, not in concert but lending each other moral support. Triangular logic suggests that for the United States to court one wing would instigate spoiling efforts by the other, either to rekindle the partnership or to compete for US favor. But reconciliation with either wing would need to be weighed in terms of the intrinsic value of that bilateral relationship as well as triangular logic. To take a well-publicized example, in 2016 Donald Trump during his presidential electoral campaign endorsed an improvement in relations with Russia, but then found it politically impossible to implement. The main obstacle was alleged Russian interference in the election, augmented by the backlog of hostility that has built up on both sides in the meantime as well as controversy over the legitimate sphere of Russian geopolitical influence.

There has been a tendency in the West to dismiss blithely the efficacy of the Sino-Russian strategic partnership. It is true that in an economic sense China still has far more trade with the United States and the EU than with Russia, and Russia, even after Putin's 2014 rebalance to the East, has more trade with Europe than with China. American interests are not as engaged with Russia as with China, but surely Russia is economically and strategically more important than Ukraine. Either country has more to gain from bandwagoning than trying to balance the lone superpower.[46] Yet though economics is without doubt important it is not in the short run politically decisive. The economic nexus between Russia and China has been historically very weak and even today remains largely a political construct. Economic sanctions as used against an economically flagging Russia have not proved effective in motivating more amenable behavior. What draws them together is not economics but analogous, though not identical, strategic interests and the pivotal role of the United States in frustrating them. Putin and Xi's June 24, 2016, meeting was remarkable because of the unusually high level of thinly disguised anti-American rhetoric. Neither country has made a secret of its discontent with the perceived unipolar distribution of global power, and it has become clear that the ambitions of both, though geographically discrete and apparently uncoordinated, clash with the status quo.

Triangular positioning is not all, of course; each nation will have certain core interests that limit its triangular latitude. For each of the three, core interests, however, have changed amid the global economic and political flux. During the last decade of the Cold War, the Sino-US relationship was perhaps at its crest, in joint opposition to the Soviet threat. The world has since shifted from bipolarity to a more multipolar balance, divided into spheres of interest dominated by a small set of global powers: the triangle is only one such conceptualization; another is pentagonal (the United States, Russia, China, Japan, and the EU), based on different notions of power and polarity.

After the fall of communist regimes in Europe in 1989–91, the concept of bipolarity was displaced by one of unipolarity, particularly in the United States. "By the grace of God, America won the Cold War," George H. W. Bush proclaimed during his 1992 State of the Union address.[47] This was the acme of triumphalism, yet it is empirically accurate to say that the United States found itself in a position of economic and strategic supremacy not seen since the end of World War II. After the Gulf War, which displayed US technological military prowess on international television, Bush spoke of a "new world order," in which democracy and human rights would displace anticommunism as the guiding ideology. American values were seen to blend in with a consensually acceptable set of rules of international conduct; hence, US strategic supremacy was deemed necessary and appropriate to enforce it for as long as possible and to impose, by economic sanction if possible or even by force if necessary, democratic governments and free markets throughout the world. Americans have clung to this worldview with considerable tenacity despite subsequent shifts in the global power balance. The triangle initially took the form of a ménage à trois with the United States in a pivot position and both wings relatively weak. Meanwhile, Yeltsin's Russia rejected the Union Treaty Gorbachev had proposed, opting for fragmentation into a loose and powerless Commonwealth of Independent States (CIS), and the advent of capitalist democracy from the top down inaugurated a decade of oligarchical takeovers and economic recession. China was in a position of international isolation and temporary economic slowdown after the bloody crackdown on its own youth at Tiananmen.

The core interests of both Russia and China in this new world order have been slower to crystalize, partly because both emerged from the Cold War at an initial disadvantage and interests depend in part on capabilities. Yeltsin's turn to Western democracy in the early 1990s was greeted by skepticism and continuing suspicion in the West, receiving substantial support only from a newly reunified Germany. By the mid-1990s, a disillusioned Yeltsin had dismissed Andrei Kozyrev and turned back to Soviet apparatchiki like Evgenii Primakov and a more Eurasian foreign policy that cultivated former Soviet clients such as China, India, Vietnam, Syria, and North Korea. Yeltsin's chosen successor, former KGB colonel Vladimir Putin, revived the economy by relying on natural resource exports in a tightening global market; thus when he proceeded to restore authoritarian state control over the pillar industries and the regions, there was only token resistance (indeed, his personal popularity neared 70 percent). Putin viewed the dissolution of the USSR as one of the great tragedies of the twentieth century and, since Russia's economic recovery in the early 2000s, identified its core interest as reasserting—and if possible in some way institutionalizing—a sphere of influence over the former Soviet sphere. In the aftermath of the 9/11 attack, Putin perceived a coincidence of threat perceptions and an opportunity for collaboration between Bush's global war on terror and his own fight against the wave of Chechen (Islamist) terrorist attacks in Russian cities. In November 2001, Putin visited the United States and was received by President George W. Bush at his Texas ranch, where the two cultivated their personal friendship and reached a verbal agreement to reduce strategic nuclear arsenals by two-thirds in the next decade. The following month the United States withdrew from the Anti-Ballistic Missile (ABM) Treaty with the concurrence of the Putin administration. The Putin administration backed the first phase of the Bush global war on terror, encouraging the Central Asian republics to provide military facilities for the United States and increasing their own assistance to the Northern Alliance in Afghanistan. This caused considerable consternation in China, where it was suspected Putin was trying to play the US card against them, especially given the US abrogation of the ABM Treaty and the movement of US forces into Central Asia (in both of which China had a shared interest).

Between September 11, 2001, and the 2003 Iraq invasion, Russia made a concerted effort to persuade the United States of the merits of a partnership in which Russia would throw its weight behind the war against Islamism in exchange for maintenance of the strategic status quo in Europe—no further NATO expansion, no theater missile defense.[48] The US response was not entirely uncompromising: NATO agreed to set up a joint committee with policy-making powers on common action, thus allowing Russia a voice on NATO's security affairs. But piecemeal inclusion in NATO had little practical impact—Russia had input but no veto. Russia noted that in every dispute between Russia and its former allies or republics (for example, over joining NATO or the EU, or emplacing antimissile sites) the United States supported the latter. To the US government's surprise and dismay, Putin then joined China, Germany, and France in opposing the invasion of Iraq, thereby commencing the gradual distancing between the two powers that was to be only temporarily allayed by the 2009 Hillary Clinton "reset."

China in the 1990s and 2000s, initially ostracized in the wake of the Tiananmen incident, was guided by Deng Xiaoping's 24-character admonition to "keep our heads down" and tend to business, which in foreign policy terms meant opening up economically to all who could be useful and limiting anti-American propaganda ("peaceful evolution," etc.) to domestic audiences. The economy after Tiananmen was recentralized under more centralized management and a liberalized policy toward FDI, for the first time permitting, for example, wholly owned foreign enterprises. This quickly gave rise to a booming foreign-invested, export-oriented industrial sector, first in four special economic zones in the southeast and then along the whole eastern "golden coast." The combination of rapid growth and the lucrative opportunities it offered so impressed the American business community that they lobbied hard to prevent persisting US human rights and labor concerns from interfering with trade, and in 2001, the Chinese were admitted to the WTO after acceding to high entry barriers. The PLA leadership was impressed by the televised US technical superiority (against Soviet weaponry) in the 2001 Gulf War, and gained a consistently larger annual budget for modernization of the Chinese military, largely through the purchase of advanced Russian weapons technology. Sino-US military-to-military confidence-building exchanges were resumed in the 1990s, though periodically interrupted by such disputes as the 1995–96 Taiwan Strait crisis, the 1999 bombing of the Chinese embassy in Belgrade, and the 2001 EP-3 incident near Hainan. The 2000s marked another decade of mutual diplomatic reassurance under China's peaceful rise/development line. Beijing needed the United States to persuade Taiwan under Chen Shuibian to abandon its drive for national independence, which Beijing proved unable to accomplish (shy of invasion) with either concessions (the Koo Cheng-fu visit to Beijing) or threats—and the United States needed Beijing to help manage the nuclear issue in Iran and North Korea.

Until the end of the decade, Washington had thus maintained its pivot position by alternating between wings without forming an irrevocable commitment to either, while China and Russia maintained their cooperative-competitive partnership. While the 1980s amounted to a quasi marriage between Beijing and Washington, Tiananmen and the dissolution of the shared Soviet threat undercut both its moral and strategic grounding. In the wake of Tiananmen, Washington largely leaned toward a newly postcommunist Russia, reviving a cordial relationship with Beijing only near the end of the 1990s with an exchange of presidential summits. But in the mid-2000s, a combination of changes in the balance of power and the growing incompatibility of perceived core interests began to dislodge the United States from its pivot position. Lofted by a global energy price spiral, Russia under the Putin-Medvedev team experienced an impressive economic resurgence in the 2000s. According to Moscow-based investment bank Troika Dialog, from 1999 to 2006 Russia's nominal GDP had grown by a factor of nearly five times from less than $200 billion to more than $900 billion, poised to exceed the $1 trillion mark in 2007. Russia's foreign exchange reserves over this period grew twenty times, from about $20 billion when Putin became president to more than $400 billion in 2007. The Russian stock market was consistently one of the fastest growing in the world, growing about 1,000 percent, while average wages increased fourfold.[49] With national self-confidence greatly enhanced by this recovery, the Putin leadership started to take more seriously the enforcement of core interests it had long harbored but not hitherto deemed politically feasible. For Putin, the core national interest was recovery of at least a sphere of influence embracing the constituent parts of the former Soviet Union. Having tried in vain to obtain the West's concurrence, he would now turn to the East. The breaking point was the color, or flower, revolutions in Georgia (2003, rose), Ukraine (2004, orange), and Kyrgyzstan (2005, tulip), together with the 2005 Andijan incident in Uzbekistan. Russia (and China) suspected Western interests—formal (e.g., NATO and the big oil conglomerates) and informal (e.g., Western NGOs)—of being behind these upheavals (which did elicit rhetorical support from the West). So in 2005, the SCO invited the United States to withdraw from its bases in Uzbekistan and Kyrgyzstan, and Uzbekistan forced evacuation the following year. In Georgia in 2008 and in Ukraine in 2014, Putin demonstrated his determination to use force if necessary to deter defections of former constituent republics of the Soviet Union to Western security alliances.

In China's case, too, an impressive rise in capabilities unleashed long cherished but hitherto repressed core interests. The Chinese growth record since the Third Plenum of the Eleventh Congress in December 1978 had been consistently among the world's highest, but particularly during the first decade of the twenty-first century, when entry to the WTO relaxed fears of retraction of most-favored-nation treatment and allowed Beijing to maintain consistently favorable terms of trade without fear of political retribution. During the Hu Jintao decade (2002–12), China accounted for some 24 percent of the entire growth in the global economy, and in 2014, China's GDP (in purchasing power parity) surpassed that of the United States, according to the World Bank. China's military spending rose apace: since 1989, there were double-digit increases in the military budget every year but one (amounting to a cumulative increase in spending of 175 percent since 2003), giving China the largest defense budget in Asia and the second largest in the world. There is no reason to think the CCP leadership was any less awed by its own achievements than the rest of the world (public opinion polls in many countries showed vast numbers of people believing China already was the world's leading power). China's growth depended on constantly increasing imports of raw materials, with annual consumption of many basic commodities such as aluminum, iron ore, and copper nearing half the world total.

Beginning in 2012, the Russian and Chinese leadership camps began to see their interests so coaligned that they could afford simultaneous bids to expand territorially in defiance of US interests. There is no empirical evidence of conspiracy or logistic support. Though Putin joined China in renouncing the PCA ruling in July 2016, Russia has declared itself neutral in East Asian maritime sovereignty disputes.[50] China has no interest in Putin's attempts to reconstruct the Soviet Union, whose disintegration was a great boon to China's national security and political economy; it is much more advantageous to negotiate with five or six small countries than with one big one, and the former Soviet republics (including Ukraine) have been receptive to China's economic deals. Yet in many respects the two regimes, one communist and the other postcommunist (but still nostalgic), find themselves on similar developmental trajectories, reaching into the past to reinforce an otherwise fragile legitimacy while pushing relentlessly to recover lost dignity. The core interests of the two partners are geographically diverse but coincide in their frustration with perceived US meddling. And this seems to have sufficed to push them into each other's arms. Fortuitously the invocation of Western economic sanctions in response to Russia's alleged violation of Ukraine's sovereignty coincided with negotiations over a new pipeline to China. This provided an opportunity for Putin to demonstrate an alternative to the European gas market, although the Chinese were not above taking advantage of his situation to bargain a low gas price. Japan, after Fukushima no less eager to take advantage of Russia's need for an Eastern market alternative (and of course still interested in negotiating a return of the northern territories), dropped out of the bidding in response to the post-Ukraine US push for sanctions, albeit with evident reluctance.

CONCLUSIONS

From a triangular perspective, the United States has allowed itself to be maneuvered into the worst possible strategic position. The Sino-Russian partnership is only as strong as the two wings' core interests conflict with US interests, so by opposing both nations' core interests at once, the United States has become the pariah in a renewed Sino-Russian marriage. And the United States is by no means as powerful as it was when it faced a united Sino-Soviet alliance alone in the 1950s, not even with the support of Western Europe and Japan (both of which are nursing difficult economic recoveries). In view of the momentous shift of national power since the end of the Cold

War, the US position, still justified in terms of ideological principle rather than geostrategic interest, may no longer be sustainable. Yet any attempt to reconfigure the triangle more favorably depends not only on triangular dynamics but also on bilateral leverage with each wing.

The logical alternatives for the United States are either to try to sustain an economically weakened and fragmented neo–Cold War coalition of democratic nations against this new Sino-Russian bloc, or try to pry that bloc apart by seducing one of the partners. The Obama choice was to tilt toward China, downplaying short-term disagreements over the South China Sea, Internet hacking, and so forth, for its cooperation in the farsighted pursuit of nuclear nonproliferation in Korea and an agreement to combat global warming. Meanwhile, the United States joined NATO in pursuing a full gamut of sanctions against Putin for retaking Crimea and besieging Ukraine. True, the United States has disapproved of China's enforcement of its maritime claims in the East and South China Seas, but US policy makers have found neither the will nor the means to halt China's subthreshold maritime expansion. The military component of the Obama pivot or rebalance strategy—the air-sea battle plan, the marine base at Darwin, the transfer of naval forces—becomes relevant only if and when confrontation escalates into warfare, which China has carefully avoided. Meanwhile, the economic component of the pivot— the Trans-Pacific Partnership (TPP)—was pursued for eight years with insufficient force to push it through Congress and now lies victim of the 2016 electoral turnover.

In many respects, the China tilt was a defensible choice: the United States has no territorial claims in any of China's peripheral waters, and China and the United States have mutual interests vested in a huge bilateral trade and investment regime, not to mention China's ownership of the largest foreign share of the US national debt. US trade dependency is much greater with China than with Russia, and China's projected future growth and potential economic rebalancing offer a potentially lucrative export market. While China has become more assertive in defense of its sovereign interests as it defines them, it has been careful not to challenge the United States directly, and the United States, while disapproving rhetorically, has been careful to draw no red lines. On the other hand, there is the issue of power transition, and the transforming nature of the Chinese system as it becomes powerful enough to challenge the system it feels itself destined to supplant. As Hugh White points out, China's size, growth, and resources make it a far more formidable potential adversary than the United States has ever faced before.[51] According to classic balance-of-power theory, it is generally deemed advisable to align with the weaker threat against the stronger—as Nixon did when crafting the original romantic triangle in 1971. After all, is Russian resistance to neighboring countries joining opposing military alliances or to the proposed emplacement of missile sites in such countries really so mysterious in the light of the Cuban missile crisis?[52]

During his successful 2016 election campaign, Donald Trump was harshly critical of the PRC and spoke positively of the Putin leadership and the prospect of improving relations with Russia, perhaps planning a rebalance of the triangle. Certainly Russia welcomed this, especially the relaxation of sanctions, as evidenced by direct interference in the US election. But the prerequisite to any such rebalance would be a harmonization of bilateral interests. And aside from the likely partisan and security establishment backlash to such a rebalance, there are many obstacles. Although the move into Crimea and eastern Ukraine is understandable from a Russian perspective, it is inconsistent with a rules-based international order, and NATO remains opposed. Trump is in favor of US energy independence, meaning he is pro-oil—offshore wells, pipelines, shale oil, Alaska, even Arctic—all of which will drive the global oil price down. The Russian economy relies on oil and natural gas to fund nearly 50 percent of its fiscal revenues (as of 2015). The global price of oil has tumbled from its mid-2014 high of $115 per barrel to $50 in 2016, causing Russia to lose more than 40 percent of its GDP. In any case, since the election the Russian option has been politically fraught. True, the United States does not buy oil from Russia, but oil prices are based on global supply and demand. In any case, the postelection scandal over Russian cyberinterference in the US presidential election has vitiated at least temporarily any rapprochement with Moscow, while the April 2017 "citrus summit" has revived the prospect of Sino-US détente.

In sum, the Great Strategic Triangle is back, and it finds the United States in the least advantageous position. If the United States were to reconfigure the triangle this would be to its advantage in getting things done in the world, but the United States faces major obstacles to doing so. The United States currently opposes both Russia and China, for analogous but discrete reasons. And for their part, Russia and China both oppose the US liberal interventionist role in the world, but from geographically distinct positions. The two are drawn together by shared conservative authoritarian value perspectives and by a foreign policy aspiration to make the world safer for that worldview, and to expand their respective spheres of influence. Each has its own national interests and their expansionist dreams are likewise geographically distinct, making their relationship a limited liability partnership. For the United States to reconfigure the triangle by improving bilateral relations with either or both wings would require a prioritization of power-political, material interests over ideal interests, and may even require partial withdrawal from certain informal US spheres of influence.

NOTES

1. Fyodor M. Dostoyevsky, *The Diary of a Writer, 1881* (New York: George Braziller, 1954), 342. Also quoted as "Russia was a slave in Europe but would be a master in Asia" (Dominic Livien, "Dilemmas of Empire 1850–1918: Power, Territory, Identity," *Journal of Contemporary History* 34, no. 2 [April 1999]: 180).

2. Exceptions include Bobo Lo, *Axis of Convenience: Moscow, Beijing and the New Geopolitics* (Washington, DC: Brookings, 2008); Gilbert Rozman, *The Sino-Soviet Challenge to the World Order* (Washington, DC: Woodrow Wilson Center Press, 2014); and Austin Jersild, *The Sino-Soviet Alliance: An International History* (Chapel Hill: University of North Carolina Press, 2014).

3. Donald Ostrowski, *Muscovy and the Mongols: Cross-cultural Influences on the Steppe Frontier* (Cambridge: Cambridge University Press, 1996), 109ff.

4. Alone among China's unequal treaties, the Peking Treaty remains unrepudiated today.

5. While it is true that Comintern advice during the late 1920s contributed to serial defeats of the CCP and that Mao's subsequent adoption of guerrilla warfare waged by peasant armies proved more successful than the Comintern policy of urban insurrections, the adoption of united front tactics at Moscow's insistence in 1936 may have rescued the embattled CCP at a crucial juncture.

6. Moscow's treaty with Nanking was a matter of considerable shock and dismay to the CCP, which had not been consulted or even informed. See Dieter Heinrich, *Die Sowjetunion und das kommunistische China 1945–1950: Der beschwerliche Weg zum Buendnis* (Baden-Baden, Germany: Nomost Verlagsgesellschaft, 1998), 99–117.

7. The Soviet Union sent one million troops into Manchukuo in 1945 to fight the collapsing Kwantung army, then gave the territory and captured Japanese munitions to the PLA (Wang Yuyan and He Ming, eds., *Sulian chu bing Dongbei shi mo* [The Soviets Sent Troops Throughout the Northeast] (Beijing: Renmin chubanshe, 2005), 142 et passim.

8. G. I. Khanin, "The 1950s—the Triumph of the Soviet Economy," *Europe-Asia Studies*, 55, no. 8 (December 2003): 1187–1212.

9. Mao Zedong, ed., "Speech at a Meeting of the Representatives of Sixty-Four Communist and Workers' Parties," November 18, 1957, Woodrow Wilson Center Digital archive, http://digitalarchive.wilsoncenter.org. Mao had articulated his cavalier attitude about the risks of nuclear warfare many times before, but not perhaps before a Soviet audience. Li Zhisui in *The Private Life of Chairman Mao* recounts that in October 1954 he told Nehru the atomic bomb was a "paper tiger" and that he was willing for China to lose millions of people in order to emerge victorious against imperialism. "China has many people. They cannot be bombed out of existence. . . . The death of ten or twenty million people is nothing to be afraid of."

10. Cf. Neville Maxwell, "How the Sino-Russian Boundary Conflict Was Finally Settled: From Nerchinsk 1689 to Vladivostok 2005 via Zhenbao Island 1969," *Critical Asian Studies*, 39, no. 2 (June 2007): 229–53.

11. "Speech by Chairman of the Delegation of the People's Republic of China, Teng Hsiao-Ping, at the Special Session of the U.N. General Assembly" (Peking: Foreign Languages Press, April 10, 1974), http://digitalarchive.wilsoncenter.org/search-results/1/%7B"subject"%3A"2652"%7D.

12. Richard Boudreau, "Russia Gets Timely Boost in German Aid: Diplomacy: Kohl Pledges Token Relief to Embattled Yeltsin in Return for Quicker Military Pullout," *Los Angeles Times*, December 17, 1992, http://articles.latimes.com/keyword/germany-foreign-aid-russia; see also Marie Elise Sarotte, "A Broken Promise?" *Foreign Affairs*, September–October 2014.

13. In 1996, Richard Holbrooke, an assistant secretary in the State Department, proposed to expand NATO by bringing in Poland, Hungary, the Czech Republic, and the Baltic nations. Secretary of Defense William Perry thought this was a very unwise move and should be deferred at all cost. A prominent group of fifty leading foreign policy authorities, including Robert McNamara, Sam Nunn, Bill Bradley, Paul Nitze, and Richard Pipes, signed a letter to Clinton opposing NATO expansion. The full text of the letter and a list of signers are available at www.bu.edu/globalbeat/nato/postpone062697.html. George Kennan told the *New York*

Times in 1998: "I think [NATO expansion] is the beginning of a new cold war. I think the Russians will gradually react quite adversely and it will affect their policies. I think it is a tragic mistake. There was no reason for this whatsoever. No one was threatening anybody else. . . . We have signed up to protect a whole series of countries, even though we have neither the resources nor the intention to do so in any serious way." But Poland, Hungary, and the Czech Republic were given immediate membership in NATO, and the Baltic states were later included under G. W. Bush. See Thomas L. Friedman, "Foreign Affairs; Now a Word from X," *New York Times*, May 2, 1998.

14. Cf. Zhimin Chen, "China's Power from a Chinese Perspective (II): Back to the Center Stage," in *Assessing China's Power*, ed. Jae Ho Chung (Basingstoke, Hampshire: Palgrave Macmillan, 2015), 271–89. Although CNP is a distinctive Chinese index, there are various estimates but no official ranking; in the Chinese Academy of Social Sciences 2010 estimate, China ranked eighth.

15. For a pioneering theoretical analysis of the international implications of asymmetry, see Brantly Womack, *Asymmetry and International Relationships* (New York: Cambridge University Press, 2016).

16. Since 2013, when Xi Jinping became president of China, in 2015 he paid five visits to Russia, and Russian president Vladimir Putin traveled three times to China. All told, Xi and Putin met twelve times, making Putin the foreign head of state whom Xi has met most frequently since assuming the presidency.

17. *RFE/RL Newsline* 9, no. 125, part 1 (July 1, 2005), https://www.rferl.org/a/1143432.html. The pattern is referred to in China as *zheng re, min leng* (warm relations among governments, cool relations with the people), which has also characterized relations with Central Asia (David Kerr, "Central Asian and Russian Perspectives on China's Strategic Emergence," *International Affairs* 86 [2010]: 127–52; 137, table 1). But public opinion has followed the elite lead: a 2015 survey found 79 percent of Russians had a positive view of China, while 51 percent of Chinese had a positive view of Russia.

18. Lo, *Axis of Convenience.*

19. A poll conducted in 2008 by Russia's Public Opinion Foundation showed that around 60 percent of Russians were concerned that Chinese migration to Far Eastern border areas would threaten Russia's territorial integrity, and 41 percent believed that a stronger China would harm Russian interests. As China's quest for new investment and trade opportunities abroad has led to increased Chinese cooperation with former Soviet republics, Russians have worried that China is competing for influence in their neighborhood. Partly as a result, Moscow initially hesitated to support Beijing's Silk Road Economic Belt initiative before ultimately embracing it in 2014. Meanwhile, some Chinese continue to nurse historical grievances regarding Russia. Chinese popular history books still invoke the unequal treaties of the nineteenth century, and Chinese commentators sometimes make critical references to the six hundred thousand square miles of Chinese territory that tsarist Russia annexed at that time.

20. "China and Russia Sign 11 Agreements, Emphasizing Joint Energy Development," *Beijing News*, June 6, 2012, accessed August 1, 2013, http://money.163.com/12/0606/02/839IJKU800253B0H_all.html.

21. As quoted in Rheanna Mathews, "The Sino-Russian Gas Agreement: Political Implications for an Asian Rebalance," Institute of Peace and Conflict Studies, May 30, 2014, http://www.ipcs.org/article/china/the-sino-russian-gas-agreement-political-implications-for-an-asian-4478.html.

22. Three years hence, the project is moving at a snail's pace. China drove a shrewd bargain, knowing Russia needed it more than China did; China got a low price, and as a result, the project is turning into a loss-making endeavor for the Russians—so Gazprom dawdles.

23. Russia's export of tanks in 1992 dropped seventy-nine-fold, and sales of combat aircraft fell 1.5 times in comparison to 1991, leaving warehouses of the military-industrial complex overstocked with unsold weapons. China was the principal buyer of Russian weapons in 1992, making purchases worth US$1.8 billion. Pavel Felgengauer, "Arms Exports Continue to Fall," *Sogodnya* (Moscow), July 13, 1993, 3.

24. Sharif M. Shuja, "Moscow's Asia Policy," *Contemporary Review* 272, no. 1587 (April 1998): 169–78.

25. Ilya Kramnik, "Russia's Arms Exports: Farewell to Arms, Hello to Profits," *RIA Novosti*, November 3, 2010, accessed August 1, 2013, http://en.rian.ru/analysis/20101103/161201525.html.

26. Tai Ming Cheung, "China's Emergence as a Defense Technological Power: Introduction," *Journal of Strategic Studies* 34, no. 3 (June 17, 2011): 296; Richard Rousseau, "The Tortuous Sino-Russian Arms Trade—Analysis," *Eurasia Review*, June 9, 2012, http://www.eurasiareview.com/09062012-the-tortuous-sino-russian-arms-trade-analysis/.

27. "Russian Official Sees China Remaining Major Arms Buyer," Interfax News Agency (Moscow), November 20, 1998, in FBIS, Daily Report/Russia, document no. FBIS-SOV-98-324, November 20, 1998; Gregory Feifer, "Russia Analysts Say Burgeoning Arms Sales Pose Security Threat," Radio Free Europe Radio Liberty, February 17, 2003, https://www.rferl.org/a/1102207.html.

28. Cf. Peggy Falkenheim Meyer, "Russia's Post-Cold War Security Policy in Northeast Asia," *Pacific Affairs* 67, no. 4 (Winter 1994): 495–513.

29. Richard F. Grimmett and Paul K. Kerr, *Conventional Arms Transfers to Developing Nations, 2004–2011*, CRS Report R42678 (Washington, DC: Library of Congress, Congressional Research Service, August 24, 2012), 10, http://www.fas.org/sgp/crs/weapons/R42678.pdf.

30. Linda Jakobson et al., "China's Energy and Security Relations with Russia," SIPRI Policy Paper no. 29 (October 2011), vi, 15, 6, 14, 19.

31. During the height of GFC in 2009, China even offered loans to Belarus, Moldova, and Ukraine, none of which are members of the SCO. The loans were later withdrawn under Russian pressure. Cf. Marcin Kaczmarski, "Domestic Sources of Russia's China Policy," *Problems of Post-Communism* 59, no. 2 (March/April 2012): 3–17.

32. The Chinese are particularly sensitive to instability here because of the ethnic overlap with the Uyghurs. China reportedly considered using force to prevent the color revolution in Kyrgyzstan in 2005, and at the time sought a base there to forestall further such outbreaks (the Russians have consistently discouraged any prospect of Chinese bases in Central Asia). China's subsequent warm embrace of Uzbek president Islam Karimov immediately after the Andijan massacre underscores that continuing dread of any upheaval in Central Asia. Younkyoo Kim and Stephen Blank, "Same Bed, Different Dreams: China's 'Peaceful Rise' and Sino-Russian Rivalry in Central Asia," *Journal of Contemporary China* 22, no. 83 (May 15, 2013): 78.

33. A treaty aiming for the establishment of the EEU was signed on May 29, 2014, by the leaders of Belarus, Kazakhstan, and Russia, and came into force on January 1, 2015. Armenia's accession to the EEU came into force on January 2, 2015, and Kyrgyzstan joined on August 6, 2015.

34. See Kim and Blank, "Same Bed, Different Dreams," 773–90.

35. According to a former Indian ambassador, the Bakiyev regime permitted the US military to use highly sophisticated electronic devices at Manas to monitor key Chinese missile and military sites in Xinjiang. K. Gajendra Singh, "Geopolitical Battle in Kyrgyzstan over US Military Lily Pond in Central Asia," *Tarafits* (New Delhi), April 11, 2010; as cited in Kim and Blank, "Same Bed, Different Dreams," fn. 45.

36. China opposed a US presence in the region as early as 2002 and has long pressured the Kyrgyz authorities to close the Manas base in particular. See Kim and Blank, "Same Bed, Different Dreams," 78.

37. David Wolff, "'One Finger's Worth of Historical Events': New Russian and Chinese Evidence on the Sino-Soviet Alliance and Split, 1948–1959," Cold War International History Project, Working Paper no. 30 (Washington, DC: Woodrow Wilson International Center for Scholars, August 2000), 73, http://www.wilsoncenter.org/topics/pubs/ACFB14.pdf.

38. In discussions with US secretary of state James Baker and German foreign minister Hans-Dietrich Genscher, Gorbachev was persuaded to accept Germany's membership in NATO on the condition (never in writing) that NATO would not move east (understood at the time to mean it would not even include Eastern Germany). See Hans-Dietrich Genscher, *Errinerungen* (Berlin: Siedler Verlag, 1995), 788–895; see also Sarotte, "A Broken Promise?"

39. For example, Russia remains Ukraine's largest trading partner, accounting for up to 20 percent of overall turnover.

40. See Samuel Charap and Mikhail Troitskiy, "Russia, the West and the Integration Dilemma," *Survival* 55, no. 6 (December 2013–January 2014): 49–62.

41. Cf. Nicholas Redman, "Russia's Breaking Point," *Survival* 56, no. 2 (April–May 2014): 235–44.

42. Alexander Abramov, Alexander Radygina, and Maria Chernova, "State-Owned Enterprises in the Russian Market: Ownership Structure and Their Role in the Economy," *Russian Journal of Economics* 3, no. 1 (March 2017), 1–23, http://www.sciencedirect.com/science/article/pii/S2405473917300016.

43. Of course China is the star in the growth sweepstakes, but Russia's economic revival under Putin, though somewhat one dimensional and short lived, should not be underestimated. The Russian economy averaged 7 percent GDP growth from 2000 to 2007. From 2008 to 2015, however, it sustained almost no growth at all, mainly due to the fall in the price of petrol, exacerbated by post-Crimea economic sanctions.

44. Jane Perlez, "Chinese President Seeks New Relationship with US in Talks," *New York Times*, May 28, 2013, http://www.nytimes.com/2013/05/29/world/asia/china-to-seek-more-equal-footing-with-us-in-talks.html.

45. See Shannon Tiezzi, "China Backs Russia on Ukraine," *Diplomat*, March 3, 2014, http://thediplomat.com/2014/03/china-backs-russia-on-ukraine/.

46. See, for example, Bobo Lo, "Ten Things Everyone Should Know about the Sino-Russian Relationship," *Policy Brief*, Centre for European Reform, December 2008.

47. George H. W. Bush, "Address before a Joint Session of the Congress on the State of the Union," January 28, 1992, American Presidency Project, http://www.presidency.ucsb.edu/ws/?pid=20544.

48. Angela Stent, "Amerika i Rossiya: partnerstvo posle Iraka?" [America and Russia: A partnership after Iraq?] *Pro et Contra* 8, no. 2 (2003): 163–77; as cited in Kerr, "Central Asian and Russian Perspectives on China's Strategic Emergence," 132.

49. Cf. Andrew Kuchins, *Russian Perspectives on China: Strategic Ambivalence* (Washington, DC: Center for Strategic and International Studies, July 2007).

50. Indeed, Russia in 2012 formed a "comprehensive strategic partnership" with Vietnam. It has sold Vietnam advanced fighters plus eight Kilo-class submarines, for which it has also contracted to build a base at Cam Ranh Bay. The last of the boats is scheduled for delivery in 2016. Rakesh Krishnan Simha, "Why Russian Submarines Are Making Waves in Asia," *Russia beyond the Headlines*, June 24, 2015, http://rbth.com/blogs/2015/06/24/why_russian_submarines_are_making_waves_in_asia_47179.html.

51. See Hugh White, *The China Choice: Why America Should Share Power* (Collingwood, Australia: Black Inc., 2012); also Hugh White, "Power Shift: Rethinking Australia's Place in the Asian Century," *Australian Journal of International Affairs* 65, no. 1 (February 2011): 81–93.

52. The crisis was preceded by an abortive US attempt to invade the island.

Chapter Four

Unsettled Sun

As in its relationship with its neighbor to the north, the historical legacy of China-Japan relations has often been ambivalent—but not at the same time in the same way. Though China "discovered" Japan during the Han, the first golden era of Sino-Japanese relations was during the great Tang dynasty, when Japan sent many students to China to study this widely admired civilization, adopting the Chinese writing system, learning from China's advanced technical expertise, emulating China's political institutions, and bringing home Buddhism, Confucianism, Chinese architecture, art, cuisine, and even sartorial fashions. In 777, the Tang court received as tribute eleven Japanese female dancers. During China's Song dynasty (960–1279), between forty and fifty trading vessels plied the waters between the two countries every year. By the time of the Yuan dynasty (1271–1368), however, Japanese pirates, known as *wako*, were pillaging the Chinese coast, to which China responded with attempted attacks on the Japanese islands. Kublai Khan, after subduing Korea, indignant at a Japanese refusal to render tribute, launched two massive amphibious invasions in 1274 and 1281, which were finally repulsed with the help of a typhoon or "divine wind" (*kamikaze*). Japanese resentment toward China reached new heights at the close of the fourteenth century, when the powerful Ming dynasty (1368–1644) induced Japan into a reluctant tributary relationship.

Japan accepted its inferior status until 1547—the year of the last recorded tribute mission—when it ended tributary pilgrimages and began competing with China for control of Korea. In 1592–98, Hideyoshi Toyotomi, one of the three "great unifiers" of Japan (with Oda Nobunaga before him and Tokugawa Ieyasu after), launched an invasion of Korea when the latter denied him passage to China, to which Korea was then a loyal tributary. Though the Japanese subdued Korean forces, the Ming then sent reinforcements, forcing eventual Japanese withdrawal. Japan then turned inward (*sakoku*), and during the Tokugawa *bakufu* (1603–1867), the two countries had virtually no official contact.

With the Meiji Restoration in 1868, Japan resolved to "leave Asia and join the West," as Fukuzawa Yukichi memorably put it, while China after the abortive Xinhai Revolution fragmented into warlordism and protracted civil/revolutionary war. While Japan's economic modernization continued to inspire the younger generation of Chinese political elites, providing passing refuge for Sun Yat-sen and other revolutionaries and assorted political outcasts, the state-to-state relationship grew asymmetrically predatory. China and Japan fought two full-scale wars in modern times, first in 1894–95 and later in 1931–45. These wars, especially the second, left both countries in ruins and one side nursing a boundless sense of grievance. After World War II, China and Japan signed defense alliances with the Soviet Union and United States, respectively, becoming strategic adversaries on opposing sides of the Cold War ideological divide. While diplomatic normalization in 1972 promised to alleviate this distressed relationship, it has proved only a respite.

The United States, as *tertius gaudens*, makes the Sino-Japanese relationship triangular, as it has also with the fractious Sino-Russian alliance. The United States played a structurally analogous pivot role in both cases. This chapter thus analyzes the relationship in triangular terms, including the United States. In simplified terms, the triangle went through three stages, to be examined in greater depth below: the 1930–45 period, when the United States and China formed a marriage against Japan; the 1950–72 period, when the United States and Japan formed a marriage against China; and the post-1972 period of ménage à trois.

THE TRIANGLE

In the aftermath of the Cold War, China, Japan, and the United States have emerged as the three pivotal actors in what remains one of the world's most economically dynamic and strategically sensitive regions. The original strategic triangle comprised the United States, China, and the Union of Soviet Socialist Republics (USSR), three great nuclear weapon states whose complicated ambitions and fears intersected. The Soviet Union, however, in 1991 disintegrated into fifteen sovereign republics, all of whom promptly fell into recession, losing as much as 50 percent of their gross domestic product (GDP) in the 1990s. The USSR before December 1991 was a giant of 8.8 million square miles and 280 million people; the surviving Russian Federation has 6.3 million square miles and 142.5 million people (as of 2015). The Russian economy under Vladimir Putin made a dramatic comeback since 2000 by capitalizing on its natural resource surplus, and in terms of strategic (particularly nuclear) power-projection capability, Russia is still the most potent foe of the United States. But its GDP ranking has slipped from second in the world to tenth, and in population it ranks ninth after Nigeria and Bangladesh. Politically, under Boris Yeltsin the Federation dismantled the Communist Party–state, announced the end of the Cold War, declared a "Charter for American-Russian Partnership and Friendship" (in 1992), and plunged into radical (and economically unfortunate) market reforms.

As we have seen in chapter 3, the post–Cold War honeymoon with liberal democracy was poorly conceived and ill fated, leaving the Russian national identity aggrieved and strategically confused. Emerging as dominant actors on the post–Cold War East Asian stage are Japan, China, and the United States. There are to be sure significant categorical differences among them. Although Ezra Vogel's *Japan as Number One* enjoyed record sales in Japan, the nation harbors deep ambivalence about regaining conventional great power status, its neighbors still more so. China and the United States are nuclear weapon states while Japan has been constitutionally limited to foreign policy pacifism; Japan and the United States have a mutual defense alliance while China renounces alliances in principle; China and Japan are longtime neighbors while the United States is a distant geographical interloper; China and the United States are on the United Nations Security Council from which China blocks Japan's ascent; and so forth. Yet for all that these three remain the largest economies (in nominal GDP) in the world and boast the region's most modern and powerful force projection capabilities. Relations between China and Japan have always been deeply influenced by their respective relationships with the United States, and the same can be said of Japan's role in US-China relations. In sum, the postwar era may be chronologically divided into four phases: the Cold War, the opening to China, the post–Cold War period, and the period of China's rise.

THE COLD WAR

Japan did not play a principal or "triangular" role in Sino-American relations during the Cold War (which, in terms of Sino-Japanese-US relations, lasted from 1945 to 1971). Two countries emerged from World War II with global ambitions and the capabilities to achieve them, the United States and the USSR, while a third, the People's Republic of China (PRC), would join them as a fully autonomous actor by the end of the 1950s. Thus Sino-US relations were premised on the position of each toward the Soviet Union, and Japan merely sought to find the most advantageous position within that triangle. During the early Cold War, from 1950 to around 1960, the Sino-Soviet alliance remained in effect, both strategically and ideologically. The United States opposed both, and Japan had little option but to support the United

States. Prime Minister Yoshida Shigeru (1948–1954) was rather more focused on economic reconstruction, summing up Japan's attitude in 1948 with
the comment "I don't care whether China is red or green. China is a national
market and it has become necessary for Japan to think about markets."[1] But
Japan was still under occupation, and while it had surrendered in September
1945, a bilateral peace treaty had not yet been signed. The United States was
wary of any reconciliation between Japan and China and held the peace
treaty in contingent abeyance. The San Francisco Peace Treaty was finally
signed in 1951, on the same day that Japan, under US pressure, signed a
bilateral peace treaty with the Republic of China on Taiwan. The terms of
this Pax Americana were set forth in the Treaty of San Francisco: the peace
treaty and the mutual security agreement signed in 1951 by the United States
and Japan. These documents ended the US occupation, defined the manner of
Japan's reentry into the international arena, and fixed Japan's subordinate
position in the American security architecture (e.g., the American military
was granted the right to retain bases in Japan and to intervene against domestic subversion).

The Yoshida Doctrine introduced by Prime Minister Yoshida Shigeru in
the early 1950s was consistent with this arrangement, focusing national energies on economic growth while offshoring defense, deferring leadership of
the free world to the United States.[2] The treaty returned Taiwan and the
Pescadores to China (which "China," the PRC or the Republic of China
[ROC] on Taiwan, has ever since been disputed) and transformed Japan from
an empire to a democratic monarchy with a constitution that (in Article 9)
denied it the right to declare war except in self-defense. The Korean War
drew Japan further away from China, as Japan served as a vital rear area for
UN forces in Korea (also helping stimulate Japan's economic recovery).

Yet Yoshida was not comfortable in a hard-line anti-Chinese position.
Although to some extent a personal beneficiary of the reverse current that
halted war crimes trials, he rejected US secretary of state John Foster
Dulles's initial proposal for full-scale Japanese rearmament (permitting only
the formation of a small "self-defense force" in 1954) and maintained economic and unofficial diplomatic contacts with the PRC. China reciprocated:
there were crises in Korea, Vietnam, the Taiwan Strait, but none between
Japan and China. Chinese official statements during this period generously
opined that ordinary Japanese people were not responsible for the war, which
they did not want, and indeed suffered grievously themselves. A content
analysis of *Renmin ribao* editorials (thirty-five were written on Japan from
1946 to 1987) reveals emphasis on a strong bond between the Chinese and
Japanese people while lambasting a small handful of militarists in cahoots
with US imperialism. Only one article mentions the Japanese invasion (in the
context of criticizing not Japan but the Nationalist Chinese government's
incompetent defense), and only one piece mentions the Senkakus/Diaoyu

territorial dispute (citing a Japanese historian who supported Chinese historical claims to the islets).[3] The Chinese Communist Party (CCP) Central Committee decided in late 1955 on two principles in dealing with Japanese war criminals: no war criminal should be executed or sentenced to life in jail, and verdicts should be limited to a very small number of ringleaders. Only forty-five of the one thousand or so Japanese prisoners extradited to China from the Soviet Union were hence sentenced as war criminals in the 1956 war crimes trials held in Taiyuan and Shenyang, while all others were pardoned and promptly repatriated.

Under the policy of separating economics and politics, Japan privately negotiated four trade agreements in the 1950s, greatly increasing the paltry initial level of bilateral commercial relations—the first in June 1952, which established a barter-based trade, and three others in October 1953, September 1955, and March 1958. Bilateral trade increased to US$60 million by 1954, US$109 million by 1955, and US$151 million by 1956. Japan became China's second-largest trade partner (after the Soviet Union), surpassing Taiwan in bilateral trade by 1956. Beijing saw revolutionary potential in Japan with its popular (if fractious) leftist parties and labor movement and directed its anti-imperialist broadsides principally against Washington. Washington for its part, having installed its largest Asian base in Japan to oversee a fragile armistice in Korea and the continuing revolution in China, chose to ignore Japan's casual enforcement of the international trade embargo on China that the United States sought to maintain at an even tighter level than the CoCom (Coordinating Committee for Multilateral Export Controls) restrictions on trade with the Soviet Union.[4]

There were always two sides of Japanese China policy in the 1950s, both conservative, but one more nationalistic than the other. With the inauguration in 1957 of Prime Minister Kishi Nobusuke—former director of the General Affairs Board of Manchukuo and Minister of Commerce and Industry in Tojo Hideki's wartime cabinet—Sino-Japanese relations deteriorated while US-Japan relations improved.[5] Beijing took particular exception to Kishi's visit to Taiwan, as well as his anticommunist stance and strong commitment to overturning Article 9 and rearming Japan (Kishi was grandfather of the normal nation ideal). Kishi's campaign to pass a revised draft of the US-Japan Security Treaty in 1960 aroused particular Chinese ire. Beijing formed a united front with domestic leftist groups to oppose it in the Diet and on the streets. The Socialist Party demanded revocation of the defense treaty on constitutional grounds, calling for complete pacifism. China vocally supported the domestic left, completely suspending Sino-Japanese relations in 1960, and trade nose-dived. Yet Kishi managed to pass the revised draft despite fierce minority opposition in the Diet and the largest student protests in Japanese history. This, however, forced the government to postpone Eisenhower's planned crowning visit and finally precipitated the fall of the beleaguered Kishi government.

The revised treaty gave Japan somewhat more equal status in the relationship[6] but did not revise the Yoshida Doctrine or rescind (indeed, it reaffirmed) Article 9 of the constitution. Meanwhile, the interrupted trade relationship with China was quickly resumed when the ideological dispute with the USSR resulted in the cutoff of Soviet aid, the Great Leap's failure incurred domestic food shortages, and China badly needed a new source of imports (e.g., complete industrial plants, machinery, steel, and chemical fertilizers) to revive its economy. Thus in 1962, Takahashi Tatsunosuke, director of the Economic Planning Agency, met with Liao Chengzhi, born in Japan and president inter alia of the China-Japan Friendship Association, in Beijing to sign a memorandum that expanded trade semi-officially by financing projects with the help of credits from the Japan Export-Import Bank. This facilitated a great expansion of memorandum trade for several years—until protests from Taiwan obliged Japan to shelve further deferred-payment exports.

During the second phase of the Cold War beginning in 1960, the Sino-Soviet alliance split asunder in a dispute that was initially ideological and quickly escalated to low-level border warfare and the threat of preemptive nuclear strikes (indeed, China reportedly detonated a nuclear test in 1969 as a warning). The PRC developed nuclear weapons and became a major strategic power with the world's third-largest military budget (after the United States and the USSR) in the 1960s. The Sino-Soviet dispute, however, left no room for an opening to the United States, as each side insisted on its own ideological variant of Marxism-Leninism and superior strategic efficacy in the struggle for leadership of the world communist movement against global capitalism. This worsened China's relations with both superpowers at once, as it promoted national liberation wars throughout the developing world that the United States felt obliged to suppress and the USSR to vie to support. Implicitly viewing Beijing's appeal to international class struggle even more dangerous than the more powerful USSR, Washington quietly began to consider some sort of collaboration with the Soviet Union in the early 1960s to eliminate Chinese nuclear capability before it materialized. But the Sino-Soviet split did not affect Japan, which remained staunchly anti-Soviet after negotiations for the return of the four northern islands (or southern Kurils) in 1956 came to naught, while maintaining unofficial commercial relations with China.

The 1961–71 decade saw Japan at the crest of its economic miracle (GDP growth averaging 10.9 percent annually) based largely on export-oriented growth. Japan sustained economic ties with an isolated China during this period based on Prime Minister Ikeda Hayato's decree separating politics from economics, while enduring some deterioration in political relations with the United States due to Japan's chronic bilateral trade surplus. The economic rise of Japan also began to provoke US demands for a more equitable sharing of the defense burden, meaning a larger arms budget and a wider geographic ambit of responsibility. This became official with Nixon's declaration of the Guam Doctrine in 1969, entailing the pullback of US forces and calling on Asians to assume greater responsibility for their own defense. While China was very much in favor of a US exit from Asia, it harbored grave reservations about the implication of a larger defense role for Japan, particularly regarding Taiwan. Japan veered rightward politically with the inauguration of Sato Eisaku in 1964, Kishi's younger brother and another staunch anticommunist who believed Japan's defense depended at least in part on Taiwan's independence. The China trade declined in the second half of the decade, partly because of Kishi's discontinuation of Export-Import Bank loans but mainly due to China's engulfment in the Cultural Revolution and the resulting politicization of trade ties.

While the Cold War did not end globally until 1989–90, the Asian cold war lost much of its propulsive force with the admission of China to the United Nations in 1971 and the Nixon visit to China in February 1972. This lanced the Sino-US "contradiction" and opened new diplomatic opportunities for Beijing. China's admission to the UN as a permanent member of the Security Council facilitated global recognition of the PRC and the diplomatic eclipse of the ROC on Taiwan. The break came not as a result of an ideological thaw but because, in the context of the threat of a Soviet nuclear preemptive strike, Chinese security considerations overrode ideology. It became possible for the United States to improve relations with both former Cold War adversaries simultaneously (a romantic triangle), thereby exacting more concessions from each than would otherwise have been possible: opening cross-curtain trade, diplomatic and cultural intercourse (détente) with both the PRC and the USSR, the first successful arms-limitation talks (SALT), and a graceful no-fault exit from Vietnam. By the end of the decade, mutual strategic interests (e.g., Washington offering Beijing extended deterrence from a Soviet preemptive strike; limited collaboration in Afghanistan, Cambodia, and sub-Saharan Africa) were supplemented by a vague ideological affinity, as the PRC regime embraced reform and opening, seemingly placing China and the United States on convergent developmental tracks. Such future aspirations aside, this "honeymoon" was, however, narrowly strategically based, and Beijing in the 1980s continued to espouse anti-American ideology and to support national liberation wars in the developing world while shifting to a more equidistant position in the triangle, undertaking normalization talks with Moscow that would eventually bear fruit in the May 1989 Beijing summit.

Japan normalized relations with China under Prime Minister Tanaka Kakuei in the wake of the Nixon visit in 1972. This was possible only because Sato, a determined opponent of the opening, failed to secure factional succession upon ending his eight-year prime ministerial tenure. The terms of the agreement represented a compromise quite favorable to China. Tokyo broke relations with Taiwan declaring that it understood and respected China's one China principle, yet the normalization agreement renounced claims to war reparations (at Japan's request) while Mao Zedong brushed off Tanaka's apology for war crimes with a jest.[7] This was, however, only the beginning of full normalization, according to Beijing. Talks then commenced in 1974 on a friendship treaty, which were protracted by China's insistence on an anti-hegemony clause explicitly addressed to the threat of Soviet hegemonism. Japan had no love for the USSR but preferred to avoid antagonizing Moscow, which still occupied its northern islands. Agreement was facilitated by the death of Mao and the rise of the pragmatic Deng Xiaoping. Deng favored a deal, accepting an anonymous anti-hegemony clause and shelving for future generations the dispute over the Diaoyu islets that first emerged in the early 1970s.

Economic needs were complementary, and signing of the Long-Term Trade Agreement (LTA) and the Peace and Friendship Treaty (PFT) in 1978 set the stage for a large and sustained expansion of commercial intercourse. The Japanese government removed all restrictions on Ex-Im Bank credit financing, and reciprocal trade agreements reduced tariff barriers by one-third. Trade rose from US$5 billion in 1978 to $13 billion in 1984, $20 billion in 1985, $15.5 billion in 1986, and $19.6 billion in 1989. Dissolution of the Soviet Union in December 1991 marked the end of the global Cold War, coinciding, however, with the popping of the Japanese asset bubble and commencing Japan's long period of relative economic stagnation. Slack domestic demand and US restrictions on Japanese imports all enhanced the value of China trade for Japan. From 1972 to 2004, Sino-Japanese trade increased 161-fold, going from $1.04 billion in 1972 to $167.89 billion in 2004 and $340 billion by 2014. After many years (since 1975) as China's leading trade partner, Japan since 1993 has slipped to second-largest trade partner, trailing the United States (unless entrepôt trade through Hong Kong is excluded, in which case the rankings are reversed). The balance of trade was generally in Japan's favor until the March 2011 Tohoku tsunami shut down Japan's domestic nuclear power supply, whereupon Japan began running an overall trade deficit (including with China) to pay for energy.

Japanese investment growth lagged trade initially due to Chinese restrictions and a jagged business cycle that sometimes forced foreign investors into bankruptcy, amounting to only $3 million in 1983. But foreign direct investment (FDI) accelerated in the 1990s after the 1985 Plaza Accord drove up the price of domestically produced Japanese exports. Japanese FDI in China reached $100 million in 1985, $1.2 billion in 1987, and $2.8 billion in 1990. In the late 1990s, there was another lull after the Taiwan Strait crisis, but China's entry into the World Trade Organization (WTO) in 2001 precipitated another FDI upsurge in the 2000s, peaking at $7 billion in 2012. FDI continues, but at a declining rate of growth since the 2012 escalation of the maritime territorial dispute in the East China Sea (see below).

During the era of the Great Strategic Triangle (1971–89), Beijing's strategic stance vis-à-vis Tokyo was contingent on its relations with the two superpowers, in essence making the Sino-Japanese-US triangle a function of Sino-US relations (Japan's relations with the USSR were all but frozen after 1956, despite its overtures in the early 1970s). Japan shuttled between Beijing and Washington to elicit the most favorable economic terms from each. Strategic and economic relations went hand in hand. During the 1950s, while China was still aligned with the Soviet Union against the United States, China strongly opposed and tried to pry apart the Japan-America Security Alliance (JASA); this opposition continued through the 1960s despite the rising salience of the Soviet threat.

In the wake of the 1969 Sino-Soviet border clash and the ensuing opening to the United States, Japan became free to upgrade its relations with the PRC, leading to early diplomatic normalization in September 1972 on terms similar to those later adopted by the United States. As Sino-US relations bloomed in joint opposition to the USSR, China lapsed into silence on the JASA and, by the end of the decade, was explicitly endorsing it, even encouraging Japan to increase its defense spending.[8] With the normalization of Sino-Soviet relations back on track after 1982, China, however, began to reconsider, once again coming to view Japan's strategic posture with foreboding. From the second half of 1982, visits to China by Japanese military delegations decreased sharply. When at the end of 1986 Nakasone Yasuhiro raised the defense budget above the tacit 1 percent limit (1 percent of GDP), Deng Xiaoping criticized this as a sign of Japanese militarism—next year the budget went down (and has not exceeded 1 percent since, despite a declining GDP). The Chinese thereafter repeatedly criticized Japan as a military threat, although China was meanwhile spending a larger percentage of their own GDP, which was growing faster. China also became critical of revisions of the JASA defense guidelines, particularly the inclusion of surrounding areas that might include Taiwan, and of the agreement to contribute to the development (and installation) of a theater missile defense (TMD) system.[9] While denouncing the US alliance system in general as a relic of Cold War thinking, Beijing, however, has not yet specifically opposed the JASA per se (despite growing disapproval, as the latter provides a fulcrum for US demands for greater Japanese burden sharing), presumably on the assumption that it might forestall Japan's development of a full-scale independent military including nuclear weaponry.

Triangular strategic relations remained relatively stable through the 1970s and 1980s. The United States was initially preoccupied with the Vietnam War, which it lost in 1975 despite détente with China and the Soviet Union, and substantially reduced its military presence in the region under the Nixon Doctrine. Affected Asian powers did not protest, seeing no immediate threat necessitating American military support. China was too preoccupied with its own Cultural Revolution and the post-Mao succession struggle to either pursue active revolutionary policies in the developing world or take full advantage of its elevation to the UN Security Council, but it did continue to cultivate the opening to the United States and, in 1982, began "normalization" talks with the USSR as well. Upon the consolidation of the reform and opening regime at the end of the 1970s, many of Mao's policies were gradually and quietly reversed without ever explicitly repudiating Mao himself. Under Deng, China seemed to have adopted its own Yoshida Doctrine, also known as peace and development foreign policy. To wit, Beijing reconciled with both superpowers, renounced the export of revolution, and befriended all countries useful to rapid domestic modernization. While this was the era of high-speed growth for Japan, it was not yet aspiring for a global role and thus became an even more attractive trade partner for China given the latter's new focus on economic modernization.

The end of the global Cold War really began in China with an overreaction by the Deng leadership to a large nonviolent protest movement that occupied the Tiananmen Square and spread throughout urban China, ignoring all orders to disperse. Though the protest was brutally repressed on the evening of June 3–4, 1989, it then spread throughout the communist bloc and, ultimately, succeeded in bringing down these socialist republics. This result had a lasting impact on the global strategic architecture. The Soviet Union disavowed communism, disintegrated into fifteen sovereign republics, and embraced democratic capitalism, declaring an end to the Cold War. For a brief period, it appeared to concerned Chinese that the triangle might shift from the strategic Sino-US coalition against the "polar bear" to a Russian-US alliance against China. Although the collapse of the Soviet Union was strategically advantageous to China in that its principal threat to national security had dissolved, the disappearance of a large communist world—even one with which Beijing had many disagreements—was highly disorienting and demoralizing. In the aftermath of Tiananmen, Sino-US relations, no longer animated by shared fear of the polar bear and shocked by Tiananmen, fell to their lowest ebb since their opening in the early 1970s. Most Western trade partners imposed sanctions, and the United States briefly attempted to withhold most-favored-nation trading status contingent on (never clearly specified) human rights reforms.

Japan joined the post-Tiananmen sanctions (without calling them "sanctions") but was first to remove them. Kaifu Toshiki was the first G7 leader to visit China, where he announced the third yen loan package after just one year's suspension. The following year Jiang Zemin exchanged state visits with Emperor Akihito in what was the first visit to China by the monarchy in its 2,600-year history. Japan in the mid-1980s launched a visionary "Plan to Accept 100,000 Foreign Students before the Beginning of the 21st Century" and simplified application procedures for student visas; thus from 1984 to 2004, more than 250,000 Chinese obtained student visas for university education or pre-university language training (though this influx damaged the position of Hu Yaobang, who had approved it). While in 1980 there were only 52,896 Chinese residents in Japan, by the end of 2007 that number had reached 606,899, overtaking Koreans as the largest group of foreign residents (28.2 percent of the officially registered foreign population). Meanwhile, Sino-US relations faltered on human rights issues, while Japan-US relations remained roiled in trade disputes. Sino-Japanese trade mounted, growing 16.3 percent per annum from 1992. By 2004, China had replaced the United States as Japan's leading trade partner and host of Japanese FDI.

Despite the reconciliation and resumption of mutually profitable commercial ties, in the 1990s the relationship began to meet headwinds. Beijing's bloody repression of unarmed student protesters at Tiananmen was a shock to the Japanese public, as was China's resort to coercive diplomacy in the 1994–95 Taiwan Strait crisis. The 1994 reform of Japan's electoral system from a single nontransferable vote (SNTV) to a mutual majority criterion (MMC; designed to facilitate a more stable two-party system) in effect wiped out the socialist and communist parties that had previously been most dedicated to close Sino-Japanese relations (although the Democratic Party of Japan [DPJ] remained relatively friendly to China). In 1995, some twenty-five million Chinese signed an online petition against Japan's inclusion as a permanent member of a reorganized UN Security Council then being considered. There were spontaneous anti-Japan mass demonstrations that involved property destruction in 1986, in 1995, in 2005, in 2010, and in 2012, the last being the largest since the normalization of relations. The Chinese state took no immediate action to curb these protests, nor were the ringleaders ever called to account as in most other popular protest movements. Though spontaneous, such outbreaks of mass hostility reflected the emphasis the party leadership had placed on patriotic education for China's young people since the early 1990s, in which memories of wartime Japanese depredations play a prominent role not only in school curricula but also in films, memoir literature, museum construction, and officially designated holidays. A visiting Japanese Diet member counted "more than 50 anti-Japanese facilities" in the form of memorial halls dealing with the war, giving him the impression that young Chinese had become more anti-Japanese than those who actually experienced the war.[10] The economic relationship, traditionally sheltered by the separation of politics and economics, evinced growing sensitivity to the political climate. There was an informal boycott of Chinese exports of rare earth elements in 2012, and bilateral trade and investment declined—Toyota's sales fell by about 30 percent in a few weeks and Japanese automakers' share of the Chinese market slipped from 23 percent to 14 percent in October–November 2012.

Since the late 2000s, the relationship has hence been characterized as economically hot and politically cold. This has not been a sudden development. At the beginning of the 1950s, Sino-US relations were ideologically polarized based on generic anticommunism, while a weak Japan was politically anti-Chinese as well but less fervently so. During the 1960s and 1970s, as Japan entered high-speed growth and became more politically weighty, the relationship equilibrated based on mutual self-interest. Japan and China had complementary needs and grew economically interdependent: Japan became the leading source of developmental aid, and this accommodative relationship acquired a certain momentum seemingly insulated from politics.

Beginning in the 1990s, however, as the political relationship became more problematic, the separation between politics and economics began to fray. Though Japanese businesspeople have remained publicly optimistic, hot economic intercourse has begun to feel the chill of cold politics. Bilateral trade volume dropped to $333.6 billion in 2012 (down from $345 billion in 2011), and it decreased another 12 percent in 2015 to $300 billion; Japanese FDI had by 2015 fallen by 33 percent since 2012. Of course there are also other factors such as the local investment climate (i.e., China's growth slowdown, higher wages, and Chinese efforts to encourage competing local industries). Japan declined to join China's Asian Infrastructure Investment Bank (which competes directly with the Tokyo-centered Asian Development Bank) and was left out of its One Belt, One Road initiative. Japan business has shifted its focus from China as factory of the world to China as market of the world. As Japanese FDI withdraws from China, Southeast Asia has reemerged as Japan's leading investment destination in Asia.[11]

In terms of public opinion, the warmest phase of the relationship began with normalization in 1972 and lasted through the end of the 1980s. Public opinion polls demonstrate consistent agreement in both countries that the bilateral relationship was vital, together with greater variance over time about whether it was succeeding. Views were mutually positive (in the 70 percent range) through the 1980s until Tiananmen, when they abruptly dropped to around 50 percent, remaining in that range until 2003, when they grew still more negative. During the decade of "peaceful development" and "harmonious world" in the late 2000s, attitudes improved somewhat, especially on the Chinese side (up to 70 percent favorable in 2008–9), before receding again after 2010. Since 2014, public opinion has become toxic, reaching 90.3 percent negative in China, 86.8 percent in Japan (numbers vary slightly in different polls).[12] To some extent, Sino-Japanese attitudes track the Sino-US pattern, though the latter never reached the same extremes: Sino-US affinity rose to 70 percent just before 1989 then abruptly dropped to the 30 percent range where it remained until 2001 when it rose to 50 percent approval; from 2011 to 2013, favorable attitudes sagged from 51 percent to 40 percent. Thus, the relationship has been highly variable but, at this point, ironically seems to have turned full circle to the beginning of the cycle— despite a high level of economic interdependence, geographic propinquity, and a diminution of the ideological, developmental, and cultural gaps.

Why has it done so? The United States has certainly played a role in this process: while the United States skillfully played pivot in the Great Strategic Triangle, thereby modulating the Sino-Soviet dispute, it has allowed Chinese provocations, reciprocal Chinese-Japanese nationalism, and its own growing sense of insecurity in the face of the rise of China to lure it from a pivot role in the China-Japan relationship and into the position of senior partner to one side of an escalating confrontation. But of course there are also other issues, as noted below.

THE ISSUES

The issues that have transformed triangular relationships from one configuration to another have varied according to temporal circumstances, some short-term episodes such as the Taiwan Strait crisis or Noda Yoshihiko's national-ization of three Senkaku/Diaoyu islets in 2012, and some long-term trends, such as the rise and fall of the Japanese economic miracle or the bigger Chinese miracle that followed. Both China and Japan are now much bigger and more advanced systems than they were emerging from the ruins of war, though they are at different stages of their developmental trajectories. There are four issue areas that have chronically recurred, and the reason they have recurred is that no one has yet found a mutually satisfactory solution. They are security, war guilt, Asian leadership, and finally (but most explosively) territory.

Security

In the wake of the only war Japan admits to having lost, at great cost to itself and to its neighbors, it conceived itself to have forever left war behind with Article 9 of the new draft constitution. Though the latter was notoriously drafted by US occupation forces and forced upon the supine nation, it has since been embraced by a large and dedicated electoral constituency. Renun-ciation was made viable for Japan in the real world by creating the small but competent Self-Defense Forces (SDF) in 1954 to fend off direct conventional threats and by forging the JASA to provide extended nuclear deterrence (the US "umbrella"). Throughout the 1950s, China vehemently opposed the JASA, and this opposition continued through the 1960s despite the rising salience of the Soviet threat. In Japan, Kishi and the Liberal Democratic Party (LDP) hawks also opposed it, arguing that Article 9 froze Japan in a position of chronic dependency and that it could not be a normal nation without armed forces.

In the wake of the Sino-Soviet border clash and the ensuing opening to the United States (followed by diplomatic normalization with Japan in September 1972), China lapsed into silence on the JASA, and by the end of the 1970s, Beijing was explicitly endorsing the alliance, even encouraging Japan to increase its defense spending. But the lack of serious threat allowed Japan to change nothing, which it did until the end of the Cold War. At that point, when the Soviet Union was no longer viewed as a security threat, China began to suspect that if JASA now had a target it was likely China. China also criticized the cooperative development of high-tech weaponry in theater missile defense (TMD), apprehending that this might neutralize its small nuclear deterrent and perhaps even be extended via warships to the defense of Taiwan. Japan thus now finds itself in a pincers between China, which harps on renascent Japanese militarism and views JASA as a pointless (or better, anti-Chinese) relic of the Cold War, and the United States, which has begun to view the rise of China (and its own overstretched alliance commitments) with foreboding and keeps prodding Japan to share more of the defense burden.

Since the 1990s, the China threat theory has become self-fulfilling. In 1992, the PRC National People's Congress passed a maritime law claiming the Senkakus or Diaoyu (which Japan had occupied since 1895) as sovereign territory, reviving a dispute Deng had postponed for future generations. In the period between 1992 and 1996, China, before signing the test-ban treaty, conducted a series of nuclear tests, to which the world's sole victim of nuclear attack was naturally sensitive, partly due to nuclear fallout over Japan. After repeated fruitless protests, Japan took the unusual step of suspending the grant portion of its loan for 1995–97. Since Tiananmen, China has rescinded its prior relegation of military modernization to last priority among the Four Modernizations with a sustained series of double-digit budget increases exceeding even its booming GDP growth rate, spending over US$1 billion per year to purchase advanced weapons systems (fighter jets, radar, submarines, tanks, destroyers, missiles) from Russia.[13] China has been the only major power not to enjoy a military spending holiday at the end of the Cold War even though reconciliation with the Russian Federation had eliminated its principal security threat. This enabled it to move forces from its northern border to the east coast and to focus more on force-projection capabilities (e.g., naval, air force, and missiles). Chinese intelligence-gathering ships and naval vessels became very active around Japanese territorial waters at the end of the 1990s.

The consensus supposition in Tokyo had long been that Taiwan was the focus of People's Liberation Army (PLA) modernization. But the Japanese noticed that they, too, were explicitly exempt from China's no-first-use pledge vis-à-vis nonnuclear states as well as from bilateral nuclear de-targeting agreements with Russia and the United States. The Taiwan missile crisis in 1995–96 alarmed Japan not only because it demonstrated China's willingness to use its military power politically but also because it occurred to SDF defense planners that if Chinese missiles could bracket Taiwan Japan was also in range. In any case, if Taiwan should come under fire it is from bases in Japan and Okinawa that US military assistance would likely be drawn, making them likely targets. Thus although since the 1990s the North Korean nuclear missile threat is Japan's greatest public security concern, the China threat theory is alive and well among Japanese political elites and defense planners (for their part, Chinese strategists consider North Korea a mere pretext for the rise of Japanese militarism).

But there are reasons for Japan to worry. Japan's SDF of around 250,000 soldiers is well equipped and trained, but in size the SDF is about a tenth the size of the PLA (2,350,000 soldiers, the world's largest standing army); SDF air force and navy force ratios are less overwhelming but likewise in China's favor (about double), and the quality gap is closing fast. In 2013, Abe Shinzo raised the military budget for the first time in eleven years (still less than 1 percent of GDP), but it has fallen from third in the world to seventh (IISS 2016) or eighth (SIPRI 2015)—less than a third that of China's.[14] In July 2014, Abe introduced legislation authorizing the exercise of collective self-defense, enabling Japanese forces to aid a country under armed attack if that attack results in a threat to Japan (left undefined), also establishing the National Security Council and Secretariat staffed by personnel from across the bureaucracy as well as a national security strategy. This legislation for the first time permitted Japan to sell weapons abroad and gave the SDF the mandate to expand overseas operations, as evidenced by participation in antipiracy patrols in the Indian Ocean and regular air patrols, port calls, and joint naval exercises in the South China Sea. China, among others, criticized these measures as evidence of Japan's congenital militarism, also playing up their impact on Japanese foreign policy. On August 2, 2016, Japan released a defense white paper devoted preeminently to the "China military threat."

Underlying the strategic threat narrative are nontraditional security issues, first and foremost the growth of the Chinese economy that provides the fiscal basis for its military power. During the 1990s, Ministry of Economy, Trade and Industry (METI) officials expressed concerns about the hollowing out of Japanese industry and the prospect of being overtaken by the Chinese economy (thus the 2001 METI white paper described China's recent economic growth as "a new threat to Japan," alluding to Beijing's efforts to assume economic leadership of the region).[15] While Japan slipped into economic stagnation in the early 1990s, China's GDP continued to enjoy double-digit growth rates. In 1973, China's GDP was one-eighth that of Japan, and by 2003, it was one-fourth and had surpassed Japan in total trade; by 2010,

China had surpassed Japan in nominal GDP and, by 2015, had become more than twice as large. Upon his second election as prime minister in 2012 Abe Shinzo pledged a commitment to Japan's economic recovery and introduced a radical program, dubbed "Abenonomics," to provide the foundation for a more assertive diplomacy and capable defense policy. After five years, the verdict is still mixed: despite the hype of Abe's "three arrows" reform agenda (comprising fiscal stimulus, monetary easing, and structural reforms), the targets have not yet been met and deflation threatens. Growth remains slow, productivity gains are limited, and debt continues to grow. Longer term, Japan faces a demographic challenge as the population ages and fails to reproduce; the population is projected to shrink from the current 127 million to 100 million by 2050. Japan has reacted to the challenges of the future with creative ambiguity, on the one hand vigorously competing with China economically and in regional politics, and on the other interceding diplomatically to prevent bilateral relations from getting dangerously volatile (as in Abe's 2014 meeting with Xi Jinping at the Asia-Pacific Economic Cooperation [APEC] summit, or again on the sidelines of the April 2015 Asian-African Summit in Jakarta).

As China's economy matures, not only does it pose the symbolic threat of further overshadowing Japan, but the two economies have become less complementary and more competitive: thus whereas China in the early 1980s sold petroleum to Japan (which was otherwise dependent on the Middle East for 90 percent of its oil), China since 1993 has become the world's largest oil importer (overtaking the United States in April 2017) and second-largest consumer, alone responsible for 40 percent of the global increase in oil demand since 2000 (i.e., while the Chinese economy grew by 9.7 percent in the first six months of 2004, its oil imports jumped 40 percent). This poses not only immediate price pressure and competition for drilling rights in disputed areas of overlapping exclusive economic zones (EEZs) but leads to the growing Chinese interest in air and naval force projection to oversee and protect sea lanes of communication (SLOCs). China and Japan have increasingly emerged as regional economic competitors, as evidenced by their nascent rivalry in securing lucrative infrastructure contracts.

The most visible sign of this has been in the railway industry: In October 2015, a Japanese consortium lost a US$5 billion contract to China to build Indonesia's first high-speed railway connecting Jakarta and Bandung.[16] Loss of the Indonesia bid to China in September 2015 spurred Japan to offer attractive loan terms and Shinkansen technology for the Mumbai-Ahmadabad high-speed railway project during Abe's visit to India in December 2015, which were accepted. Japan won this as an exemplar of the Partnership for Quality Infrastructure (PQI) project Abe has been promoting throughout the region. Japan is also due to begin construction of a high-speed rail link in Thailand going east to west while Chinese companies have begun work on a railway project in Laos going south. Both countries along with South Korea also are engaged in a bidding war over a high-speed rail link between Singapore and Kuala Lumpur. To counter China's cost advantage, Japan has pledged better technology and safety standards and operational support over the full life-cycle of its projects, purportedly making them cost effective in the long term. It has also offered more benefits to local economies by hiring and training local workers, as opposed to the common Chinese practice of importing labor for Chinese-funded infrastructure projects. This competition to sell high-speed rail infrastructure has emerged as a microcosm of a broader Sino-Japanese rivalry for industrial supremacy in Asia. Having lifted a seventy-year ban on military exports in 2014, Japan competed (unsuccessfully) for a contract to sell Soryu-class submarines to Australia. Deals have so far been limited to the sale of surveillance aircraft to the Philippines and India. China has a clear lead in arms sales, having emerged as the world's third-largest exporter of arms, with shipments growing by 143 percent in the last five years, according to SIPRI.[17]

Guilt

Japan's imperial army committed a great many atrocities during the war, of which both its former victims and the Japanese leadership are well aware. When Tanaka Kakuei offered an apology on the occasion of diplomatic normalization, Mao dismissed it with a joke, but subsequent leaders have been less forgiving. The Chinese have become assiduous students of Japanese history texts, alleging that the government textbook authorization system has been used to reject textbooks that depict imperial Japan in a negative light. In 1982, 1984, 1986, 1995, 2001, 2005, and 2015, whenever the Japanese education ministry reviews or approves a new series of textbooks, Japanese textbooks are assailed for failing to acknowledge Japanese indemnity for atrocities committed during the invasion of China. While the Chinese (and the Koreans) criticize Japanese textbooks for historical amnesia, the Japanese right wing believes too much self-abasement (what Abe once called "self-torturing views of history") is deleterious to the national identity. The result of the constant criticism and resulting revisions has been the publication of texts that are not only innocuous but also bland. In an attempt to resolve the controversies, historians from China, Japan, and South Korea launched a collaborative project in 2002 that resulted in simultaneous publication in the three countries of a volume of supplementary teaching materials on the modern history of all three. From the Japanese perspective, these exchange programs served as a vehicle for attacks by Chinese historians and progressive Japanese historians on Monbusho and Japanese conservatives, while criticism of historical distortions or omissions in Chinese textbooks was notably absent.

In 1985, Prime Minister Nakasone together with members of his cabinet made an official visit to the Yasukuni Shrine, where Japanese war dead have been honored since 1869. China protested, and Nakasone refrained from additional visits. His visit was, however, neither the first nor the last: among Japanese prime ministers, Miki Takeo first visited in 1975, as did Emperor Showa. But in 1978, fourteen convicted Class A war criminals were interred at the shrine. The emperor thereafter abstained from further visits, but Ohira Masayoshi visited in 1979; Suzuki Zenko in 1980, 1981, and 1982; Hashimoto Ryutaro in 1996; and Koizumi Junichiro six times (2001–6). This was considered disrespectful to the victims of Japanese aggression, but China's greatest fury was enflamed by Koizumi, perhaps because he continued his annual visits in the face of Chinese public protests and diplomatic requests to refrain. Abe Shinzo visited once as prime minister in December 2013, meeting fierce Chinese criticism and even "disappointment" from Secretary of State Hillary Clinton.

China has also reacted indignantly to a series of insensitive statements extenuating Japanese war guilt by leading politicians: in 1986, Minister of Education Fujio Masayuki stated publicly that whoever complained about Japanese history books should first look back to see whether they had not committed such a thing in their own history; Nakasone dismissed him amid a storm of protest after he refused to resign. In 1988, China was shocked by a series of statements by National Land Agency director Okuno Seisuke, who contended that Japan had not intended to invade China; Okuno was forced to resign. In 1994 then justice minister Nagano Shigeto said the Nanjing massacre was fabricated (he resigned), and in 2014 Abe's government asked a United Nations special rapporteur to revise a 1996 report on wartime comfort women (she refused).

Japanese war guilt is invoked not only apropos of the war itself but many other seemingly unrelated issues. In 1995, Japan's application to be included in a proposed reorganization of the UN Security Council was linked to textbook issues to trigger the first major Chinese student protest movement since Tiananmen, along with objections to the second Japanese (commercial) invasion. China has even linked the recent dispute over the Senkaku/Diaoyu islets to Japan's incorrect view of history, even though the dispute has more to do with competing interpretations of international sovereignty laws.

Contrary to accusations that Japan has never apologized there have been many high-level official apologies: by Yoshida, by Kishi, by Tanaka, by Kono (specifically addressing the comfort women issue), most famously by Murayama (1994, 1995), by Obuchi (1995), and most recently by Abe in March 2014, when he reaffirmed the apologies by his predecessors without adding new language of his own. There are at least eleven different ways of saying "sorry" in Japanese, and the critics parse these to question the sincerity of Japanese apologies. Part of the reason for Chinese sensitivity to this issue may be because apologies specifically addressed to China seem to be relatively fewer than those addressed to Korea. Thus in the wake of the unprecedented issuance of a formal written apology to the South Korean Kim Dae Jung regime in 1998 the visiting Jiang Zemin delegation in November 1998 immediately demanded an analogous apology, which Prime Minister Obuchi declined to provide on grounds that in view of the sudden request the requisite diplomatic preparations had not been made (though he did tender a prompt oral expression of remorse), resulting in the Chinese delegation returning in dudgeon without a joint communiqué. (Obuchi then discovered from the media that his refusal was domestically popular, and he dug in his heels.) Another possible reason for suspicions of Japanese insincerity is that Japan, unlike Germany, which paid billions to Israel and other countries, never paid a cent of war reparations to China. Japan has negotiated (and paid) reparations to Korea, Thailand, the Philippines, Myanmar, and many others, but China under Mao renounced reparations claims (at Japan's request) and neither side has officially revisited the issue.

In tacit compensation for China's magnanimity, however, Japan made China the biggest single recipient of Japanese official developmental aid (ODA), representing more than 60 percent of the total assistance China ever received from both bilateral and multilateral foreign sources. The aid began one year after the Japan-China Peace and Friendship Treaty was signed in 1978. According to the Japanese Ministry of Foreign Affairs, ODA from 1979 to 2015 totaled some $76.6 billion in subsidized yen loans, $14.7 billion in grant aid, and $1.7 billion in technical cooperation. ODA projects in China have included large-scale economic infrastructure projects, including the building of roads, airports, and power stations, as well as medical and environmental complexes. In 2005, Japan publicly announced its intention to suspend ODA in 2008 in light of China's rapid economic development (China put a man into orbit in 2005), China's foreign aid to Africa and Southeast Asia, its claims to territory occupied by Japan, and its public lack of gratitude for Japanese assistance.[18] Indeed, Chinese media seldom mention and more rarely express gratitude for Japanese aid, but this is partly because while Japan views ODA as generous benefaction China views it as blood money owed them in lieu of reparations. Chinese also point out that much of these funds are tied to the purchase of Japanese goods, technology, and industrial plants, creating substantial technology dependence.

In any event, ODA has clearly failed to serve one of its implicit goals: that of allaying Chinese accusations of Japanese guilt. Such accusations have tended to increase over time and at opportune moments in particular. The first textbook protest in 1982 came on the heels of the Baoshan controversy, for example.[19] The 470-billion-yen Nakasone loan package of 1984 helped soothe Chinese hurt feelings; the 810-billion-yen Takeshita aid package of 1988 similarly coincided roughly with the second textbook crisis, the Okuno public misstatement, and the Kokaryo dormitory incident. The 1998 apology brouhaha chronologically overlapped the negotiation of the terms of the next yen loan. Chinese demands for apologies are understandably insatiable, but only partly based on haunting memories of wartime suffering. Upon the collapse of world communism in 1989–91, the CCP became aware of the lack of popular enthusiasm for Marxism-Leninism and launched a sustained patriotic education movement to shift the basis of political legitimacy to popular nationalism. Museums were built, books were written, and films were made (two hundred Japanese war films were made in 2012 alone). From elementary school to higher education, children are taught about Japanese war crimes in vivid detail. Thousands of children are bussed to the Museum of the War of Chinese People's Resistance against Japanese Aggression in Beijing by their elementary schools to view photos of war atrocities such as the Nanjing massacre.

Regional Leadership

As trade and investment boomed in the era of high-speed Chinese growth and relative Japanese industrial stagnation, China became more active in regional multilateral diplomacy. Both China and Japan joined the Association of Southeast Asian Nations (ASEAN) Regional Forum, ASEAN's first attempt to replicate the ASEAN Way in the rest of East Asia in the security realm, at its founding in 1994. Since then ASEAN has organized several other "plus" vehicles to try to organize relations beyond ASEAN: the ASEAN Regional Forum (ARF) provides a venue for security discussions, the ASEAN Plus Three (APT) processes discuss community building in economic and functional areas, and the East Asia Summit (EAS) adds a broader strategic dimension. After the 1995–96 Taiwan missile crisis sent shudders through the region, China pursued "peaceful rise/development" and "harmonious world" rhetoric globally and a charm campaign in Southeast Asia in the late 1990s to alleviate the China threat theory. China was the first non-ASEAN country to sign the Treaty of Amity and Cooperation (TAC) in 1993 and joined the nonbinding Declaration on the Conduct of Parties in the South China Sea (DOC) the same year. During the Asian financial crisis in 1997–98, Japan (with more at stake, as the largest Asian investor at this point) remained the largest financial underwriter, contributing some US$43 billion in financial aid to overcome the Asian crisis, while China contributed some $4 billion and refrained from further currency devaluation. Japan also proposed the Asian Monetary Fund in 1967, a proposal jointly opposed by the United States and China (for different reasons); thus, the project was abandoned and the Chiang Mai Initiative (CMI; a mutually contributed fund to provide emergency bailouts) was adopted instead. China and Japan cooperated to set up the CMI but began to compete when it was multilateralized (as the CMIM) in 2008. Each wanted to be the largest contributor in order to have the greatest weight on the board.

But China was less interested in new financial architecture than in regional free trade agreements. In November 2001, China proposed a free trade agreement (FTA) with ASEAN at an ASEAN Plus Three (APT) summit that was then endorsed by ASEAN leaders, which sent a major shock wave throughout Japan. Given its protected agriculture and fishery sectors Japan has always had greater difficulty negotiating FTAs—the ASEAN-Japan Comprehensive Economic Partnership Agreement was not proposed until 2002, and only then in response to China's initiative. But Koizumi soon rose to the competitive occasion to propose not only a Japan-ASEAN FTA but also an APT FTA and an ASEAN Plus Five—namely, ASEAN, Japan, China, South Korea, Taiwan, and Hong Kong—none of which aroused much Chinese enthusiasm.[20] (China has generally prioritized ASEAN Plus One over ASEAN Plus Three.) In 2003, China formed a strategic partnership with ASEAN. When the ASEAN-China FTA (ACFTA) came into operation in 2010 (derived from ASEAN Plus One), an FTA for ASEAN Plus Three (which Japan had been pushing), expanded to become the sixteen-member Regional Comprehensive Economic Partnership (RCEP), which is still in negotiation with improved prospects since US withdrawal from the TPP. The ACFTA has been highly successful in promoting economic integration between ASEAN and the PRC, quickly making China ASEAN's leading trade partner. China's trade with ASEAN increased almost tenfold from US$32 billion in 2000 to US$319 billion in 2012, while Japan's trade with ASEAN increased from US$116 billion in 2000 to US$216 billion in 2012, trailing ASEAN-China trade in terms of both quantum and rate of growth. While China's share of ASEAN's total trade increased from 4.3 percent in 2000 to 12.9 percent in 2012, Japan's share decreased from 15.3 percent to 10.6 percent for the corresponding period. On the other hand, Japan clearly remains ASEAN's largest foreign investor: while China's FDI to ASEAN from 2010 to 2012 increased from US$2.5 billion to $4.3 billion, Japan's FDI jumped from US$10.8 billion to US$23.1 billion.

The rivalry has roiled international as well as regional associations. The UN in 1992 began to deliberate a reorganization of the Security Council, where the limit to five members since founding of the organization was considered anachronistic and out of touch with subsequent developments. On March 21, 2005, then UN secretary-general Kofi Annan called on the UN to reach a consensus on expanding the council to twenty-four members. He mooted two possible proposals, one of which would include six new permanent members. Japan, the second-largest financial contributor to the UN (after the United States), which had been elected eleven times to two-year terms as a nonpermanent member, was one of the six. At this time, some twenty-five million Chinese signed an online petition against Japan's inclusion as a permanent member of the UN Security Council, while others took to the streets in a brief but vociferous and mildly destructive anti-Japanese protest movement. Japan's support for UN Security Council reorganization was perceived in China as part of a Japanese-US plot to seize Asian leadership. China, still the only Asian member of the Security Council, has consistently opposed reorganization and particularly the elevation of Japan to that status (while maintaining an equivocal view of the admission of India). In retaliation, Japan was not above twitting China for its use of developing country status to rationalize a very modest assessment of its dues to the UN (less than 1 percent of total dues before 2000, compared to Japan's usual assessment of around 20 percent). But as China became the world's largest economy in purchasing power parity (PPP), this has changed: dues increased from 1.54 percent in 2001–3, to 3.19 percent in 2004–12, and to 5.15 percent after 2013. In 2015, China protested a proposed hike to 7.92 percent in 2016, making its assessment third largest after the United States and Japan, noting that per capita incomes in China are still relatively low.

Since the issue of territorial sovereignty claims over the South China Sea or parts thereof was raised at the second ARF meeting of foreign ministers of participating states in 2010, China has objected to Japan, while not a claimant to any territory in the South China Sea, voicing the complaint that the dispute may affect freedom of navigation. Due to Chinese opposition, discussion on the South China Sea dispute has moved slowly, and Japan has failed to gain access to various ARF working groups that discuss this issue.[21] China has promoted a diversionary focus on nontraditional security (NTS) within the ARF (e.g., terrorism, piracy, transnational crime), while Japan prefers to focus on transparency, confidence-building measures (CBMs), and other aspects of military security. While the two countries have both vied for leadership of the various extended ASEAN forums, they have used different approaches. China pursues a strategy of minimizing the size of the association in order to minimize opposition while Japan has pursued the exact opposite strategy in order to minimize China's relative influence. Koizumi first called for an "East Asian community" in 2002 in a Singapore speech. Based on the final report of the East Asia Study Group (EASG) established by the APT countries in 2002, an East Asia Summit (EAS) was scheduled for 2004, originally consisting (in accord with the ideas of the EASG) of only the APT 13. The proposal was enthusiastically supported by China, with the support of Malaysia.[22]

In November 2004, Malaysia's prime minister, Abdullah Badawi, announced that an agreement had been reached and that the first EAS would be held in Kuala Lumpur in December 2005. The agreement included no mention of a possible expansion of the ASEAN Plus Three forum. The Japanese objected, pursuing Koizumi's vision of a broadened community including Australia, New Zealand, and India. Eventually, the Japanese view prevailed over the Chinese-Malaysian coalition. When China failed to convince AS-EAN countries not to invite non-APT countries to the first EAS in Kuala Lumpur in 2005, it favored a draft declaration for the summit that would elevate the APT states as a "core" group having a dialogue with a secondary group made up of Australia, New Zealand, and India.[23] This position foundered on strong opposition from Japan. Beijing then offered to host the second summit, but this, too, was vetoed by Japan. When Japan then bid to cochair the first EAS with Malaysia, this proposal was vetoed by China.[24] ASEAN then stipulated that only ASEAN countries could host EAS summits. With that, further Chinese resistance to expanding the membership collapsed, and both Russia and the United States joined in 2011 (China could not accept one and not the other). But when the Japanese foreign minister floated the idea of establishing a maritime regime in the South China Sea for the prevention of maritime conflicts, the proposal was not introduced into the meeting's agenda due to Chinese objection and lukewarm response from Southeast Asian countries eager not to offend China.

In the contest for leadership of East Asia, Japan has fought a skillful defense as the once-dominant but declining Asian power, the United States has played a peripheral role content to use Japan as its stalking horse, and China has taken full advantage of its size, power, and booming growth rate. China has largely outmaneuvered Japan on the trade issue by being more willing to expose protected sectors and generally less cautious about terms before signing. Japan, on the other hand, has a big lead in FDI stock in East Asia, though if current trends continue China will eventually overtake it there, too.

The competition has continued since 2008 in the form of multilateral FTA construction, though how that will evolve with the 2016 departure of the United States from the Trans-Pacific Partnership (TPP) is unclear. On the territorial issue, Japan's strategy has been to cling tenaciously to the territory it occupies with the support of the JASA in the East China Sea and in the South China Sea to help build a coalition in support of the territorial status quo in ASEAN extended forums. China's organizational tactics have been an evolving mix, beginning with increasingly active participation in ASEAN forums in the 1990s and 2000s but then since 2010 participating mainly in order to block movement detrimental to its interests while setting up its own forums. Since 2013, China has shifted from attempting to lead ASEAN through such mechanisms as APT and ACFTA to splitting and sidelining ASEAN's prized centrality with its Belt and Road Initiative and the Asian Infrastructure Investment Bank (AIIB), augmented by discrete bilateral economic arrangements.

Territory

Japan has altogether three unresolved territorial disputes in Asia. First, Japan contests Korean occupation of the tiny uninhabited island Tokdo/Dokto (Takeshima in Japanese); second, Japan claims the Northern Territories/southern Kurils occupied since 1945 by Russia (Etorofu, Kunashir, Shikotan, and the Habomais islets); and third, it claims the Senkaku/Diaoyu (hereinafter S/D) islets, southernmost in the Ryukyu chain about one hundred miles from Taiwan. The S/D dispute is the only one in which Japan is the current stakeholder, and it is the most sensitive and passionately contested of the three. There are at least four reasons for this: first, the S/D are part of the maritime glacis that is perceived to inhibit the blue-water strategic ambitions of the PLA Navy (i.e., the first island chain); second, the historical circumstances surrounding Japan's claim are controvertible, on historical if not legal grounds; and third, the islands lie athwart vast subsurface hydrocarbon deposits that both countries need, as largest and third-largest oil importers in the world. Fourth (and perhaps most important), this confrontation pits Japan against China, its strongest and most dangerous rival in the region. Thus, it compounds and gives a solid empirical basis for all the growing tensions mentioned earlier.

Japan staked legal claim to the eight tiny S/D islets in January 1895. Japan's narrative is that a businessman, Koga Tatsushiro, discovered the islands to be unoccupied in 1884, and that they were incorporated into the country's territory only after having been surveyed for more than ten years. Japan then occupied the islets uncontested from 1895 to 1945. After World War II, administration was provisionally transferred to the United States (which used them for occasional gunnery practice). In May 1969, the UN Economic Commission for Asia and the Far East (ECAFE) announced, based on its investigations, that the area might contain one of the richest oil and gas deposits in the world. In 1972, the United States returned the islets to Japanese administrative control along with Okinawa. Taiwan first officially challenged Japan's control of the islands in 1971, and the PRC followed suit several months later. Before that time the islets were clearly identified on Chinese and Taiwanese maps as Japanese territory.[25] China, however, now traced Chinese contact with the islands back as far as 1372, arguing that the islands were to be sure not settled by but used as shelters by Chinese fishermen and part of the coastal defense system against pirates and smugglers.[26] Noting that all territories gained during the imperialist era according to the Potsdam Declaration (1945) and the San Francisco Peace Treaty (September 1951) were to be restored to their former owners, China demanded their return. Japan argued that they were not spoils of war annexed in the Treaty of Shimonoseki in 1895 but incorporated three months before that treaty based on *terra nullius*. This is certainly an intriguing chronological coincidence, but the Japanese point out that they were not mentioned in any of the Shimonoseki documents in 1895 nor in the San Francisco Peace Treaty, and that neither Chinese government raised any objections to such omissions at the time or for the next seven decades.

The Chinese claim based on historic rights is augmented by a geological one based on natural prolongation: the S/D are alleged to rest on the East China Sea continental shelf, with the Okinawa Trough separating them from the Japanese continental shelf and the Ryukyu archipelago. This interpretation would bring Chinese claims to the shores of Japan. Japan, on the other hand, claims that because the two-hundred-nautical-mile EEZs of the two nations overlap, the maritime boundary should run along a median line between the two countries, and this is the line that its coast guard and the Japan Maritime Self-Defense Forces (JMSDF) or navy have endeavored to protect.

The UN General Assembly's acceptance of Beijing's bid to the China seat on the Security Council in 1971 and Japan's decision the following year to sacrifice diplomatic relations with Taiwan in favor of the mainland put an end to Taiwan's ability to play an effective legal role in the S/D dispute. Meanwhile, Chinese objections to Japan's claim have been repeatedly suspended but never relinquished. They were first suspended for the sake of normalization of diplomatic relations between Beijing and Tokyo in September 1972. In the negotiations for the 1978 friendship treaty, right-wing LDP members tried to condition the inclusion of the anti-hegemony clause on Chinese acceptance of Japanese claims to the islets but China demurred, dispatching about one hundred armed fishing boats to the islets. A Japanese right-wing group, the Japan Youth Federation, retaliated by building a lighthouse on Uotsuri/Diaoyu, the largest of the islets. Finally, Japan accepted the anti-hegemony clause in the friendship treaty (without naming any hegemonist), and in return, Deng proposed that the dispute be shelved for future generations to resolve. The issue resurfaced with the National People's Congress (NPC) drafting of the Territorial Waters Law in late February 1992, which reaffirms China's claim to the S/D (Article 2), including twelve nautical miles of territorial sea and another twelve nautical miles of contiguous zones (Articles 3 and 4). Japan took this to be an unnerving departure from Deng's shelving of the claim and protested this as a clear infringement of Japan's sovereignty. China dismissed Japanese protests, asserting that its sovereignty over the islands was indisputable. In 1996, Japan proclaimed an EEZ around S/D, resting its counterclaim on the fact that it exercises effective control of the territory. The Jiang Zemin regime in 1998 retreated to Deng's shelving of the issue but never agreed to repeal the law as Japan demanded. Japan accepted this ambiguous outcome with the conclusion that "there does not exist any territorial problem with China in the first place," and with that "no dispute" has since refused to acknowledge Chinese claims. In a subtle diplomatic shift, Abe did, however, acknowledge "differing views over the recent tension" over the islets as the price of a meeting with Xi Jinping on the sidelines of the December 2014 APEC meeting.[27]

Yet the Japanese have hitherto refrained from any attempt to exploit the subsurface deposits for fear of provoking China, while criticizing China for drilling and extracting oil on their side of the maritime boundary line (as defined by Japan). One Japanese coping mechanism has been checkbook diplomacy: thus in 2000, the Foreign Affairs Committee of the LDP conferred a 17.2-billion-yen loan package to China contingent on cessation of Chinese survey vessel intrusion in Japanese waters. The Chinese authorities agreed (without accepting Japan's position) to notify Japan before entering its territorial seas, but then ignored their agreement in practice. Beijing offered joint exploration of the region on the precondition that China has sovereignty, while Japan continued to emphasize sovereignty based on effective control. Concerned at the increasing number of incidents, the two sides reached what seemed to have been a breakthrough agreement for peace, cooperation, and fellowship in 2004: the terms included provision for Japan to cooperate with the Chinese National Offshore Oil Company (CNOOC) in the development of the East China Seas oil fields. Talks were held for joint development beginning in 2006, and in June 2008, a consensus was reached outlining a 2,700-kilometer joint development zone (JDZ) roughly bisecting the intermediate line. Negotiations thereafter seem to have fallen apart due to reemergence of the sovereignty issue.[28] But Chinese intrusions without notification continue with growing frequency. The disputed boundaries, rivalrous patrols of armed vessels and aircraft, and growing mutual public antipathy generate risk of a clash that could escalate beyond control.

Since the 2010 Asian Olympics in Guangzhou, tensions have heightened to a new level. On the morning of September 7, 2010, a Japanese coast guard patrol vessel found a Chinese trawler, the *Minjinyu 5179*, operating about 7.45 miles northwest of S/D. The Japanese coast guard asked the trawler to leave the disputed area, but it then rammed the patrol vessel *Yonakuni*. When the coast guard ordered the trawler to stop for inspection, its captain, one Zhan Qixiong, opted to flee; in the course of his interception, the *Minjinyu 5179* collided with another patrol boat before Japanese sailors boarded the vessel. The captain and fourteen crew members were then placed under arrest for illegal fishing and evading arrest. The incident then escalated with unusual speed. Between September 8 and 19, 2010, Beijing summoned the Japanese ambassador on no less than six occasions—including a summons by State Councilor Dai Bingguo at two o'clock in the morning on September 12—demanding the immediate release of the trawler and its crew and restating China's historical claim to the islets. China canceled talks on joint resource exploitation in the East China Sea, canceled a number of people-to-people exchanges, and suspended exports of rare earth elements (REEs) to Japan, hitherto the largest REE consumer in the world and importer of 65 percent of China's REE exports (China has a virtual monopoly on REEs, about 95 percent of the world supply). China also arrested four employees of a Japanese company in north China for alleged espionage and rejected a Japanese ambassador's request for a meeting. Even after the Chinese captain was released on September 24, 2010, the Chinese demanded an apology and compensation from Japan for the captain's so-called illegal detention. This claim was roundly rejected as groundless, and the Japanese demanded reparations for damage to their patrol boat. The unofficial embargo on REE exports continued for over a month. Meanwhile in Japan the media played up the issue and there were also anti-Chinese demonstrations, and approval ratings for Kan Naoto's coalition government fell thirteen points (from 66 percent to 53 percent), while 87 percent of the public expressed distrust of China, the largest negative response since the question was added to the survey in 2004.[29]

Tensions then escalated still further in a second crisis in 2012. Ishihara Shintaro, then mayor of Tokyo and an outspoken nationalist, was raising funds in a plan to purchase three of the islets and erect structures clearly identifying them as Japanese territory. Unable to dissuade him, Prime Minister Noda Yoshihiko on September 11 nationalized the three islets by purchasing them from the Kurihara family for ¥2.05 billion (US$26.2 million), arguing that this change in ownership had no bearing on sovereignty. Although Beijing reportedly was apprised of this plan in June, Beijing reacted with immediate outrage, to Tokyo's astonishment, calling this a unilateral change (betrayal) of the status quo.[30] Mass demonstrations erupted in more than a hundred Chinese cities and, to a lesser extent, in Japan as well. China claimed the islets as indisputable Chinese territory and, in September 2012, declared territorial baselines and began patrolling surrounding waters; in 2013, it also unilaterally declared an air defense identification zone (ADIZ) including the islets (which it has not consistently endeavored to enforce). Two months later Noda was defeated in a flash election and forced to step down.

The change of administrations, however, brought Abe Shinzo—a relative hard-liner who took steps to boost defense capabilities—back to power, prompting a Chinese publicity campaign recounting Japan's wartime atrocities and warning of the rise of Japanese militarism. The US position on the issue had been inconsistent in Japanese eyes, declaring itself neutral on the islets' sovereignty but then nonetheless assuming responsibility for their security; to make this odd position clear, Barack Obama became the first president to state it publicly in 2015. Abe and Xi have met twice since 2012 in polite, cool encounters, but a risk reduction agent for the two militaries in the East China Sea has yet to materialize. The escalatory spiral has been stabilized, but the crisis was frozen in place rather than de-escalating, as the PRC persisted in flying aircraft (in the first three months of 2016 alone, Japan scrambled its fighter jets a record 193 times to intercept Chinese aircraft in its airspace, more than double that of the same time period in 2015) and boats (fifty times in 2013, fifty-seven times in 2015, and over one hundred times in 2016) into the territorial space surrounding the islets. China apparently maintains this routinized brinkmanship as an expression of sovereignty; many Chinese experts avow that China has thus achieved contested administration of the islets. Patrols now take place on a weekly basis, and the Japan Air Self-Defense Force (JASDF) intercepts daily. In addition to coast guard patrols, the People's Liberation Army Air Force (PLAAF) and Navy (PLAN) aviation and the State Oceanic Administration all regularly have planes operating in an airspace that was in the past exclusively controlled by Japan.

CONCLUSIONS

From a triangular perspective, the Sino-Japanese-US relationship began as an arranged marriage, consisting of the Japan-America Security Alliance (JASA) on one side facing an opposing Sino-Russian alliance on the other. Yet even during the Korean War, when Japan served as a vital base, the level of tension was lower than one might have anticipated. To China, Japan was not at this time a threat (digging out of the ruins of American nuclear and fire bombings and constrained by Article 9 of a superimposed constitution) while the United States decidedly was; from Japan's perspective, China was less threatening than the USSR (which attacked Manchukuo, violating their neutrality pact in the waning weeks of the war, and proceeded to annex Sakhalin and the Kurils) and a complementary trade partner to a recovering trading nation. Beijing tolerated the JASA as preferable to unilateral Japanese rearmament, and during the Sino-Soviet split, it was a useful deterrent to the USSR, which displaced the United States as China's main security threat. The heyday of Sino-Japanese relations was reached in the 1970s and 1980s, facilitated by the United States opening to China and strategic triangular collaboration against the USSR, in which Japan participated.

As junior partner in the marriage, Japan's opening to China was implicitly contingent on the attitude of the United States. Whenever Sino-US relations improved, Japan has promptly endeavored to improve relations with China for fear of being cut out of a Sino-US deal. Of course there were always other issues—war guilt, geographical proximity and trade complementarity, the fraternal embrace of Japanese socialist and communist parties, the SNTV electoral system that had allowed the latter to survive, Japanese ODA, and certainly the volatile territorial factor.[31] But US approval has always been sine qua non. Thus, the end of the Cold War was a challenge to both allies, because the shared anticommunist animus of the alliance was no more (Japan was slow to accept this because of its lingering dispute over the Northern

Islands). For a while, it seemed that economic complementarity could replace strategic necessity. After Deng Xiaoping's "southern voyage" (*nanxun*) to stimulate reform and opening, Sino-Japanese trade became the fastest growing bilateral trade nexus in Asia. By 2004, China had replaced the United States as Japan's leading trade partner and host of foreign direct investment. Meanwhile, political relations cooled, in correlation with the cooling of Sino-US relations. There was a perceptible drop in favorable Japanese views of China after June 4, 1989, and again after the 1996 Taiwan Strait crisis, mirroring the simultaneous fall in US public opinion. But correlation does not mean causation, and the issues have not always been the same. The rise in Chinese perceptions of Japanese war guilt reflected nationalistic textbook selections in 1982, 1984, 1986, 1995, and 2005, stimulated at home by the state-led revival of Chinese nationalism in the wake of the post–Cold War recession of Marxism-Leninism. Koizumi's six visits to the Yasakuni Shrine, comfort women, and the whole politics of war guilt and historical amnesia are all specific to Sino-Japanese relations. Equally specific is the maritime territorial dispute.

Comparing the Sino-Soviet-US triangle with the Japan-US-China triangle, it seems clear that whereas the United States played its pivot role very well in moderating the Sino-Russian dispute, its role in the increasingly volatile Sino-Japanese dispute has been less successful. This is certainly not to say that Washington was responsible for all the issues that have arisen since 1989 to plague the relationship. Yet it is worth noting that all these issues were already present during the heyday of the relationship in the 1970s and 1980s, but were not then fatal.[32] At least one (not the only) significant change is that the Sino-US relationship has become more defensive and critical as China's GDP and military capabilities have neared the tipping point, and this apprehension has been subtly conveyed to Japan. Most critical has been the mutual strengthening of the JASA instigated by Washington since the 1980s, partly to download part of the East Asian defense burden to a perceived alliance free rider, partly because Japan's leadership hungered for greater responsibility as a normal nation. In 2014, Japan increased its defense budget for the first time in many years, and Abe succeeded in passing legislation reinterpreting constitutional restrictions to permit collective self-defense. The Chinese saw this, together with the Obama pivot/rebalance, as part of a broader strategic encirclement. The war on terror, from a Chinese perspective, was used by the United States for the same purpose, establishing bases in South and Central Asia to augment those in the northeast, all around China's periphery. Meanwhile, India's violation of the nonproliferation treaty was quietly overlooked (the United States even supported India's application for membership in the Missile Technology Control Regime and the Nuclear Suppliers' Group) while focusing international opprobrium on the Democratic People's Republic of Korea's analogous violation.[33] China has been particularly critical of the 1996–97 revision of the JASA guidelines that authorized the use of SDF forces to maintain peace in the region surrounding Japan, accusing Japan of including Taiwan within its defense perimeter. These suspicions were heightened by the issuance of a joint security statement in February 2005 including Taiwan as a shared security concern.[34] Not to mention the South China Sea maritime territorial dispute, in which China perceives the United States and Japan to have jointly taken sides against its righteous claims.

How can we best account for a successful triangulation in the first case and failure in the latter? The two triangles occurred in different times and circumstances. In both cases, the United States was threatened, but in the Sino-Soviet-US triangle it was China that was most directly threatened, and China made substantial concessions (opening to the capitalist world, reducing aid to North Vietnam, offering peaceful reunification with Taiwan) to facilitate détente. The Soviet threat to the United States, though overestimated in retrospect, was still manageable, and the opening to China made it still more so. As objectively the least threatened of the three, Washington could take a more disinterested, pivot stance.

In the subsequent Sino-Japanese-US triangle, the Japanese trade imbalance with the United States faded with Japan's economic lost decades, and it is now Japan that feels itself most threatened. And no wonder: China is more populous, has a faster growth rate (already twice Japan's aggregate GDP), has a larger military (including nuclear weapons), and is rapidly overtaking Japan technologically. Before 2010, when the bilateral relationship was more balanced, the United States could and did play a more pivotal role, for example, with the "Nixon shocks" of 1971 or the 1998 "Japan passing" (when the United States colluded with China to block Japan's proposal for an Asian Monetary Fund, and when Clinton symbolically overflew Japan for his summit in Beijing). After 2012, the United States can no longer easily play a balancing, pivotal role and impartially modulate the relationship because it is now a rising China that is perceived to be the most dangerous challenger of the US-led status quo.[35] Thus the China-Japan triangle has not become "romantic" with the United States at pivot; instead, it is moving toward locking in the Japan-US "marriage."

NOTES

1. As quoted in William R. Nester, *Japan's Growing Predominance over East Asia and the World Economy* (New York: Macmillan, 1990), 78.

2. Masaru Tamamoto, "Japan's Search for a World Role," *World Policy Journal* 7, no. 3 (Summer 1990): 493–520.

3. Tadashi Ikeda, "Getting Senkaku History Right," *The Diplomat*, November 26, 2013, https://thediplomat.com/2013/11/getting-senkaku-history-right.

4. According to state and defense department documents cited by Gordon Chang, the United States was at this time implementing a "wedge strategy" designed to detach China from the Soviet Union by being tougher on China. See Gordon H. Chang, *Friends and Enemies: The United States, China, and the Soviet Union, 1948–197*2 (Stanford, CA: Stanford University Press, 1990).

5. Japan's more critical stance toward China in the 1950s also owed to the international environment, specifically the first Taiwan Strait crisis, which began in 1954 with exchanges of artillery fire. The crisis intensified in early 1955 when China captured nearby I-jiang and Dachen Islands and threatened to attack Jinmen and Mazu. The United States warned China that it would use military force, even atomic weapons if necessary, to defend those islands. The tension was only temporarily reduced when Zhou Enlai called for talks in April 1955, at the Bandung Conference. China was during this time still in full public support of the USSR, which in 1957 launched the world's first intercontinental ballistic missile and first orbital satellite, *Sputnik.*

6. The new document eliminated the passage in the 1951 treaty (Introduction) that assigns the United States responsibility for Japan's defense, omitted a provision permitting the US military to assist in putting down internal disturbances, and limited the duration of the treaty.

7. Mao said, "Don't be sorry. Japanese militarists in China brought great benefits to the Chinese people [enabling them to] seize power. Had there been no Imperial Army, we could not seize power. In this, I have a different opinion from you and the two of us have a contradiction. (Laughter, animation.)" [毛： 沒有什麼抱歉。日本軍國主義給中國帶來瞭很大的利益，使中國人民奪取瞭政權。沒有妳們的皇軍，我們不可能奪 取政權。這一點，我和妳們有不同的意見，我們兩個人有 矛盾。（眾笑，會場活躍)]" (Mao Zedong greeting Japanese prime minister Kakuei in Nanjing, 1972, "Talk: Mao Zedong" [translated into Chinese from Japanese]), *Wikiquote*, https://en.wikiquote.org/wiki/Talk:Mao_Zedong. Mao was known for his ironic sense of humor. Tanaka, however, did render a formal apology to the Chinese people on this occasion.

8. In 1980, China's deputy chief of general staff, Wu Xiuqian, suggested to Nakasone that Japan should increase its defense spending to 2 percent of GNP. Drifte, *Japan's Foreign Policy*, 52–55.

9. The first guidelines were issued in 1978 in order to specify the division of labor between the two signatories. Revised guidelines were issued in 1997, following the 1994–95 North Korean crisis and the 1995–96 Taiwan Strait crisis, and more sweepingly in 2015. In the 1997 revised guidelines, Japan agreed to take responsibility to survey its airspace up to several hundred miles and its sea lanes up to one thousand miles, arousing Chinese accusations that Japan now included Taiwan within its defense perimeter—an allegation Japanese spokespersons disputed but did not categorically deny. These suspicions were heightened by the issuance of a joint security statement in February 2005 that included Taiwan as a shared security concern. See Wu Xinbo, "The End of the Silver Lining: A Chinese View of the US-Japan Alliance," *Washington Quarterly* 29, no.1 (Winter 2005–6): 119–30. In April 2015, Japan and the United States published a new joint statement and updated guidelines that emphasized bilateral and trilateral collaboration in security capacity-building efforts in the South and East China Seas.

10. Tsuchida Ryushi (Liberal Democratic Party), as cited in Karl Gustafsson, "Memory Politics and Ontological Security in Sino-Japanese Relations," *Asian Studies Review* 38, no. 1 (2014): 71–86.

11. For a third straight year, in 2015 the amount of foreign direct investment from Japan to the ten-member Association of Southeast Asian Nations (ASEAN) exceeded such investment in China and Hong Kong, according to figures compiled by the Japan External Trade Organization. In 2013, Japanese corporate investment in Southeast Asia was three times that in China, and the pace has been accelerating: the outstanding amount of Japanese investment to ASEAN nations almost tripled (to US$180.9 billion) from 2010 to 2015, according to the Bank of Japan.

12. Cf. The Genron NPO, in collaboration with Public Opinion Research Institute Corporation in Japan and *China Daily*, Horizon Research Consultancy Group, *The 10th Japan-China Public Opinion Poll Analysis Report on the Comparative Data*, September 9, 2014, http://www.genron-npo.net/en/opinion_polls/archives/5317.html.

13. For example, the latest arms budget increase, in 2015, is 10.1 percent, at a time of GDP growth of 6.5 percent.

14. International Institute of Strategic Studies, *Strategic Survey: The Annual Assessment of Geopolitics* (London: International Institute of Strategic Studies, 2017), 84ff; Stockholm International Peace Research Institute, *SIPRI Yearbook 2015: Armaments, Disarmament and International Security* (London: Oxford University Press, 2016), electronic summary, https://www.sipri.org/sites/default/files/2016-03/YB-15-Summary-EN.pdf, p. 14.

15. Allen S. Whiting and Xin Jianfei, "Sino-Japanese Relations: Pragmatism and Passion," *World Policy Journal* 8, no. 1 (Winter 1990–91): 107–35.

16. The Chinese high-speed rail project in Indonesia, however, reportedly has run into difficulties, which has raised concerns that it could follow in the footsteps of an infamous contract for the Northrail Project in the Philippines that China won in 2004 but ultimately shelved in 2012.

17. Siemon T. Wezeman, "Developments in Arms Transfers," 2015, *SIPRI Yearbook Online 2016*, https://www.sipri.org/yearbook/2016/15.

18. Overseas Economic Cooperation Fund, *kaigai keizai kyoroku binran*, 1987, 251; as cited in Ogata Sadako, "Regional and Political Security Issues: Sino–Japanese–United States Triangle," unpublished paper, Institute of East Asian Studies, University of California, Berkeley; also see Joshua Keating, "China Sends Japan $1.2 Billion in Aid Every Year," *Foreign Policy*, December 2, 2010, accessed December 2, 2010, http://blog.foreignpolicy.com/posts/2010/09/28/japan_sends_china_12_billion_in_aid_every_year.

19. In 1978, China contracted with Japan's biggest steel manufacturer to build a big steel complex in Baoshan, but the deal ran into problems because of a budget deficit aggravated by factional disputes over Hua Guofeng's "foreign leap forward" and was canceled. Deng Xiaoping then hinted that the decision might be reversed if Japan could provide assistance. Thus, the first ODA loan was authorized in 1979.

20. Naoko Munakata, "Seize the Moment for East Asian Economic Integration," *PacNet 5A*, February 1, 2002, as cited in Soeya Yoshihide, Jianwei Wang, and David A. Welch, "A New Look at the US-China-Japan Triangle: Toward Building a Stable Framework," *Asian Perspective* 27, no. 3 (2003): 177–219.

21. Joel Rathus, *Japan, China and Networked Regionalism in East Asia* (Basingstoke: Palgrave Macmillan, 2011), 144–45, as cited in Chien-Peng Chung, "China-Japan in 'ASEAN Plus' Multilateral Arrangements: Raining on the Other Guy's Parade," *Asian Survey* 53, no. 5 (September 1, 2013): 801–24.

22. Jae Cheol Kim, "Politics of Regionalism in East Asia: The Case of the East Asia Summit," *Asian Perspective* 34, no. 3 (2010): 128.

23. Bruce Vaughn, "East Asia Summit: Issues for Congress," *CRS Report*, December 9, 2005, 2.

24. Eric T. C. Cheow, "East Asia Summit's Birthing Pains," *Straits Times* (Singapore), February 22, 2005.

25. See replicas of these maps in Ko-Hua Yap, Yu-Wen Chen, and Ching-Chi Huang, "The Diaoyutai Islands on Taiwan's Official Maps: Pre- and Post-1971," *Asian Affairs: An American Review* 29 (May 31, 2012): 90–105.

26. See the legal exposition by Jerome Cohen and Jon Van Dyke in the *South China Morning Post*, November 10, 2010.

27. Reiji Yoshida, "Tokyo Admits 'Differing Views' on Senkakus, Opening Door to Abe-Xi meeting," *Japan Times*, November 7, 2014, https://www.japantimes.co.jp/news/2014/11/07/national/politics-diplomacy/tokyo-admits-differing-views-on-senkakus-opening-door-to-abe-xi-meeting/#.WfZujymAMuw.

28. On negotiations toward joint development, see Gao Jianjun, "A Note on the 2008 Cooperation Consensus between China and Japan in the East China Sea," *Ocean Development and International Law* 40 (2009): 291–303.

29. *Yumiuri Shimbun*, November 7, 2010. When asked which country was most likely to pose a threat to Japan, 81 percent thought North Korea, but China placed second at 79 percent. Among Chinese respondents, 81 percent thought bilateral ties were bad and 79 percent opined

that Japan was untrustworthy. The survey was conducted by phone in Japan October 22–24, 2010, and in China October 19–26, 2010.

30. International Crisis Group, *Dangerous Waters: China-Japan Relations on the Rocks*, Asia Report no. 245 (April 8, 2013) thus refers to China's "reactive assertive" tactics.

31. China has been the biggest single recipient of Japanese official developmental aid (ODA) since 1982, representing more than 50 percent of the total assistance China received from both bilateral and multilateral sources. Since 2000, Japan has publicly announced several times its intention to suspend ODA in the light of China's rapid development, its own foreign aid to Africa and Southeast Asia, and its public ingratitude about Japanese aid, yet ODA continued as late as 2010 at the rate of about US$1.2 billion per year. Overseas Economic Cooperation Fund, *kaigai keizai kyoroku binran*, 1987, 251; as cited in Ogata, "Regional and Political Security Issues"; also see Keating, "China Sends Japan $1.2 Billion in Aid Every Year."

32. The Diaoyu/Senkaku issue first came up during normalization talks in 1972, with the powerful conservative antinormalization group arguing that Japan should not agree to formal diplomatic relations until China conceded ownership of the islands. Zhou Enlai agreed to shelve the issue. It came up again in 1978 when the Chinese were pressing Japan to sign a Peace and Friendship Treaty with an anti-hegemony clause implicitly directed against the USSR. But Japan was at the time hoping for the return of the Northern Territories from the USSR and negotiating various trade agreements with Moscow. Again Japanese conservatives argued that the Senkaku issue had to be settled before signing a treaty. In April, an armada of Chinese fishing boats suddenly appeared near the islands, arousing great uproar in Japan. The boats withdrew, with Beijing explaining that they had been pursuing a school of fish and gone off course. China agreed to insert a clause in the treaty stating that it was not directed against a third party, the Senkaku issue was shelved (but not conceded), and the treaty was signed.

33. See Rex Li, *A Rising China and Security in East Asia: Identity Construction and Security Discourse* (New York: Routledge, 2009), 215 ff. et passim.

34. See Xinbo Wu, "The End of the Silver Lining: A Chinese View of the US-Japan Alliance," *Washington Quarterly* 29, no. 1 (Winter 2005–6): 119–30.

35. Japan has also at times aspired to a mediatory pivot role. Under DPJ leadership in 2009–12, for example, Tokyo proposed an all-Asian "East Asian community" and a less dependent alliance relationship in a transparent appeal to China. However, China did not reciprocate Japan's overture but instead escalated the bilateral territorial dispute, while US refusal to consider compromise on the Okinawa base issue made this venture untenable.

Chapter Five

Divided Identities

Taiwan and Korea are categorically different from the other countries in Asia in that they are both divided nations. Thus from the outset, their foreign policy preferences are distinctive in that one of their inherent national preoccupations is reunification.[1] All nations have a foreign policy to deal with other countries, but divided nations make special governmental arrangements to deal with their nonforeign but severed parts. All four of these states are constitutionally founded on a commitment to "one country." The People's Republic of China (PRC) has included a Taiwan delegation in its National People's Congress (NPC) since the Fourth NPC in 1975, and also offers Taiwan province and its municipalities official representation in the Chinese People's Political Consultative Conference (CPPCC). The Republic of China (ROC; now more commonly referred to as Taiwan) has continued to represent all mainland provinces in its (largely ceremonial) National Assembly until its dissolution, and the ROC constitution is committed to "one China."[2] In the Democratic People's Republic of Korea (DPRK), the unification goal has been incorporated into the fundamental documents of both party and state. The preamble to the charter of the Korean Workers' Party (KWP) states that "[t]he present task of the KWP is to ensure the complete victory of socialism in the Democratic People's Republic of Korea and the accomplishment of the revolutionary goals of national liberation and the people's democracy in the entire area of the country." Nominally South Korean delegates were ensconced in the first national legislature, and although the DPRK's seat of government has always been Pyongyang, the DPRK constitution from the outset stipulated that "the capital of the [future] Democratic Federal Republic of Korea shall be Seoul."[3] Both Koreas and both Chinas have established many institutions to handle the issue (the Ministry of National Unification in South Korea; the Committee for Peaceful Reunification of Korea in the DPRK; the Taiwan Office of the State Council and the Association for Relations across the Taiwan Strait in China; and the National Unification Council, the Mainland Affairs Council, and Strait Exchange Foundation in Taiwan). Taiwanese, whether native (*bensheng ren*) or more recent migrants (*waishengren*), are distinguished from foreigners (*waiguo-ren*) on the mainland as "compatriots" (*tongbao*). At the same time, in both dyads there has been keen competition for international recognition, mutual-ly successful in the Korean case, where both sides have won United Nations (UN) seats and are widely recognized diplomatically, but not in the Chinese (where the Republic of China in Taiwan was at first successful in excluding the mainland from recognition, and the People's Republic since 1972 has become increasingly successful at denying recognition to Taiwan). Yet nei-ther side (of either dyad) has ever recognized the other as a state (in contrast to the two Germanys under Willy Brandt and Erich Honecker), though nei-ther state in either dyad has been completely successful in preventing other states from doing so.[4]

Three countries were divided by the Cold War: East and West Germany, North and South Korea, and China and Taiwan, all riven and yet drawn together by this teleological magnetism. National unity is not a tautological truth but an empirical one, for it is of course quite possible for a nation to be divided with no particular interest in reunification. This was true in the early division of Pakistan and India, the split between Pakistan and Bangladesh, the divorce of Malaysia and Singapore, and the post–Cold War breakup of Czechoslovakia. But in all these cases, the division was voluntarily enacted by the two halves. In the case of the four divided nations, the split was involuntary, structurally imposed by outside forces.

Due to the bifurcated global ideological framework that divided them, reunification remained difficult to imagine during the Cold War, but its con-clusion opened new options. The communist bloc was left in shambles (in-cluding the Warsaw Pact and the Council for Mutual Economic Assistance), to be replaced by untamed markets and renascent nationalism.[5] North and South Vietnam, divided by the powers upon the defeat of the French at Dienbienphu by the Geneva peace talks in 1954, were reunited by armed force during the Cold War. East and West Germany, divided by the victors of World War II, were reunited upon its conclusion. Taiwan and China and the two Koreas remain divided. The Asian divided nations have remained di-vided for three reasons: lasting emotional antipathy rooted in their violent origins; continued ideological and structural cleavages; and the different end-ing of the Asian cold war. While in Europe the communist regimes collapsed and gave way to a redistribution of spheres of influence, in Asia they sur-vived via economic reform and nationalist revitalization and remain power-ful. Because the complexities and strains of the divided nations have made them such perennial global trouble spots, the international community would in principle welcome peaceful reunification.

Taiwan and the two Koreas are relatively small countries surrounded by great powers, and their foreign policy options are naturally constrained by this fact. The most relevant great powers are China and the United States, which take opposite positions in the two cases. China supports reunification in the Taiwan case while in the Korean case it prefers continued division; the United States supports reunification in the Korean case while it supports continued division in the Taiwan case (in both cases, public rhetoric differs). These allegiances are based not on ideology but on security commitments: China is allied to the DPRK while the United States is allied to the Republic of Korea (ROK) and retains an informal defense commitment to Taiwan.

What, then, do the two cases have in common? Besides both being divided nations with incompatible ideologies and political-economic systems, both are located on China's eastern periphery, both were Japanese colonies throughout the first half of the twentieth century, both are perceived by China to be sources of potential instability and vulnerability, both have frustrated and ambivalent feelings toward each other and toward the great powers surrounding and constraining them. Both were originally divided by civil war (in Taiwan before division, Korea after), then integrated into opposing camps during the Cold War. Both are divided into what have become quite unequal halves (albeit in each case still strong enough to deter forceful reunification). Both are constitutionally committed to reunification but, in practice, the national interest of the divided halves tends to take precedence.

This chapter is not focused on reunification per se, but that is the issue that makes these cases distinctively complicated. The two divided nations both deal with their shared intranational problem in a great power context that is analogous in their juxtaposition between China and the United States and their consequent tendency to equivocate (hedge), but in other relevant respects quite different. We examine each case in turn, predominantly during the post–Cold War period when both became open to reconfiguration, focusing on the relationship between internal and external power dynamics.

TAIWAN

This overview of the Taiwan-China split, noncommittally referred to by both as the "cross-Strait relationship" (*liangan guanxi*), consists of three parts, chronologically ordered. The first covers the period of mutual hostility from 1949 to 1970, when the relationship represented essentially a continuation of the civil war, rife with threats, raids, spying expeditions, and barely suppressed collective violence. The second involves the advent of a strategic triangle from 1971 to 1989, when Taiwan's Cold War patron essentially abandoned Taipei in the interest of building a relationship with the more strategically significant PRC. It was during this period that the PRC launched its first plausible offer for peaceful reunification. Although Taipei did not immediately accept the offer, Beijing did not rescind it, and it turned out to be a game changer. The third period is focused on the post–Cold War period (1989–present), still within a strategic triangular framework, now however unleashed from "great" triangular context after the Soviet bloc collapsed and the cross-Strait issue became detached from the international power game.

The Chinese claim to Taiwan (and Taiwan's claim to be part of China) is both ethnolinguistic and historical. All but some 2 percent of the Taiwanese are ethnic Han Chinese, speak a local dialect of Mandarin, and observe Chinese ceremonial rituals. Some mainland historians claim Taiwan has been part of China since the beginning of the Sui dynasty (598–618), yet official dynastic histories as late as the Ming make no reference to Taiwan in the section on administrative geography (the *dilizhi*, which comprehensively lists all provinces, prefectures, subprefectures, and counties of the Ming state), so it seems reasonable to assume it was then no more than an insignificant outlying frontier region. By the thirteenth century, there were, however, a significant number of Chinese settlements on the island, where fertile virgin land and mild climate attracted economic migrants. The island also attracted various European imperialist interests (in 1622 the Dutch drove out some Spanish settlers and established a colony). A rebel named Zheng Chenggong (known in the West as Koxinga) established a pirate garrison near Tainan in the name of the recently defeated Ming, but the Qing dispatched a naval force under Admiral Shi Lang to destroy the Zheng fleet in the Battle of Penghu (1683), thereafter annexing the island as part of the province of Fujian. In 1887, Taiwan finally became a province, only to be annexed by Japan eight years later, following China's defeat in the Sino-Japanese War. It remained a colony until 1945, when it was returned to China.[6] Mao Zedong offered in 1936 to assist in the struggle for independence of Taiwan and Korea (from Japan). This changed when the Nationalists retreated to the island in 1949, after which the liberation of Taiwan was subsumed in the incomplete Chinese civil war.

The reestablishment of the Republic of China by the defeated Kuomintang (KMT) was not entirely welcomed by the indigenous population. Having brutally reasserted Chinese sovereignty in the wake of the February 28 [1947] Incident, the KMT avowed the intention of reversing its military setback at the first opportunity. For its part, the victorious PRC fully expected to liberate the island as soon as it had consolidated control of the mainland, thereby completing the revolution and ending the so-called hundred years of humiliation, including the unequal treaty of Shimonoseki ceding Taiwan to Japan. The mainland was, however, unable to make good on this threat and, in recent years, has shifted to more emollient tactics, which have proved economically compatible with bilateral modernization agendas. In view of ethnic homogeneity, geographic proximity, historical origins, and above all the balance of power, the Chinese claim that Taiwan is part of China is quite plausible and has been diplomatically accepted by most countries in the world, including Japan, South Korea, and the United States. It is, however, energetically (and thus far successfully) contested by the people and government of Taiwan.

The Cold War

The first three decades, when the leaders of the civil war remained at their respective helms, may be characterized as a period of mutual antagonism amid shared consensus about how it should be resolved; in other words, both sides concurred on the provisional and unsatisfactory nature of the division and the necessary end-state of reunification ("one China"). Both sides expected it to be resolved by force, and the only remaining issue was this: Who wins? The Chinese Communist Party's (CCP) military ambitions were echoed by the KMT government on the island, still claiming to be the Republic of China and maintaining all formal structures of legislative democracy, including representatives from Outer Mongolia and Tibet, educating children to learn Chinese literature and geography, and enforcing the pronunciation of Mandarin Chinese. China took advantage of the Nationalist occupation of two islands within artillery range of the mainland (Jinmen and Mazu) to precipitate two crises by shelling them, first in 1954–55 and more concertedly in 1958, but found any attempt to move beyond that frustrated by the United States, whose command of the sea and the air made invasion unrealistic. Taiwan conducted raids and espionage (including high-altitude surveillance by U-2 spy planes, in cooperation with the CIA) on the mainland and frequently reiterated its desire to recover the mainland, particularly during the three black years of famine following the Great Leap Forward (1959–62), calculating that an invasion would trigger an irrepressible popular uprising; however, these schemes were opposed by the United States, without whose backup any such foray would be highly risky (as the 1961 Bay of Pigs fiasco illustrated). Meanwhile, both sides engaged in their quite different approaches to socioeconomic modernization, involving socialization of the means of production and Soviet-style central planning on the mainland and state-directed capitalist export-oriented growth on Taiwan. The latter approach appears to have been more effective economically, raising per capita income from around US$50 per annum in 1950 to $200 in 1964 and more than $3,000 by the mid-1980s, when China's own highly successful export-oriented growth surge began.[7] The ROC government represented China in the United Nations (including on the Security Council) and in most foreign embassies from 1949 to 1971, enforcing a "one China policy" by breaking diplomatic relations with any country that recognized the PRC. The PRC thereafter adopted the same tactic toward the ROC.

Strategic Triangle

During the period from 1970 to 1990, Taiwan was in effect deserted by its principal security guarantor and patron, the United States, which turned to the PRC as a more useful strategic partner in its bipolar contest with the Soviet Union.[8] Thus began the Great Strategic Triangle between the United States, the PRC, and the Union of Soviet Socialist Republics (USSR), as the United States opened relations with China while continuing détente with the Soviet Union, taking advantage of the resulting ambiguity to enhance its negotiating position with both. This grand design was initiated during Richard Nixon's visit to China in February 1972, a "week that changed the world."[9] Both sides had other pressing issues in mind, but Zhou Enlai made clear Beijing's priority on the Taiwan issue at the outset, and the United States responded with a formula in which it acknowledged Beijing's position that both China and Taiwan agreed that there was only "one China" and that Taiwan was a part of it. This formula, vainly opposed by Taipei, was designed to extricate the United States from the issue and permit the relationship to evolve in accord with the balance of power, anticipating that the KMT regime would soon collapse and be peacefully absorbed into the PRC.[10] This formula, the centerpiece of the 1972 Shanghai Communiqué, was reaffirmed in the second and third communiqués in 1979 and 1982, which, together with the 1979 Taiwan Relations Act, were to form the basis for future US relations with the two opposing sides of the Taiwan Strait.

Yet the subsequent evolution of the relationship did not proceed according to plan. The Beijing side, having been informally assured of US concurrence in the eventual realization of their dream of reunification, avoided further military forays and turned to united front tactics to recover their prize. China, in fact, played the issue quite low key during the first decade, attempting to sustain the plausibility of its Three Worlds revolutionary foreign policy while beginning cautiously to explore the opportunities of UN Security Council membership, for the most part preoccupied domestically with the twists and turns of the Great Proletarian Cultural Revolution and with the succession to Mao and his cohort of first-generation revolutionaries. Only after succession was resolved and formal US recognition secured in January 1979 did Beijing's post-Mao leadership launch a more comprehensive new package for peaceful reunification, consisting of three direct links (*tong*) across the Strait (mail, transportation, and trade) and "one country, two systems"—Taiwan could retain its own capitalist system after unification and function with a high degree of autonomy, merely changing flags and sovereignty. Thus Beijing suspended artillery bombardment of the offshore islands and invited Taipei to talk.

Taiwan's response to these dramatic developments was unexpectedly defiant. Despite having been dealt a near-fatal diplomatic setback involving not just the loss of US support but eviction from the United Nations and loss in the course of the next two decades of formal diplomatic recognition by most nations in the world, Taipei did not evolve a new foreign policy strategy to cope with this crisis of international survival. To do so would have necessarily involved a shift from exclusive reliance on a single (manifestly unreliable) patron to alternative security partners, but given the bipolar structure of world power, Taipei's realistic options were limited. Yet Taiwan did not collapse or sue for favorable reunification terms as a result of its declining international status. The immediate response to Beijing's offer of "three links" was "three noes": no contact, no talks, and no compromise.

To the dismay of Beijing and Washington, Taipei maintained its stubborn rejection for nearly a decade. There were three reasons for this. The first was personal: Chiang Ching-kuo, who like his father, was a veteran of a long, circuitous, and ultimately bitterly disappointing relationship with the CCP on the mainland, and was deeply anticommunist: there could be no rapprochement during his lifetime. A second factor was the hedged quality of the US shift of recognition, the terms of which maintained (over strident PRC objections) the right to continue to sell arms to Taiwan. This was followed by the Taiwan Relations Act, signed by a reluctant executive after almost unanimous legislative approval, which unilaterally stipulated a US "grave" interest in peaceful resolution of the issue and tendered assurances of continued military and quasi-diplomatic support for the island. Third, the domestic economic conjuncture was not conducive to capitulation—though internationally ostracized, Taiwan's economy was (in contrast to that of the mainland, at this point still trying to reconcile economic development with cultural revolution) booming and globalizing, shifting from textiles and extractive industries to more technologically advanced lines of production (e.g., microelectronics, personal computers, and peripherals). Whereas in 1962, Taiwan had a per capita gross national product (GNP) of $170, ranking between Zaire and Congo, by 2005 Taiwan's per capita GNP, adjusted for purchasing power parity (PPP), had soared to $27,600, vastly exceeding that of the mainland.

All the same, it was hard to see any upside to Taiwan's diplomatic situation. Beijing proceeded to occupy the Chinese seat in the UN and all its ancillary agencies while nation after nation shifted diplomatic recognition from Taipei to Beijing, given the latter's refusal to accept dual recognition. Although a landslide of other recognitions was set off by the Nixon visit in 1972, formal US recognition did not follow until 1979, but the terms negotiated in 1972 became the template for both that and for most other countries' recognitions: China would tolerate continuing informal contacts (e.g., trade missions) with Taipei but no formal diplomatic ties. Taiwan was hence ousted from all international organizations for which statehood was a prerequisite, retaining its seat in a few (e.g., the Asian Developmental Bank [ADB], Asia-Pacific Economic Cooperation [APEC]) only by agreeing to call itself "Taipei, China" or "Chinese Taipei." Taiwan's only saving grace was its ability to establish informal trade missions in around 130 countries as functional substitutes for ambassadorial representation. Beyond occasional weapon sales, the United States did little on Taiwan's behalf.

Though Taipei remained unmoved by China's overtures, US abandonment may have helped precipitate a momentous domestic political transmogrification, which at once facilitated and complicated cross-Strait relations. Taiwan's claim to be recognized as "China" having been so roundly rejected by the international diplomatic community set off a quest for alternative bases of legitimacy. Augmented by factors such as US prodding to improve its observance of human rights (particularly after the assassination of a dissident biographer of Chiang Ching-kuo in California was traced to Taiwanese intelligence operatives) and the democratic wave that swept Asia in the wake of the overthrow of the Marcos dictatorship in the Philippines and the election of Kim Dae-jung in Korea, Taiwan in the waning years of the Chiang Ching-kuo presidency undertook a gradual and fairly seamless transition to democratic government. The process began with localization (i.e., the appointment of native Taiwanese to political positions) and *dang wai* elections (elections that non-KMT candidates without partisan affiliation were permitted to contest) in the early 1980s. By 1988, martial law was lifted and opposition parties permitted to form.

The impact on cross-Strait relations was mixed. In an economic sense, it was positive because democratization empowered Taiwan's business community to skirt Chiang Ching-kuo's "three noes," by engaging the mainland via Hong Kong: trade took off in the early 1990s, followed by investment. China soon became the island's most important trade partner. On the other hand, democratization proved to be a setback to reunification in at least two ways. First, "one country, two systems" was designed to accommodate capitalism but not necessarily democracy—the former was compatible with the reforms launched at this time on the mainland but the latter was not (as underscored by the sanguinary end to the May 1989 Tiananmen protests). This meant Taiwan's democratic progress was viewed suspiciously from the mainland. Second, democratization resulted in the political emancipation of the island's majority of "natives" (*benshengren*) whose ancestors had lived on the island since the Ming and long harbored resentments against the "outsiders" who fled the mainland with Chiang Kai-shek, and it proved politically feasible to turn these subethnic resentments against the equally authoritarian PRC. Beijing was understandably upset by this and periodically threatened to punish Taiwan's electorate if it voted the wrong way, precipitating a politically counterproductive backlash.

After the Cold War

The post–Cold War period unleashed the cross-Strait stalemate from the collapsing bipolar global system, allowing it to evolve autonomously based on the interests and ambitions of the three parties involved. Thus arose a "mini-triangle" between the United States, Taiwan, and the PRC. Though highly asymmetric (in 1990 Taiwan's gross domestic product [GDP] was only 40 percent that of China, and the United States was ten times that of both), in some ways this was a very pure triangle, because (thanks to Beijing's successful diplomatic isolation campaign) Taiwan's fate was so exclusively dependent on two countries—the PRC (as security threat and would-be unifier) and the United States (as security provider). And with Taiwan's economic opening to China in the 1990s, the Taiwan triangle prefigured the dilemma that would face the rest of East Asia with the rise of China: a thriving economic relationship coexisting with a potential security threat. Yet at the same time, the Taiwan triangle is unique in one sense: in this case, one actor is expressly dedicated to eliminating the sovereign existence of another.

Given the wide range of open possibilities after the Cold War, the Taiwan triangle changed continuously, evolving through four phases: (1) thaw, (2) freeze, (3) rethaw, and (4) refreeze.

Thaw, 1988–94

The end of the Cold War resulted in cross-Strait détente. This was facilitated by both international and domestic factors. The CCP crackdown at Tiananmen was followed by similar uprisings throughout Eastern Europe that resulted in the wholesale collapse of those regimes, followed within two years by the end of the Soviet Union itself. The PRC survived, one of a mere handful of communist regimes, defying widespread expectations that it, too, would collapse. This had an alienating effect on Sino-American relations, for two reasons. First, use of lethal force against unarmed demonstrators at Tiananmen was very well publicized by Western media in Beijing to record the Sino-Soviet summit, and had a lasting impact on Western public opinion, the net effect of which was to underline the leadership's determination to resist "peaceful evolution" (*hoping yanbian*) to liberal democracy. This was a shock to Western expectations that economic reform implied political convergence. Second, the collapse of the Soviet Union meant that the mutual strategic basis for the Sino-US quasi alliance was no longer necessary, as neither China nor the United States needed each other to deter a shared threat. Indeed, China had already launched a long process of reconciliation with the Soviet Union, climaxing in a normalization summit in Beijing on the eve of the crackdown. The irrelevance of the Sino-US strategic partnership facilitated greater US support for Taiwan (e.g., weapons sales) without the previous level of sensitivity about upsetting the PRC, while Taiwan's democratization newly endeared it to American liberals.

Assured of stronger US ideological backing, Taiwan was ready to take a new and more confident approach to cross-Strait policy. Without revoking the "three noes," an institutional mechanism was found to engage the communists without officially talking to them: a Mainland Affairs Council (MAC) was set up in the Executive Yuan to supervise the nominally private Straits Exchange Foundation (SEF) in 1991, and the PRC promptly reciprocated by establishing the Taiwan Affairs Office under the State Council and a private Association for Relations across the Taiwan Straits (ARATS). After preliminary discussions in Hong Kong about how to finesse Beijing's precondition that Taiwan accept the one China principle (resolved by agreeing on one China with different interpretations of "China," since referred to in Taiwan as the "1992 Consensus"), the two sides began to meet regularly to resolve technical problems in Singapore, culminating in a summit meeting of the leaders of the two organizations, Wang Daohan (ARATS) and Koo Cheng-fu (SEF), in April 1993. To oversee this process, the KMT government established the cabinet-level National Unification Council to draft the National Unification Guidelines, outlining a three-stage timetable for reunification contingent upon a cross-Strait peace treaty and prior democratization of the PRC. Underlying and facilitating this momentous shift from armed confrontation to negotiation was an acknowledgment that Taiwan no longer had effective political jurisdiction over the mainland anyhow, and the government thus stated that it did not actively challenge Chinese sovereignty on the mainland but only over Taiwan and assorted adjoining islands. However, Beijing did not reciprocate with recognition of the ROC's de facto sovereignty in Taiwan, objecting that this shift to geopolitical realism endangered the "one China" principle and legitimated separatism. Thus it was rescinded by the accommodative KMT regime in 2008, in line with its affirmation of the "one China" principle (with different interpretations).

Trade and mainland tourism accelerated dramatically in the early 1990s, avoiding formal acceptance of the three links (and complicating trade statistics) by routing everything through Hong Kong. By the end of 2010, a total of 61,048,742 Taiwanese residents had visited the mainland. Considering Taiwan's total population of 23,000,000, this is the equivalent of saying that every Taiwanese has visited the mainland almost three times.[11] Trade was followed by Taiwanese investment, which drew further trade. Beijing welcomed both, creating a trade and investment climate even more optimal for Taiwanese compatriots than for Western investors in order to cultivate economic dependency, under the Marxist assumption that political integration would inevitably follow economic integration. Business interests were whetted by the US forced revaluation of the New Taiwan dollar (driving up export prices) and by the temporary vacuum of foreign investment on the mainland as the West and Japan imposed post-Tiananmen sanctions and Western investors fled. Trade and investment were to grow rapidly over the next twenty years with only relatively minor and temporary declines during crises. Moreover, the current account has been consistently imbalanced in Taiwan's favor, generating a huge foreign exchange surplus.

What drove cross-Strait détente? The major domestic factor on the mainland at this time was the policy of reform and opening to the outside world, including the establishment of special economic zones and a socialist market economy, which created domestic opportunities for outside investment while stressing multilateral friendship with all useful trade partners abroad. The accelerated industrialization after years of international economic isolation during Mao's quest for ideological purity generated a great need for capital and technology, which the more advanced Taiwan economy was well equipped to supply. The absence of a language barrier and the low wage rate, which the government was willing to keep low, were very attractive to Taiwan businesspeople facing rising living standards and industrial pollution concerns at home. On the Taiwan side, the major domestic factor was, ironically, democratization. The previous KMT dictatorship had been based on the assumption that the nation was still engaged in civil war, an emergency condition based on the threat of imminent communist attack necessitating the imposition of martial law. The lifting of martial law and the state of emergency implied that the threat was no longer potent: in the bloom of democratization, the immediate attraction to things previously forbidden was pervasive. Tourism boomed, Chinese literature and popular culture became accessible, and there was a lively interest in things Chinese, a "mainland fever" (*da lu re*). Taiwan's opening to China in the early 1990s slipped under the radar of the United States, which was then leading its allies in the imposition of economic sanctions on China for televised human rights violations.

Freeze, 1995–2005

While trade and investment continued to thrive, beginning in the mid-1990s political-diplomatic relations broke down almost entirely, and instead of moving further toward unification, Taiwan took tentative steps toward independence, which China condemned with increasing shrillness without being able to deter them. The immediate reason for this chill was that Taipei, well aware of the eventual political price of economic integration, was determined to "hedge" each step toward the mainland with another step toward integration with the global community, frustrating the mainland's sequestration strategy. Informal "vacation diplomacy" in Southeast Asia was followed by the summer 1995 visit and alumni address of Lee Teng-hui at Cornell University, his alma mater, in which he publicly lauded Taiwan's political and economic progress. Beijing was outraged by this alleged violation of the sovereignty they claimed over Taiwan (which the United States had acknowledged in the three communiqués), and they not only protested but also conducted a series of amphibious landing drills off the coast of Fujian province and launched short-range missiles to splash down off the coast of Taiwan's major ports. This exercise of coercive diplomacy lasted for months and finally was suspended after President Clinton sent two carrier groups to the vicinity of the island in February 1996. In Taiwan, this in effect chilled the economic climate and drove down support for the Democratic Progressive Party (DPP) presidential candidate, but it did not defeat Lee Teng-hui, who won Taiwan's first popular presidential election by a comfortable margin. Beijing attempted to get the relationship back on track by inviting SEF chair Koo Cheng-fu to the mainland in late 1998, but the following spring Lee Teng-hui again upset Beijing by asserting that China and Taiwan were both "states" (*guojia*) with a special state-to-state relationship. Thus the cross-Strait relationship was once again derailed.

The underlying domestic factor accounting for the freeze was that Taiwanese democracy proved to be a fickle ally of Beijing's reunification-through-economic-integration scheme. The Taiwanese public, initially entranced by the emergence of a dynamically reforming new China, was shocked by such incidents as the 1994 kidnapping and murder of thirty-two tourists and staff at Qiandao Lake in Zhejiang and by the botched official investigation. The greatest shock was, however, the 1994–95 missile crisis. Beijing's reunification strategy emphasized a warm socioeconomic welcome to Taiwanese "compatriots" (*tongbao*) while forbidding their diplomatic integration with the rest of the world or dangerous experiments with domestic democracy, which the electorate resented, and politicians learned to mobilize that resentment to win office. Thus, for example, Chen Shui-bian, the charismatic presidential candidate of the opposition DPP, won elections in 2000 and again in 2004 based on appeals to hold a referendum to endorse Taiwanese independence, redraft the constitution for an independent Republic of Taiwan, and win a Taiwanese seat in the United Nations. Thus the subethnic cleavage between *benshengren* and *waishengren*—namely, natives and mainlanders—based on simmering resentment of the Chiang dictatorship, was brought into alignment with the majority future nation preference for independence versus unification by identifying the KMT with contemporary China. Having won the presidency, Chen used his executive powers to try to remold the island's national identity from Chinese to Taiwanese, shifting education and research funding streams to Taiwanese history, and renaming streets, parks, museums, and holidays after distinctively Taiwanese heroes or events.

Beijing, for its part, responded with understandable alarm to this shift of national identity, which began in the 1990s after the missile crisis under Lee

Teng-hui and went into high gear under Chen Shui-bian. But warnings of possible imminent invasion turned out to be electorally counterproductive, and Beijing then lost credibility by failing to carry them out. Beijing, however, succeeded in appealing to the United States to help curb Taiwan's independence yearnings by in effect warning of the inevitability of cross-Strait war in that case while at the same time proffering a peaceful solution. This tricky position meant muting threats against Taiwan's independence advocates while accusing the DPP of courting a disaster that the PRC would then be "forced" to inflict. But the United States, fully engaged in Iraq and the global war on terror, needed China to help cope with North Korea and was not inclined to endorse a Taiwanese break for independence if it meant war with China. After the 2000 electoral setback, Beijing lapsed for the most part into dignified silence, refusing to negotiate with a deeply distrusted DPP government but no longer reacting so belligerently (and counterproductively) to Taiwanese provocations. From a triangular perspective, having aroused domestic sentiments to embrace a politically impossible dream, Taiwan thus fell into the worst possible position of a pariah facing a Sino-US marriage.

Rethaw, 2005–15

The rise of Hu Jintao and Wen Jiabao at the Sixteenth Party Congress in September 2002 marked the introduction of a more conciliatory foreign policy rhetoric (China's "peaceful rise," in a "harmonious world"), as well as a corresponding shift in China's Taiwan policy. In the 2004 election, Beijing tried to avoid making threats in the face of the DPP's sponsorship of two parallel referendums, relying instead on Washington to keep Chen in line. After Chen's narrow reelection in March 2004, Beijing revised its blanket hard line in favor of a more nuanced policy mixing carrots and sticks. In March 2005, the National People's Congress unanimously passed an anti-secession law, formalizing the threat of nonpeaceful means should Taipei declare independence, yet also omitting reference to the "one China" policy as a precondition for talks in a subtle signal accepting the "1992 Consensus" (one China, different interpretations). The CCP then revived their old history of united fronts in the form of the KMT-CCP Forum, which culminated in the 2005 Pan-Blue China visits including meetings between Hu and KMT chairman Lien Chan in April 2005 and a May meeting with People First Party (PFP) chair James Soong. When Chen Shui-bian reversed course and resumed his symbolic drive for independence by suspending the National Unification Council and National Unification Guidelines in early 2006, Beijing protested but avoided threats of force, relying on the United States to rebuke Chen for violating the "five noes" he had made after his election in 2000 and again in 2004. By thus lowering the temperature of cross-Strait relations and depriving the DPP of an obvious mainland threat to inveigh against, Beijing contributed to the KMT's landslide electoral victory in both legislative and presidential elections in 2008. All the same, Beijing maintained its military buildup against Taiwan, along with a quietly effective policy of isolating the island diplomatically.

The response of Taipei to Beijing's tactical shift was circumspect. Instead of talking about ultimate unification, successful presidential candidate Ma Ying-jeou advocated a status quo of neither unification nor independence that most people in Taiwan favored, attempting to redefine Taiwan's politics by shifting its central cleavage from national identity to the economy. The court case against Chen Shui-bian was a late-breaking windfall for the KMT that underscored its claims of the DPP's managerial incompetence with judicially supported allegations of high-level corruption. Because the performance of the DPP government in managing the economy left much to be desired, Ma calculated that his new strategy would win the 2008 presidential election, and he was right. But upon taking office after his 2008 victory, Ma and his new administration lost no time pursuing reconciliation with the mainland along the lines anticipated in the 2005 Pan-Blue visits to China, justifying this departure from campaign rhetoric by arguing that improved cross-Strait relations would improve the island's economy. Ma issued his "three noes"—no unification, no independence, no war (*butong, budu, buwu*)—in his inauguration speech to assure the electorate, maintaining silence about the ultimate destination of cross-Strait rapprochement. The cap was lifted on Taiwanese trade and investment with the mainland, and the SEF-ARATS negotiating forum was reconvened; by the end of 2009, the two sides had implemented the "three links," facilitating Chinese tourist visits of nearly three million in 2013 and nearly four million in 2014. Negotiations resulted in over twenty cross-Strait agreements, culminating in the summer of 2010 in the Economic Cooperation Framework Agreement, which reduced bilateral trade barriers and opened the way for Taiwan to negotiate analogous trade agreements with various Southeast Asian countries beginning with New Zealand and Singapore.

Economically, the upshot was an immediate acceleration of cross-Strait trade and investment and a marked upsurge in the island's GDP in 2008 and 2010, interrupted and followed by severe economic downturns. Taiwan's GDP growth since 2010 has lagged its peer group of "four tigers" (South Korea, Hong Kong, and Singapore),[12] falling well short of Ma's "633" campaign promise in 2008 (an annual GDP growth of 6 percent, a 3 percent unemployment rate, and an increase of per capita income to US$30,000). Taiwan's GDP, nearly half that of the PRC at the end of the Cold War, declined to a quarter of the PRC by 2000 and to less than a tenth by 2008.[13] Cross-Strait integration continued: Taiwan's trade dependency ratio is 70 percent, some 40 percent of which is with the PRC (up from 29 percent in 2010), while some 80 percent of Taiwan's foreign direct investment (FDI) goes to China (versus 50 percent in 2003). Economic dependency is asymmetrical—corresponding ratios for the mainland are lower and declining with its faster growth rate. While that puts Taiwan at a relative disadvantage, trade has stimulated the island's GDP growth, and the balance of trade remains in its favor.[14] Part of Taiwan's economic dismay can be attributed to the steady slowdown of the mainland economy each year since 2010.

The political-strategic implications of closer alignment with its greatest national security threat have also been questioned. China's arms buildup has quietly continued: by the end of 2014, the People's Liberation Army (PLA) had around 1,200 ballistic missiles aimed at Taiwan's cities, ten times more than in 2000; most of these are Dong Feng (DF) 11 and 13 medium-range missiles, more precise and destructive than those launched in 1995–96. Ma has repeatedly called for the PRC to dismantle its missile arsenal (most recently in the November 2015 Singapore summit with Xi Jinping), to no avail. The United States remains Taiwan's strongest strategic supporter, but US arms sales to Taiwan have declined over time.[15]

The result was that Ma's personal popularity steadily declined since his reelection in 2012, reaching a nadir of 9.2 percent in September 2013, adversely affecting his ability to advance his agenda. The Services Trade Agreement (STA), the intended next step toward economic integration after the Economic Coooperation Framework Agreement (ECFA) passed in 2010, stalled in the KMT-controlled legislature, reflecting factional splits over parliamentary procedure and declining public support. The sunflower student movement that occupied Taiwan's legislature for three weeks in March 2014 seems to have crystallized public opinion against the bill. In sum, the cross-Strait rethaw seems to have foundered on three flaws. First, the economic benefits of the program declined, and given the modest sociocultural and political appeal of closer cross-Strait relations this proved very costly. Second, the Ma administration proved politically incapable of educating the electorate to the value of the thaw, and voters came to oppose it for what may well have been empirically unfounded reasons. Third, in the wake of the more assertive PRC sovereignty claims in its near seas (with which the KMT identified), the United States shifted its publicly neutral position from crypto-support for the KMT in 2012 back to a more truly neutral position in the 2016 elections.

Refreeze, 2016

Taiwan, at just the time it seemed to have put the endlessly nettlesome cross-Strait problem to rest after a decade of cordial and mutually beneficial relations, appears to have resurrected it with the landslide defeat of its Pan-Blue sponsors. President Tsai Ing-wen has made clear her preference for no trouble with the mainland, but at the same time, she has failed to comply with the "one China" formula the mainland considers the bedrock of détente. Tsai is by nature a deliberate and cautious person not prone to the incendiary oratory or provocative proposals of Chen Shui-bian. But Beijing is deeply suspicious of Tsai as the former author of the two states theory in 1999 and as chair of the MAC at the time of Chen's repeated denials of the existence of any "1992 Consensus" as well as his 2001 "one country on each side" formulation. She has refused to endorse the 1992 Consensus that Beijing stipulates as prerequisite to talks, and cross-Strait communication channels have remained mute since her election. Beijing has effectively cut off tourist traffic to the island nation. With its March 2016 recognition of Gambia (and Sao Tome and Principe nine months later), Beijing has broken the diplomatic truce. Consensus expectations are that Beijing will proceed quietly but deliberately to cut off all diplomatic and economic lifelines at its disposal in order to teach the island a lesson. Not many nations are likely to protest, given that 172 of them have acknowledged that there is but one China and Taiwan is only a part of it. Will Taipei return once again to a thaw? Unfortunately the standoff is likely to last for some time. The KMT was defeated in 2016 by the largest majority in Taiwan's democratic history, and this must be attributed in part to Ma's cross-Strait policy, if only because it occupied such a central place in his agenda. The Tsai presidency thus marks a deliberate departure from Ma's policy that she is unlikely to forsake soon or cheaply. We may stand at the threshold of a brave, perilous new era in cross-Strait relations.

KOREA

Korea is similar to Taiwan in being an unstable outlier to China and source of potential instability, reliant on a distant security patron toward which there is some popular ambivalence. But it is different in many other respects. Most important, it is not part of China and China has no revisionist design to incorporate it.[16] The People's Republic of China's (PRC) relations with Korea are vital from historic, economic, and political perspectives. In October 1950, China sent its People's Volunteer Army to rescue the Democratic People's Republic of Korea (DPRK) from otherwise certain defeat, at a cost of some 390,000 casualties (according to official Chinese figures) and the lost chance to take Taiwan. The DPRK has since remained beholden to the PRC for its national security and, to a considerable extent, for its economic livelihood. China is the DPRK's largest trade partner by far and, since 2004, also the largest trade partner of South Korea, which (like Taiwan) enjoys a favorable trade balance with China.

Korea was historically a tributary state to China in its prime and an invasion route when China was vulnerable, from Hideyoshi Toyotomi in the sixteenth century to the Kwantung Army in the twentieth century. In many respects, China is now integral to the resolution of Korea's future, either as crucial facilitator of reunification or formidable veto power. On the other side is of course the United States, a more recent ally that blocked one violent attempt at reunification by a PRC-DPRK coalition in 1950, encouraged the democratization of the South, and is likely to retain veto power over any revision of the status quo not in its interest. Like China, both Koreas are relatively new to nation-statehood and, also like China, hungry for greater power and status. The South has sought that through one of the most rapid and successful economic modernizations in history; the North seeks it by becoming an internationally recognized nuclear weapon state. Both deem reunification a prerequisite to achieving their full national identity.

In all these divided nations, the prime impetus for reunification generally comes from the most successful half, under the plausible assumption that it can then dominate the reunified whole. We have seen this in the China-Taiwan case, where the former has consistently taken the initiative because of its asymmetric size and power despite a slower initial modernization. In the Korean case, on the other hand, the initiative has shifted between two more equal halves as their relative power balance has shifted. The DPRK— larger in area than the South, more abundantly endowed with natural resources, beneficiary of Japanese infrastructure investment during the colonial period,[17] and recipient of generous support from communist bloc countries,[18]—outpaced the South in GDP growth for its first two decades, thanks to these advantages plus the headlong mobilization of all these assets in extensive growth via command planning. The DPRK's policy was to seek immediate reunification by revolutionary violence to establish a centralized Federal Republic of Koryo, and has from the outset and fairly consistently thereafter placed a higher priority on reunification than the South.

While the Taiwan Strait impasse fits a triangular model very well, the Korean case is complicated by the involvement of more actors with a stake in the solution. The Korean War locked the balance of power into a relatively stable two plus two configuration: the North Korea–China alliance versus the South Korea–US alliance (plus relatively passive supporters on either side— Russia in the north, Japan in the south). This balance between North and South made any strictly bilateral attempt at coercive reunification highly risky. Thus the prerequisite to any plausible reunification scenario on the Korean peninsula, whether peaceful or violent, has always been to mobilize a decisive coalition on one side sufficient to overcome anticipated opposition from the other side. By June 1950, Kim Il-sung believed he had achieved that: first, he got Stalin's permission and promise of support (contingent on Chinese approval), and then he used this as leverage to procure Chinese support.[19] Meanwhile, the public US omission of Korea from its defense perimeter gave him reason to presume the United States would remain neutral.

Thus Kim launched the Korean War with a massive blitzkrieg designed to eliminate all resistance preemptively. It nearly succeeded, driving South Korean forces down to the tiny Pusan perimeter on the southern tip of the peninsula. But the United States unexpectedly mobilized a broad counter-coalition in the UN, and General Douglas MacArthur's counterattack was equally stunning, outflanking the North with an amphibious landing near Inchon and then proceeding to cut off the invasion force and drive north toward the Yalu River bounding Korea and China. This, in turn, precipitated intervention by a half million Chinese People's Volunteers, which again drove UN coalition forces south before a stalemate was finally achieved near the original line of demarcation. The deadlock lasted until Stalin's death in 1953. While in the initial postwar period the North, like the South, was preoccupied with domestic reconstruction (only two buildings remained standing in Pyongyang at the end of the war), in the following two decades the North launched a massive buildup aimed at achieving military superiority. In the early 1960s, the Korean People's Army (KPA) manpower is thought to have been just over three hundred thousand, while by the late 1970s the KPA was approaching one million, backed by a high and steadily rising share of economic output devoted to war readiness. Clearly the North had not given up its goal of revolutionary reunification. Yet the North refrained from a second invasion because neither China nor the Soviet Union, having gambled much and gained nothing in the first invasion, would support one.[20] Instead Kim's strategy was to launch a series of limited provocations, designed to weaken the South and perhaps trigger a casus belli for a second attack (e.g., the two tunnels discovered under the demilitarized zone [DMZ] in the 1970s, large enough for tanks). There are many lengthy lists of such provocations: in January 1968, North Korean commandos penetrated the Blue House in an assassination plot against the president, Park Chung-hee; in August 1974, DPRK agents attempted again to assassinate Park, instead killing his wife; in October 1983, seventeen senior members of Chun Doo Hwan's entourage in Rangoon were killed by a North Korean bomb; in November 1987, a Korean Airlines commercial jet flying out of Baghdad exploded in midair killing 115 passengers; and in 1996, twenty-six North Korean commandos infiltrated the South from an offshore submarine. More recently, in 2010, the North torpedoed the South Korean frigate *Cheonan* and, later that year, launched an unprovoked artillery barrage at Yeongpyong Island; both of these incidents took place just outside North Korean territorial waters, where the South had been holding military exercises. Provocations have continued against both hard-line and soft-line regimes in the South, during freeze or thaw.

Meanwhile, the economic modernization policy of the North slowed precipitously in the 1970s (nearing bankruptcy by the end of the decade),[21] while the South launched a more successful economic takeoff under the developmental dictatorship of Park Chung-hee. The cumulative result was that, by 2015, estimates of per capita GDP in the North were US$1,224 while the figure for the South was US$27,200, according to the Bank of Korea. The most critical period for the North was the 1990s, following the Tiananmen uprising in China and the ensuing collapse of communism in Eastern Europe and the Soviet Union. Both former economic patrons cut the North loose in their preoccupation with domestic crises. This coincided with a shift of the correlation of forces globally with the collapse of the communist bloc; particularly noteworthy from the Korean perspective was the peaceful reunification of Germany under democratic auspices. This inspired speculation that the North, too, would collapse and be absorbed by the South.

South Korea, having reached its era of high-speed GDP growth in 1988–98, took advantage of its relatively strong position to launch a bold new diplomatic strategy in July 1988 named Nordpolitik, in homage to the policy of Ostpolitik launched by Willy Brandt in the early 1970s to normalize relations with East Germany. This signature policy initiative of Roh Tae-woo overturned the doctrine of "the enemy of my enemy is my friend" to cultivate relations not only with the North but with both of Pyongyang's allies, the PRC and the USSR. The initiative proved surprisingly successful, garnering a breakthrough in the ROK's relations with both patron states: the USSR recognized South Korea in 1990 (at the price of a $3 billion loan) and the PRC recognized it in 1992. In 1991, Eastern Europe followed suit as well, as South Korea exchanged ambassadors with (now postcommunist) Poland, Yugsolavia, Romania, (then) Czechoslovakia, Bulgaria, and Outer Mongolia. In the same year, both South and North Korea gained admission to the United Nations. This was immediately followed by an increase in trade: South Korea's trade with China reached $3.1 billion in 1989, while trade with the USSR and Eastern Europe rose to $800 million. And trade has continued to flourish, particularly with the PRC: China-ROK trade increased from $6 billion in 1992 to over $300 billion in 2014, larger than South Korea's trade with the United States and Japan combined, according to the Korea International Trade Association (KITA).

The South Korean opening to the North, though welcomed by the PRC and the USSR, had a counterproductive impact in Pyongyang, where it was perceived as a serious threat. Kim Il-sung, stung by perceived betrayal and loss of face, reportedly even threatened to counter Beijing's recognition of Seoul by recognizing Taipei (it never happened). Coinciding with the upsurge in South Korean trade with both patron states was a precipitous drop in each country's trade with the DPRK, with catastrophic economic consequences for the North. The hitherto annual summits between Pyongyang and Beijing were suspended from 1992 until 2000, with Moscow still longer.[22] At the onset of the 1990s—and particularly in the wake of the first nuclear crisis (1993–94), when the United States branded the DPRK part of an "axis of evil"—a pattern of international ostracism set in. China began decreasing military aid to the DPRK (while continuing to provide economic support in the form of consumer goods). Pyongyang again requested military weapons in March 2003 at the end of the Iraq war, but China refused, advising Pyongyang to maintain a posture of self-restraint. The former Soviet Union, trying to cope with the unexpectedly devastating consequences of its abandonment of communism in 1991, cut off subsidized oil shipments to the North. North Korea plunged into famine, during which the economy averaged a negative 4.1 percent growth from 1991 to 1999, cutting GDP in half. Up to a million Koreans are estimated to have starved to death.

In the wake of economic catastrophe and abandonment by former patrons, the DPRK adopted the *songun* (military first) policy, spending around 25 percent of a stagnant budget on its large military establishment and redoubling efforts to develop nuclear weapons. This probably exacerbated the economic disaster by diverting scarce resources but may have saved the regime. Both China and Russia opposed North Korea's efforts at nuclear weapon development but were politely ignored. The International Atomic Energy Agency (IAEA) monitors detected these clandestine efforts and protested, whereupon Pyongyang kicked them out and opted to rescind its accession to the nuclear nonproliferation treaty. At this point, the United States considered a preemptive strike on Yongbyon to destroy the North Korean nuclear complex but also had to consider that this would likely start another Korean war with serious collateral damage to Seoul, home of nearly one-third of the South Korean populace. Yet when Jimmy Carter offered to mediate a dangerously escalating standoff, he found the doors to Pyongyang open. Carter then negotiated the Agreed Framework with Kim Il-sung in 1994 for the North to give up its quest for nuclear weapons (not nuclear power) in exchange for various diplomatic concessions from the United States, Japan, and South Korea. However, neither side then fulfilled its pledges.

For the next twenty years, Pyongyang would manage with great tenacity to pursue a covert nuclear weapons program while at the same time negotiating with the United States and the South to discontinue that program, first under the Agreed Framework and, after its collapse in 2002, under the six-party talks initiated in 2003 by Beijing. The ultimate upshot is that Pyongyang launched nuclear tests in 2006, 2009, 2013, twice in 2016, and 2017, along with numerous missile tests to find a capable delivery vehicle. Throughout this period, the North was dependent on foreign aid from the same countries opposing its nuclear program, using a combination of dire humanitarian need and the promise to negotiate an end to nuclear weapon development as leverage. None of the inducements introduced during either of these negotiation regimes—neither the sunshine policy (1992–2008) nor the contingent incentives policy of Lee Myung-bak and Park Geun-hye—had more than a superficial impact on nuclear development.

At the same time, though the North received a great deal of aid that might not have otherwise been available, none of the major incentives offered to compensate the North for giving up the bomb—diplomatic recognition, an end to sanctions, light-water reactors—was ever forthcoming. The DPRK's first nuclear test in 2006 was followed by renewed six-party negotiations leading to a denuclearization agreement in 2007, which broke down the following year over verification procedures. Rather than reviving talks to persuade the North to give up weapons it now vowed never to give up ("buying the same horse twice," as Robert Gates put it), the United States, after the second nuclear test in 2009, adopted a policy of strategic patience.[23] While urging unconditional resumption of the six-party talks and agreeing with the UN and other members of the talks to impose stringent sanctions, China has become the North's leading trade partner, foreign investor, and aid provider, with an increasingly positive balance of trade that has incited suspicion China is forgiving mounting North Korean debt.[24] Japan cut off trade with the North during the controversy over the abduction and imprisonment of Japanese citizens in 2004, and the South cut off trade after the second nuclear test, after which China became the North's main (ca. 92 percent) trade partner.

But there have always been two interdependent issues in Korea, and the nuclear issue is important but ancillary to the more basic issue of North-South reunification. On this issue, the relationship has been consistently antagonistic, sometimes clad in rhetorical raiments of tragically severed brotherhood for which reunification is offered as the ultimate solution but more often simply vituperative. The impact of the recently added nuclear issue has been to raise the international profile of the Korean problem while eclipsing the prospect of reunification. For the South and the West, nuclear disarmament becomes a prerequisite to further progress toward reconciliation; for the North, progress toward diplomatic recognition and a peace treaty is a prerequisite to discussion of the nuclear issue. Reflecting the shift in the peninsular balance of power since the Cold War, the South's interest in reunification has increased while since the late 1980s Pyongyang's view of national unification has become increasingly securitized.

South Korea's proposals have taken two forms, which can be characterized as hard and soft. The hard approach, under Roh Tae-woo and Kim Yong-sam, assumed that the North would collapse and be peacefully absorbed into the South, which would then assume the financial burden of rehabilitation and democratic modernization in the North. The soft approach, introduced by Kim Dae-jung and then followed by Roh Moo-hyun, assumed the North would survive indefinitely despite its economic difficulties and reunification must necessarily take place by mutual consent, thus promising never to try to undermine or absorb North Korea. Both, however, assumed the need for a preliminary period of economic and social integration. On September 11, 1989, Roh presented the Korean National Community Unification Formula (*Hanminjokgongdongchae tongilbangan*), a formula for unification through preliminary formation of a national community, which was passed in 1992 and has (in revised form) remained South Korea's official unification formula throughout the Kim Dae-jung, Roh Moo-hyun, Lee Myung-bak, and Park Geun-hye eras.[25] The Roh administration also initiated regularly scheduled prime ministerial talks with the North, culminating at the sixth round in February 1992 in signing two important documents: the Basic Agreement on Reconciliation, Nonaggression and Exchanges, and the Joint Declaration on the Denuclearization of the Korean Peninsula, as a result of which all American tactical nuclear weapons were withdrawn from Korea by the end of 2001.[26] The Kim Dae-jung approach, quickly dubbed the "sunshine policy" in reference to Aesop's famous fable, was premised on the separation of politics from economics and the principle of flexible reciprocity, seeking to insulate economic integration from political tension. And indeed, over the next decade, stimulated by some two hundred inter-Korean political talks and two summit meetings in Pyongyang, forty-two inter-Korean agreements were signed between the two Koreas—seventeen during the Kim Dae-jung administration and twenty-five during the Roh Moo-hyun administration. A joint venture was set up to facilitate tourism to Mt. Kumgang, and the Kaesong Industrial Complex (KIC) was jointly established near the DMZ to exploit South Korean capital and North Korean labor. Inter-Korean trade increased: by 2002, the ROK had become the DPRK's second-largest trading partner after China; by 2008, after Japan bowed out on the abductee issue, China (40 percent) and South Korea (26 percent, or around $1.82 billion) became the DPRK's two leading trading partners, together claiming 66 percent of Pyongyang's total trade.

But the two issues could not easily be detached. Public support for "sunshine" dropped steadily in the 2000s as the North continued nuclear development while engaging in talks not to do so.[27] With the election of Lee Myung-bak in 2008, all momentum toward inter-Korean economic integration leading to political accord was lost. After reaching its acme in 2008, trade plummeted after the second test in 2009, leaving China the DPRK's main trade partner. Based on evidence that aspects of the previous sunshine regime (including the 2000 summit) had been underwritten by covert political subsidies and that the separation of politics and economics had been largely illusory, the new president attached demands for political reciprocity.[28] These were promptly met by indignant refusals and threats from the North. All joint North-South economic ventures were closed save for KIC (which ultimately also closed in 2015). Lee was succeeded as chair of the Grand National Party (GNP; now Saenuri, or New Frontier Party) and president by Park Chung-hee's oldest daughter Geun-hye. She distanced herself from Lee to introduce Trustpolitik, a diplomacy based on incremental progress and rhetorical moderation. Strict reciprocity remained, but Park agreed with the soft line in seeking to detach reunification from the issue of nuclear disarmament. She gave a major speech outlining her vision in Dresden and, in 2014, convened the National Unification Advisory Council to pursue it. Both Kim and Park suggested another summit in their 2015 New Year's addresses, though subsequent events were not propitious, with two North Korean nuclear tests and the impeachment of President Park Geun-hye. Park's Trustpolitik had been embedded in a strategy analogous to Nordpolitik in bracing inter-Korean détente with an end run to Beijing. This appeared highly successful in Beijing, as Park had seven visits with Xi Jinping (including attending in China a 2015 military parade celebrating victory over Japan) while Kim Jung-un has yet to visit Beijing. It was, however, utterly unsuccessful in moving toward either nuclear disarmament or North-South reconciliation.

The year 2017 ushered in new leadership in both the United States and South Korea. Barack Obama alerted Donald Trump during their transition talks that North Korea would be his most urgent issue, tacitly conceding that the strategic patience policy he had pursued for the last eight years had been a failure. This urgency was underscored by the January 1 announcement by Kim Jung-un that within the next year the North would test an intercontinental ballistic missile (ICBM) capable of delivering a nuclear missile on the continental United States. "It won't happen," tweeted Donald Trump. Over the next several months, the Trump administration applied a combination of hard and soft power to induce Pyongyang to move toward nuclear disarmament. Trump sent carriers to North Korean waters, declared that strategic patience was over, and adjured Xi Jinping to put pressure on the North, warning that if the Chinese could not solve the problem the United States would do so. At the same time, he made clear that his demands were limited to security, that regime change was not in the cards, and that he would be honored to meet with Kim Jung-un under the right circumstances. The North responded that it, too, would be willing to talk under the right circumstances and continued its missile tests. In the South, the new president, Moon Jae-in, elected on promises of implementing "sunshine 2.0," has yet to elicit interest in rapprochement from the North and, meanwhile, is trapped between Chinese demands that he reverse installation of the terminal high-altitude area defense (THAAD) antimissile system and US demands that he uphold the sanctions regime, which would make any revival of intercourse with the North impossible. Moon is also beset by all the other problems of a new Korean presidency—prosecuting his predecessor, staffing a cabinet with honest officials, reviving a slowing economy, and fulfilling campaign promises to take down the chaebols. The situation has become very labile.

Thus after a period of innovation and diplomatic realignment under Nord-politik, the Koreas seem to have returned to their original "two versus two plus" configuration, with the United States supporting the South and China in effect protecting a North that it publicly condemns. Russia's position mirrors China's, and Japan's essentially follows the United States (with more focus on the abductees issue). North Korea, though having used its development of nuclear weapons to avoid potential collapse, remains on economic life support. Trade with the South as well as the West has collapsed in the sanctions regime, and China has become North Korea's most important ally, biggest trading partner, and main source of food, arms, and energy. While Seoul continues to rely on the United States for security protection, it now looks chiefly to Beijing to solve the riddle of the DPRK threat and beyond that, reunification. The sanctions policy has not deterred the DPRK's nuclear program; rather, it has ironically neutralized the influence of the United States, Japan, and the ROK while enhancing the diplomatic indispensability of China, because China still offers something to the North that can be withheld (e.g., Beijing briefly cut off oil supplies in 2003 and 2006–7, and threatened to do so again in April 2017) while the others are bereft of direct diplomatic access, carrots and sticks. The failure of sanctions to achieve results is attributed to Beijing, which continues normal trade with the North while giving lip service to sanctions, allowing the DPRK to survive and continue nuclear and missile development.[29] The chief beneficiary of this outcome (aside from North Korea) is China, which now monopolizes North Korean trade. Yet blaming Beijing, as the United States continues to do under Trump, has achieved very little so far aside from enhancing China's political and economic impact on the North.

CONCLUSIONS

Both the China-Taiwan and the Korean case have schizoid foreign policies, oriented both to outside powers and to the other half; both have tried (inconclusively) to bring them into alignment. To do so might offer stability and resolution of their national identity dilemma. But the two have now been split more than sixty years, divided not only by war and ideology but by different socioeconomic systems. In both cases, the larger and stronger half has taken the initiative, anticipating that it would then lead the reunified whole (as in the German precedent). The boldest initiative in the Taiwan case was the "three links" and "one country, two systems" initiative of Deng Xiaoping in the early 1980s, offering a path to peaceful reunification with considerable autonomy. In the Korean case, initiative passed from North to South with the relative economic rise of the South; here the most spectacular initiative was Seoul's Nordpolitik, which attempted to dislodge the North from its traditional alliance system. But in both cases, old alignment patterns proved resilient. In the China-Taiwan case, China's rise has in effect blocked any feasible path to independence in Taiwan while at the same time making peaceful reunification less attractive because a now relatively smaller and weaker Taiwan can no longer realistically hope for the mainland to make many accommodations to Taiwan's democracy. In the Korean case, Nordpolitik successfully isolated the North but also posed such a serious threat to its existence that it turned to nuclear weapons for security. And the South's sunshine diplomacy was never really trusted by the North, which took advantage of the South's largesse without making sincere or lasting concessions, keeping the South at bay with a series of provocations and with the development of nuclear weapons (which have served the same function).

The Taiwan Strait imbroglio is ideally suited to triangular analysis, as China and the United States loom above all other states in any realistic appraisal of the island's security outlook. The original configuration was embedded in the Cold War ideological and treaty framework, as Taiwan formed an alliance with the United States and China allied itself with the Soviet Union, thereby locking the Taiwan triangle in place. Both sides strove for reunification on zero-sum terms but neither could put together a strong enough coalition to achieve this. Though prepared to defend the island against unprovoked attack, the United States had no interest in unleashing Chiang for a high-risk attempt at reunification, while the Soviet Union was even less interested in honoring its alliance commitments if China tried to take a Taiwan linked to the United States. Indeed, that was among the main reasons the alliance became moot. In the wake of the Sino-Soviet dispute, reunification prospects essentially dissolved: China, now a triangular pariah, was severely weakened after the Great Leap failure and in no position to confront the United States over Taiwan without Soviet nuclear protection.

The end of the Cold War, however, substantially improved triangular mobility. China exited the strategically useless alliance with the USSR while still maintaining cordial relations with its northern neighbor, but more important, normalized diplomatic relations with the United States. With American tacit approval, China offered Taiwan its most attractive package for peaceful reunification: a high degree of autonomy in a "one country, two systems" framework. And Taiwan responded positively, after initial hesitation. Under a political framework both sides could tentatively agree upon, trade and tourism led investment and cross-Strait economic integration took off. China's political objective was to change the triangle from a Taiwan-US marriage into a Chinese-US marriage, and for a while, it seemed time was on its side. But the reunification train has run off the rails, for one essential reason: all three sides wanted more than their initial agreement set forth. The United States wanted above all for the problem to be peacefully resolved without further trouble, but China was unwilling to give up its sovereign right to use force to coerce Taiwan, optimally to reunify but at least not to declare independence. China ultimately wanted "one China," meaning sovereignty over Taiwan within the existing People's Republic. And Taiwan ultimately wanted sovereignty, with full participation in regional and international affairs. While all three were temporarily willing to repress their ultimate goals for short-term gain, the submerged presence and periodic reemergence of these end goals created a climate of bad faith and suspicion that impeded further integration.

Triangular logic applies to Korea as well, but only with poetic license. In the Korean case, the initial framework has proved ultrastable, as a China-DPRK alliance faced a US-ROK alliance, and both alliances have remained more credible than the Sino-Soviet alliance. So the goal has been triangular construction rather than manipulation (i.e., to put together a coalition of at least two great powers while neutralizing the great power support of the opposition). The DPRK thought it had achieved this by July 1950, having secured the support of both China and the USSR while the United States was believed to be neutralized. Faced with armed assault the United States, however, shed its neutrality and even obtained UN endorsement for a defense of the South, and the war ended in stalemate. At the end of the Cold War, Roh Tae-woo changed the balance to the South's advantage via a diplomatically shrewd Nordpolitik. The consequent alienation of both former patrons (coinciding with their manifest weakness during this period of worldwide communist collapse) had catastrophic consequences on the North. Although this breakthrough was followed up by conciliatory approaches to the North under Kim Dae-jung and Roh Moo-hyun, including movement toward economic integration, the changed power balance aroused an acute sense of insecurity in the North that inspired the drive to nuclear weaponization. This drive more than anything else induced US intervention, which in turn prompted Chinese countervailing intervention as host of the six-party talks. Despite subsequent attempts to detach the two issues, nuclear disarmament has subsequently upstaged and obstructed any attempt at North-South reconciliation, let alone reunification.

Hyug-Baeg Im and Yu-Jeong Choi are correct in deeming the two Chinas to have made greater progress toward peaceful reunification than the two Koreas.[30] Modernization has facilitated economic integration and brought the two sides of the Strait to an economically convergent course, with growing intermixing of populations, even families. Lifestyles and living standards are now comparable in Taipei and Shanghai, with career opportunities sometimes better in the latter. Certainly one of the world's largest trade and investment linkages inhibits any resort to coercive reunification. Yet paradoxically, after a decade of seemingly successful cross-Strait socioeconomic integration, interest in reunification in Taiwan has not waxed but waned—it is substantially lower than in South Korea. Part of the reason is that while the economic inducements the mainland offers Taiwan compatriots were attractive, since the relationship is so exclusively economic, once the economy slows down (as it has since 2010) there is little left to hold it together. What is left is political cultural convergence, which remains relatively tenuous, interrupted by threats and contingent on hopes for meaningful Chinese political cal reform. And the fate of reform amid the post-2010 economic slowdown has not been encouraging. The loss of performance legitimacy leads to a resort to nationalism and a narrowing of the political cultural spectrum.

Both divided nations are perennial trouble spots not only because of the tensions attending reunification but because they have complicating links to great powers, and local crises can hence reverberate into great power conflict. Both patron states support reunification and nonproliferation in principle, but their core interests are in their own national security; given the risks, they prefer not to get involved unless that is tangibly threatened. Their intervention hence tends to be triggered only by a perceived shift in the balance of power in the two dyads. And at bottom the United States and China have different interests regarding Taiwan and Korea. From the US perspective, the reunification of China will make Taiwan China's open door to the Pacific and the first step in its ambition to win uncontested control of its peripheral waters and break through the first island chain, entailing a shift in the East Asian power balance. From Beijing's perspective, a united Korea must be expected to lean South, bringing US troops to the banks of the Yalu (from which China chased them at great cost in 1950–53). If Pyongyang needs nuclear weapons to forestall reunification, Beijing may be able to swallow its principled misgivings more easily than the United States, especially as those weapons are unlikely to be aimed westward.[31] While the United States is comfortable with the status quo in Taiwan China is comfortable with the status quo in Korea. Thus a resolution of these local flashpoints ultimately presupposes the resolution (or compromise) of the larger struggle between the powers. A triangular configuration can provide some measure of protection to smaller powers, but it cannot heal national division.

NOTES

1. On divided nations, see, among others, John J. Metzler, *Divided Dynamism: The Diplomacy of Separated Nations: Germany, Korea, China* (Lanham, MD: University Press of America, 1996); Jaushieh Joseph Wu, ed., *Divided Nations: The Experience of Germany, Korea, and China* (Taipei, Taiwan: Institute of International Relations, National Chengchi University, 1995); Weiqun Gu, *Conflicts of Divided Nations: The Cases of China and Korea* (Greenwood, CT: Praeger, 1995); and Samuel S. Kim, *The Two Koreas and the Great Powers* (New York: Cambridge University Press, 2006).

2. Holding CPPCC membership is a violation of Taiwanese law that bars citizens from taking positions in state or party bodies in China. The Association of Taiwan Investment Enterprises on the Mainland (ATIEM), which lists some 130 Taiwanese business associations across China as members, met with Taiwanese president Ma Ying-jeou in December 2012 to

try to change that. But the Mainland Affairs Council announced that same month that Taiwanese could not sit on the CPPCC. It is, however, legal to be an honorary, nonvoting CPPCC member, and some Taiwanese businesspeople are honorary members.

3. Charter of the Workers' Party of Korea, https://en.wikipedia.org/wiki/Charter_of_the_Workers%27_Party_of_Korea. There are two DPRK constitutions: a People's Constitution (1948) and a Juche Constitution (1972). Cf. Constitution of North Korea, https://en.wikipedia.org/wiki/Constitution_of_North_Korea#1972_Juche_Constitution.

4. Not a single country recognized both Seoul and Pyongyang in the 1950s and 1960s, but by 1976 some forty-nine countries had already done so without incurring diplomatic severance from Pyongyang or Seoul, and in 2001, both gained simultaneous representation in the UN. By 2005, the number of states recognizing both Koreas reached 152, 80 percent of UN membership. Kim, *The Two Koreas and the Great Powers*, 345. Yet since the Cold War, the South, with its export-oriented growth strategy, has pursued a more active foreign policy than the North.

5. The ideas of "united" and "divided" nationalism are not mutually exclusive. For example, in the China-Taiwan case, "united" nationalism was evoked by the dispute over China's claims in the East and South China Seas, which are identical with Taiwan's claims—and Ma Ying-jeou concomitantly rose to defend them, to Beijing's delight. But "divided" nationalism has generally been a more powerful electoral force.

6. It remains, however, unclear to which "China" Taiwan was returned. The Cairo Conference (November 1943) promised the return of "all the territories Japan has stolen from the Chinese," and this was reaffirmed in the Potsdam Declaration in 1945. ROC troops accepted the Japanese surrender on Taiwan in October 1945. The CCP interpretation is that, having won the civil war, the People's Republic of China that was established in Beijing on October 1, 1949, was the legitimate successor of the Nationalist government and rightful claimant of all Chinese territory including Taiwan. The Nationalist interpretation is that, although temporarily defeated and forced to seek refuge on Taiwan, the civil war had not been concluded: Nationalist forces would regroup and recover the mainland from the "Communist bandits" (*gong fei*); meanwhile, Taiwan was the provisional headquarters of the exiled Republic of China. The CCP leadership also recognized the provisional status of their victory and fully expected to invade Taiwan and finish the job—and the United States, despite having supported the losing side, shared that expectation, evacuating extraneous US diplomatic personnel as early as May 1950. But when the Korean War broke out in June 1950, the Truman administration quickly changed its tune, ordering the Seventh Fleet to defend the island. Yet despite its recognition of the ROC as the legal government of China, the United States oddly refused to acknowledge its sovereignty over Taiwan, whose status remained undetermined. Steven M. Goldstein, *China and Taiwan* (Malden, MA: Polity Press, 2015), 20–22.

7. John F. Copper, *Taiwan: Nation-State or Province?* (Boulder, CO: Westview Press, 2009), 86.

8. Taiwan was deserted diplomatically but not militarily (see below).

9. Cf. Margaret MacMillan, *Nixon and Mao: The Week That Changed the World* (New York: Random House, 2007).

10. Nancy Bernkopf Tucker, *Strait Talk: United States–Taiwan Relations and the Crisis with China* (Cambridge, MA: Harvard University Press, 2009), 41–51.

11. Yitan Li, "Constructing Peace in the Taiwan Strait: A Constructivist Analysis of the Changing Dynamics of Identities and Nationalisms," *Journal of Contemporary China* 23, no. 85 (2014): 119–42.

12. Since 2008, Taiwan's economic performance has been volatile, moving from 7 percent in 2008 to minus 7 percent in 2009 to 9 percent in 2010 to 7 percent in 2011 to around .01 percent in 2012. Growth has also been less equally distributed, with a Gini index of 0.32 in 2000, increasing to .35 in 2001 and remaining around .34 since then.

13. China's gross domestic product (GDP) was $1.198 trillion in 2000 and $4.519 trillion in 2008. By contrast, Taiwan's GDP in 2000 was $326 billion in 2000 and a little more than $400 billion in 2008. World Economic Outlook Database, International Monetary Fund, http://www.imf.org/external/pubs/ft/weo/2011/02/weodata/index.aspx.

14. By classification, 37 percent of Taiwanese exports are electronic equipment, which is also Taiwan's main export to China. China's largest export is also electronic equipment, accounting for 25 percent of all exports. At least seven of the top ten electronic equipment exporters are Taiwanese-owned companies. The reason is simple: China is the final assembly point in the global supply chain that is the modern information technology industry. Any drop in Taiwanese exports to China would soon be reflected in China's exports. Moreover, collectively Taiwanese companies employ more than seventy million Chinese, making them by far the biggest private sector employers in the country.

15. The United States delivered $4.3 billion in weapons to Taiwan in the 2004–7 period and $3.7 billion in 2008–11. Shirley A. Kan, *Taiwan: Major U.S. Arms Sales since 1990* (Washington, DC: Congressional Research Service, July 23, 2014). The Obama administration made the only major sale in over four years in December 2015.

16. The 2001–4 scholarly discourse claiming the ancient kingdom of Koguryo as a Chinese province, however, has been interpreted by some South Koreans as a potential claim on Korean territory.

17. The post–World War II division of the peninsula resulted in advantages and disadvantages for both the North and the South. In 1945, about 65 percent of Korean heavy industry was in the North but only 31 percent of light industry, 37 percent of agriculture, and 18 percent of the peninsula's total commerce. Tino Sanandaji, "North Korean Economic History," *Tino Sanandaji* (blog), June 27, 2010, http://tino.us/2010/06/north-korean-economic-history/.

18. North Korea was dependent on fraternal assistance for more than 80 percent of its industrial reconstruction needs between 1954 and 1956, the period of its first three-year plan. China was the second-largest contributor after the Soviet Union, the rest of the Council for Mutual Economic Assistance (COMECON) countries a close third. During this period, Kim Il-sung shrewdly balanced Pyongyang's dependency on foreign patronage, purchasing most weaponry from the USSR, for example, because it was more technically advanced.

19. Cf. Sergey Radchenko, *Two Suns in the Heavens: The Sino-Soviet Struggle for Supremacy, 1962–1967* (Stanford, CA: Stanford University Press, 2009); and Lorenz Luethi, *The Sino-Soviet Split* (Princeton, NJ: Princeton University Press, 2008). For a perspective underscoring intra-alliance differences during even this early period, see Thomas J. Christensen, *Worse than a Monolith: Alliance Politics and Problems of Coercive Diplomacy in Asia* (Princeton, NJ: Princeton University Press, 2011).

20. Kim reportedly frequently lobbied Beijing to support a second invasion, notably, after the fall of Saigon in 1975.

21. In 1980, Pyongyang defaulted on all of its loans except those from Japan. By the end of 1986, hard-currency debt had reached more than US$1 billion. Pyongyang also owed more than US$2 billion to communist creditors, principally the Soviet Union. The Japanese also declared North Korea in default.

22. Jin Moo Kim, "North Korea's Reliance on China and China's Influence on North Korea," *Korean Journal of Defense Analysis* 23, no. 2 (June 2011): 257–71.

23. Robert Gates: "I'm tired of buying the same horse twice," quoted by David E. Sanger, "US Weighs Intercepting North Korean Shipments," *New York Times*, June 7, 2009, http://www.nytimes.com/2009/06/08/world/asia/08korea.html.

24. The DPRK's trade dependency on China reached US$5.63 billion in 2011, an increase of 62.5 percent over the previous year. China's trade with North Korea rose to $3.1 billion in the first half of 2012, a rise of 24.7 percent; the 2011 trade figures of $5.7 billion represent a 62.4 percent gain over 2010. Meanwhile, trade with South Korea, hitherto North Korea's second-biggest trade partner, stopped growing in 2007 and dropped by 10 percent in 2011. Korea Trade Investment Promotion Agency (KOTRA) estimates indicate an increase of trade dependency on China from 42 percent in 2008 to over 70 percent in 2011.

25. Young Ho Park, "South and North Korea's Views on the Unification of the Korean Peninsula and Inter-Korean Relations" (Korean Institute for National Unification Paper 21, January 2014), 8, http://www.brookings.edu/~/media/events/2014/1/21%20korean%20peninsula%20unification/park%20young%20ho%20paper.pdf.

26. Roh Tae-woo, "July 7, 1988 Declaration in the Interest of National Self-Esteem, Unification, and Prosperity," in *Korea under Roh Tae-woo: Democratisation, Northern Policy, and Inter-Korea Relations*, ed. James Cotton (Canberra: Allen and Unwin, 1993).

27. Public support for the sunshine policy dropped sharply from 76.9 percent in 1998 to 33.9 percent in 2001. See Alec Axelblom, "Republic of Korea's Sunshine Policy: The Sweeping Fall in Support for the Sunshine Policy and the Role of the Ministry of Unification during the Tumultuous Sunshine Years," Master's thesis in Asian studies, University of Lund, http://lup.lub.lu.se/luur/download?func=downloadFile&recordOId=8922967&fileOId=8922968.

28. In his 2014 presidential memoir (roughly translated, My Time as President), Lee Myung-bak disclosed North Korea requested an inter-Korean summit five times, but he refused because Pyongyang requested corn, rice, fertilizer, and US$10 billion to fund a development bank. The proposals ended after Lee demanded an apology for sinking the *Cheonan*.

29. See the UN's recent report on compliance with the sanctions resolutions. The report lists Chinese involvement in six out of nine cases of prohibited arms transfers, and twelve out of sixteen cases of activities abroad by North Korean entities under sanction. The report's observation that there have been no changes in the pattern of air force sorties by the DPRK also seems to contradict China's claim that it has strictly limited aviation fuel sales to the regime.

30. Hyug-Baeg Im and Yu-Jeong Choi, "Inter-Korean and Cross-Strait Relations through the Window of Regional Integration Theories," *Asian Survey* 51, no. 5 (September–October 2011): 785–811.

31. To be sure, after the test of Pyongyang's midrange Hwasong-12 missile in early May 2017, a North Korean lecturer assured a group of state officials that China's cities are within range of DPRK missiles.

Chapter Six

Moralist Center

Southeast Asia, like China, joined the sweepstakes of the newly industrialized countries (NICs) in the late twentieth century. Previously it had been something of an exotic backwater, a cultural and economic meeting point between South Asia and East Asia. Geographically the region is divided into maritime Southeast Asia (the Philippines, Malaysia, Brunei, East Timor, Papua New Guinea, and Indonesia) and mainland Southeast Asia, also known as Indochina (Vietnam, Laos, Cambodia, Myanmar/Burma, Singapore, and Thailand). In terms of religious impact, the region owes to South Asia the influence of Theravada Buddhism, Hinduism, and Islam; from Northeast Asia comes Mahayana Buddhism and Confucianism; and from the West, Christianity in all its forms. Influential modern idea systems include democratic liberalism, capitalism, and communism. Linguistically, economically, and ethnoculturally it is perhaps the most diverse region on earth, ranging from Singapore, a highly developed city-state with a per capita gross domestic product (GDP) approaching that of the United States, to largely agrarian developmental states like Cambodia or Laos.

All but two of the sovereign states of the region (East Timor and Papua New Guinea, both candidates for membership) are members of the Association of Southeast Asian Nations (ASEAN), an intergovernmental organization (IGO) established in 1967. With a combined GDP of US$2.9 trillion in 2015 (3 percent of global GDP) and a combined population of 625 million and a healthy foreign direct investment (FDI) to gross domestic product (GDP) ratio of 52 percent, Southeast Asia now has the fourth-largest GDP in Asia after China, India, and Japan, and the seventh largest in the world. The GDP of the region is projected to grow by more than 5 percent per annum over the next five years, well above the expected global average, while intra-ASEAN trade is expected to exceed US$1 trillion.

Southeast Asia was previously intersected by the political and cultural influences of India and China. But China isolated itself since the end of the Ming dynasty, and the influence of India was broken during the colonial era, when both South and Southeast Asia fell under the sway of Western imperialism. Since post–World War II decolonization, the predominant outside influences on the region have come from the north (China) and the east (the United States). Of course other great powers have also been influential: Japan, after militarily overrunning the region during World War II, has limited its postwar presence to diplomatic and commercial penetration, particularly after the 1985 Plaza Accord revaluation of Japanese currency made it an attractive investment opportunity. Russia's influence during the Cold War, on the other hand, was mostly strategic, with a submarine-launched ballistic missile fleet in the Sea of Okhotsk (based in Vladivostok) and mutual defense alliances with China, North Korea, and Vietnam.[1] After gaining independence in 1947, India was a leader (along with China, Indonesia, and Burma) of the nonaligned movement in such forums as the Bandung Conference but tended to neglect Southeast Asia during much of the Cold War. Beginning in 1991, the Rao government sought to revive interest with a Look East policy (upgraded to the Act East policy in 2014 by Narendra Modi), in 1996 India was included in the ASEAN Regional Forum (ARF), signed ASEAN's Treaty of Amity and Cooperation (TAC) in 2003, and was included in the East Asia Summit (EAS) in 2005.

In view of the predominant contemporary outside influence of China and the United States, international politics in Southeast Asia takes place mainly in three arenas: the intraregional or intra-ASEAN arena, Sino-ASEAN relations, and ASEAN-US relations. Hence the organization of this chapter will consist of three parts: The first part will outline the foreign policy predispositions of the three principals: ASEAN, China, and the United States. The second presents the triangular format that will be used to analyze the interaction between the three. The third part analyzes seriatim each of three successive patterns of interaction over time. A brief conclusion follows.

POLITICAL DISPOSITIONS

A foreign policy predisposition refers to a nation's general orientation toward relevant other nations in the international firmament; the term "relevant" is defined by geographic propinquity, economic interests, population, history, and national identity. There is perpetual conflict about and demands for redefinition of a foreign policy disposition, as different constituencies contend to stretch identity to fit their own material and ideal interests. But once it takes coherent form, it can be used (or misused) to build consensus around a policy course and sanction dissidents as unpatriotic. It can also in some cases imbue a lasting sense of "mission" to proselytize one's national identity to relevant others, or to strengthen one's identity by nesting it among some set of similar identities.

Southeast Asia, to begin with the most challenging and controversial case, is heir to an ancient literate civilization in which vast empires (the Srivijaya in Indonesia, the Pagan in Myanmar, the Angkor in Cambodia) long contended for dominance. The region succumbed to imperialist rule (with the lonely exception of Thailand) in the nineteenth century, but this was not a unifying experience as each European power carved out its own colony: the Dutch in Indonesia, the British in Burma and Malaysia, Spain followed by the United States in the Philippines, the French in Indochina, and the Germans in Papua New Guinea. The Japanese invasion emancipated these colonies from Western imperialism only to impose one of their own, but the 1945 Japanese defeat did not immediately end hostilities. The return of European imperialism was violently but successfully resisted, followed by ethnic and ideological insurgencies and other intramural conflicts (e.g., the 1962–66 Konfrontasi between Indonesia and newly created Malaysia). The creation of the Association of Southeast Asian Nations (ASEAN) in 1967, initially consisting of the five leading southern nations, then including Brunei, enhanced internal cooperation as set forth in the Declaration of Bali Concord 1976, and admitted the four Indochina states—Vietnam in 1995, followed by Laos and Myanmar in 1997 and Cambodia in 1999. The association was to some extent patterned after the European Union but less ambitious, employing a staff of only about three hundred at its Jakarta headquarters. Never explicitly aiming at a fully integrated superstate, ASEAN aspired to speed economic growth, social progress, regional peace, and stability among its members. Organizationally it is an anarchic regime based on consensual democracy or unit veto, sometimes criticized as a "talk shop" that has many meetings but gets little done.

However fragmented, ASEAN has been ambitious to spread its influence into the post–Cold War world. To do so, it has aspired to forge its own collective identity, and to socialize its members and associates to adhere voluntarily to a common set of norms—to a culture of restraint and to the three Rs of the ASEAN Way: restraint, respect, and responsibility. These norms are set forth in the treaties, declarations, and agreements in ASEAN, starting with those outlined in the 1967 Bangkok Declaration and elaborated in subsequent declarations and agreements. This so-called ASEAN Way was defined by Malaysian academic Noordin Sopiee as the "[p]rinciple of seeking agreement and harmony, the principle of sensitivity, politeness, non-confrontation and agreeability, the principle of quiet, private and elitist diplomacy versus public washing of dirty linen, and the principle of being non-Cartesian, non-legalistic."[2] This spirit suffuses all ASEAN statements of diplomatic principles, such as the 2002 Treaty of Amity and Cooperation

(TAC), to which all members or associates must commit in order to join: (1) respect for sovereignty and territorial integrity, (2) noninterference in internal affairs, (3) settlement of disputes by peaceful means, and (4) renunciation of threat or use of force. And the transformation has indeed been impressive: since 1967 no interstate wars have been fought in Southeast Asia, a respectable rate of growth has been achieved, and economic cooperation has increased.

The US historic disposition to Southeast Asia is similar to that to the rest of Asia—somewhat more intimate perhaps, as it became engaged in colonialism, taking advantage of the 1898 Spanish-American War at a time of intense domestic nationalism to seize Guam and the Philippines (after five years of fierce resistance). As in the China case, the Orient (as it was then called) was prized for its exoticism and frequented by traders and Christian missionaries. After World War II, the United States was ideologically inclined to support decolonization (it did withdraw from the Philippines), only to backtrack after the 1950 invasion of South Korea to support the French and the British in their efforts to suppress communist liberation movements that arose against Japan and then turned against returning Western imperialism. The United States soon became the main cheerleader and bankroller of Western anticommunist resistance. Vietnam was the main theater of militant US anticommunism, but it also veered into Cambodia and Laos. After this bitterly unsuccessful intervention, the United States withdrew militarily from the region under tacit agreement with China during the Nixon visit to do likewise. Led now by its private sector, the United States has continued an active economic engagement in the region. ASEAN is the leading Asian recipient of US foreign direct investment (FDI), with around US$150 billion (more than China, India, South Korea, Taiwan, and Hong Kong combined); the United States is ASEAN's fourth-largest overseas market (generating exports worth roughly the same as those of China and nearly four times those of India), with total two-way trade in goods and services of $260 billion (as of 2015), and its third-largest trade partner. The United States also gives about four times as much developmental aid to the region as China, which specializes in subsidized loans. Moreover, the region is a favored business location for American multinationals (3,700 in Singapore alone). In 2007, the United States was the first country to nominate an ambassador to ASEAN, later given official residence in Jakarta. The Barack Obama administration elevated US engagement with ASEAN, signing the Treaty of Amity and Cooperation, paving the way for participation in the East Asia Summit, and inaugurating annual Ten Plus One ASEAN-US summits. American political interest in the region, however, has been episodic.

China's disposition toward Southeast Asia actually has been quite similar to the American, seeing it as a region of economic opportunity. While China has historically been invaded or threatened from the west, the east, and the north, it has never been threatened from the south. Contrariwise it has some-times represented a security threat to its southern neighbors, notwithstanding its own conception of its historical identity as a harmonious, peace-loving civilization. China invaded and occupied Vietnam for nearly a thousand years, penetrated as far as Java under the Yuan, and had four wars with Burma during the eighteenth century. On the other hand, it is true that most Southeast Asian states were respectful tributaries of imperial China and that vast waves of Chinese migrated to the region in the aftermath of the seven voyages of fifteenth-century Ming admiral Zheng He, many of whom pros-pered and still render residual loyalty (including cash remittances) to the homeland. China has historically been viewed as more advanced and hence a source of enlightenment and occasional danger to its Southeast Asian neigh-bors, an image that China's post–Mao Zedong economic miracle has helped to revive. In sum, China's historical disposition to Southeast Asia is that of a culturally superior neighbor, entitled to deference and compliance.

China's relations with Southeast Asia, politically constrained during the Cold War, have rebounded vigorously since. Economic trade has thrived, particularly since China and ASEAN formed the ASEAN-China Free Trade Agreement (ACFTA) in 2010, with investment following. But China's politi-cal interest in the region has been, like that of the United States, episodic. In the immediate postwar era, China supported national liberation movements in Vietnam, Burma, Malaysia, Indonesia, and the Philippines, often with the support of overseas Chinese populations, leaving a widespread sense of dread. But during the Cultural Revolution, China became preoccupied with domestic turmoil and reduced its material involvement in these movements (though rhetorical support continued). During the Deng Xiaoping era, Chi-na's rhetorical support was finally muted (with the temporary exceptions of Cambodia and Afghanistan) as China became preoccupied with domestic reform and cultivating relations with the advanced industrialized democra-cies that would provide the most lucrative markets and sources of capital and innovation. When the West shunned China in the wake of Tiananmen, China turned to the developing world. In 1990, Indonesia resumed diplomatic rela-tions suspended in the wake of the 1965 coup, and Singapore established relations. With the establishment of diplomatic ties with Brunei in 1991, Sino-ASEAN relations entered a new era: China managed to have official ties with all ASEAN states at a time when Western Tiananmen sanctions were still in force. China and Southeast Asia have had conflicting territorial claims since 1947, but Beijing tactfully shelved them until 2009. China's disposition to Southeast Asia today is a contradictory hybrid of mutually beneficial commercial penetration and sweeping territorial claims, forcibly but cautiously implemented. Thus China's relations with Southeast Asia have become a test case for what kind of great power a rising China will ultimately turn out to be.

WHAT STRATEGIC TRIANGLE?

A strategic triangle may be said to be operational if three conditions exist: (1) all three participants are sovereign (i.e., free to decide their own national interests and foreign policy preferences), rational actors (i.e., ideology, religion, and such do not limit linkage options); (2) each actor takes into account the third actor in managing its relationship with the second; and (3) each actor is deemed essential to the game in the sense that its defection from one side to the other would affect the strategic balance. Can the relationship between ASEAN, China, and the United States be conceived as a strategic triangle? The second and third conditions clearly exist: each actor takes into account the third in its relation to the second (e.g., ASEAN takes into account the interests of China in dealing with the United States, and certainly vice versa), and each actor is essential in the sense that a defection would imply a critical shift in the balance of power. The relationship, however, runs into serious difficulty with the first condition. China and the United States are clearly sovereign actors, but ASEAN is not a unitary actor and is, instead, a collection of small or medium nations concerting together to attain greater influence in a region otherwise dominated by great powers (e.g., China, Japan, and India).

When ASEAN can cobble together an internal consensus it can make binding decisions like any other sovereign actor, as it did, for example, in the formation of the ASEAN Free Trade Agreement (AFTA) in 2015, eliminating all internal tariff barriers, or when it forced Myanmar to adopt democratic elections in 2010. Since 2013, ASEAN has moved to give its collective identity a solid legal basis by adopting a charter (2008) and by pledging to construct an ASEAN community by 2020, upon three pillars—namely, the ASEAN Economic Community, with a single market and production base; the ASEAN Political-Security Community (APSC), and the ASEAN Sociocultural Community (ASCC). ASEAN's claim to be treated as a unitary actor is demonstrated not only in its efforts at internal integration but also in the agreements the association has formed with other actors, such as ASEAN Plus Three (APT), the ASEAN–European Union talks, the ADMM Plus (ASEAN Defense Ministers plus ARF defense ministers), and the free trade agreements (FTAs) with China, Japan, and Korea. Acting as a unitary actor is a force multiplier for the Southeast Asian community: thus, the agreements it forms with outside actors are invariably based on ASEAN centrality, an assertion other actors can accept because ASEAN poses no threat to them. ASEAN has also attempted to negotiate the maritime sovereignty dispute with China as a unitary actor even though ASEAN per se has no sovereignty claims to any of the territory in question. But it is true that without consensus it cannot act, as China has astutely recognized.

But is this a difference in kind or a difference in degree? Not having a coherent foreign policy certainly incurs opportunity costs. But sovereign actors also face this difficulty in the sense that there may be partisan or factional divisions among domestic participants in the foreign policy–making process, resulting in ambiguous policies or even protracted policy paralysis. ASEAN does try very hard to synthesize a consensus to act as a sovereign entity because it is aware that as a unit it has more international influence than it would otherwise. Many countries, including China and the United States, now send ambassadors to ASEAN. So as far as the triangle is concerned, ASEAN can thus be considered a collective identity with *aspirational sovereignty*, whose members share many interests and threat perceptions and hence can often (but not always) muster a concerted response to outside challenges.

Let us now outline a rough periodization. Stage 1 is the period of the Cold War, from 1950 to 1980; stage 2 is the post–Cold War period, from roughly 1980 to 2010; and stage 3 is the rise of China period, from 2010 to the present. We next examine each period more closely to determine the basis for the triangular configuration at the time, how it came into being, and why it eventually shifted to a new configuration.

Stage 1: Cold War, 1950–80

The Cold War period constituted a marriage between the United States and Southeast Asia against the People's Republic of China (PRC) as a pariah. The basis of the antagonism was the communist revolution that was successfully concluded in China in 1949; the revolution constituted a major shift in the world balance of power and was intended to have what Lenin called a "domino effect" of continuing revolution throughout the world, which communist regimes in Moscow and Beijing backed with both organizational and logistic support. The Cominform (Communist Information Bureau) was formed in response to the US Marshall Plan in September 1947 to coordinate international revolutionary activities, based on the Zhdanov Doctrine that there were but "two camps" ideologically and all others must choose between them.[3] This was viewed with great (in retrospect exaggerated) alarm in both the United States and in the fragile new nations of Southeast Asia. As in China, auspicious conditions for communist revolution were originally created by the Japanese invasion and creation of a short-lived Greater East Asian Co-Prosperity Sphere, which in wartime conditions turned out to be even more rapacious than Western imperialism. Communist insurgencies began in Southeast Asia—namely, Burma, Malaya, Vietnam, the Dutch East Indies, and the Philippines—against Japanese occupation forces, often in united front coalitions with US and European (erstwhile colonial) forces. When

Japanese occupation forces departed in 1945, resistance continued against returning Western colonial authorities.[4]

These insurgencies were loosely based on the Chinese communist revolutionary model, combining class struggle at the grassroots level with nationalist mobilization against the Japanese invaders. And as the largest Asian state and the first to establish an independent new regime after Japan's defeat, China aspired to leadership of so-called national liberation movements in the developing colonies and semi-colonies that became known as the Third World. In 1936, Mao explained to Edgar Snow the "unique position" of the Chinese Communist Party (CCP): "The Chinese revolution is a key factor in the world situation and its victory is heartily anticipated by the people of every country, especially by the toiling masses of the colonial countries. When the Chinese revolution comes into full power, the masses of many colonial countries will follow the example of China and win a similar victory of their own."[5] Even before victory in China, the Moscow "center" advised communist parties in the colonial world to "study the experience of the Chinese Communist Party."[6] The assertion of the leading role of the communist revolution became a vehicle for the consolidation of Mao Zedong's Thought as a winning formula for launching peasant insurgencies in developing countries (as well as for his personal ascendancy within the CCP). Mao was said to have created a revolutionary theory applicable not only to the special characteristics of China but also to other new nations in similar circumstances.

The crowning public assertion of the CCP's unique leadership role was made by Liu Shaoqi in his Report to the Party's Seventh Party Congress in 1945, in which he referred to Mao Zedong or his Thought no less than 105 times: "The Thought of Mao Zedong . . . will . . . make great and useful contributions to the cause of the emancipation of the peoples of all countries, and of the peoples of the East in particular."[7] In the revised Party Constitution (which Liu also drafted), Mao's Thought was put on the same footing with Marxism as a "guiding principle for all the works of the Party." A meeting between Stalin and Liu Shaoqi in the summer of 1949 produced an agreement that while the Union of Soviet Socialist Republics (USSR) would be the leading socialist power internationally, China would assume responsibility for the communist revolution in East Asia.[8] After the liberation of China was proclaimed in October 1949, Stalin encouraged Mao to lead similar revolutionary movements throughout the Third World, where conditions were deemed analogous to those in China. These efforts were greeted by indigenous supporters of revolution in all the new nations of Southeast Asia. Only Japan, South Korea, and Taiwan were proof against this revolutionary appeal by dint of being occupied by US forces in the closing phases of the war.

After liberation, the CCP leadership made international revolution with a particular focus on the Third World the centerpiece of Chinese foreign policy, employing the full panoply of state resources including extremely generous foreign aid for such a poor country.[9] The Chinese model of peasant war surrounding the cities was successfully implemented in Vietnam, Cambodia, and Laos, the former constituents of French Indochina, and unsuccessfully applied in the Philippines, Burma, Indonesia, Thailand, Singapore, and Malaysia. The resulting conflicts defined the contours of the Asian cold war cleavage for more than three decades; it also created two mutually exclusive economic blocs in which the Council of Mutual Economic Assistance (Comecon), formed in 1949 as a communist counterpart to the Marshall Plan and the European Economic Community (EEC), faced an informal arrangement in which developing Asian nations were given privileged access to US consumer markets in return for their support for the US anticommunist coalition. The conflict was deeply divisive and protracted. In triangular terms, this was a Southeast Asian–US marriage against a pariah of communist forces (the PRC, the USSR, the Socialist Republic of Vietnam).

A simplified bottom-line verdict would be that the pariah lost and the US–Southeast Asian marriage ultimately won the Southeast Asian cold war (as one might expect from the relative size and strength of the two coalitions): indeed, even in cases of communist victory, the outcome was not necessarily helpful in terms of Chinese foreign policy (take Vietnam, for example, with which the PRC had a fierce border war only four years after victory). Critical to this ultimate victory was not only the superior power and resources of the United States as anticommunist coalition leader but ideological schisms and lack of coordination within the international communist coalition. Ironically, although the communist ideological appeal transcended nationalism to focus on internationally shared class interests, repressed nationalism split the communist camp between its leading powers so deeply that there was armed conflict among communists (not only the two principals but their agents). At the end of the Cold War, the repudiation of Marxism-Leninism in the former Soviet Union and its revision in the PRC finally discredited the already weakened transnational revolutionary argument. Circumstances in Southeast Asia were also less favorable: communist revolution had succeeded in the Chinese case not only because of its superior military strategy of "people's war" but because at critical junctures revolutionary forces were able to form united fronts with class enemies, but this was left out of the romanticized export version of the China model. The Chinese revolution was, in fact, not a mass uprising around the country based on class struggle but a series of military battles. Moreover, in Burma, the Philippines, and Malaysia, the revolutionary appeal was limited to ethnic minorities; only in Indonesia could a semblance of grassroots class struggle and elite united front be achieved (and there only until the abortive coup attempt in 1965).

Although the post-Mao leadership in 1979 opted to repudiate the unsuccessful, now even counterproductive "export of revolution," the experience was not without positive consequences. First, the threat of revolution seems to have inspired land reform, educational investment, and labor reforms in those countries in order to preempt communist appeals. Second, a counterrevolutionary international political economy was created in the Asian Pacific Rim consisting of open US consumer markets and economic assistance in tacit exchange for political commitments to market economic development and eventual democratization. Third, China's involvement in global revolution coined an image of China as champion of the poor and oppressed and a tribunal for the interests of developing countries that has proved surprisingly resilient, despite the evolution of a more nationalist foreign policy and a more hierarchical distribution of wealth, power, and other values in China itself in the course of its economic development. This image of China having a unique moral mission in the world has arguably endured in China as well, even as the content of that mission has evolved. China's generous aid to other developing nations in the course of promoting international class struggle established very few proletarian dictatorships, but it did prove useful in generating the 1971 majority vote in the United Nations General Assembly to evict Taiwan from the China chair in the UN and install the PRC on the Security Council, and China has maintained rhetorical solidarity with this increasingly heterogeneous grouping, for example, in its UN General Assembly roll call voting record.

Post–Cold War, 1980–2010

The Cold War ended earlier in Asia than in Europe, thanks largely to Sino-US détente. The early phase of the post–Cold War period, from around 1980 to 2010, was a ménage à trois, in triangular terms, in which the United States, the PRC, and the ASEAN countries enjoyed mutually cordial interrelations. Yet it was a ménage not of active cooperation but of mutual withdrawal by tacit agreement of the two superpowers. This new configuration did not suddenly appear ex nihilo; the seeds to the transformation were planted by the epoch-making 1972 Nixon visit to China. And the repercussions were not instantaneous. It initiated a Sino-US détente narrowly limited at the outset to the strategic necessity of thwarting the perceived rise of a Soviet Union that was deemed a threat to both countries but most acutely to the PRC. In triangular terms, the United States tacitly agreed to protect China from a Soviet preemptive nuclear strike while at the same time maintaining détente (and strategic arms limitation talks) with the USSR. This engendered a romantic triangle with the United States at the pivot position balancing two antagonistic "wings." Although this was strategically imperative for China given the Soviet threat, the Maoist leadership was wary of US manipulation and determined to limit détente to the strategic dimension. Thus although the two countries opened trade missions in each other's capitals and limited trade began (including nonlethal security technology), China's ideological crusade against Soviet socialist imperialism—a threat which had grown to eclipse opposition to capitalism—continued and even intensified, now with US support. Thus in 1974, Deng Xiaoping outlined Mao's Three Worlds theory in a speech to the UN General Assembly, in which the world was seen divided into a first world of maleficent hegemons (the United States and the USSR), a second world of medium powers that might tilt either way, and a proletarian third world of developing countries led by the PRC.

The impact on Southeast Asia, a geographically accessible piece of the third world, was ambiguous. Proxy wars continued through the 1970s and well into the 1980s, in which the PRC and the USSR sought to undermine each other's proxies and protect their own. China's rhetorical support (e.g., radio broadcasts) for guerrilla insurgencies in Burma, Malaysia, Thailand, and the Philippines continued through the late 1980s, but in former French Indochina, Hanoi came to distrust Chinese patronage after the Nixon visit and drifted increasingly into the Soviet camp. Chinese strategic advice to Hanoi had been to continue the guerrilla insurgency indefinitely, but Vietnam, now with predominantly Soviet logistic and advisory assistance, disregarded Chinese counsel after the Tet Offensive and shifted to a more conventional military strategy for its crowning victory over the south. When China's genocidal client Khmer Rouge regime in Cambodia precipitated border conflict with Vietnam and the latter countered by invading Cambodia and overthrowing the Khmer regime in 1979, China made Vietnamese evacuation of that country one of three fundamental obstacles to reconciliation with the USSR in its 1982–89 normalization negotiations with Moscow. Vietnam finally pulled all troops out of Cambodia in fall 1989.

The decline in Cold War tensions during the 1980s suggested that economic rather than military power would determine regional leadership, a role for which Japan was ideally suited. During the decade, Japan displaced the United States as the largest provider of new business investment and economic aid in the region, although the US market remained a major source of Asia-Pacific dynamism. Especially following the rise in value of the yen relative to the dollar in the late 1980s (after the Plaza Accord), Japan's role as a capital and technology exporter and as an increasingly significant importer of Asian manufactured goods made it the core economy of the Asia-Pacific region. There was even fear in parts of Asia that Japan's systematic economic penetration into the region would eventually lead to something akin to its pre–World War II scheme to create a Greater East Asian Co-Prosperity Sphere. After a reassessment of policy, the Japanese leadership appeared to have decided that more emphasis ought to be given to helping the developing countries of the region modernize their industrial bases to increase their self-reliance and economic resilience. Japan decided in the late 1970s that bilateral aid in the form of yen credits (usually tied to purchase of Japanese goods), tariff reductions, larger quota incentives for manufactured exports, and investments in processing industries, energy, agriculture, and education would be the focus of its aid programs in Asia. In 1977, Japan adopted the Fukuda Doctrine, assuming no military role and setting up the Japan-ASEAN Forum to pursue equal partnership with ASEAN based on mutual trust. From 1960 to 2011, Japan provided 34.9 percent of its global official development aid (ODA) to ASEAN. Between 1976 and 1986, Japan's total ODA to ASEAN increased five times. By fiscal year 1988, Japanese aid to the ASEAN countries totaled US$1.9 billion versus only US$333 million in aid from the United States. Japan also became the number one provider of FDI to ASEAN countries, with cumulative investment as of March 1989 of about US$14.5 billion, more than twice that of the United States. Japan's share of total foreign investment in ASEAN countries in this period ranged from 70 to 80 percent in Thailand to 20 percent in Indonesia. In the early 1990s, the Japanese government also made a concerted effort to enhance its Asian diplomatic stature. Kaifu Toshiki's much publicized spring 1991 tour of five Southeast Asian nations—Malaysia, Brunei, Thailand, Singapore, and the Philippines—culminated in a May 3 major foreign policy address in Singapore, in which he called for a new partnership with the Association of Southeast Asian Nations (ASEAN) and pledged that Japan would go beyond the purely economic sphere to seek an "appropriate role in the political sphere as a nation of peace."[10] As evidence of this new role, Japan took an active part in promoting negotiations to resolve the Cambodian conflict.

The overall trend during this period was toward greater peace and prosperity. It was to be sure an empty détente, based more on supervening outside priorities diverting the powers than on any explicit understanding among them. China was engulfed in the Cultural Revolution, the United States was in global retreat under pressure from a domestic antiwar movement, and the Soviet Union was under fresh leadership preoccupied with the China threat. In 1969, Nixon announced the Nixon Doctrine, urging US allies to rely on their own self-defense efforts and less on US protection. Although Vietnamization, the most prominent would-be exemplar of this doctrine, failed with the collapse of the Saigon republic in 1975, the United States did reduce its military commitment to East Asia and urge its allies to assume responsibility to defend themselves (with the help of booming US weapons sales). Former proxies, no longer urgently needing security protection from the powers, began to withdraw from the strategic umbrellas of the great powers. The United States was pushed out of its bases—Clark Air Force Base (1991) and Subic Bay Naval Base (1992) in the Philippines—while the Soviet navy was evicted from Cam Ranh Bay by Vietnam in 2002. Meanwhile, Sino-Soviet normalization talks engendered the necessary Soviet diplomatic pressure to facilitate Vietnamese withdrawal from Cambodia, ultimately resulting in Sino-Soviet normalization and the emergence of a pro-PRC neo-Khmer regime under Hun Sen, a defected Khmer officer. FDI from Japan, Taiwan, and the West flooded into Southeast Asia after Tiananmen, and the 1990s were boom years for the "small dragons": Thailand, Singapore, Malaysia, and Indonesia. There may have been some sense of abandonment about the withdrawal of the great powers from Southeast Asia, but the overall feeling was one of relief.

Southeast Asia, for the first time in decades disencumbered of external security threats and now under more coherent leadership, proceeded in the next two decades to construct a bold new East Asian architecture based on ASEAN centrality. They selected an elite group of wise men (Eminent Persons Group) to formulate the ambitious Vision 2020 and proceeded to act to integrate the rest of East Asia peacefully to ASEAN norms. Beyond the original five members, Brunei Darussalam became the sixth member in January 1984, barely a week after becoming independent. Vietnam became the seventh member in 1995, Laos and Myanmar joined in 1997, and Cambodia joined in 1999; Papua New Guinea and East Timor are candidate members seeking accession. This will make the organization regionally inclusive of all twelve Southeast Asian nations.

The ASEAN vision has been to go beyond Southeast Asia to restructure all of East Asia around the ASEAN Way. ASEAN began by expanding the Post-Ministerial Conference (PMC) external dialogues to include four new dialogue partners, including China. The PMC then formed the basis for Asia's first multilateral security dialogue, the ASEAN Regional Forum (ARF), established in 1994. Other frameworks that emerged in the 1990s were the South China Sea Workshops, Asia-Europe Meetings (ASEM), Asia-Pacific Economic Cooperation (APEC), and the ASEAN Plus Three (APT, meaning China, Japan, and Korea) meetings, established in 1997 and institutionalized to form a multilateral FTA in 2010. The ASEAN Charter came into force in 2008, as well as the East Asia Summit (EAS), including ASEAN Plus Three plus three more: Australia, New Zealand, and India (adding Russia and the United States in 2011). The ASEAN Economic Community (AEC) was established in December 2015, creating a common Southeast Asian market. ASEAN undertook to delve into delicate security issues in "plus" meetings of defense and foreign ministers, which formally approved a number of agreements. The Framework Agreement on Comprehensive Economic Cooperation and the Memorandum of Understanding on Nontraditional Security Issues were signed with China in 2002, paving the way for the ACFTA. In the same year, the nonbinding Declaration on the Conduct of Parties in the South China Sea (DOC) was signed. As this nonbinding document failed to resolve the escalating territorial dispute, in 2011 the Guide-lines for the Implementation of the DOC were agreed after protracted negoti-ations, which were, however, also nonbinding and ineffectual. Negotiations on a binding Code of Conduct (COC) continued, with a new target date for completion of 2017. This deadline succeeded in producing only a nonbinding "framework" for a COC. All these attempts to broaden the compass of AS-EAN included China, disregarding the post-Tiananmen sanctions imposed by the West, and were meant to socialize its giant neighbor in a culture of restraint. They have been implemented, however, in the ASEAN Way, mean-ing many meetings and discussions but no decisions except by unanimous consent and little or no executive power to enforce decisions. This has creat-ed the opportunity for a proud and determined dissident to stymie majority consensus.

Rise of China, 2010–Present

The period from 2010 to the present can be characterized as a romantic triangle, with ASEAN adopting a *passive pivot* position. Although ASEAN has continued its outreach, this shift to a more passive position was set in train by the rise of China. During the ten-year term of the leadership of Hu Yaobang and Wen Jiabao (2002–12), China achieved the highest sustained growth rate in its recorded history, averaging 10.4 percent nominal GDP growth per annum and 10.1 percent per capita growth. This achievement was particularly impressive in the global context: while the global financial crisis cast the developed world into recession, in China, although trade dived deep into negative territory in 2009, late that year China launched a four-trillion-yuan (around US$640 billion) stimulus package. The short-term impact was to offset falling exports with domestic infrastructure investment, and it spared China from any single year of recession throughout the crisis period, with an understandable bracing effect on public opinion—China surpassed Japan in aggregate GDP in 2010. While in 1980 China's share of global GDP was 2 percent—far less than the United States at 22 percent—by 2014, China had overtaken the United States in GDP (in purchasing power parity [PPP]); from 2004 to 2015, China's share of global trade nearly quadrupled from US$600 billion to US$2.2 trillion. The first decade of the new millennium saw a threefold increase in China's military expenditures (from US$42 bil-lion in 2001 to around $130 billion in 2011), far exceeding the combined expenditures of all Southeast Asian nations over the same time period (US$28 billion).[11] China had arrived, much faster than anticipated.

The upshot for Southeast Asia of China's rise was two major policy initiatives, one welcome, the other rather less so. The political strategic in-itiative was apparently focused on realizing China's emergent great power aspirations by expanding physically into its near seas. The political economic initiative consisted of an ambitious financial outreach designed to establish a China-led economic circle on China's periphery and find a way out of industrial overcapacity by exporting surplus capital and services.

Territorial Expansion

In the context of its economic rise and growing need for natural resources, China became concerned about what Hu Jintao in 2005 called the "Malacca dilemma." In 1968, oil was discovered in China's peripheral seas. The PRC's Geology and Mineral Resources Ministry estimated that the Spratly area held oil and natural gas reserves of 17.7 billion tons compared to the 13 billion tons held by Kuwait, placing it as potentially the fourth-largest reserve bed in the world (Western estimates have been considerably less optimistic). The Philippines discovered oil off the Palawan coast in 1976, and by 2010, these fields were supplying 15 percent of all petroleum consumed by that country. Subsurface hydrocarbons were also discovered in the East China Sea near the putative maritime boundary with Japan just north of the Senkaku/Diaoyu islets; after several years of ultimately fruitless bilateral negotiations over joint development, China began exploiting these fields unilaterally. By 2012, the competition for natural resources between China and its neighbors had become increasingly acute. China began to use a wide variety of means to assert its claims. The changing of the guard at the Eighteenth Party Congress in 2012 provided an opportunity for a reassessment of this assertive and regionally upsetting course, but the new leadership of Xi Jinping, instead of shelving the dispute as his predecessors had done, vowed to pursue China's sovereignty claims with unprecedented vigor. It has done so since.

In 2009, China responded to the Asian unfolding of the United Nations Convention on the Law of the Sea (UNCLOS) to launch a vigorous attempt to claim exclusive sovereignty over some 80–90 percent of the South China Sea, or at least to the land features in the South China Sea and their territorial waters. No one is too clear on the exact extent of China's claims, and China has not been helpful in clarifying them. Though its claims are unusually sweeping, China is hardly unique: the Philippines began the process of creating facts in the sea in 1978, Vietnam followed in 1982, and Malaysia in 1983. In 1988, China intervened to halt the further expansion of Vietnam's holdings near Johnson South Reef in a skirmish sinking two ships, killing sixty-four Vietnamese sailors, and taking nine prisoners (later repatriated). Since then, China has firmly established its occupancy of the Paracel Islands in the north and seized seven land features in the South China Sea. It has not attempted to dislodge other claimants from any of the four dozen outposts that they have planted in Chinese-claimed maritime territories, and has been careful not to provoke military confrontation with them or with the US Navy.

The legal basis of China's maritime claim includes the following points: First is the claim that have been Chinese waters since ancient times, as demonstrated by the discovery of potshards and diary or logbook references to the islets by ancient travelers. Historical claims are typically given short shrift by UNCLOS for fairly obvious reasons (e.g., in 1936 Benito Mussolini justified his invasion of Ethiopia by reference to imperial Rome). All the littoral states make similar historical claims based on similar evidence; the Chinese physical remains found on some of the islets may also have been cargo carried by Arab traders. In any case, there is no indication that Chinese explorers who named the islets or mentioned their existence ever laid claim to them on behalf of previous Chinese dynasties or established permanent settlements there. The modern concept of sovereignty was not even coined until the Treaty of Westphalia ending the Thirty Years' War in 1648. Second is a maritime map with a (then eleven-dash, now nine-dash) or "cow's tongue" line sketched on it by the Chinese Nationalist regime in 1947, which resembled a similar map drawn by imperial Japan after conquering the littoral territories from European colonial regimes. China inherited the map from the defeated Nationalists in 1949, who continue to make an identical claim in Taiwan, though neither seriously attempted to enforce this claim until much later. And the original claim was to the land features enclosed by the line, while China since the 1990s has expanded the claim to include "historical waters" encompassing some 85 percent of the South China Sea. Though the map overlaps the two-hundred-nautical-mile exclusive economic zones (EEZs) of four littoral states as well as maritime areas previously considered high seas, China since 2009 has claimed exclusive sovereignty and refused to compromise, calling its claim "indisputable." To be sure, China has agreed to joint exploitation of subsurface resources with other claimants contingent on prior acknowledgment of Chinese sovereignty. The contesting littoral states prefer the rules set forth by UNCLOS in 1982, which define sovereignty based on a specified distance from land features, according to which China would be entitled only to an EEZ of two hundred miles around Hainan Island, the southernmost land feature over which it has undisputed sovereignty. In 2013, the Philippines challenged Chinese occupation of Scarborough Shoal after failing to negotiate a bilateral compromise. Although China refused to accept UNCLOS jurisdiction after three years of deliberations, the Permanent Court of Arbitration (PCA) of the International Tribunal for the Law of the Sea issued a ruling in June 2016 in favor of Manila.

There are at least three reasons for China's more energetic recent efforts to enforce its claims. First, in 1968 rich subsurface hydrocarbon deposits were discovered by the United Nations Economic and Social Commission for Asia and the Pacific (ESCAP)—the exact size of these deposits is still unclear, but China takes the optimistic view that they amount to the largest deposit in the world outside Saudi Arabia. Other littoral states have already begun to exploit these deposits, often in joint ventures with major international oil companies. PetroVietnam, now the country's largest state-owned enterprise (SOE), accounts for about 20 percent of the country's GDP and 25–30 percent of annual government revenue, largely from the Bach Ho (White Tiger) offshore field in the South China Sea. In the Philippines, a recent discovery of natural gas reserves in the Malampaya oil fields off the island of Palawan is being used to generate electricity in three gas-powered plants. Malaysia and Brunei also exploit offshore petroleum fields within China's nine-dash line. China, which has not yet seen a drop of oil from the South China Sea, has expressed indignation at this lucrative infringement of its blue-water territory.

Second, from a strategic perspective, at least since the rise to the Politburo Standing Committee of Admiral Liu Huaqing in the 1990s, China has declared a national interest in establishing control over its near seas, including the East China Sea, the South China Sea, and the Yellow Sea. Liu saw the People's Liberation Army (PLA) Navy (PLAN) trapped by three island chains and even proposed a timetable for breaking through each of them to the high seas in order to become a global naval power (according to which it is behind schedule). The South China Sea commands a strategic premium as the largest and deepest body of water among China's near seas. That is why it is the most strategically important sea for China's navy, a refuge for its nuclear missile submarines to patrol in relative safety and a potential buffer against the US Navy and other foreign navies. It offers a strategically centered location from which China's naval and air forces can project their reach into both the Western Pacific and Indian Oceans. The PLAN's most important naval base faces onto the South China Sea from Sanya on Hainan Island, and its southern fleet is equipped with its newest and most capable ships, submarines, and aircraft. That is why China objects to US surveillance craft entering its EEZ near Hainan and sometimes harasses or chases them away when they do so.

Third, since the Tiananmen crackdown in 1989, there have been double-digit increases in China's military (slowing to single-digit since 2015), giving China the largest military budget in Asia and the second largest in the world. China's military budget increased more than threefold since the beginning of the century, from $41 billion in 2001 to around $146.6 billion in 2016, according to official PRC figures (which are often deemed understated). By 2017, China had launched its second aircraft carrier and had begun its first nuclear submarine deterrent patrols. Breaking past convention against military bases in other countries, China announced in 2014 that arrangements had been made for its first military support base abroad, in Djibouti. Now, with a locally dominant navy and air force, Beijing for the first time has the power (and it thinks the right) to enforce its claims against neighboring claimants and has proceeded to do so.

Though adamant about the righteousness of its claim, China has proceeded cautiously and incrementally. This caution is attributable in part to China's preference to maintain cordial relations with neighbors with conflicting claims, and partly to the intrusion of the United States into the dispute, for the United States does have the power to block China's enforcement of its claims and has chosen to declare a strong national interest in protecting freedom of navigation. Chinese maritime vessels, typically belonging to the coast guard and fisheries police and other maritime agencies while keeping the navy in reserve as an escalation deterrent, in 2010 began detaining fishing vessels, confiscating fish, cutting cables, setting up oil drilling rigs, and in effect annexing small islets by patrolling near them and blocking other vessels from doing so. Of the forty-eight major incidents identified in the South China Sea from 2010 onward, at least one Chinese coast guard (or other Chinese maritime law enforcement) vessel was involved in 77 percent of the incidents; four additional incidents involved a Chinese naval vessel acting in a maritime law enforcement capacity, raising that number to 85 percent. China further reinforced its claims in 2014 with the reclamation of many of the seven reefs and islets it occupies, dredging land from the surrounding ocean floor to augment their size by a total of some 3,200 acres, after which harbors, airstrips, lighthouses, and, most recently, anti-aircraft missile systems and close-in defensive weaponry were added. This project was made possible by China's acquisition around 2000 of a large and impressive fleet of dredging ships. The model for this project is Mischief Reef, a coral atoll submerged at high tide located 135 miles from the coast of the Philippines' Palawan Island. China built a small structure on stilts there in 1995, and when Manila protested, Beijing responded reassuringly that the structure was a mere fishermen's shelter. Recent satellite images unveil China's reclamation of approximately 5,580,000 square meters of land on the island and the construction of a 9,800-foot runway, radar nests, anti-aircraft guns, and preparations for a future naval base. It is now the largest island in the South China Sea.

The dominant Chinese foreign policy discourse since the late 1990s had been that of "peaceful development" and "harmonious world," hoping thereby to disarm the China threat theory that arose after Tiananmen and the Taiwan missile crisis and demobilize the network of bilateral alliances with the United States left over from the Cold War, which Beijing called anachronistic, no longer relevant to a new era of win-win cooperation. But in the late 2000s, a more muscular narrative began to emerge that was more consistent with the activist enforcement behavior Beijing has adopted since 2009. First, there was a rising emphasis on core interests, which could not in principle be compromised, one of which was the defense of sovereignty over China's various territorial claims but particularly Taiwan, Tibet, and Xinjiang (also, it was implied in 2010, the East and South China Seas). Second, after a long period of identification with the internationally oppressed developing countries in the global south, China's leaders around 2012 began acknowledging that China was indeed a great power, having great power relations of a new type with other great powers. Such new-type relations included mutual respect for respective core interests, including China's sovereignty claims. Third, the rhetorical hallmark of Xi Jinping's rise was the invocation of the great rejuvenation of the Chinese nation and the China Dream. The context of this rhetoric has been a revival of memories of unequal treaties and the "hundred years of humiliation" narrative, that after enduring bitter injustice China now has the right and the power to reclaim its rightful place in the world. China's rhetoric still contains the "win-win" narrative that the more China grows the more it will create development opportunities for the rest of Asia; and it is true that the blossoming of north-south economic relations has brought higher growth rates and economic prosperity, but its sovereignty claims have been more controversial.

The response of the other two wings of the triangle to Beijing's attempt to expand its sphere of influence has been generally cautious and diplomatic. Although no one actually agreed with the nine-dash line except Taiwan (which distanced itself from China's attempts to enforce it), few have dared to publicly disagree with it, even after the PCA ruling. The United States has responded with a show of force—in the form of freedom of navigation operations (FONOPs) voyages of naval ships in the vicinity of China's expanded islets despite Chinese warnings—in a demonstration of its refusal to recognize any claim to maritime sovereignty. ASEAN was at sixes and sevens—some countries agreed with Beijing's contention that maritime territorial disputes should be settled bilaterally. Vietnam and the Philippines were vocal in their objections, and Manila, after failing to generate support for a Code of Conduct at an ASEAN ministerial meeting in 2011, took its claims to the UNCLOS PCA in 2012. But although the resulting verdict favored the Philippines, it was vociferously spurned by China and hence proved politically unenforceable. Thus newly elected president Rodrigo Duterte disregarded the 2016 ruling and joined Cambodia, Laos, and Brunei in signaling a preference for accommodation with China while distancing himself from the US alliance. Beijing promptly rewarded him with pledges of $24 billion in aid and investment. But when Duterte told Xi he still wanted to drill for oil in adjacent waters, Xi said, "We want to maintain the present warm relationship. But if you force the issue, we'll go to war."[12] Duterte has tried to balance, not following through on earlier threats to abandon the US alliance (despite no assurance of US military support for Filipino territorial claims) and has earmarked $35 million to upgrade Filipino facilities in the Spratly Islands. Vietnam, having lost bloody naval skirmishes with China in 1974 and 1988, has also sought a balance between resistance and negotiation.

Those states whose EEZs were interdicted by the nine-dash line and entered into bilateral negotiations with Beijing for joint development soon found Beijing's terms (recognize Chinese sovereignty) unappealing, and hence sought to mobilize multilateral resistance via ASEAN to even the playing field. But Beijing was skillful in neutralizing the mobilization of multilateral resistance. In view of the inefficacy of the ARF, the ASEAN defense ministers operationalized the expanded ADMM Plus (ASEAN plus defense ministers from eight other Asian powers) as a new security process, whereby the latter would meet with their ASEAN Plus colleagues to discuss issues unsolvable within ARF. ADMM Plus has the same membership composition as the EAS, but the defense forum is likely to be more firmly and specifically focused on the solution of conventional security matters. It was indeed able to discuss the issue more frankly and confidentially but likewise lacked enforcement power. Whatever the forum, those ASEAN countries that had no conflicting maritime territorial claims and enjoyed expanding economic relations with the PRC stood ready to block any discussion offensive to their patron.

Thus after the nonbinding implementation guidelines to the Declaration on Conduct (DOC) passed in 2011 failed to alleviate mounting tensions, efforts shifted to the formulation of a binding Code of Conduct (COC). Passage, however, became contingent on China's approval (as one of the major claimants), and talks stalled for the next seven years, reportedly finally nearing completion of a framework for a COC after twenty-one years of barren negotiations in June 2017. When in a 2012 ASEAN meeting the Philippines tabled a resolution criticizing China's behavior, Cambodia refused, and for the first time, the meeting adjourned without a communiqué. Again in an ASEAN foreign ministers' meeting in 2015, the issue of land reclamation was raised by several states but was deleted from the communiqué, and again at the July 2016 ministerial meeting, Cambodia blocked any resolution critical of Beijing. Beijing does not hesitate to scold publicly any countries, like Singapore, that question China's policies or bring up the PCA ruling. Not only Beijing's cultivation of proxies but also the integration of China itself into such expanded forums as the ARF and ADMM Plus has given it a voice in the issue, which it has used like a diplomatic rapier.

In 2016, Wang Yi visited Brunei, Laos, and Cambodia, reaching a four-point consensus that the territorial disputes were not an issue between China and ASEAN as a whole. When Singapore criticized China for splitting ASEAN by meddling in its internal affairs, China indignantly denied any such intention. At an ADMM Plus foreign ministers meeting in Yunnan in June 2016, China was particularly on edge, warning ASEAN against any joint statement on the PCA ruling about to appear. When ASEAN prepared a joint statement criticizing China's behavior, it was vetoed by Cambodia and Laos. In September 2017, an article appeared in the *Global Times* accusing Singapore of raising the South China Sea dispute at the Non-Aligned Movement summit in Venezuela, which Singapore denied. Thus ASEAN has proved unable to concert a united resistance to China's incremental advances.

What does China want and why does it want it? Unlike classical imperialism as practiced by, say, Great Britain with its British East India Company (1600) or Holland's Dutch East India Company (1602), in which commercial exploitation of natural resources brings in the state to protect civilian enterprises once they are threatened by indigenous resistance, in China's case the expansion into the East and South China Seas has been led from the beginning by military forces for apparently strategic objectives.[13] True, fishing boat fleets are also sometimes involved (China now boasts the largest fleet in the world), but their sudden, massive appearance and disappearance lead one to suspect that they, too, are under central command. From this we may infer that China's objectives have at least hitherto been primarily strategic. China did deploy the Haiyang Shiyou 981 drilling rig in Vietnam's EEZ (an area that China also claims) in the spring of 2014 before suddenly withdrawing it without explanation three months later. So perhaps China also has commercial ambitions. If so, given that almost every land feature in the South China Sea is occupied or controlled by one claimant or another, China's next step may be to authorize its oil giants like the Chinese National Offshore Oil Company (CNOOC) to deploy and drill in waters where they see hydrocarbon potential. A China coast guard ship has been at anchor near Malaysia's Luconia Shoals, 120 kilometers off the coast of Borneo, since August 2013, not engaged in any perceptible activity but warning Malaysian fishermen away. The huge Chinese base at Mischief Reef is just one hundred kilometers from the known gas reserves of the Reed Bank, off the Philippines, which Manila also claims. And Vietnam is concerned that China has designs on the oil fields under the Vanguard Bank off its southwestern coast. Though it has not drilled again since 2014, China has intervened to prevent Vietnam or the Philippines from new drilling in waters within its nine-dash line. However, given the low price of oil at the time, there is little commercial incentive for China or anyone else to develop these fields.

The United States, seeing its strategic and logistic interests at risk, reacted with unusual sharpness to China's salami-slicing advances. The US position on the question of sovereignty had hitherto been consistently passive and neutral. The United States had no maritime territorial claims and avoided involvement. When China defeated Vietnam in 1988 and occupied the Paracels, the United States said little and did nothing; when China stealthily occupied and then fortified Mischief Reef in 1995, well within the EEZ of the Philippines, a US ally,[14] the United States objected verbally but did nothing. Then in 2010, Secretary of State Hillary Clinton at a meeting of the ARF in Hanoi asserted that the United States had a national interest in the defense of freedom of navigation in the South China Sea and urged disputants to reach a peaceful multilateral settlement. The following year President Obama announced a "pivot" (later rebalance) of US forces designed to strengthen the US military and economic commitment to the Western Pacific. This rebalance included beefing up US forces in Singapore and establishing new defense facilities in northern Australia; economically, the focus was on crafting a Trans-Pacific Partnership (TPP), to which China was not invited. The United States strengthened its bilateral alliances with Japan, the Philippines, Thailand, and Australia, made port visits, weapons sales, and naval exercises with frontline states. When China used a ruse to take effective command of Scarborough Shoal from the Philippines in 2012, the United States attempted (unsuccessfully) to mediate the standoff in Manila's favor. All this clearly indicated one-sided support for the anti-China position, a departure from customary neutrality, and Beijing was visibly annoyed. Beijing's rhetoric became sharply antagonistic to US meddling while attributing Southeast Asian resistance to US manipulation.

It is too soon to say which way the Trump regime will tack on the maritime issue: Donald Trump's campaign rhetoric seemed at least in part to embrace a neomercantilist position similar to the Nixon Doctrine. The US withdrawal from the TPP and the apparent collapse of the Obama rebalance policy has clearly resulted in at least temporary decline of confidence in US leadership in the region. Xi Jinping has taken prompt advantage of the leadership vacuum with a rhetorical embrace of two projects previously identified with the United States, globalization and international cooperation to prevent climate change. While the United States remains the largest investor and foreign aid donor in ASEAN, there has in recent years been a huge influx of Chinese trade and investment from China. China in recent years has become the biggest investor in Laos, Cambodia, and Myanmar, the linchpins of an apparent strategy to neutralize ASEAN resistance. If Trump opts for strategic withdrawal à la Nixon's Guam Doctrine, the ASEAN states may increasingly move toward neutrality along the lines of Finland or Switzerland. Or they may, of course, opt to bandwagon with China. As an alternative to the TPP, China has advocated the Regional Cooperative Economic Partnership (RCEP), a multilateral FTA that ASEAN originally introduced. But Trump is unpredictable, and other parts of his campaign rhetoric as well as his National Security Council appointments suggest a possible return to a more traditional Republican posture of staunch support for allies, defense of perceived US strategic interests, and upholding such principles as freedom of navigation. Rex Tillerson, the fledgling secretary of state, has criticized China's island reclamation campaign in the South China Sea, both in his confirmation hearings and in a May 2017 ASEAN ministerial meeting.[15] The top Trump priority has been to halt North Korean progress toward a nuclear second-strike capability, and although the United States resumed naval patrols to monitor Chinese-occupied islands in May 2017, Trump may conceivably opt to soft-pedal anti-PRC moves in the south so long as he deems Chinese support useful in bringing Pyongyang to the negotiating table.

Political Economic Expansion

The second, more welcome impact of China's rise on Southeast Asia has been a massive upsurge of commercial intercourse with the region, contributing to the growing economic integration of Northeast and Southeast Asia. The headline event has been the announcement in 2013 of Xi Jinping's visionary One Belt, One Road (OBOR) initiative. The sequencing of China's two initiatives, greater territorial assertiveness beginning in 2009 followed by OBOR in 2013, might lead one to suspect that OBOR was introduced to counter the largely negative reaction to its sovereignty claims. But although the timing of the rollout invites such suspicions, the OBOR actually has had its roots in China's political economic outreach since the turn of the millennium. China first became economically interested in Southeast Asia around the time of the Asian financial crisis in 1997–98, to which it responded with loans of altogether US$4 billion to Thailand and Indonesia (and by refraining from joining them in devaluing its currency), to the relief of these stricken export economies. General discontent with the terms of International Monetary Fund (IMF) loans aroused interest in alternative regional financial solutions, which China encouraged, and in 1997, ASEAN Plus Three talks were initiated, out of which grew the Chiang Mai currency swap agreement and the ASEAN-China Free Trade Agreement (ACFTA).

The global financial crisis (GFC), set off by the collapse of Lehman Brothers in September 2008, also inflicted damage on China's economy, stimulating Chinese interest in rebalancing its investment strategy. Chinese exports were beset by dumping complaints in the World Trade Organization (WTO) in the wake of global overcapacity while exports to the European Union (EU) and the United States fell by 19.4 percent and 12.5 percent, respectively, contributing to a rise in China's current account deficit. [16] At the same time, China had to fight domestic inflation. In 2008, the Chinese economy was overheating. Property prices, wages, land prices, property rents, and power prices were all rising, and Chinese policy makers realized they needed to do things differently. A plunge in global asset prices stimulated a wave of outgoing FDI into Southeast Asia and Africa. This meant four things. First, as the cost of production was now lower in Southeast Asia, Chinese firms could gain by shifting their production bases outside China. China's excess capacities in steel, cement, and infrastructural engineering fit well with the needs of the infrastructure deficient economies of Southeast Asia. Second, investing in these regions meant access to bigger markets for Chinese firms and more uniform regional development. The relatively underdeveloped Kunming region in Yunnan, for example, has emerged as a major rail terminal with direct lines to Singapore as well as connections to Yangon, Phnom Penh, Ho Chi Minh City, and Hanoi. These development investments also mean Chinese bankers are able to make better use of their excess liquid funds (which otherwise command a lower return invested in China). Third, Chinese firms could evade protectionist measures targeted at their exports if they started exporting from Chinese-invested facilities in Southeast Asian countries instead. Finally, investing in Asia reduced some of China's energy requirements while improving access for raw material imports.

China also wanted its own trade and investment vehicle to structure its financial expansion. Instead of promoting bilateral FTAs with individual ASEAN nations, the approach favored by Japan, China focused on building the region-wide China-ASEAN FTA. First proposed by Zhu Rongji in 2001, ACFTA came into effect in 2010 as the largest FTA in the world in terms of people involved and third largest in GDP, encompassing some two billion customers. China's economic engagement in ASEAN quickly deepened, remarkable not only for the cumulative dollar total but for its swift acceleration. China became the region's largest individual trading partner by 2013, with 14 percent of ASEAN trade (accounting for 10.7 percent of China's total trade). During the ten-year period from 2005 to 2014, bilateral trade tripled—reaching US$366 billion by 2014, according to ASEAN trade figures. At the same time, trade has become increasingly imbalanced. According to ASEAN aggregate trade statistics, in 2014 China accounted for more than one of every five dollars of imports coming into Southeast Asia, while Southeast Asian exports to China pale by comparison, resulting in a deficit amounting to 20 percent of total bilateral trade. Chinese FDI into ASEAN started later but has since crescendoed. Between 1995 and 2003, China's cumulative FDI flows into ASEAN amounted to a mere $631 million, less than 0.2 percent of the region's total global inflows. By 2012, China's cumulative stock of investment in ASEAN had reached $28.2 billion. (US FDI in ASEAN has nearly doubled since 2008 with a total stock of over $226 billion, more than in China, India, and Japan combined. Although Chinese FDI has grown faster since 2015, it still ranks in third place behind the United States and Japan.)[17]

While China's early economic relations were predominantly with the more developed "small tigers" in the south (Thailand, Malaysia, Singapore, and Indonesia) the focus since 2009 has shifted to the less developed CLMV tier (Cambodia, Laos, Myanmar, and Vietnam). This shift coincides with Chinese reliance on these countries to block progress on a COC. In 2009, Hu Jintao launched the bridgehead strategy, moving from Yunnan southward in the construction of infrastructure (dams, high-speed rail, roads, mineral extraction) designed to foster connectivity between China (particularly Yunnan and Guangxi) and mainland Southeast Asia. The East-West Economic Corridor (EWEC) has been built connecting Myanmar, Thailand, Laos, and Vietnam; three South-North Economic Transportation Corridors have been constructed (linking China-Vietnam, China-Laos-Thailand, and China-Myanmar). The Southern Economic Corridor between Cambodia, Thailand, and Vietnam is also under construction. In Laos, Chinese investment rose from just below 1.5 percent of total FDI in 2003 to 77 percent by 2012; in Cambodia, it grew from over $59 million in 2003 to $2.9 billion in 2013. China is the largest investor and aid donor in Cambodia; Cambodian officials and businesspeople frequently visit China seeking further investment. Chinese interests have secured potentially lucrative oil exploration rights both in the Tonle Sap and offshore in secretive Cambodian deals. Now the world's largest producer of hydropower and the largest dam, road, and high-speed rail builder,[18] China already has four dams on the upstream part of the Mekong, is currently investing in three hydropower dam projects in Laos and another one in Cambodia, and has plans for a further twelve dams along the river. Downstream from China's massive dam-building efforts is the fertile Mekong delta, where Vietnam, its interests more vulnerable to the downside of China's expanding influence than its neighbors, has complained of water diversion and salinization. Chinese FDI in CLMV, mostly by SOEs, tends to be focused on infrastructure (e.g., dams, high-speed rail) and resource extraction (e.g., oil, mining).

The dramatic unveiling of One Belt, One Road, now known as the Belt and Road Initiative (BRI), by Xi Jinping in 2013 put an illustrious name on China's various economic outreach projects evoking the pre-Han Silk Road from western China through Central Asia to Europe—some old, some new, all now in enhanced symbolic packaging. This vast network of infrastructure projects is projected to create the world's largest economic corridor, covering a population of 4.4 billion with an economic output of $21 trillion—two-thirds of the world's population, 50 percent of its GDP, and 75 percent of known global energy reserves (on imports of which China is increasingly dependent). And as OBOR makes progress, it will also increase the global use of Chinese currency, another Chinese economic objective. More than forty countries and international organizations have signed cooperation agreements or memorandums of understanding (MOUs) with China so far on the BRI. China has also signed industrial capacity cooperation agreements with over twenty countries. China has already invested heavily in port expansion and development throughout Southeast Asia: $2 billion in maritime Silk Road funding was earmarked to expand the port in Kuantan, on the east coast of western Malaysia, for instance, and China promised to invest in the $7.2 billion Malacca Gateway Deep Sea Port project. According to the World Bank, China by July 2016 already had invested $51.1 billion in various OBOR megaprojects. Officials boast that there are up to nine hundred deals under way, worth $890 billion, such as the three-thousand-kilometer high-speed rail from Kunming to Singapore.

To fund this vast project, Beijing provides several financial instruments. The China Development Bank (CDB) will receive $32 billion, the Export-Import Bank of China (EXIM) will take on $30 billion, and the Chinese government will also pump additional capital into the Agricultural Development Bank of China (ADBC), altogether totaling some $62 billion. To underwrite the China-Pakistan Economic Corridor (CPEC) is a $46 billion fund (subsequently increased to $55 billion). Funding will also be provided via two new multilateral banking projects, the Asian Infrastructure Investment Bank (AIIB), to which China has committed at least $50 billion toward a projected total of $100 billion, and the BRICS bank or New Development Bank (NDB), which also aims for a $100 billion currency reserve pool. While the BRICS bank is limited to BRICS countries (Brazil, Russia, India, China, and South Africa), others were invited to join AIIB, and after a year's hesitation, some fifty-seven founding members jumped in immediately, including twelve NATO members. Beijing will not have formal veto power; however, the bank is located in Beijing, and China holds a 30.34 percent stake in the bank while the articles of agreement require 75 percent support for a major policy decision. The total funding China has put on offer in this visionary project, sometimes referred to as China's Marshall Plan, exceeds US$6 trillion, though it has not yet stated on what financial terms or by when.[19] According to the CDB, around $900 billion in loans is already committed to ongoing or planned projects. Although about $1 trillion has left the country one way or another since 2014, China still has a $3 trillion cache of foreign exchange reserves to draw upon that it cannot easily expend domestically.

To be sure, the OBOR project is in its early stages and pitfalls lie ahead. China's projects entail infusions not only of capital but also equipment and whole labor crews, which are often imported from China and then left in the country; and China prefers to retain a controlling interest in the project infrastructure and land. Chinese investments in ASEAN tend to have relatively low spillover effects on local economies compared with Japanese and South Korean investments—there is typically little interaction with local firms, resulting in low transfer of knowledge and technology. One of the problems China confronts is how to achieve mutuality. OBOR clients typically receive only announcements flowing downward of China's intentions. Current and proposed exchanges have also been largely Sinocentric, earning the sobriquet "one belt, one way." Indeed, Chinese news articles about the initiative highlight other countries' interest in learning from China. Most of China's investment in international education goes to providing scholarships for students from OBOR countries to study in China, or in support of Chinese study programs abroad through Confucius Institutes or in opening international campuses of Chinese universities. The separate deals are negotiated with no strings attached but bilaterally, state to state with little concern for transparency. Interest rates on Chinese loans seem to vary depending on the temperature of the bilateral relationship.

China still has plenty of capital to invest, but the ability of recipient countries, many in fragile financial straits, to absorb the loans necessary to finance such massive investments is often inadequate, leaving them in a position of permanent indebtedness. In neighboring Laos, China accounted for over 40 percent of Laos's public external debt as of 2015, up from 35 percent in 2012, pushed up by debt service payments on infrastructure and power investments like the China-Laos railway, stretching (when finished, work started in 2015) 257 miles from the Chinese border to Vientiane, 70 percent of it through tunnels and bridges (at a cost of over half the country's $10.5 billion 2015 GDP). Chinese aid to Cambodia amounted to US$320 million in 2015 or roughly 30 percent of all foreign aid received. And Beijing accounts for the largest proportion of foreign investment in Cambodia and about 43 percent of the country's total debt stock, mainly in the form of loans from the CDB to Cambodia's government. Anecdotal evidence as well as econometric analysis indicates that these investments will indeed improve the economic prospects of the recipients—when they are paid for.[20] Another problem is caution on the part of overleveraged and risk-averse Chinese lending institutions. Aside from the obvious problem of moral hazard, there is the problem of "one belt, one (debt) trap." The top-down, closed-door negotiation of the deals makes them susceptible to elite corruption, reducing any trickle-down effect on the populace. And the neocolonial composition of trade (raw material exports and manufactured imports) that must be expedited to pay for these investments is conducive to a natural resource curse, trapping these economies at a lower stage of development.

What does this rapidly changing relationship look like from a triangular perspective? The currently operant configuration of the relationship between ASEAN, China, and the United States has shifted from a ménage to a romantic triangle. In other words, ASEAN is now able to maintain better relations with the United States and the PRC than the latter have with each other. This is rather ironic because the bone of contention between China and the United States in this part of the world is something belonging to neither—namely, the South China Sea. Previously no one could be said to own the South China Sea, which was defined as a public good. While the Monroe Doctrine certainly tried to discourage further European colonization of the Americas (and the Mediterranean was once called a "Roman lake"), there is no legal precedent for claiming formal title of an unenclosed sea. Without claiming sovereignty, the Southeast Asians previously derived greatest nonexclusive use-value from the sea based on physical proximity.

In a sense, US intrusion into the dispute was a clear misalignment of interests and capabilities in that the United States has no territorial claims in the dispute. This intrusion seems rather to have been based on a combination of a belief in the strategic value of Southeast Asia, a commitment to the international norm against territorial aggression, and power transition anxiety. It is conceivable that the future well-being of Southeast Asia hinges on control of the South China Sea. But it is unclear that the fate of the region is a core interest of the United States that it would fight to defend—while it may be one of the PRC. US complaints of constraint on freedom of navigation have been met by Chinese insistence that they have no intention of interfering with commercial shipping.[21] And this is technically true, though the Chinese have blocked vessels engaged in fishing or oil exploration. US commitment to the Cold War norm of nonaggression is conflated with a defense of the strategic status quo. Underlying this is the US perception that the PRC is determined to push the US Navy out of the South China Sea, an area it has hitherto dominated. As noted in chapter 2, this has evoked fears of a power transition and a shift in the global power balance. From a Chinese perspective, they are simply protecting their sovereign territory, and US meddling is even more annoying than the resistance of Southeast Asian countries because they believe the latter would otherwise not dare to resist. China believes the United States tends to embolden otherwise feckless small countries to defy an otherwise overwhelming balance of power.

ASEAN thus paradoxically becomes the pivot balancing between two polarized wings even though it is ASEAN that also holds the major stake in the game. As pivot, Southeast Asia benefits both from Beijing's economic largesse and from US security, and it cannot afford loss of protection nor is it willing to forgo Chinese economic inducements. Both are attractive, while the outbreak of war between these two giants would be an unmitigated disaster in which ASEAN loses both. Thus for ASEAN as a whole, the need for balance and harmony (the ASEAN Way) may outweigh its interest in defending maritime sovereignty claims. That said, in the long run exclusion from local high seas will limit developmental prospects for these trade-dependent economies. A key motivation for the Philippines to bring the arbitration case was the need to clarify the legal situation of the Reed Bank, for example. The Malampaya gas field offshore from Palawan, which provides one-third of the electricity for Manila and the island of Luzon, is running out and needs to be replaced. According to the tribunal, the gas under the Reed Bank belongs to the Philippines, but any attempt to extract it is likely to incur Chinese wrath. Vietnam derives some 24 percent of GDP from oil production, most of which is pumped offshore; Malaysia gets 45 percent of its revenue from the government-owned oil company Petronas, also pumping from offshore fields; and all Southeast Asian countries have thriving fish industries. Continuing Chinese attempts to gain monopoly control of maritime resources will minimally imply continuing friction.

CONCLUSIONS

Southeast Asia has always been a meeting point. Historically it was a meeting point between East Asia and South Asia, absorbing Hinduism, Theravada Buddhism, and Islam from the south and Confucianism and Mahayana Buddhism from the north. Western colonialism opened the region to the West and to the winds of global modernization. Since Japan's uninvited liberation from Western imperialism during World War II, the dominant outside influences have come from the United States and the PRC. The United States, as the strongest world power to emerge unscathed from the war, represented an odd mix of democratic liberalism and a defense of lingering Western imperialist interests, while China sought to divest itself of its tributary traditions and represent the forces of world revolution (with Chinese characteristics). Both tended to ignore the force of indigenous nationalism, which shaped events in complex and unexpected ways.

The Chinese revolutionary project was a vastly ambitious one aimed at transforming the entire Third World, but Southeast Asia in particular for reasons of geographic proximity and historic patterns of confluence, and it significantly impacted postwar developments in Indonesia, Burma, Malaysia, the Philippines, Thailand, and Vietnam. In the long run, however, it succeeded only in Vietnam. And it was here that Chinese interests clashed most directly with US interests, as the United States stumbled into defense of a holdover neocolonial regime. ASEAN came into being in 1967 independently but with Western support, in part in reaction to the perceived communist threat. This confrontation with China over former French Indochina was ultimately resolved in a bilateral compromise in which both powers tacitly agreed to withdraw, a solution that was sabotaged, however, by Vietnamese nationalism. This outcome not only created enduring friction for the Socialist Republic of Vietnam with both China and the United States but also split Southeast Asia between south and north, a cleavage that was not resolved until the end of the Cold War.

The post–Cold War era began with a withdrawal of both PRC and US power projection from the region, facilitating the configuration of a triangular ménage à trois. ASEAN took advantage of the power vacuum to expand vigorously but peaceably, resolving the ideological breach with the northern tier states to include all Southeast Asian states and introducing a number of extended forums intended to socialize the rest of East Asia into the ASEAN Way. On the basis of ASEAN centrality, the ARF, ACFTA, EAS, and other forums were instituted to engage Japan, Korea, and China and, ultimately, Russia, the United States, India, and Australia–New Zealand as well. The rise of China as a geopolitical juggernaut occurred within this friendly context, as China joined ARF in 1990 and helped innovate the APT and ACFTA at the end of the decade. Beijing's generous assistance to stricken Southeast

Asian economies during the Asian financial crisis helped to dispel lingering mistrust of the communist giant and economic intercourse took off, benefiting both sides.

But beginning around 2010, the strategic implications of the rise of China began to appear more problematic. The crux of the problem is, of course, China's mounting determination to turn the South China Sea into a Chinese lake, converting tiny subsurface islets into naval and air bases commanding their own EEZs. China has not yet attempted to take over land features already occupied by other Southeast Asian claimants, but it has attempted to pave over previously unoccupied islets and claim fishing and petroleum bounties. Yet the incorporation of China into various ASEAN forums, designed to socialize China into the Asian Way, has also afforded Beijing the political wherewithal to prevent a majority from forming that could question its claims or oblige it to negotiate a more mutually acceptable compromise. China has implemented an active diplomacy and economic statecraft to prevent any such majority from forming, including One Belt, One Road and other such generous mega-investment projects. This has for the time being succeeded in blocking any Code of Conduct or multilateral sanctions and thrown ASEAN centrality into serious question. The invocation of the UNCLOS seems to have resulted only in a further weakening of the authority of international law. ASEAN emerges as a passive pivot between an ambitiously expansionist China and an alarmist United States, which sees the geopolitical balance in Asia shifting to its enduring disadvantage. Yet there is serious question, particularly in the light of the unexpected results of the 2016 presidential election, whether the United States has the interest, will, or strategy to counter the power-political implications of the China Dream. The ASEAN hope must be that its practically feckless but visionary diplomacy may in the long run penetrate the more ruthless policies of Beijing.

NOTES

1. The mutual defense alliance with China, activated in 1950, remained operational for only about a decade. The alliances with Vietnam and the Democratic People's Republic of Korea (DPRK) terminated at the end of the Cold War. But Russia has since endeavored to build strong relations with India, Vietnam, and North Korea.

2. Quoted in Hadi Soesastro, foreword to *ASEAN in a Changed Regional and International Political Economy*, ed. Hadi Soesastro (Jakarta: Centre for Strategic and International Studies, 1995), iii–iv.

3. The communist-led Malayan People's Anti-Japanese Army, for example, received guerrilla training as well as arms from the British during the war but ended up forming the main body of the Malayan National Liberation Army, the armed wing of the Malayan communists who engaged in the insurgency in Malaya from 1948 to 1960. Even though the British would eventually win their counterinsurgency campaign, they had to pay the price of at least 1,860 British and allied deaths and over 2,400 wounded.

4. See Karl Hack and Geoff Wade, "The Origins of the Southeast Asian Cold War," *Journal of Southeast Asian Studies* 40, no. 3 (October 2009): 441–48.

5. Edgar Snow, *Red Star over China*, rev. and enlarged ed. (New York: Grove Press, 1968), 181.

6. Kermit E. McKenzie, *Comintern and World Revolution, 1928–1943: The Shaping of Doctrine* (New York: Columbia University Press, 1964), 137; cited in Steven M. Goldstein, "The Chinese Revolution and the Colonial Areas: The View from Yenana, 1937–1941," *China Quarterly*, no. 75 (September 1978): 594–622, fn. 12.

7. Liu Shaoqi, "On the Party," (May 1945), in *Collected Works of Liu Shaoqi*, vol. 2 (Hong Kong: Union Research Institute, 1969).

8. Shen Zhihua and Xia Yafeng, "Leadership Transfer in the Asian Revolution: Mao Zedong and the Asian Cominform," *Cold War History* 14, no. 2 (2014): 195–213.

9. For example, the highest proportion of GNP the developed Western nations gave in foreign aid barely exceeded 0.5 percent, and the US figure at the turn of the millennium was far below .01 percent. Under Mao, China's foreign aid reached 6.92 percent (in 1973), the highest amount (as a proportion of GNP) the world has yet seen. Dangdai Zhongguo, ed., *Dangdai Zhongguo de duiwai jingji hezuo* [China today economic cooperation with foreign countries] (Beijing: Zhongguo shehui kexue chubanshe, 1989), 68. For a classic analysis, see Peter Van Ness, *Revolution and Chinese Foreign Policy: Peking's Support for Wars of National Liberation* (Berkeley: University of California Press, 1970).

10. Toshiki Kaifu, "Japan and ASEAN: Seeking a Mature Partnership for the New Age Policy Speech by Prime Minister Toshiki Kaifu Singapore, 3 May 1991," *ASEAN Economic Bulletin* 8, no. 1 (July 1991): 87–94.

11. See the Swedish International Peace Research Institute (SIPRI) Database, http://www.sipri.org/databases/milex.

12. "Duterte and Xi Talk War," *Philippine Daily Inquirer*, May 24, 2017, https://www.pressreader.com/philippines/philippine-daily-inquirer/20170524/281719794526122.

13. See Eugene Staley, *War and the Private Investor: A Study in the Relations of International Relations and International Private Investment* (Garden City, NY: Doubleday, Doran & Co., 1935).

14. The Philippines, however, is an ally that had evicted the United States from Clark Air Force Base in 1991 and from Subic Bay Naval Base in 1992, hitherto its largest overseas military installations.

15. Nick Wadhams, "Tillerson 'Emphatic' about Need to Halt South China Sea Buildup," *Bloomberg*, May 4, 2017; cf. https://www.bloomberg.com/news/articles/2017-05-04/tillerson-emphatic-about-need-to-halt-south-china-sea-buildup.

16. According to the Global Trade Alert, a database which tracks protectionist measures, 659 measures have been initiated against Chinese exports since the 2008 crisis.

17. According to ASEAN figures for net FDI inflow, in 2015 Chinese FDI inflow totaled US$8,256.5 million, up from $6,990 million in 2014; this compares with Japanese inflow of $17,559 million in 2015 ($15,705 million in 2014) and US FDI of $13,646 million in 2015 ($14,748 million in 2014).

18. China has built the world's largest hydropower project (the Three Gorges Dam), the world's highest railway, the world's highest and longest bridges, and an eight-hundred-mile canal from the Yangtze River to Beijing in part of the world's largest water transfer project. But although such projects—only the most conspicuous of a vast modern infrastructure—have boosted GDP and added to industrial efficiency, they also provide opportunity for cadre corruption and the accumulation of debt beyond feasible repayment costs. Chris Buckley, "China's New Bridges: Rising High, but Buried in Debt," *New York Times*, June 10, 2017, https://www.nytimes.com/2017/06/10/world/asia/china-bridges-infrastructure.html.

19. Li Su, Huang Jiangnan, and Zhao Gang, *Xi Jinping jingjixue di wu hang guoce yu shi da guoli* [Xi Jinping's economics: Five national policies and ten national powers] (Hong Kong: Xing hui tu shu you xian gong si, 2015).

20. See Chien-peng Chung and Thomas J. Voon, "China's Maritime Silk Road Initiative: Political Economic Calculations of Southeast Asian States," *Asian Survey* 57, no. 3 (May–June 2017), 416–50.

21. Indeed, China has not yet threatened commercial shipping through the South China Sea. A recent report showed that the shipping industry is not too concerned about US warnings that

Beijing is seeking to exert control in the South China Sea. Even if China does eventually take over the South China Sea, shipping firms don't think that this would affect the passage of merchant ships. Cf. "Shipping Unscathed as China Flights Raise South China Sea Tension," Reuters, January 13, 2016, http://www.reuters.com/article/southchinasea-shipping-idUSL8N14R17X20160114. That said, Beijing has started warning aircraft or vessels approaching its now occupied islets off, now implicitly claiming EEZs for them—there may be a slippery slope.

Chapter Seven

Enduring Ambivalence

Beginning as fraternal founding leaders of the nonaligned bloc, what we see emerging since around the turn of the century in terms of India-China-US relations is beginning to look broadly like a classic triangle, mutatis mutandis. Among the changes that must be made, India's foreign policy architecture has never been too clear. India's national identity emerged from its colonial experience with lingering ties to the West, as it had taken some pride in being recognized as the largest and most important constituent of the British Empire (the "jewel in the crown") and has remained a dominion of the Commonwealth since 1947. Upon establishment of a fully independent republic in 1950, India's identity was primarily oriented to the so-called Third World of postcolonial developing nations. That vast conglomeration, however, has become more diverse over time. As a culturally heterogeneous socialist democracy intent on distancing itself from both liberal democracy and Leninist socialism, defined more in terms of what it was not than what it was, India has preferred to define its national identity by abstract ideals (secular, democratic, peace loving) rather than any pattern of interstate relationships. This vaguely idealistic identity has arguably served the country well, enabling it to follow its national interests from one relationship to another as opportunities and risks appear without any sense of ideological strain. The foreign policy course at any given time is set by the elected prime minister (the presidency is largely ceremonial) and implemented by the Minister (and Ministry) for External Affairs. Thus it tends to vary with his/her personal characteristics and political priorities. As founding leader, Jawaharlal Nehru, India's prime minister for seventeen years, set the course of Indian foreign policy in terms of two principles: nonalignment and self-reliance. Still revered, his founding principles have had a lasting but not consistent impact on India's foreign policy.

There have been three distinct stages in the development of Indian foreign policy since independence.[1] The first, or "Nehruvian," stage began in 1947 and lasted until the Sino-Indian War of 1962. The second, or "Gandhian," stage (headlined by the leadership of Indira and her son Rajiv) lasted from 1962 to 1991. The third stage began with the 1991 economic reforms and continues to the present. While the first stage saw the high and low of the Sino-Indian relationship and the second was on the whole characterized by a low-level freeze, in the third stage India's diplomatic architecture began to take a recognizably triangular shape. This chapter is hence focused on the third stage, divided into three sections. The first will focus on Sino-Indian relations, the second on US-Indian relations, and the third on the triangular interaction among the three.

SINO-INDIAN RELATIONS

Cultural and economic relations between China and India date back centuries. Around the second century, Hindu and Buddhist influences spread to China and from there to Korea and Japan. Chinese scholars visited Indian universities Nalanda and Taxila and other Buddhist centers to study Buddhism. During the first millennium, Sino-Indian relations were limited to religious exchanges, but in the second millennium (1100–1500), they gave way to trade and commercial relations. While religious pilgrimages occurred over land, commercial relations took place primarily through maritime routes during the Song dynasty (960–1278), the Yuan dynasty (1279–1368), and the early Ming dynasty (1368–1644), as the Silk Road was closed by the Islamic invasion of Central Asia and by a powerful Tibetan kingdom.[2] During the nineteenth century, China's growing opium trade with the British raj triggered the First and Second Opium Wars, coinciding with India's unsuccessful first war of independence (the Sepoy Mutiny, 1857–59).

Sino-Indian relations during the Nehruvian era began most auspiciously: India was the second country outside the communist bloc to end formal ties with the Republic of China on Taiwan and recognize the People's Republic of China (PRC) as the legitimate government of China, and it persistently urged Beijing's admission to the United Nations (UN), including to its Security Council (a favor India would now like returned). Nehru envisaged that India and China could work together to lead a postwar, postcolonial Asia. The early phase of Sino-Indian relations was warm, despite China's military takeover of Tibet in 1950. Both were socialist planned economies (indeed India adopted its first five-year plan in 1950, three years before China) beginning at a low level of development but with soaring ambitions. The slogan of the day was *Hindi-Chini Bhai-bhai* (Indians and Chinese are brothers). In 1954, the two countries (represented by Nehru and Zhou Enlai) signed an agreement on trade and intercourse with Tibet in which India signed away inherited imperial privileges there and recognized Chinese sovereignty. The Five Principles of Peaceful Coexistence (*Panchsheel*, in Sanskrit) emerged from that meeting and were reaffirmed at the Bandung Afro-Asian Conference (to which Nehru arranged to have China invited) the following year. The five principles have been written into the preamble of every Chinese constitution since.[3]

In the late 1950s, however, relations deteriorated, beginning with the Dalai Lama's 1959 flight from Tibet with some eighty thousand followers and subsequent permanent refuge in Dhramsala. Beijing blamed India for inciting the Tibetan revolt and for hosting the exile community, and the subsequent propaganda barrage then accumulated other issues. In the context of promoting revolution in the Third World, China supported a communist movement in neighboring Nepal and the Naxalbari (Naxalite) rebellion in West Bengal (which still continues, without official Chinese support). This was followed by a succession of regrettable events: China secretly began constructing a road across the barren Aksai Plain connecting Xinjiang to Tibet in 1957, and ambushed Indian border patrols sent to surveil the perceived infringement of Indian territory in 1959. The territorial dispute gathered momentum. India initiated a forward policy in which it placed outposts along the border, including some to the north of the so-called Line of Actual Control (LAC) proclaimed by Zhou Enlai in 1959. The Chinese suddenly launched simultaneous offensives in Ladakh in the west and across the McMahon Line in the east on October 20, 1962. China quickly defeated and humiliated Delhi, annexed the Aksai Chin, but withdrew from the Tawang area it had taken in the east. Diplomatic relations were suspended for the next decade as India nursed its wounds and hurt pride. China conducted its first nuclear tests in 1964, and backed Pakistan in Indo-Pakistani War in 1965.

This led to a reevaluation of India's place in world politics, to an informal distancing from the policy of nonalignment and adoption of a more "realistic" approach to China. During the 1962–87 period, under the leadership of Prime Minister Indira Gandhi and other Congress Party stalwarts, India pursued an arms buildup facilitated by closer alignment with the Soviet Union, culminating in a friendship treaty in August 1971. Meanwhile China, domestically preoccupied with the Cultural Revolution (which tended to sharpen the contradiction with India as a perceived proxy of the "revisionist" USSR), cultivated a countervailing relationship with Pakistan in the form of arms sales and defense cooperation. Aroused by China's nuclear test in 1964, India tested its first "peaceful nuclear explosive" in 1974. The years 1962 to 1976 may be considered the relationship's nadir, during which the two did not even exchange ambassadors. A somewhat more benign relationship commenced after 1982 (ambassadorial representation was resumed, and a Joint Working Group established), though trade remained minimal and border talks made little progress. Since the 1980s and 1990s when China and India respectively embarked on their economic reforms, strategic rivalry was amplified by a competitive scramble for resources in Asia and Africa.

The downward spiral was stemmed by Rajiv Gandhi with his 1988 prime ministerial visit to China, the first such visit since Nehru's visit in 1955. During this trip, both sides agreed that the Joint Working Group (JWG) for settlement of the border dispute would meet regularly and hopefully make some progress. Meanwhile, relations in multilateral forums ironically seemed more amenable to betterment than bilateral relations. Although China has not supported India's aspiration to join either the Asia-Pacific Economic Cooperation (APEC) forum or the UN Security Council, both countries were founding members of the Non-Aligned Movement in the 1950s and subsequently both joined the BRICS (Brazil, Russia, India, China, and South Africa) and the Group of 20. China invited India as an observer and finally a member of the Shanghai Cooperation Organization or SCO (along with Pakistan). China became an observer at the South Asian Association for Regional Cooperation (SAARC) while India joined the Association of Southeast Asian Nations (ASEAN) Regional Forum (ARF) and (with Australia and New Zealand) the East Asia Summit (EAS).[4] India has joined the BRICS Development Bank and the controversial Asian Infrastructure Investment Bank (where it is the second-largest investor, with 8 percent of voting rights), but has shown no interest in the One Belt, One Road megaproject. The two have taken mutually complementary positions on such issues as global warming, noninterference in the internal affairs of other nations, the need to right the global north-south gap, antiterrorism, and nuclear nonproliferation.[5]

Yet there is a persisting deficit of strategic trust. In 2004, a BBC World Service poll calculated that 66 percent of the Indians saw China's increasing influence in the world as "mainly positive"; this favorable response declined to 44 percent in 2005.[6] In a BBC poll in December 2006, carried out only a few weeks after the cordial visit by Hu Jintao, this share shrunk further to 36 percent.[7] According to a July 2014 Pew Global poll, just 30 percent of Chinese hold a favorable view of India and 31 percent of Indians hold a favorable view of China. This is partly because of old wounds, partly because there is so little interaction between the two populations. Of the 100 million Chinese who traveled overseas in 2013, just 160,000 came to India, while in contrast 1.4 million visited France. Of the 270,000 Indian students studying abroad in 2013, just 9,200 were in China, and only 2,000 Chinese students were studying in India.[8] In terms of policy, the lack of trust may be attributed to three basic factors: (1) the persisting border dispute (the only land-based territorial dispute China has not settled aside from tiny Bhutan), (2) geostrategic competition, and (3) an ambivalent economic relationship.

The Border Dispute

The border dispute, though not intrinsically related, immediately followed and was apparently exacerbated by the flight of and Indian sanctuary for the Dalai Lama, after which the PRC accused India of expansionism and imperialism in Tibet and throughout the Himalayan region. China claimed 104,000 square kilometers of territory over which India's maps depicted Indian sovereignty and demanded rectification of the entire border. The two territories in dispute are the Aksai Chin in the northeastern section of Ladakh district in Jammu and Kashmir (also contested with Pakistan, which subsequently proved more amenable to territorial concessions than India), and in the eastern sector a region China calls "Southern Tibet" that India renamed Arunachal Pradesh and made a state. Zhou met with Nehru in 1960 and proposed a swap: China would relinquish its claim to Arunachal Pradesh in exchange for India's abandonment of its claim to Aksai Chin. The eastern section is much larger (three times the size of Taiwan) with greater economic potential than the barren and sparsely populated Aksai Chin, and both areas have acquired nationalist symbolic importance. Nehru demurred at the time, and the offer is now moot since China took what it wanted in the Aksai Chin and has nothing to trade for Arunachal (which it still wants).[9] As the two sides entered into negotiations, it became clear that an underlying cartographic problem was China's consistent refusal to accept the McMahon Line as the final line of border demarcation, counting it among the unequal treaties imposed by imperialist powers.[10] Indians argue that China claims the territory on the basis that it was under Chinese imperial control in the past, while Chinese argue that India claims the territory on the basis that it was under British imperial control in the past. Nehru also argued that since China had accepted the McMahon Line in its settlement with Burma it should be willing to use the same yardstick here.

The escalating dispute culminated in a short, sanguinary border war between China and India in October 1962. India's crushing defeat, followed by a vituperative Chinese propaganda campaign against India, shattered Nehru's image at home and abroad. Between 1962 and 1969, Sino-Indian relations remained in a deep freeze, interrupted by recurrent artillery exchanges (1967, 1971, and 1975). There were skirmishes at Nathu La and Cho La in 1967 and in 1987 at Sumdorong Chu in the eastern sector, both inconclusive, Indian forces acquitting themselves somewhat better than in 1962. In 1990, the Chinese and Indian military tentatively started mending fences by exchanging middle-rank officers from the National Defense College in New Delhi and the National Defense University in Beijing, and there have been no fatal encounters since 1986 (unlike the Indo-Pakistani border area).[11]

After the Cultural Revolution and the death of Mao Zedong, bilateral relations gradually improved. In 1976, China reopened its embassy in New

Delhi, and India consequently sent an ambassador to the People's Republic. A year later, Beijing offered to start talks for resuming border trade. In 1978, it invited Foreign Minister Atal Bihari Vajpayee to discuss bilateral political and economic relations. At the same time, China modulated its pro-Pakistan stand on Kashmir. Beginning in December 1981, officials from both countries have held annual talks on the border issue. The Agreement on the Maintenance of Peace and Tranquility along the Line of Actual Control was signed on September 7, 1993, during the landmark visit of Prime Minister P. V. Narasimha Rao. It affirmed that the India-China boundary question should be resolved through peaceful and friendly consultations and that the LAC should be strictly observed. During President Jiang Zemin's visit to India at the end of November 1996, the governments of China and India signed the Agreement on Confidence-Building Measures in the Military Field along the Line of Actual Control (LAC) in the China-India Border Area. During Chinese premier Wen Jiabao's visit in April 2005, the two sides signed an agreement on political settlement of the boundary issue, affirming joint readiness to seek a fair, reasonable, and mutually acceptable solution to the boundary issue through equal and friendly negotiations. Since 2003, more than a dozen rounds of talks had been launched to resolve border disputes. The issue remains basically intractable but it has been more successfully managed: notwithstanding recurrent border incursions, reciprocal troop mobilizations (as in 1986–87), and continuing efforts by both sides to strengthen their militaries' respective capabilities on the borders, since 1967 recurring confrontations have been defused diplomatically without further bloodshed.[12] Still the Chinese continue to press forward, keeping the issue alive with periodic subthreshold incremental incursions.[13] Thus in June 2017, a tense military standoff occurred when China attempted to extend a road on the Doklam plateau southward near the Doka La pass in Bhutan and Indian troops deployed to prevent it.

Geostrategic Competition

There are two basic strategic issues underlying continuing bilateral distrust: (1) the shifting balance of military power, and (2) the mutual use of suspected "proxies" to build encircling and counterencircling regional coalitions. Although the power asymmetry between the two is less than that between China and Southeast Asia, the current and immediately foreseeable balance of military power is tilted in China's favor simply because China can extract a larger defense budget from what has been a larger and faster growing gross domestic product (GDP).[14] There are two relevant aspects of the strategic power balance: nuclear and conventional.

Nuclear

India tested its first "peaceful nuclear explosion" in 1974, ten years after China, but refrained in principle from weaponization at that time. A quarter century later, in May 1998, the nationalist coalition government led by the Bharatiya Janata Party (BJP) tested five bombs and thereafter proceeded to weaponization. The immediate justification was offered by Foreign Minister George Fernandes, calling China India's "potential threat number one." This understandably provoked outrage from Beijing, which froze diplomatic relations until 2000. Actually Fernandes may not have known of the forthcoming tests (May 11–13) at the time of his (May 3) speech, but in his May 11 letter to Clinton, Vajpayee claimed that China had placed medium- and intermediate-range missile systems in Tibet: "We have an overt nuclear-weapon state on our borders, a state which committed armed aggression against India in 1962."[15] China ever since has consistently opposed India's quest to legitimate its nuclear status, while the United States in contrast lifted initial sanctions and in 2008 helped secure a temporary waiver to India's admission to the Nuclear Suppliers' Group (NSG) and later to its full membership in the Missile Technology Control Regime (MTCR).[16] The issue of Indian power has hence become a useful wedge issue for the United States. It has also incited some Chinese suspicion of its closest strategic partner, Russia. The two have long been the top arms customers of the Soviet Union/Russia, India displacing China as number one since the decline in Chinese purchases after 2007, and the Chinese sometimes suspect the Russians of tilting against China by selling the Indians more sophisticated hardware. Actually, one of Russia's basic strategic objectives since the mid-1990s has been to build a strategic triangle (specifically, a ménage à trois) including both India and China, so Moscow has generally supported Indo-Chinese harmonization.

But it would be an oversimplification to attribute Indian nuclear weaponization exclusively to the China threat.[17] Other contributing factors certainly include the virtually simultaneous acquisition of a Pakistani bomb, the rise of Hindutva nationalism under the BJP, and a factor difficult to measure but hard to dismiss: international prestige. In the postwar global status hierarchy, the five acknowledged nuclear weapon states—which happen also to be the five permanent members of the United Nations Security Council—rank near the top. And India's quest for status is particularly relevant to its position vis-à-vis China: the two countries, once equal, since the 1950s have grown at differential speeds, and Indians are sensitive to China's perceived triumphal condescension.[18] As of 2015, China was 4.66 times richer than India in nominal method and 2.20 times richer in purchasing power parity (PPP) method, ranking India as the seventh-largest economy in the world (nominal GDP) and China as second largest. The military gap has widened correspondingly. In 2015, China's defense spending was US$145.8 billion compared to India's US$47.9 billion, according to the Stockholm International Peace Research Institute (SIPRI). China, in contrast to India, has taken little note of the bilateral nuclear threat, declaring that its nuclear forces are oriented entirely toward the United States: "The mission of China's strategic nuclear force is to ensure the United States is adequately concerned by its retaliatory strike capabilities."[19]

In the draft nuclear doctrine articulated in August 1999, then prime minister Atal Bihari Vajpayee committed his country to a credible minimal deterrent deliverable by a triad of launch vehicles: aircraft, land-based missiles, and sea-based assets—namely, submarines yet to be built—with an emphasis on quick reaction time and survivability. At the same time, New Delhi calls for universal nuclear disarmament and has pledged no first use. According to India's own assessment, it now possesses a fully operational triad.[20] In December 2014, the Indian military conducted its first successful test of the land-based 2,500-mile-range Agni-IV, the first Indian ballistic missile capable of delivering nuclear or conventional warheads into proximate Chinese territory; as of November 2015, it was still undergoing trials. In January 2015, India successfully tested the road-mobile delivery platform of its first true intercontinental ballistic missile, the Agni-V; with a range of up to 3,500 miles, it will extend India's strategic reach to the rest of China. (China's rocket force has included nuclear missiles with a range equivalent to India's Agni-V since 1980.) SIPRI estimates that India has between 90 and 110 relatively low-yield nuclear weapons, compared to China's more than 260 warheads. The newest element of India's nuclear arsenal is the INS *Arihant*, India's first domestically built ballistic-missile-carrying nuclear submarine (SSBN), which underwent trials in the fall of 2016. This will give India a second-strike capability that can survive a land-based nuclear exchange. *Arihant*, the first of an expected four SSBNs, will carry twelve Sararika missiles, ranging from five hundred to one thousand miles depending on payload. Neither Pakistan nor China has plausible antisubmarine warfare capabilities for tracking or sinking the boats. China, as in other respects slightly ahead, first sent its four "boomers" (SSBNs) on patrol in December 2015.

In sum, although India remains behind China both quantitatively and qualitatively (India's 1998 test of a thermonuclear device or H-bomb was less than satisfactory), India can now be said to have a minimal deterrent. Moreover, India's highly advanced space program makes technically possible the acquisition of comprehensive surveillance capabilities, and the precision of its guidance systems facilitates counterforce as well as countervalue options. But India's security outlook has always been complicated by the fact that it also balances against China's "all-weather friend" Pakistan, which has an estimated stockpile of 100 to 120 deliverable nuclear weapons. Hedging, India also has a strategic partnership (one of its twenty, to China's fifty) with

China, and conducts naval exercises with the People's Liberation Army Navy (PLAN) as well as with Japan and the United States.[21]

Conventional

The conventional force balance is less likely to be definitive but likely to be deployed first in the event of hostilities. Although China has the largest unsated territorial claim, having occupied the Aksai Chin in the west, it is unlikely to use the People's Liberation Army (PLA), largest in the world, to pour across the Himalayas like Hannibal over the Alps just to seize Arunachal Pradesh. But China and India do have overlapping naval ambitions that now rival their land-based disputes. India has historically implicitly assumed de facto dominance in the Indian Ocean, while China has been attempting to exert the same power over its coastal waters generously conceived. China also seems intent on developing its economic and military interests in the Indian Ocean in a manner likely to have a major impact on the regional balance of power, disregarding India's historic regional prerogatives. As the world's largest oil importer (82 percent of its imports go through the Strait of Malacca), China has become concerned about securing its sea lanes of communication (SLOCs) against pirates in the Gulf of Aden as well as potential threats of interdiction by a certain meddlesome superpower under foreseeable future contingencies, and has thus acquired a powerful "blue-water" navy, sending intermittent submarine probes into Indian Ocean waters. As early as 1993, General Zhao Nanqi, director of the Chinese Academy of Military Sciences, maintained that, "we are not prepared to let the Indian Ocean become India's Ocean."[22] China's 2015 defense white paper, *China's Military Strategy*, signaled a shift from "offshore waters defense" to a more capacious "open ocean protection."[23] China is using its antipiracy deployments and its resource import dependency as justification for expanding its naval presence in the region and making it permanent. China has developed a number of military and civilian seaports since 2008, financing infrastructure developments in Kyaukpyu, in Myanmar; Colombo and Hambantota, in Sri Lanka; and Mahe, in the Seychelles. In 2015, China contracted to build its first naval facilities in Djibouti, on the Horn of Africa, overlooking the pirate-infested Gulf of Aden.[24]

The other projects are still mainly commercial, providing harbors to resupply merchant and naval shipping, thereby advancing China's economic, diplomatic, and military purposes in the region (however, the distinction between commercial and military may be fungible in Chinese eyes, as they have used Chinese-funded commercial ports in Sri Lanka to dock their submarines). In the process, such outreach helps Beijing amass goodwill with South Asian governments, all of which now have more trade with China (invariably imbalanced in China's favor) than with India. Still, since December 2008, the PLAN has continuously deployed two to three surface vessels in the Arabian Sea in some nineteen different deployments and, in February 2014, awoke Indian attention with a three-ship naval exercise in the East Indian Ocean. A PLAN conventional submarine docked twice in Colombo the same year without prior notification. Chinese submarine visits to Pakistan are increasing as well and will likely continue, as demonstrated by the docking of a Chinese nuclear-powered submarine in Karachi in May 2016.

China's naval capabilities are now marginally greater than India's in nearly all categories. As fleet queens, both now field refurbished Soviet aircraft carriers. Over a decade ago, India bought the thirty-eight-thousand-ton former Soviet *Admiral Gorshkov* for $1.6 billion. After an extensive refit, it joined the Indian navy in 2013 as the INS *Vikramaditya* ("Almighty"), hosting an air wing of thirty Russian-built Mikoyan MiG-29K fighters. INS *Vikramaditya* is the Indian navy's second aircraft carrier, complementing its aging 28,700-ton aircraft carrier INS *Viraat* ("Giant"). Built for Britain's Royal Navy as HMS *Hermes* in 1959, it fought in the Falklands in 1982, was decommissioned in 1985, and was transferred to India two years later. Beijing acquired the hull of the much bigger (67,500 tons) two-thirds completed *Varyag* from Ukraine in 1998. Towed to China, extensively refitted, and renamed the *Liaoning*, it is the Chinese navy's first aircraft carrier. The PLAN also plans three domestically constructed carriers, the first of which was launched in Dalian in April 2017. India has noticed China's buildup in the Indian Ocean with growing wonder about its conceivable strategic purpose. Just as China aims to make the South China Sea a Chinese lake, India wants to make the Indian Ocean an Indian lake, and as in the Chinese case, economic as well as strategic considerations weigh heavily. As Holslag has pointed out, more than 95 percent of its exports are shipped through the surrounding waters, and India drills up to 70 percent of its domestic hydrocarbons in offshore blocks.[25]

Taking a cue from China's island building in the South China Sea, India is reinforcing its defense facilities (i.e., airstrips, ports, etc.) on its Andaman and Nicobar Islands strategically located in the Bay of Bengal near the Malacca Strait. India has been carrying out joint naval exercises with Singapore near the Andaman Islands for two decades. India has also announced it will be building a new port at Chabahar in Iran, near to Gwadar and like it a logistics point linking Central Asia to the Indian Ocean. When China approached India to solicit cooperation in its massive Maritime Silk Road (MSR) in 2014, India's response to what it conceives as a revival in new clothing of the so-called string of pearls strategy has been noncommittal. With the biggest chunk of the MSR's first phase well under way in Pakistan—and partly through parts of Kashmir still claimed by India—a green light would be politically difficult for India's Prime Minister Narendra Modi. Hitherto the Chinese buildup in the Indian Ocean and Bay of Bengal has been low key, and there is as yet no indication of any attempt to challenge Indian vessels publicly in the way the Chinese maritime police fleet routinely challenges Japanese coast guard or US surveillance vessels or Southeast Asian fishing boats in peripheral waters.[26]

While the overall military balance clearly favors China, India is striving to remain competitive in the quiet arms race and at the same time to balance externally. Thus India has engaged in greater strategic cooperation with Japan and the United States, though security cooperation has been somewhat inhibited by fear of provoking China.[27] India and Japan issued the Joint Declaration on Security Cooperation in October 2008, and in 2009, the two signed a strategic partnership agreement and held their first bilateral naval exercise. India was the first country outside South Asia that Abe Shinzo paid a state visit to in 2014, upgrading the relationship to a special strategic and global partnership.[28] In August 2016, India and the United States signed the Logistics Exchange Memorandum of Agreement (LEMOA), providing access to each other's military facilities for fueling and logistic support on a reimbursable basis. Along with Russia, India cultivates good relations with mutual friend Vietnam. Military cooperation includes sale of military equipment, sharing of intelligence, joint naval exercises, and training in counterinsurgency and jungle warfare. During his September 2016 visit, Modi awarded a $500 million credit line to Vietnam, and the two formed a comprehensive strategic partnership. India also regularly deploys its warships for goodwill visits to Vietnamese ports. Over vociferous Chinese complaints, India has also cooperated in oil exploration in Vietnamese waters, tacitly recognizing Vietnamese maritime sovereignty claims over China's.[29]

Although India has avoided involvement in the East China Sea territorial dispute, it has taken increasing interest in the South China Sea, refusing to endorse China's position on freedom of navigation and preaching respect for international law—specifically, the 2016 Tribunal Award to the Philippines. India signed a strategic partnership with ASEAN in 2012, but it views the South China Sea as a secondary sphere of influence, its priority being the Indian Ocean/Bay of Bengal area. It realizes it does not have the naval capability to stake any kind of claim as a significant military power in the South China Sea, but by inserting itself into the ongoing controversy India can undermine China's "peaceful rise" narrative and enhance its relative strategic and economic value to Southeast Asia while leveraging strategic pressure on China to offset the latter's drive into the Indian Ocean region. Trade between India and ASEAN has reached US$76 billion (as of 2013–14), up more than 20 percent since a decade ago. This has been facilitated by the India-ASEAN Free Trade Agreement (IAFTA) in goods, which targeted trade of US$100 billion by 2016. India has begun to place special emphasis on Cambodia, Myanmar, Laos, and Vietnam (whose current leading trade partner is China). But it is not yet a serious economic competitor to

China in Southeast Asia: India constitutes just 2.7 percent of ASEAN's total trade volume, whereas China constitutes 10.4 percent.

Like China, India fears strategic encirclement, by China in particular. Yet in an asymmetric relationship the weaker power has more reason to fear than the stronger, and unless the latter redoubles its conciliatory efforts the logical course for the weaker is to raise defense spending and coalesce with others to form an external balance. In India's case, this has contradictory implications: on the one hand, India must logically balance externally with its neighbors against China, but on the other hand, India's neighbors need to externally balance with one another against India, the subregional hegemon. In this tacit competition, China has so far been more persuasive in building a balancing coalition than India. It was with the support of this coalition that China gained observer status in the SAARC over Indian resistance. Three cases in China's encirclement strategy are worth considering more closely: Pakistan, Bangladesh, and Sri Lanka.

Pakistan   The linchpin of China's coalition is Pakistan, which separated from India for sectarian reasons in 1947 and has since had four major conflicts with its giant neighbor, all unsuccessful. Sino-Pakistan ties gained particular momentum after the 1962 Sino-Indian war, when China and Pakistan signed a boundary agreement recognizing Chinese control over portions of Pakistani-administered Kashmir. Beginning in 1965, China has steadfastly supported Pakistan in its wars with India, though never to the extent of sending Chinese troops. Pakistan helped facilitate China-US détente in 1971 and has also been instrumental in warming China's relations with the Muslim world. China has provided clandestine assistance in Pakistan's development of nuclear and missile technology and remains Pakistan's largest defense supplier, with joint projects including the (nuclear-capable) JF-17 fighter, an airborne warning and control system, the Shaheen-1 ballistic missile, and the Babur cruise missile. Pakistan is now the world's leading purchaser of Chinese weapons; from 2006 to 2016, Pakistan accounted for no less than 35 percent of China's total arms exports. These include short-range M-11 missiles, the third-generation J-10 fighter (then China's most advanced), and eight Yuan-class SSBNs (some of which may be fitted with nuclear-tipped missiles).

China has also constructed and subsequently (after Singapore withdrew) contracted to operate a new port at Gwadar, having secured the land rights to the port and surrounding areas until 2058, where it also plans to build a commercial and manufacturing hub similar to the special economic zones in China. Through the China-Pakistan Economic Corridor (CPEC) introduced by Xi Jinping in 2013, Gwadar is to be linked to Kashgar in Xinjiang via a network of railroads, highways, and pipelines. The project is expected to result in the creation of more than seven hundred thousand direct jobs between 2015 and 2030, Pakistani officials promise, and add 2 to 2.5 percentage points to the country's annual economic growth. Once fully implemented, the value of CPEC projects is anticipated to equal all foreign direct investment (FDI) in Pakistan since 1970, or 17 percent of Pakistan's 2015 GDP. The project, funded by a US$42 billion Chinese loan (hiked to $62 billion since December 2016) plus some Pakistani cofunding, is a cornerstone of China's ambitious One Belt, One Road (OBOR) project; indeed, it will link the twenty-first-century Maritime Silk Road to the overland Silk Road Economic Belt. The China Overseas Ports Holding Company has expanded the Gwadar port in Pakistan and has an operating lease until 2059. The Chinese money for CPEC is largely on commercial terms. Local and international companies can bid for these projects as well, but with China loaning the funds, Chinese state-owned enterprises (SOEs) will get most of the contracts. CPEC will provide not only Chinese capital but also Chinese labor and steel.

Though China's links to Pakistan are the oldest and strongest in South Asia, they are notoriously vulnerable to terrorism, particularly in poor Balochistan, richly endowed with natural resources from which the Balochs have benefited little. Over ten thousand Chinese expatriates reside in Pakistan, where they have endured more terrorist attacks than in any other country between 2004 and 2010.[30] When the United States dismantled the Taliban regime in Afghanistan, a large number of Central Asian Islamist groups (including Uyghur groups fighting for an independent Eastern Turkestan in Xinjiang) took refuge in the Pakistan-Afghanistan border areas. To guard CPEC projects Nawaz Sharif was providing a "special security division for Pakistan-China economic projects," comprising more than fifteen thousand army and civil forces.[31] China has also begun to deploy thirty thousand of its own security personnel to protect the projects along the CPEC route, raising the specter of a permanent military establishment. Symbolizing this security relationship, a ninety-member PLA honor guard marched in Pakistan's national day military parade in Islamabad on March 23, 2017. India has rejected CPEC because some of the territory being traversed by the corridor (in Pakistan-occupied Jammu and Kashmir) is still claimed by India. But more fundamentally, the project seems designed to turn a weak opponent into a strong one—while at the same time sealing that neighbor's all-weather friendship to a still stronger rival to the north.

Bangladesh China is the main supplier of military hardware to Bangladesh; it is Bangladesh's largest trading partner and continues to make large investments. Since 2010, Beijing has supplied Dhaka with five maritime patrol vessels, two corvettes, forty-four tanks, and sixteen fighter jets, as well as surface-to-air and antiship missiles. Bangladesh, in return, has granted China oil/gas exploration rights at Barakpuria, as well as naval access to Chittagong port, thereby giving China a closer proximity to Myanmar oil fields and the seas around India. China currently has a $705 million contract to build a two-lane, underwater tunnel connecting Chittagong port and Kar-naphuli River valley. In May 2016, the Hasina government approved the $4.47 billion Padma Bridge rail link project, and in her October trip to Beijing, Sheikh Hasina signed an additional twenty-seven deals. Driven by the uneasy China-India relationship, thriving China-Bangladesh relations have inspired India to offer a $2 billion credit line as well; and India is financing and building a deep-sea port in Sittwe, in Myanmar's Rakhine State, which also fronts on the Bay of Bengal to the north of Chittagong, including plans for a special economic zone upstream. This port is one part of the Kaladan Multi-modal Transit Transport Project (KMTTP) in western Myanmar, which aims to connect Mizoram in landlocked northeast India to the Bay of Bengal. These megaprojects are financed by massive increases in governmental debt loads. The AIIB recently granted a $66 million loan for two power distribution projects and the improvement of transmission lines in Bangladesh. Needing a deepwater port, Bangladesh had previously agreed to assign the Sonadia deal (near Chittagong) to China, but Sheikh Hasina did not sign the scheduled agreement when she visited Beijing in 2014 opting first to consider competing offers. Again, geostrategic rivalries enhanced Dhaka's leverage: Japan offered to build a new port in Matabari, a few miles from Sonadia. Beijing also wanted to develop another port at Payra, a few miles away, and India also made a counteroffer. In the spring of 2016, Bangladesh finally signed a contract with a Dutch company to build the Payra port.

Sri Lanka   In Sri Lanka, China led in the rebuilding of Sri Lanka's infrastructure after the fourteen-year civil war ended in 2009 as India and the West shied away, citing the victorious government's human rights abuses. China earned then president Mahinda Rajapaksa's gratitude for its unwaver-ing support of his brutal war against the Liberation Tigers of Tamil Eelam. Land and labor were both relatively cheap, the government friendly, and Chinese money started flooding in, seemingly a win-win deal with no strings attached. Rajapaksa could rely on the steady flow of Chinese money to solidify his power while Beijing gained access to one of the most valuable geostrategic positions in the Indian Ocean. Among the big-ticket Chinese projects was a port in Rajapaksa's hometown of Hambantota at Sri Lanka's southern tip, built at a cost of around $1 billion by the SOE China Harbor Engineering; China's Export-Import Bank provided 85 percent of the fund-ing at 6.3 percent interest. Other key projects included the Mattala Rajapaksa International Airport in Hambantota and a new railway. Additionally, the $1.4 billion Colombo Port City Project, including a 2.4-million-container-per-year capable terminal, was started in 2013, the single-largest foreign investment in Sri Lankan history, including an adjacent industrial zone cov-ering fifteen thousand acres of land. In 2015, China conducted a combined counterterrorism exercise with the Sri Lankan army called Silk Road Cooperation 2015, a harbinger of future plans. But development stalled amid controversy over the tender procedures and environmental impact; the project was left in limbo when Rajapaksa was unexpectedly voted out of office in early 2015.

In sum, the upshot of these three Chinese inroads on India's periphery, from the Indian perspective, has been to continue to the old pattern of strategic encirclement. The Indians suspect that the political implication of China's assistance to neighbors on all sides is to transform economic capital into political and strategic influence. From an economic perspective, while India's neighbors are in dire need of improved infrastructure and grateful for Chinese assistance in the construction of turnkey projects, the financing has been long term and risky for both lender and recipient. China has thus far insisted on negotiating these projects bilaterally, optimizing its asymmetrical bargaining advantage. To take CPEC, for example, all materials in the project (except cement, which is locally sourced), including workers, equipment, and building materials, are imported from China. This raises at least two important issues. First, will Gwadar eventually host PLAN ships and subs? The so-called string of pearls scenario assumes the Maritime Silk Road will be militarized, which China denies, but it is true that Chinese submarines have occasionally docked in Gwadar just as they have used Chinese-constructed ports in Sri Lanka. Pakistan reportedly welcomes Chinese military engagement. The risk of militarization will be greatest if and when indigenous resistance arises, as in the case of xenophobic terrorism. Second, as in some other BRI megadeals, how financially sustainable is the project going forward? The Pakistani government, recognizing that CPEC may end up draining its resources rather than increasing them, interceded two successive years to reduce the amount of Pakistan's money committed to the corridor. Trade with China has increased rapidly but is imbalanced and neocolonial, exporting raw materials and importing manufactures. The grant portion is often tied, meaning a stipulated percentage must be used to purchase Chinese goods and services. In 2016, the International Monetary Fund (IMF) published a report on its three-year loan to Pakistan, noting that CPEC-related imports (machinery and natural resources) could be so large and costly as to push the current account deficit to 1.5 percent of GDP by 2017. Investment would likely boost growth and attract FDI in the short term, but medium-to-long-term issues like increasing capital outflows "could arise from CPEC-related repayment obligations and profit repatriation."[32] Because China does not want to draw down its foreign exchange surplus ($3 trillion in 2017) any further, it may have to tap international bond markets. That would greatly increase China's external debt and expose it to exchange rate risks.

In Sri Lanka, Rajapaksa was voted out, and the new Maithripala Sirisena government tried to renege on the megaprojects he had contracted, claiming they were environmentally problematic and made no immediate contribution to development (e.g., the empty Mattala Rajapaksa International Airport at Hambantota). But Sri Lanka had fallen into a debt trap. Sirisena was reminded that Sri Lanka had acquired a legally binding US$8 billion debt at 6.3 percent interest, which the Chinese lenders expected Sri Lanka to repay. Indeed, Sri Lanka's debt-to-GDP ratio increased from 36 percent in 2010 to 94 percent in 2015, with more than one-third of government revenue going to service Chinese loans. Then when Sri Lanka's GDP growth rate slowed from an annual average of 6.4 percent in 2010–15 to 4.5 percent in 2016, the nation suffered a debt and balance-of-payment crisis, its financial position only temporarily stabilized by a $1.5 billion IMF emergency loan. The high debt load made Sri Lanka even more beholden to China. On his first trip abroad, Sirisena visited India, and India's Prime Minister Modi came through, offering $318 million in credit for rail construction and a $1.5 billion currency swap between the central banks of the two nations. But Sri Lankan debt came to $64.9 billion, about $8 billion owed to China. Thus 2016 found Sri Lanka back wooing Chinese investments. The government revived the port city project, and followed up with a visit to China by Prime Minister Ranil Wickremesinghe in April 2016, who hoped to negotiate a reduction in the $125 million penalty incurred for previously suspending work on the megaproject. In October, the government announced a debt-for-equity deal in which China would take an 80 percent stake in the $1.5 billion Hambantota port and take over the airport for ninety-nine years, thereafter renewable for another ninety-nine years. Barring an unexpected growth surge, the same debt trap awaits the Colombo project. But this triggered mass protests in Colombo, leading to renegotiations. An agreement was reached for China to reduce its stake in the project by 20 percent after ten years. Still China remains majority owner and will manage the project going forward.

In some instances, China's ambitious political economic expansion plans coincide with Indian interests; in others, they arouse Indian suspicions and countervailing efforts (often both). On the one hand, both are members of the BRICS, the AIIB, the ARF, ADMM (ASEAN Defense Ministers Meeting) Plus, the EAS, and so on. As EAS members, both are in the process of negotiating the Regional Comprehensive Economic Partnership (RCEP), where China blames India for dragging its feet, refusing to bring its high tariff rates down. Both are also members of the BCIM (Bangladesh-China-India-Myanmar Corridor), engaged in building a road from Kunming through Mandalay (Myanmar), Dhaka (Bangladesh) to Kolkata, formerly Calcutta. (The point from China's perspective is to short-circuit the Malacca Strait, which can be cut off by the US Navy.) BCIM is now subsumed by the OBOR. Modi is uncomfortable with the OBOR, shifting in 2017 from non-signatory to opponent, not only because of the Kashmir territorial issue but also due to an underlying geostrategic distrust.

There is hence a growing tendency, particularly under Modi, for India to set up its own competing tent. This began with Modi's inauguration in 2014, to which he invited all SAARC members (including the political head of the Tibetan government in exile, Lobsang Sangay, to China's indignation). India, under Modi, also has taken increasing interest in China's sphere of interest, in 2015 changing its Look East policy to an Act East policy. Modi also initiated an Act West policy in 2016 with a deal to modernize the port in Iran's Chabahar, and build road and rail links from there to Central Asia. India is also committed to the International North-South Trade Corridor, linking Mumbai in India via Bandar Abbas in Iran to Moscow in Russia. Instead of BCIM, India promotes the Bangladesh–India–Myanmar–Sri Lanka–Thailand Economic Community (BIMSTEC) as an avenue linking the South Asian economy to vibrant Southeast Asia. BIMSTEC, founded to promote trade and development in 1998 and expanded in 2005 to include security measures, is similar to China's BCIM corridor but without China. India also promotes the Mekong-India Economic Corridor (MIEC) proposal, which would link Myanmar, Thailand, Cambodia, and Vietnam with India— also leaving China out. MIEC dovetails with Mekong-Ganga Cooperation, which from 2000 has worked to improve connectivity and economic and cultural exchanges between its member countries India, Laos, Myanmar, Thailand, Cambodia, and Vietnam. Also planned is an India-Myanmar-Thailand trilateral highway. In place of OBOR, India has envisaged its own grand global initiative called Mausam, which aims to reestablish its ancient maritime routes and visualizes an India-centered link connecting with historic sea routes in Asia, Europe, and Africa. In 1994, India also initiated unofficial relations with Taiwan, to Beijing's displeasure, establishing an India-Taiwan association.

Economic Relationship

India's economic relations with China developed relatively late but have recently accelerated powerfully. China and India actually chose similar economic development strategies in the 1950s—namely, economic self-reliance and state-led industrialization—steered, however, by Leninist and democratic socialism, respectively, but growth rates were roughly comparable. China then came out of isolation and began reforming its economy in 1978. India's hesitant and piecemeal reforms, initiated in the 1980s, became systemic and broader after July 1991, though like China's they have been incremental. Since 1980, China has grown at an average rate of around 10 percent per annum while India in its own reform era (1995–2015) has averaged 7 percent (however exceeding China's growth in 2014–17). China became the world's largest exporter by 2012. India's exports also grew, though much less than China's—at this point, India is still perhaps the least globalized major economy. While the two countries remained on a par economically from their origins to the late 1970s, China has, since its reform and opening, outdistanced India, and its economy is now about five times India's. From a trickling US$2 billion in 2001, the combined trade volume between the two Asian giants surged to US$70.08 billion by 2016. Trade between the two countries has expanded annually by 15 percent from 2007 to 2015, according to the Confederation of Indian Industry.

Yet there is a huge and growing trade deficit. In the fiscal year ending March 2016, India's exports to China reached $8.86 billion while China's exports were US$61.54 billion, for a gaping bilateral deficit of $52.67 billion. As growth slows in China, the gap is expected to widen, *caeteris paribus*, as China will import less while still seeking to export its overcapacity. This means India cannot depend on China to develop export-oriented growth. Moreover, while China exports telecommunications equipment, computer hardware, industrial machinery, and other manufactured products, India sends back mostly raw materials such as cotton yarn, gems, copper, and iron ore. Although China has increased outgoing foreign direct investment (OFDI) considerably since 2010 (it now exceeds incoming FDI), India has received relatively little of it (with $1.25 billion in 2016, India was seventeenth on China's FDI list), although India surpassed China as a global destination for FDI in 2015. India's investments in China are even more paltry, at around US$0.564 billion. Without strong investment ties, the relationship is deprived of an important lobby with a vested interest in strengthening bilateral economic relations. Also lagging is growth in people-to-people exchanges (e.g., tourism and immigration). But in 2014, Prime Minister Modi struck a deal with visiting Chinese president Xi Jinping for $20 billion of Chinese investment over the next five years (which is somewhat disappointing amid prior rumors of $100 billion and after having made a similar deal with Japan netting $35 billion). In sum, economic interdependency is growing fast from a modest beginning—but asymmetrically. China's trade and especially investment is greater with India's neighbors Pakistan, Bangladesh, Sri Lanka, and Myanmar, proportionate to their economies, than the trade of those countries with India. This creates a perplexing political economic dilemma for Delhi.

US-INDIAN RELATIONS

India and the United States are the world's two largest functioning democracies. India began as a socialist democracy, however, and although it has since adapted as the world has changed, it retains some nostalgia for the Gandhian values of self-reliant socialism. This is one of the reasons why although they have never been enemies they have long been somewhat estranged.[33] India's nonaligned policy, which regarded the Soviet Union and China as natural allies of the Non-Aligned Movement and was distrusted by the United States, further distanced the two countries. The US parallel alignment with India's longtime nemesis Pakistan is another irritant. Pakistan's designation as a Central Treaty Organization treaty ally and its long association with the United States pushed India toward the other superpower. When the communist bloc was then split by the Sino-Soviet dispute, India sided with the Soviet Union, signing a friendship treaty in 1971, while the United States with the Nixon visit played the China card (arranged with Pakistan's covert assistance). India's victory in the Bangladesh Liberation War in 1971 against Pakistan, then a close ally of both China and the United States, established India's preeminent position in South Asia but further dampened the possibility of India-US cooperation.

Since the end of the Cold War, however, the United States has shifted from favoring Pakistan to India, while maintaining cordial relations with both countries.[34] Indeed, the United States conducts more joint exercises with India than with any other country (including allies), and India is now the largest purchaser of US arms among developing nations (around US$93.5 billion in 2008–15). There are at least three reasons for this. First and most important, as China's rise came within striking distance of overtaking the United States in GDP and in theater military capability, the United States, in its growing apprehension over a prospective rising threat (a concern India shares), has sought external balancers.[35] In view of their converging threat perceptions, India was the apt choice. Second, as the US anticommunist ideology was eclipsed in 2001 by the global war on terror, India was able to join in that effort more convincingly than devoutly Muslim Pakistan. Pakistan's proximity to Afghanistan led the United States to rely on it both in its proxy resistance to Soviet occupation in the 1980s and in its war on terror after 2001, but seemingly inextricable ties between Pakistan's Inter-Services Intelligence (ISI) and terrorist bands in both countries eventually frayed strategic trust. This fear of religious extremism and its access to a "Muslim bomb" also came into play in the slanted US approach to Non-Proliferation Treaty (NPT) enforcement. Finally, India's own impressive economic and political rise, its geopolitical position, and its naval capabilities all made it a pivotal (and ideologically convivial) partner.

What changed the equation was the disintegration of the Union of Soviet Socialist Republics (USSR) at the end of the Cold War, the rising importance of the Asia-Pacific region, and India's own economic reform and liberalization, initiated in the early 1990s following the discrediting of state socialism and with the catalyst of a local financial crisis stemming from the shock of the Gulf War.[36] The rise of the BJP opposition—more nationalistic, more economically liberal, more politically conservative than the Congress Party—facilitated reconciliation. Prime Minister Atal Bihari Vajpayee, at the helm of the BJP-led United Progressive Alliance (UPA) government, called the United States a "natural ally of India," and President Bill Clinton agreed that India and the United States would be partners in peace in the new century.[37] On the other hand, the UPA government initiated nuclear testing at Pokhran in 1974, in defiance of the NPT (which India has never signed). India's Pokhran-II nuclear tests prompted the invocation of UN and then US economic sanctions, and a sharp reproof from China. But there was a domestic political consensus behind the bomb, India is not heavily trade dependent, and the sanctions were not rigorously enforced by most other countries (including China) and soon lifted. Ironically the simultaneous Pakistani tests seem to have somewhat diffused international pressure on India. The United States then supported India against Pakistan in the Kargil War of 1999, signaling the changing US attitude. In March 2000, President Bill Clinton visited India, opening a new chapter in Indo-US relations.

But the US president who did the most to advance the relationship was George W. Bush. A landmark event in the bilateral relationship was the announcement of the Next Steps in Strategic Partnership (NSSP) in January 2004, after protracted negotiations. This facilitated cooperation in four fields—civilian nuclear energy, civilian space programs, high technology trade, and missile defense—where India's possession of nuclear weaponry had previously made meaningful cooperation all but impossible. On July 18, 2005, President Bush thus announced that he would work to achieve full civil nuclear energy cooperation with India and would also seek agreement from Congress to adjust US policy in the context of a broader, global partnership with India in order to promote stability, democracy, prosperity, and peace. After intense legislative controversy on both sides, India and the United States jointly announced on July 27, 2007, that they had reached agreement on the text of a nuclear cooperation agreement. India agreed to allow close international monitoring of its nuclear weapons development in tacit exchange for the revocation of sanctions and undertook plans in 2005 for civilian nuclear cooperation, though it refused to give up its nuclear arsenal. The ascendancy of Narendra Modi injected new life into the strategic relationship, as the two agreed in 2014 to codevelop and coproduce certain advanced weapons systems, including Javelin antitank guided missiles and unmanned aerial vehicles and agreed to renew their decade-old Defense Technology and Trade Initiative (DTTI) as well as extend the India-U.S. Defense Framework of 2005. During Modi's June 2016 visit to Washington, Barack Obama announced that India would henceforth be classified as a major defense partner, allowing it access to technology on a par with the closest allies and partners of the United States. Although this designation was especially created for India, it is assumed that it will be equivalent to the major non-NATO ally designation that Pakistan has long enjoyed.

Economically, due to the early Indian emphasis on economic self-reliance and the later partnership with the Soviet Union, the India-US trade relationship is still relatively underdeveloped. Though one of the original parties to the General Agreement on Tariffs and Trade (GATT) 1948, India's record in multilateral trade negotiations has largely been protectionist, and its FTAs have reflected low levels of ambition. Nonetheless US-India trade has grown from $19 billion in 2000 to $64.3 billion in 2015, still distant from the express goal to reach $500 billion in the next decade. The trade is imbalanced, but unlike India-China trade, it is in India's favor: US exports to India totaled $22 billion in 2015 while Indian exports to the United States doubled that, for an Indian surplus of $21.6 billion. Also US FDI is much greater than China's and also imbalanced in India's favor—cumulative U.S. foreign direct investment into India in 2014 totaled $28 billion while Indian FDI in the United States was a mere $7.8 billion. The United States attributes the still relatively modest level of FDI to the Indian government's caps on foreign direct investment, which Modi has been pressing to remove. Both are working on a bilateral investment treaty (BIT), but progress is slow. While Russia has historically been India's main military hardware supplier, India-US defense trade has increased steeply under the Defense Technology and Trade Initiative (DTTI), passed in 2012, reaching $14 billion by 2015. The two are collaborating on such strategic projects as aircraft carrier and jet engine designs. In April 2016, India agreed in principle to open up its military bases to the United States. Boeing and Lockheed recently offered to manufacture F-16 and F/A-18 fighters in India. China views this rapid improvement in India-US relations with understandable concern over the possibility that it is its target, which both of course deny. New Delhi, always worried about Sino-US (and, correlatively, US-Pakistan) collusion, is nonetheless gratified by the new, more serious attention its US connection piques from its admired northern rival.

No international relationship is without problems. Some argue that India's strategic proximity with the United States has created a chasm between India and China; certainly this is true, though the causal nexus runs both ways. Indo-US rapprochement has also complicated Indo-Pakistani relations. Excluding Pakistan from the 2008 civil nuclear deal pushed Pakistan into the arms of China, and now both are bidding for admission to the NSG, each with its own sponsor. On the other hand, the Obama administration's 2016 decision to supply F-16 fighter jets to Pakistan over India's objections prompted an irate response from New Delhi. And of course, India is leery of the China-Pakistan relationship, while the United States looks askance at India's cordial relationship with Iran. The US business community objects to the imbalance of trade, complaining of Indian nontariff and bureaucratic barriers to US imports and investment. After getting the civil nuclear deal passed, India in 2010 passed a nuclear liability law that does not cap liability for nuclear suppliers, making it risky for US nuclear operators to function in India. US investors have many of the same complaints as in China, of "compulsory licenses" and the use of patent law to compel forfeiture of intellectual property rights to Indian competitors. For its part, India would like to expand production of generic medicines opposed by the US pharmaceutical industry and is unhappy with US immigration law restrictions, now heightened by Trump. In regional security politics, the United States has tried to persuade India to play a greater role in the Afghan quagmire (e.g., by training Afghan security forces), which New Delhi has largely ignored.

TRIANGULATION

Whereas the superpower rivalry was bipolar and comprehensive, tending to cleave the world into two relatively comprehensive rival alliance networks, the Indo-China rivalry coincides chronologically with the Cold War but is no simple spinoff of proxies. Its strategic architecture is complicated by patron-client linkage to both regional and extraregional powers. During the Cold War, Pakistan was China's client and main arms customer, as India was the Soviet Union's. This is still partly true—Pakistan and China remain all-weather partners, but no longer unconditionally, while meanwhile the rapprochement between China and Russia has meant that India's apprehensions about China are less likely to elicit Russian support. The United States, meanwhile, has become more sympathetic to India as its romance with China cooled. All these alignment shifts are nuanced and relative, however: India still values its relations with China, its main trade partner, as does the United States. And while both India and the United States find the China threat useful to cultivate closer bilateral relations, neither wants its relationship with China to deteriorate further.

The sine qua non in any patron-client relationship is that the patron be viewed as superior in relevant ways to the client, in this case as measured in terms of relative technological advancement and economic-strategic capabilities. This qualifies the patron as the logical source for weapons sales, technology transfer, developmental aid, and possibly military support. Thus focusing only on patronage, we have the following food chain: the United States at the top, followed by China, India, and Pakistan. Along this food chain, solidarity links may be forged based on political, ideological, or even religious affinity, as long as these links do not disregard patronage requirements. India could thus form a link with either China or the United States, and Pakistan could form a link with India, China, or the United States. But the pattern has been for clients, in order to avoid the possibility of domination by a powerful neighbor, to seek the more geographically distant patron:

thus Pakistan turns to China or the United States rather than India, and India turns to Russia or the United States rather than China.

The devil is thus in the politics, which interrupts the chain of patronage with historical strategic antipathies (based largely on the unresolved territorial dispute that exploded in the 1962 border war). These break the patronage chain in two, leading to the formation of two interlinked triangles: a "small" regional triangle consisting of India and its two local threats, and a "large" global triangle consisting of India's global relationships as an emerging great power. The two triangles are linked together by the Sino-Indian link they both share, forming a quadrangle.[38] In the small triangle, India confronts China and Pakistan, which it has for many decades deemed to be its two principal national security threats. Thus India is the pariah in this triangle, facing two opposing wings. But they are unequal ones: as India is bigger and stronger than Pakistan, China is also bigger and stronger than India, an asymmetry that has increased since China initiated reform and opening in 1978, accelerating its economic growth rate and military force projection capability. Thus, although China consistently spends a smaller percentage of its budget on defense than either India or Pakistan, that smaller percentage of a larger total budget translates into greater arms expenditures. In 2015, while India spent $51.3 billion on defense, an increase of 0.4 percent from 2014, China spent $215 billion, an increase of 10 percent.[39] India's hostility to both countries has been reciprocated, strengthening the all-weather friendship China and Pakistan have enjoyed for the past half century. In view of the asymmetric balance between India and Pakistan, this alignment has helped stabilize the antagonistic status quo, to India's net disadvantage. Thus the triangle takes the form of a stable marriage between China and Pakistan, facing pariah India.

The small triangle is not a formal defense alliance but an all-weather friendship. China has been Pakistan's patron since 1964 and the relationship remains close, such that nearly 70 percent of Pakistan's conventional armament is of Chinese design and 90 percent of its missile production is based on PRC aid of some sort. And it has naturally been reinforced since the advent of the BRI, and the CPEC in particular. The United States, while claiming Pakistan as a non-NATO ally, has sanctioned Pakistan twice in the past—in 1965 and again in 1990—whereas China has consistently supported Pakistan's military modernization. China was the only country to join Pakistan in protesting US violation of Pakistani sovereignty in the assassination of Osama bin Laden, although Al Qaeda had explicitly targeted Xinjiang. While Indian strategic thinkers attribute this friendship to Chinese strategic ambitions in South Asia, the Chinese (and the Pakistanis) see the PRC role as that of a necessary counterbalance to an Indian drive for regional hegemony. But though it is true that Chinese military support for Pakistan has been consistent and robust and perhaps even in occasional violation of international arms control regimes (the NPT, which China has signed, and the MTCR, which China has agreed to observe without signing), the relationship is loosely formalized in a friendship treaty, not a mutual defense alliance, and China has never dispatched Chinese troops in support of Pakistan, even when the latter was subjected to dismemberment in 1971. And though both states have conflicts of interest with India, they do not dispute the same things: China and India share the longest contested border in the world, whereas Pakistan's territorial dispute with India is essentially confined to Kashmir, where the two have engaged in chronic conflict held below the nuclear threshold by the "stability-instability paradox."[40] Tibet is an issue in Sino-Indian relations, largely because of the presence of the Dalai Lama and a Tibetan refugee community in northern India, but largely irrelevant to Indo-Pakistani relations.

The other, "large" triangle is again between India and China, now with the United States in an outside position pivoting between the two. Given the strained current relations between India and China and between India and Pakistan in the small triangle, if the Indo-US relationship is positive it helps to balance the otherwise adverse balance in the small triangle. Both triangles have become stable marriages. The escalation is driven by two fraught situations: first, terrorist incidents along the border and within India launched by such extremist Muslim organizations as the Lashkar-e-Taiba or Jaish-e-Mohammed, which are allegedly manipulated by Pakistan's shadowy Inter-Service Intelligence (ISI), and second, India's brutally repressive peace-keeping efforts in Indian-occupied Kashmir, which produce a violent backlash that these terrorist bands have strived to support. China has supported Pakistan on both antiterrorism policy and the Kashmir issue, as beneficiary of a generous border settlement in Pakistan-occupied Kashmir. Both triangles have been stable marriages, which is no accident. New Delhi uses the large triangle not only to facilitate its global ambitions but to counter the Sino-Pakistani marriage in the small triangle. Although the triangles are thus balanced, the asymmetrical distribution of power gives rise to a spiral: India, facing Pakistan and China, prepares to fight China, intimidating Pakistan; Pakistan externally balances with China to defend itself against India; India must double down to balance against both Pakistan and China: each arms against its most powerful conceivable foe (or coalition). During the Cold War, the Sino-Soviet dispute made the Soviet Union a reliable great power supporter in the large triangle against the China-Pakistani marriage in the small triangle, but since Sino-Soviet reconciliation at the end of the 1980s, Russia's relations with Pakistan have begun to improve concomitantly. Russia has been increasingly replaced by the United States as Sino-US relations deteriorate in maritime East Asia. The US role might advantageously seek to shift to a benign pivot, facilitating better relations in both triangles. This, however, has been inhibited by the United States' own insecurities: its terrorist obsession complicating relations with Pakistan, on the one hand, and its fears of China as a peer challenger to US leadership on the other. Both of these fears have braced the positive Indo-US partnership, but are otherwise destabilizing.

One logically possible resolution to the escalating negative dynamic in both large and small triangles would, of course, be an improvement in the Sino-Indian relationship, which is the side shared by both triangles. If this relationship could be genuinely improved and strategic mistrust allayed, China would no longer have a need to send its submarines and warships into the Indian Ocean or to bolster the economic and defense capabilities of India's neighbors Pakistan, Sri Lanka, Bangladesh, and Nepal. The old Indo-Pakistan antipathy could be de-escalated and possibly even reconciled absent Indian suspicions of Sino-Pakistani collusion. With an improved Sino-Indian relationship, China might even reach one of its central goals—of freezing US forces out of Asia—for without the China threat India would no longer need the United States. China could then pivot its South Asia strategy on the central strategic partnership with India, facilitating mutual cooperation with smaller neighboring states rather than pitting them all against the other regional superpower.

In terms of political reality, this is all unfortunately rather fanciful, for Sino-Indian mistrust has been one of the underlying constants (varying in intensity, to be sure) in South Asian politics since 1962. Any attempt to get to the bottom of the reasons for the inconclusive stagnation of border negotiations, now in progress for seventeen years, is likely to incite a mutual exercise in finger pointing. India thinks that it is incumbent on China to be more forthcoming since it has already taken what territory it claims in the west, yet China still demands the return of Arunachal Pradesh and has allegedly initiated most of the border incursions that still periodically recur. That is India's perspective, but China sees its role in South Asia as vulnerable and defensive. China is the geostrategic outlier, on the margins of the subcontinent, land access blocked by the Himalayas, long maritime logistic lines of supply, with an East Asian rather than a South Asian ethnocultural disposition. India's control of Arunachal, site of Dawang, the birthplace of the Dalai Lama (whose return visits China is powerless to prevent), threatens its continued control of Tibet, a core interest.

Yet if there is to be any real improvement in the Sino-Indian relationship it must come from China, simply because China has been most impatient with the status quo. In tune with its 2000s campaign to disprove the China threat theory and win acceptance as a responsible great power, the Chinese leadership has shown occasional interest in such a role, moving gradually toward a more equidistant position. At least up until the inception of OBOR, China showed little interest in propping up Pakistan's economy and, although China has consistently been its largest arms supplier, provided little substantial economic aid, even during crisis periods. Since 1990, China has refused to be drawn into the Kashmir dispute, no longer supporting Pakistan's demand for a plebiscite, calling rather for Indo-Pakistani rapprochement modeled on the 1972 Simla Accord.[41] In the 1999 Kargil conflict, China's public neutrality facilitated a relatively swift settlement. China disapproved of India's but also Pakistan's nuclear tests in 1998, which cast unwelcome light on China's prior assistance in Pakistan's nuclearization. Since 1998, after Pokhran-II and a brief period of sharpened polemics following India's identification of China as its leading security threat, Sino-Indian relations improved perceptibly. Thus we have seen reactivation of the Joint Working Group (JWG) to discuss the Sino-Indian border, an exchange of summits and high-level diplomatic visits, Indian recognition of Chinese sovereignty over Tibet, and Chinese recognition of Indian sovereignty over Sikkim.[42] As noted previously, there has been an impressive upsurge of bilateral trade.[43] As both sides resolved to let the relationship forge ahead where opportunities appear ripe despite continuing obstacles preventing resolution of basic issues, the outlook warrants cautious optimism.

There has even been some Chinese empathy for Indian geostrategic grievances over China's increasingly intrusive stance in the region. Some Chinese India specialists believe China should accept India's ambitions for regional dominance and international great power status in exchange for at least a limited global partnership ("Chindia"), according to Yuan.[44] At bottom India and China share perspectives on a fairly wide range of international issues, they argue, such as opposition to US unilateralism and preference for a more multipolar world. This would entail a recalibration of the Sino-Pakistani strategic alliance, which should be possible with requisite Indian reassurances to Islamabad. On the intractable border issue, both sides agreed in 1993 and 1996 to respect the Line of Actual Control (LAC) leaving the Aksai Chin under de facto Chinese control, yet China continues to insist on sovereignty over Arunachal Pradesh as well. Thus China sends periodic patrols across the LAC, and both sides strengthen their border fortifications. For the time being, Chinese supporters of a more comprehensive Sino-Indian rapprochement seem to be in a minority position, and this seems unlikely to change in the foreseeable future, if only because it would necessitate the modification of policies grounded in the still canonical Deng Xiaoping era. Broadly speaking, those scholars and strategic thinkers who are more optimistic about prospects for Sino-Indian détente tend to be affiliated with the State Council, academic research institutes, or civilian think tanks, while advocates of a more pessimistic or realist perspective tend to be concentrated in the defense and security fields. There is very little popular domestic support for a basic shift in Chinese South Asia policy, but then Chinese media coverage of the issue has hardly been encouraging.

The large triangle embracing the United States, India, and China has historically been a romantic one, in which Washington cultivated better relations with Beijing and New Delhi than the latter had with each other. But to speak of US participation in a triangular relationship requires a bit of poetic license, inasmuch as US involvement in the South Asian region has not been consciously triangular or indeed animated by any particular strategy besides indiscriminate anticommunism. Until recently, the USSR was deemed the major threat, and China seems to have been deeply discounted as a factor in the formulation of US South Asia policy, as the Indian alignment with the Soviet Union put Indo-US relations into hibernation during much of the Cold War. During the period of the Sino-Soviet split and the strategic triangle (1971–89), the Sino-Pakistani all-weather friendship dovetailed with an on-going Pakistani-US alliance (dating back to Ayub Khan in the 1950s) against a perceived Soviet geostrategic drive through Afghanistan to the Indian Ocean, and Pakistan played a key role facilitating the 1971 Sino-US rapprochement. None of this helped Indo-US relations.

Meanwhile, India's friendship with the USSR made the world's largest democracy an unlikely strategic fit for the world's most populous dictatorship. The Indo-Soviet Friendship Treaty, signed August 9, 1971, was prompted by Chinese and US collusion in support of Pakistan in the 1971 Bangladesh war, when Washington sent the Seventh Fleet steaming into the Bay of Bengal and even quietly intimated to Beijing that if China were to open a second front in the north in support of Pakistan the United States would contain any Soviet countermeasures. US relations remained warm with China and Pakistan and cool toward India throughout the resurgent Soviet-US Cold War of the 1980s, focusing on support for the anti-Soviet mujahideen (including Osama bin Laden with the help of Pakistan's Inter-Services Intelligence [ISI] in Afghanistan). In triangular terms, the United States was tilting toward China (and its ally Pakistan) against India, but India was actually incidental to US security interests, which were focused on countering Soviet initiatives. Though India was distrusted as a client of the Soviet Union, Indian and American interests per se did not clash. The South Asian region, like Cambodia or Outer Mongolia, was peripheral to the global triangular chessboard.

Thus when the Soviet Union collapsed, to be replaced by a Russian Federation initially eager to be embraced in a strategic partnership with the United States, the US perspective on both China and India changed; for the first time, the United States saw these two rising powers in terms of their respective national interests rather than solely in terms of their possible use value vis-à-vis the USSR. In this reassessment, the relationship became more authentically triangular, as both China and Pakistan lost strategic utility for the United States (concomitantly also losing their own need for US military support), while India could be appreciated for itself outside the Soviet shadow. India's opening to the outside world and economic growth surge began in 1991, about a decade after China's, and in the decades since, GDP growth averaged an impressive 7 percent per annum, making India an increasingly important trade and investment partner (Indo-US trade in 2013 totaled $96.7 billion, tiny compared to Sino-US trade of $560 billion, almost nine times Indo-US trade—still, up more than 400 percent from a mere $23.9 billion in 2003). The trade discrepancy has mainly to do with India's failure to get plugged into global value chains due to a holdover attachment to socialist self-reliance. Yet India's developmental future holds great economic and political potential: India is a democracy with a firmly institutionalized rule of law, human rights issues are not salient, and India does not make sovereignty claims over areas strategically important to US interests or threaten US perceived primacy in a power transition contest. Since 9/11, Indo-US defense collaboration has increased considerably, with the announcement of a series of measures usually reserved for allies, ranging from joint exercises in Alaska to sales of military hardware; in 2014, the United States surpassed Russia as India's largest arms supplier, and India became the second-largest US arms customer.[45]

As noted previously, the two triangles share a Sino-Indian link, which thus becomes the key relationship on which the quadrangle pivots. At present, Islamabad's and Washington's involvement on the outside angles of the quadrangle is fueled by Sino-Indian ambivalence. Given Sino-Indian polarization, China supports Pakistan and the United States supports India; if Sino-Indian détente should blossom by some political miracle, that would jeopardize both US and Pakistani security interests as currently defined. Meanwhile, suspicions abound. Beijing is of course concerned with the threat of Indo-US collusion, and India has for its part suspected Sino-US collusion against Indian interests since 1971. It is also conceivable that Washington may shift from its pro-India tilt to a more equidistant pivot position under Trump, maintaining good relations with both India and China without tilting to either side. Such a shift naturally presupposes a long-term cultivation of positive Sino-US relations. While the collapse of the Soviet Union made such a configuration feasible, the possibility of simultaneous good US relations with both India and China did not arise until Washington perceived the need for international cooperation in the light of the war on terror. While that so-called war is still in progress, it has had surprisingly little permanent impact on global strategic architecture.

Whereas these two interlocking large and small triangles help to clarify China's strategic choices and their implications for South Asia, the region also includes two other triangular relationships relevant to the US and Pakistani roles in the region: the US-India-Pakistan relationship, and the US-China-Pakistan relationship. The US relationship with New Delhi and Islamabad, given the historical antagonism with the latter, seems a strong candidate for a romantic triangle with Washington in a benign pivot position. Washington never really grasped that possibility, tending rather to tilt one way (toward Pakistan) during the Cold War and the other (India) thereafter. Not until the war against terrorism brought to light a convergence of interests between the two subcontinental powers against transnational terrorism was the United States able to move into a balancing role, which elevated US subcontinental influence for as long as the antiterrorist animus remained salient for both. If the US-Indo-Pakistani relationship has not realized its potential for strategic leverage, this is even more so of the relationship between Washington, Beijing, and Islamabad. In retrospect, this triangle fits into three stages: the period from the early 1950s to the early 1960s, consisting of a Pakistani-US anticommunist marriage against both China and India; the relatively brief period of the late 1960s, consisting of a romantic triangle with Islamabad in a benign pivot position between Washington and Beijing; and the 1970s through the late 1990s, when Sino-US strategic triangulation facilitated a ménage à trois between Washington, Beijing, and Islamabad that was now anti-Soviet and anti-Indian. This emergent triangle broke down at the end of the Cold War for obvious reasons already explicated. These two triads failed to become operationally significant partly because the actors did not accept each other as strategically significant, in part because both revolve around a Pakistani-US axis that is too weak to sustain them.

CONCLUSIONS

There are two inflection points in the relationship between China, India, and the United States. The first is the end of the Cold War, which reduced the strategic utility of both China and Pakistan and weakened India's link to the USSR. This deprived the tacit US-China-Pakistan anti-Indian and anti-Soviet coalition of its motive power, giving India (indeed, all actors) wider diplomatic room for maneuver. This marked the beginning of Sino-Indian rapprochement. While Sino-US relations survived, the rationale shifted from a geostrategic to a commercial one, as China's reform and opening unleashed China's stupendous rise, creating new economic opportunities. The second inflection point was 9/11, which initially created the basis for an inclusive ménage, uniting the United States, India, China, Pakistan, and Russia against a nonstate terrorist threat. This threat, however, has not proved great or constant enough over time to preserve any such grand alliance. Though its position in Xinjiang and Tibet has clearly been endangered by the rise of Islamist fundamentalism China has retained close ties to Pakistan despite the risks as a sort of inoculation against growing sectarian divisiveness at home. The United States also has a vested strategic interest in Pakistan (which hosts US military bases). Although Pakistan's religious heritage was initially deemed useful, its ambivalence in the continuing war on Islamist extremism has given rise to distrust and a US tilt toward India.[46] Meanwhile. Chinese

and Russian great power ambitions opened a breach with the relatively declining American superpower, making tacit Indian-US external balancing
appear more useful.

South Asia, within the past two decades, has posed a double-barreled
challenge to the international nonproliferation regime: On the surface were
the 1998 nuclear tests, the world's first public violation of this well-en-
trenched international regime. Underlying and justifying this challenge is the
more potent discursive challenge articulated largely by India—that it is inherently unfair to divide the world into two categories of nation-state, those
who have nuclear weapons and those who have not, decreeing that the
monopoly of the former should be protected while the latter should be eter-
nally deprived. The implication of the discursive critique is that for as long as
some states have the security of nuclear weapons and some do not, those
without them will want them, that so long as demand exceeds supply there
will be a market bidding prices high enough to service those demands; in
short, there will always be proliferation, as is the case with narcotics, organs,
sex, and other scarce commodities. All prohibition can do is drive up the
price. The nuclear tests themselves make up the direct challenge, saying in
effect that those unfairly excluded from the market are now claiming their
due; in other words, the tests are a step away from the principled position of
total abstinence to the more realistic stance that so long as this weapons of
mass destruction (WMD) monopoly is not being eliminated as it ought to be,
we want a share. In the wake of 9/11, the reaction of the international NPT
regime, led by the world's lone superpower, seems to have been to punish
those countries with whom the United States is not on good terms while
quietly acquiescing to proliferation for those countries with which it is. Of
course this is not a mere capricious preference; there are reasonable objective
reasons why some nations can more safely be trusted with nuclear weapons
than others. Still, it is bound to be viewed by the have-nots as arbitrary and
unfair, and to drive up demand for WMDs among those countries with which
the United States is not on good terms. Why they are not on good terms is not
solely an ideological or even a strategic question, but involves a judgment
that while proliferation may be bad in principle, if our adversaries have
WMDs we must have them to ensure our survival.

What lessons can be drawn from South Asia's last five years of experience with nuclear weapons escalation control is not yet entirely clear. On the
one hand, it may well be claimed that this is indeed still one of the most
dangerous places on earth, in view of the proximity of two nuclear weapon
states, the lack of transparency and technical checks on accidental launch, the
lack of assured second-strike capability on either side, and finally the presence of irreconcilable conflicts for the sake of which each side is still prepared to fight and die. All these conditions are still present, and although the
situation at the beginning of 2016 was somewhat less precarious, this may be

due not to any structural change in the triangular relationship but merely to the prudence of the current leadership of the major powers. But it might also be argued that what is most noteworthy is that despite all these serious drawbacks nuclear war has after all *not* taken place. My own tentative interpretation is that the South Asian experience has shown that escalation control at the top end of the ladder (e.g., from conventional war to nuclear exchanges) has proved to be surprisingly robust under exceptionally trying circumstances. That is not grounds for self-congratulation or complacency—the nuclear balance in the region is fragile, badly in need of regularized intercourse among national security officials and other confidence-building measures. Escalation control at the bottom end of the ladder, in contrast (i.e., from terrorism or guerrilla warfare up to conventional war), is much less firmly institutionalized, partly due to failure to take responsibility for outbreaks of violence by irregular forces, partly because of the failure to take into account the bilateral implications of counterinsurgency efforts (e.g., India's Kashmiri policies). The prospect is unfortunately for continuing volatility at this level, in which the state with conventional superiority can prevail by threatening to escalate to a level at which it can bring its superiority into play, blithely assuming that hostilities will not escalate to the top of the ladder simply because they must not.

With regard to strategic triangulation, the decisive qualifier of the two triangles describing South Asia is not that they are asymmetric but that they are both nuclear. The acquisition of nuclear weaponry has been a great equalizer. The South Asian experience since 1998 has also demonstrated the tenability of minimal deterrence; in other words, in all but worst-case scenarios (i.e., nuclear war fighting) a minimal deterrent is as good as a much bigger one, certainly sufficient to deter a preemptive first strike. That is what accounts for such apparently successful escalation stability at the top end of the ladder, despite the perhaps decisive asymmetries that would come into play if nuclear war actually broke out. There are two possible implications to be drawn. On the one hand, it seems that all three actors in either triangle over time are becoming more strategically autonomous (e.g., Pakistan becomes less dependent on China), more secure of their sovereignty, and more willing to take bold foreign policy risks (such as Kargil). On the other hand, it seems that they also become less willing to accept painful losses (or risks of loss), meaning that irredenta such as Kashmir or the Sino-Indian border dispute become more intractable if concessions are entailed. Which of these two implications is decisive may depend on the balance of power, the quality of political leadership in the contending states, and other changing environmental factors.

NOTES

1. Cf. Nitya Singh, "How to Tame Your Dragon: An Evaluation of India's Foreign Policy toward China," *India Review* 11, no. 3 (2012): 139–60.

2. Mohan Malik, *China and India: Great Power Rivals* (Boulder, CO: First Forum Press, 2011), 12–13.

3. Amitav Acharya and See Seng Tan, "Introduction: The Normative Relevance of the Bandung Conference for Contemporary Asian and International Order," in *Bandung Revisited: The Legacy of the 1955 Asian-African Conference for International Order*, ed. See Seng Tan and Amitav Acharya (Singapore: National University of Singapore Press, 2008), 5. The Five Principles of Coexistence, as formulated by Nehru and Zhou Enlai in Beijing in April 1954, are as follows: (1) mutual respect for each other's territorial integrity and sovereignty, (2) mutual nonaggression, (3) mutual noninterference in each other's internal affairs, (4) equality and cooperation for mutual benefit, and (5) peaceful coexistence.

4. India acquiesced to granting China observer status in SAARC as part of a deal in which Pakistan agreed to Afghanistan's full membership. But to ensure that China did not become a dominant presence, India also enlisted Australia, Myanmar, the European Union, Iran, Japan, Mauritius, South Korea, and the United States as observers to SAARC. See Swaran Singh, "Paradigm Shift in India-China Relations: From Bilateralism to Multilateralism," *Journal of International Affairs* 64, no. 2 (Spring/Summer 2011): 155–68.

5. George Gilboy and Eric Heginbotham, "Double Trouble: A Realist View of Chinese and Indian Power," *Washington Quarterly* 36, no. 3 (Summer 2013): 125–42.

6. PIPA, "22-Nation Poll Shows China Viewed Positively by Most Countries Including Its Asian Neighbors," http://www.pipa.org/OnlineReports/China/China_Mar05/China_Mar05_rpt.pdf.

7. Rory Medcalf, "What Indians Think about China," *The Diplomat*, May 27, 2013," https://thediplomat.com/2013/05/what-indians-think-about-china.

8. "How Asians View Each Other," Pew Research Center, July 14, 2014, http://www.pewglobal.org/2014/07/14/chapter-4-how-asians-view-each-other.

9. The Chinese, however, value Aksai Chin strategically as the only land link between the country's two troubled western regions of Tibet and Xinjiang, between which it has since built a highway.

10. In 1913–14, representatives of Britain, China, and Tibet attended a conference in Simla, India, and drew up an agreement concerning Tibet's status and borders. The British negotiator Henry McMahon drew the eponymous line between Tibet and India for the eastern sector on a map attached to the agreement. All three representatives initialed the agreement, but Beijing then objected to the proposed Sino-Tibet boundary and refused to sign the more detailed final map. After approving a note that stated China could not enjoy rights under the agreement unless it ratified it, the British and Tibetan negotiators signed the Simla Convention and more detailed map as a bilateral accord.

11. Sujit Mansingh, "India-China Relations in the Post–Cold War era," *Asian Survey* 24, no. 3 (June 1994): 269; as cited in Jonathan Holslag, "The Persistent Military Security Dilemma between China and India," *Journal of Strategic Studies* 32, no. 6 (December 2009): 811–40.

12. Office of the Secretary of Defense, *Annual Report to Congress: Military and Security Developments Involving the People's Republic of China 2016* (Washington, DC: U.S. Department of Defense, 2016), http://www.defense.gov/Portals/1/Documents/pubs/2016%20China%20Military%20Power%20Report.pdf.

13. Singh, "How to Tame," 149–53. An annual average 250–300 PLA intrusions took place as of 2013. Most recently (April 15, 2015) the PLA established a camp on the Depsang plain in the Daulat Beg Oldi (DBO) sector of Ladakh, which India considers its side of the Line of Actual Control, a standoff that lasted for nearly three weeks before the PLA dismantled the camp.

14. According to the International Institute for Strategic Studies (IISS) Military Balance 2016, China accounts for 41 percent and India for 13.5 percent of all defense spending in Asia; in 2015, China spent US$145 billion vs. India's $47 billion.

15. George Perkovich, *India's Nuclear Bomb: The Impact on Global Proliferation* (Berkeley: University of California Press, 1999), 415, 417.

16. China's opposition to Indian nuclear weaponization, and its 2016 blockage of India's admission to the NSG, rest on its violation of the Non-Proliferation Treaty (NPT), which India opposes in principle and has never signed. China, which disregarded the nuclear test-ban treaty and conducted many tests before joining in 1996, also violated the NPT in providing Pakistan with fissile materials and technology to develop its nuclear deterrent.

17. More credible to Indian strategic analysts than the threat of a Chinese nuclear attack is the prospect of Chinese nuclear blackmail. A 2003 report from the Indian Ministry of Defense claimed that every major Indian city was within range of Chinese missiles based in Tibet, a claim supported to some extent by Central Intelligence Agency (CIA) estimates, while it could not be said the Chinese cities are reciprocally vulnerable to Indian missiles. Agence France Presse, "All Major Indian Cities within Range of Chinese Missiles: Report," New Delhi, May 30, 2003. The first report of nuclear weapons in Tibet was made by the Soviet news agency in 1974, and US intelligence concurs that China currently has sixty-six missiles that can hit all major Indian cities and military areas. China has consistently denied both the presence of missiles in Tibet and the targeting of India. Waheguru Pal Singh Sidhu and Jing-dong Yuan, *China and India: Cooperation or Conflict?* (Boulder, CO: Rienner, 2003), 50–51.

18. China's annual rate of growth between 1953 and 2009 was 8.1 percent, and India's annual rate of growth during the same period was 4.8 percent. As of 2014, China's (nominal) GDP was around US$10 trillion versus India's $2 trillion. By 2003, China's real per capita GDP reached US$5,321, and India's real GDP per capita was US$3,213.

19. Yang Yi, "Bridging Historical Nuclear Gaps," in *The China-India Nuclear Crossroads*, ed. Lora Saalman (Washington, DC: Carnegie Endowment for International Peace, 2012), 22.

20. See Ajey Lele Parveen Bhardwaj, "India's Nuclear Triad: A Net Assessment," IDSA Occasional Paper 31, Institute for Defense Studies and Analyses, April 2013.

21. Rajat Pandit, "Top Chinese Military Delegation Headed for India to Discuss Measures for Peace on Border," *Times of India*, November 13, 2015, 1, http://timesofindia.indiatimes.com/india/Top-Chinese-military-delegation-headed-for-India-to-discuss-measures-for-peace-on-border/articleshow/49762755.cms.

22. Arun Prakash, "China's Maritime Challenge in the Indian Ocean," *Maritime Affairs: Journal of the National Maritime Foundation of India* 7, no. 1 (Summer 2011): 14.

23. Information Office of the State Council of the People's Republic of China (PRC), "China's Military Strategy," China Daily, last modified May 26, 2015, http://www.chinadaily.com.cn/china/2015-05/26/content_20820628.htm.

24. Pakistan has actually suggested that Gwadar could be upgraded to a naval base for Chinese use. China, however, immediately rejected this offer. Farhan Bokhari and Kathrin Hille, "Pakistan Turns to China for Naval Base," *Financial Times*, May 22, 2011, http://www.ft.com/intl/cms/s/0/3914bd36-8467-11e0-afcb-00144feabdc0.html.

25. Holslag, "Persistent Military Security Dilemma," 825.

26. Francine R. Frankel, "The Breakout of China-India Strategic Rivalry in Asia and the Indian Ocean," *Journal of International Affairs* 64, no. 2 (Spring/Summer 2011): 1–17.

27. The annual Malabar exercise between India and the United States was first held in 1992. In 2007, it was broadened to include Japan, Australia, and Singapore. However the proposed 2007 Quadrilateral Security Dialogue (QSD), which would have brought together Australia, India, Japan, and the United States in some sort of undefined coalition, dissolved upon Australia's withdrawal, while India abandoned the Malabar naval exercises, in both cases from fear of provoking China.

28. Hoo Tiang Boon, "The Hedging Prong in India's Evolving China Strategy," *Journal of Contemporary China* 25, no. 101 (2016): 792–804.

29. India's state-owned ONGC started a joint oil exploration project in 1988 in Vietnam's territorial waters in the South China Sea also claimed by China. Beginning in the early 2000s, China has objected to India's role in this venture. India has responded in two ways. First, it has asserted the right of its state-owned enterprise to carry it out as part of India's legitimate economic interests. Second, it has begun to sell patrol boats to Vietnam in order to bolster the latter's coast guard capability. India's warships have also made port calls to Vietnam and

defended its right to do so. India has asserted that it will use its navy to defend installations related to this venture in the eventuality that these come under any threat.

30. See Mathieu Duchatel, "The Terrorist Risk and China's Policy toward Pakistan: Strategic Reassurance and the 'United Front,'" *Journal of Contemporary China* 20, no. 71 (September 2011): 543–61.

31. Khurram Husain, "Hidden Costs of CPEC," *Dawn*, January 5, 2017, http://www.dawn.com/news/1286698.

32. Saibal Dasgupta, "Chinese Investments May Hurt Rather than Help Pakistan, Say Think Tanks, IMF," *Times of India*, November 6, 2016, https://timesofindia.indiatimes.com/world/china/Chinese-investments-may-hurt-rather-than-help-Pakistan-say-think-tanks-IMF/articleshow/55276325.cms.

33. Dennis Kux, *India and the United States: Estranged Democracies* (Washington, DC: National Defense University Press, 1993), xvii.

34. Most prominently, Pakistan expected but did not get the same civil nuclear deal as India. This has pushed Pakistan further into closer cooperation with China, including arrangements for China's construction of two nuclear reactors in Pakistan. Cf. Rizwan Naseer and Musarat Amin, "Sino-Pakistan Maneuvering to Balance the Power in South Asia," *South Asian Studies* 30, no. 2 (December 2015): 329–42.

35. In a recent Lowy Institute poll, China ranked only second to Pakistan in terms of countries that people considered threatening to India, with 60 percent indicating China would be a major threat over the next decade (an additional 22 percent identified it as a minor threat). Seventy-three percent of those surveyed identified war with China as a big threat over the next ten years. Almost three-quarters believed that China wants to dominate Asia. Fifty-eight percent felt that China's growth had not been good for India. (The India Poll 2013 reports the results of a nationally representative opinion survey of 1,233 Indian adults conducted face-to-face between August 30 and October 15, 2012.) Rory Medcalf, India Poll 2013, Lowy Institute for International Policy, http://www.lowyinstitute.org/publications/india-poll-2013.

36. Sumit Ganguly and Manjeet S. Pardesi, "Explaining Sixty Years of India's Foreign Policy," *India Review* 8, no. 1 (2009): 4–19.

37. "Address by Shri Atal Bihari Vajpayee," Asia Society, accessed July 16, 2012, http://asiasociety.org/policy/address-shri-atal-bihari-vajpayee">shri-atal-bihari-vajpayee.

38. For insightful analyses of the triangular dimension of these relationships, see Vena Rajmony, "India-China-US Triangle: A 'Soft' Balance of Power System in the Making," Working Report, Center for Strategic and International Studies, March 15, 2002; and Guihong Zhang, "US Security Policy towards South Asia after September 11 and Its Implications for China: A Chinese Perspective," *Strategic Analysis* 27, no. 2 (April–June 2003): 145–71.

39. "Military Expenditure," SIPRI, April 1, 2016, as cited in "India World's Sixth-largest Military Spender: Report," *Dawn*, April 4, 2016, http://www.dawn.com/news/1250119.

40. Because both sides recognize that a nuclear exchange would be catastrophic, they paradoxically feel able to engage in subnuclear conflict with relative impunity. See Sumit Ganguly and D. T. Hagerty, *Fearful Symmetry: India-Pakistan Crises in the Shadow of Nuclear Weapons* (New Delhi: Oxford University Press, 2005).

41. Previously China always supported Pakistan's demand for self-determination in Kashmir. By the 1990s, however, China had developed an aversion for the concept of self-determination, lest it be applied to its occupation of Tibet or Xinjiang, or its claims to Taiwan, now defined as core issues.

42. On June 12, 1999, when the Pakistan foreign minister, Sartaz Aziz, went to Beijing to seek Chinese support, China told Pakistan to "settle its disputes with India peacefully through dialogue and negotiations." China's shift was likely decisive in forcing Islamabad to come to terms. Bhartendu Kumar Singh, "Chinese Views on the Kargil Conflict" (Institute of Peace and Conflict Studies Paper 211, June 25, 1999), http://www.ipcs.org/article_details.php?articleNo=211.

43. Yasheng Huang has argued, however, that the relative strength of secondary (industrial) and tertiary (service) sectors (China's industrial sector and India's service sector) does not bode well for economic complementarity but for intensified competition. See Yasheng Huang, "The

Myth of Economic Complementarity in Sino-Indian Relations," *Journal of International Affairs* 64, no. 2 (Spring/Summer 2011): 111–24.

44. See Jing-dong Yuan, "Foe or Friend? The Chinese Assessment of a Rising India after Pokhran II," in *South Asia's Security Dilemma*, ed. Lowell Dittmer (Armonk, NY: Sharpe, 2005), 150–75.

45. Ramananda Sengupta, "How America Replaced Russia as India's Largest Arms Supplier," *Swarajya*, September 27, 2015, http://swarajyamag.com/section/politics.

46. In FY 2002, Pakistan received an estimated US$624.5 million in developmental assistance and economic support funds, compared to $164.3 million for India. Guihong, "US Security Policy towards South Asia," 155. From 1946 to 2012, India has been the top recipient of US aid at $65.1 billion, according to USAID, while Pakistan has been the fifth-largest recipient. "India Biggest Recipient of US Economic Assistance over 66-year Period: USAID," *Dawn*, July 14, 2015, http://www.dawn.com/news/1194228. But since the 2003 escalation of the war on terror, Pakistan has been the third-largest beneficiary of US aid (after Israel and Afghanistan).

Chapter Eight

Happy Country

Since the 1990s and with accelerating speed since the turn of the millennium, Australia has been pressed by a series of challenges to reassess its strategic and geopolitical position in the world. Asia, since the 1970s, has supplanted Great Britain and Europe as Australia's most important trade network, led by Japan in the 1980s and surpassed by China beginning early in the twenty-first century. The rise of China has made an even stronger impression on Australia than the previous ascensions of Japan and the "Asian tigers." For this there are at least three reasons. First, China's rise seems to have been equally steep and more sustained than the previous ascent of Japan and the newly industrialized countries (NICs); indeed, the gross domestic product (GDP) growth rate has only recently shown signs of flagging, though China still remains among the world's fastest growing nations. Having overtaken Japan as a trade partner in 2007, within four years Chinese trade with Australia exceeded Japan's by one-third (over US$76.3 billion in 2011 versus $50.7 billion with Japan and $38.3 billion with the United States). China surpassed Japan in 2010 to become the world's largest trading nation and second-largest economy in nominal gross domestic product (GDP) and the largest in purchasing power parity (PPP), with good prospects of becoming the world's largest (in both categories) by the end of the decade. Second, China is much bigger than either Japan or the NICs, and its aggregate impact on world markets has hence been greater. And third, unlike Japan or the NICs, all of which at the time could be assumed to be formal or informal constituents of the US hub-and-spokes Asian alliance network (like Australia), the People's Republic of China (PRC) consistently has pursued an outspokenly independent foreign policy, while acquiring its own strategic power-projection capabilities and nuclear deterrent. This combination of factors, particularly the third, has raised the possibility that China's diverging material and ideal interests may, current PRC assurances to the contrary notwithstanding, pre-cipitate a break with the US-led East Asian status quo. And this in turn has raised the issue of what, in this perhaps unlikely and distant but still not inconceivable scenario, Australia is to do. How should Australia—a vast, bountifully endowed, economically developed nation, with a population about equal to that of Taiwan—best safeguard its national interests?[1] Strate-gically, this could conceivably entail a decisive shift in Australia's foreign policy orientation to bring its economic requirements into better correlation with its perceived security needs.

Inasmuch as such a reorientation would necessarily involve some trade-off between the nation's largest trade partner and its main security partner, the decision would seem to fit our triangular framework quite well. What makes these three a triangle is the interests and threats that draw them togeth-er. China is Australia's largest trading partner and the United States its larg-est foreign investor and source of imports (including weapons); the United States is also China's largest trade partner. Australia has preferential trade agreements with both (with China most recently, signed November 2014 after nearly ten years of negotiations). Strategically the United States has been formally allied with Australia since 1951, and there has long been a healthy mutual appreciation of their shared economic, strategic, and cultural interests in Asia and the Pacific. China and Australia were allies during World War II but adversaries during the Cold War (indeed, Australia sent troops to fight in both Korea and Vietnam). Since the Sino-Soviet split and China's economic opening to the outside world, mutual economic interests and the apparent absence of any conflicts have brought them together. The three are roughly comparable in size (China is the world's third-largest coun-try; the United States is fourth; and Australia is sixth) but asymmetric in population, GDP, and strategic force-projection capability. The United States and Australia are developed market economies with high per capita incomes while China is a developed economy in aggregate terms but still a developing nation in per capita terms. While both the United States and Australia support the existing rules-based international order (i.e., the status quo), China, though an active and increasingly influential participant in that order, has also signaled an interest in crafting a new order it can more easily control. In sum, while there is a triangular dynamic it is an eccentric regional triangle with a growing discrepancy between the strategic and the economic dimen-sions.

Thus the following discussion begins by looking more closely first at the economic and then the strategic dimensions. After this, we turn to the more complicated issue of how these two mutually interpenetrating sectors inter-act. In the final section, we analyze the logic of the Australian triangle.

ECONOMICS

The boom in China trade coincides with two developments: China's industrial modernization under the reform and opening policy launched at the Third Plenum of the Eleventh Congress in December 1978, and Australia's natural resource extraction boom, which took off in 2003 when prices for commodities like iron ore and coal began rising worldwide. From 2005 to 2011, the Australian mining sector grew by 85 percent and the export of commodities derived from mining increased by 100 percent. In comparison, overall GDP increased by a more modest 41 percent. Per capita disposable income rose by 13 percent and real wages rose by 6 percent while unemployment dropped by 1.25 percent, all thanks to the mining boom. This gave rise to the locution "two-speed economy." Meanwhile China's industrialization soon exhausted domestic sources of supply, and in Australia it found the raw materials it needed to sustain growth. The economic relationship is complementary and mutually profitable but asymmetric, meaning that, because China is the world's biggest trading state, the relationship is more important to Australia's economy than it is to China's.

A rapidly industrializing China was the main beneficiary of the mining boom. The China trade surpassed Australian-US trade in 2009 and is still climbing with no end in sight.[2] China and Australia signed a free trade agreement in 2015 and a comprehensive partnership agreement the same year. China's trade with Australia, driven largely by the "workshop of the world's" resource hunger (largely for iron ore and coal), has increased along with a positive Australian trade balance (keenly appreciated domestically in view of the country's chronic current account deficit overall). Exports boomed from 5 percent of the total in 1996 to more than one-quarter by 2012 and from around US$5.4 billion in 2000–2001 to nearly $513 billion in 2015, accounting for 34 percent of Australia's exports in 2014. Australia is the G20 country most dependent on China in terms of export revenue. The last time a single export market was this important was the United Kingdom (UK) in 1952–53, according to the Australian Trade Commission. US trade with Australia has fallen into third place (since 2010) and has been heavily imbalanced in favor of the United States, accounting for only about 5 percent of Australia's exports. The merchandise that China exports to Australia is mainly industrial products, such as clothing, electronic components, computers, toys, and sports equipment, while the goods that China imports from Australia are mainly natural resources like iron ore, wool, farming products, and copper.[3] An estimated 54 percent of Chinese demand for iron ore is met by Australian exports.

Though Australian-Chinese trade is complementary and imbalanced in Australia's favor, there are certain risks in its neocolonial composition. First, China's demand for iron ore, coal, and so forth, could decline, as indeed it has been declining as overall economic growth declines, partly due to China's massive industrial overcapacity. Even if China's demand is sustained despite overcapacity for the sake of sustaining a high growth rate, should *world* demand contract the commodity price will come down. Second, Australia could fall victim to the so-called Dutch disease, meaning an overreliance on natural resource extraction will come at the expense of growth in the secondary and tertiary sectors of the economy (in 2014 the Reserve Bank of Australia calculated that the manufacturing sector had lost 5 percent growth during the mining boom).[4] Finally, China could opt to politicize the trade relationship. True, the premise of China's successful rise since the advent of the reform and opening policy has been the strict separation of politics and economics, but there have been recent signs that this may be changing.[5]

But trade was yesterday's news, and today's has been investment. China's steel industry expanded at an extremely rapid pace in the 2000s, as the country rose to a position of global dominance. China produced approximately 823 million metric tons of crude steel in 2014, accounting for almost 50 percent of world production. Among the top ten global steelmakers, by 2013 seven companies were from China, producing 568 million tons. Originally self-sufficient in the resources needed for steel production, China's import dependency has been rising and, by 2014, reached 78.5 percent. Given its enormous cache of foreign reserves (around US$3 trillion as of 2017) and in view of gyrating prices amid the global commodities boom, China since 2009 has made clear its interest in investing heavily in the Australian economy (particularly the resource extraction sector), with the evident intention of controlling price fluctuation by owning the source of supply. The Heritage Foundation's China Global Investment Tracker estimates that between January 2005 and December 2010 Chinese foreign direct investment (FDI) to Australia was around US$34 billion, in that year the largest single destination for outgoing Chinese FDI. According to official Chinese figures, Chinese FDI in 2015 reached a record $118 billion, 14.7 percent up from 2014. Australia is second only to the United States as a host country for large-scale Chinese overseas direct investment (2017), and the majority of this investment has been conducted by state-owned enterprises (SOEs). That said, as a percentage of total cumulative FDI stock, Chinese investment in Australia is still relatively modest at 2.5 percent (2015), behind not only the United States but six other countries.[6]

China's upsurge in interest in Australian economic opportunities has been generally welcomed, with some caveats. As in the United States and the European Union (EU), there has been some unease about the mercantilist propensity of the Chinese state to organize its foreign investments strategically. Most Chinese FDI is conducted by SOEs under direct control of the state, and one of the purposes of investment has been to take supply sources (e.g., mines) out of the market. Some 78 percent of Chinese investment in

Australia over the 2005–15 period was in the resources sector. More recently commercial real estate has attracted Chinese interest, mostly private. Neither are sectors that carry high security risk. When strategic Chinese investment excites public controversy, as in the February 2009 Rio Tinto and Oz Mineral bids, or the blocked $10 billion 2016 sale of a 50.4 percent stake in Australia's largest energy network (Ausgrid), the political establishment intercedes to veto the deal and Beijing complains but abides.[7] Notwithstanding this regulatory intervention, Chinese investment behavior on the whole has been market rational. China does not recognize dual citizenship and has not hesitated to prosecute Chinese nationals employed by Australian business firms for infractions of Chinese law, to Australian consternation.

Of course the relationship has not been purely pecuniary. There are roughly one million Australians of Chinese ancestry (around 5 percent of the population), up from 669,890 in 2006. Close to half a million residents were born in the PRC, and China has remained a leading source of fresh immigration.[8] Mandarin is the second most commonly spoken language. Chinese were initially lured to Australia by the 1851 gold rush. (Since the mid-nineteenth century, Australia was dubbed the New Gold Mountain after the Old Gold Mountain of San Francisco in the United States.) Some 150,000 Chinese students now study in Australia. And Chinese interest is reciprocated, albeit in smaller scale. As of 1995, China was not even in the top ten destinations for Australians studying abroad, but student numbers surged 83 percent since 2011 (37 percent in 2015 alone), with up to five thousand Australians studying in Chinese universities by that year, according to China's Ministry of Education. China is the second-largest source of foreign tourists (over one million in 2015), who injected nearly US$7 billion into the local economy. Over the past four decades, 115 sister-city and sister-state relationships have formed between Australia and China, including a partnership between Wagga Wagga, a town of sixty-three thousand residents, and Kunming, a provincial capital with one hundred times that population. Australian Chinese are widely regarded as a model minority, with low crime rates and relatively high educational levels and per capita incomes. Recently expansive PRC foreign policies have been more controversial, contributing in the spring of 2017 to public consternation over Chinese political influence in domestic politics, particularly by lobbyists and tycoons with state security connections, sometimes involving nationalist student activism organized by the Chinese embassy. The CCP's united department has made it a priority to gain control of Chinese-language media and voluntary associations in Australia. Canberra is reportedly planning to introduce a law against foreign interference activities.

SECURITY

Strategically, the United States and Australia are bound by an alliance while China in principle rejects the alliance system as outmoded and conflict prone. Australia has had many alliances but, following the East Asian pattern, only one mutual defense alliance at a time, fitting explicitly into the patron-client paradigm. The first alliance was with Great Britain, but inasmuch as it was no longer able to protect its commonwealth during World War II (vide Singapore) thereafter with the United States. Australia supported US security commitments in both world wars and, later, in Korea, Vietnam, and the global war on terror. While the alliance is popular and generally assumed to have served Australian interests, it has at times fallen into disfavor in Australia's quest for a more independent international role, as, for example, during the Whitlam tenure, or in the wake of the 2003 Iraq invasion.[9] An alliance is typically predicated on a shared threat, whether explicit or (for diplomatic purposes) unnamed.[10] In the 1940s, the obvious threat was Japan, which flew sixty-four raids on Darwin (including its largest attack since Pearl Harbor, in February 1942) and thirty-three raids on other targets in northern Australia and, at one point, seriously considered an invasion. During the Cold War, China threatened the regional strategic status quo by supporting national liberation movements in Southeast Asia, with particularly intimate ties to the largest communist party outside the bloc, the Communist Party of Indonesia. After the Cold War, China opened to the outside world, at first only commercially but gradually also as an active participant in regional strategic regimes such as the Association of Southeast Asian Nations (ASEAN) Plus forums, taking a prominent leadership role in multilateral arrangements such as the Shanghai Cooperation Organization (SCO) or the Conference on Interaction and Confidence-Building Measures in Asia (CICA).

On the other hand, China's revived territorial claims since 2009, as they have been defined by China, are inconsistent with international law and a threat to the territorial status quo as understood in Australia and in Australia's adjacent Southeast Asian neighborhood. As in the US case, the threat to Australian interests is less clear than it is to those neighboring states whose exclusive economic zones (EEZs) are intersected by China's nine-dash line, as Australia has no sovereignty claims at stake and its lifelines are not intersected by Chinese sovereignty claims. But 54 percent of Australian trade passes through the South China Sea, including more than 90 percent of its iron ore and coal exports, much of it actually bound for China. If the South China Sea becomes a Chinese lake, Australia's peripheral security as well as its economic interests will be affected, and Australia for many years has deemed defense of the Southeast Asian neighborhood (particularly Indonesia) second only to self-defense.[11]

Accordingly, since the turn of the century, Australia has been upgrading its defenses. The Australian Defense Force (ADF) is relatively small given the population base but technologically advanced and well trained (the navy and air force are probably the best in the region). But the ADF budget and future strategy have become controversial in the light of changes in the Asian power balance and the revolution in military affairs that has shortened the strategic distance that previously insulated the country from threats. There have been four Defence White Papers since the Cold War (in 2000, 2009, 2013, and 2016). The Labor 2009 Defence White Paper of Kevin Rudd first recommended a sizable increase in military spending (the Chinese response was officially noncommittal, informally "incandescent"). The successor government of Julia Gillard conducted the first major review of the ADF's posture in over twenty-five years in 2011. The final report released in 2012 (and echoed in the 2013 White Paper) attempted to shift the emphasis to engagement with Asia, but also recommended new weapons purchases and a strengthened ADF presence in the north and northwest facing the South China Sea.[12] The 2016 White Paper, initiated under Tony Abbott and approved by Malcolm Turnbull, is even more pointed than its predecessors. The White Paper's focus is on the military rise of China and the militarization of its maritime disputes—particularly "the unprecedented pace and scale of China's land reclamation activities." Perceived to be at stake is the "rules-based global order."[13] To contribute to national defense, from 2000 to 2015 defense spending has increased by 75 percent in real terms, defense personnel numbers are up by 18 percent, and military modernization has accelerated. In 2016, the government budgeted $24.8 billion for defense, much of which will be used by the navy to build twelve submarines, nine frigates, and twelve offshore patrol vessels.[14]

As the increasingly transparent object of this buildup, what has been China's reaction? Beijing views both Australia and the United States as potentially positive contributors to its central objective, the rise of China: the United States is still China's biggest national trade partner with which it enjoys a large positive trade balance, and Australia is a rich source of raw materials to supply the world's leading importer of coal, iron ore, gold, wool, copper, aluminum, and other raw materials.

Notwithstanding occasional complaints of US financial mismanagement, China's dissatisfaction with the United States is mainly strategic, based on a perceived US challenge to China's fragile postcommunist national identity as a major power of a new type adrift of the democratizing mainstream. China is particularly sensitive to perceived strategic encirclement, interpreting both the expansion of the Japan-US security alliance to permit the dispatch of Self-Defense Forces (SDF) to United Nations (UN) peacekeeping efforts and the US use of basing facilities in Uzbekistan and Kyrgyzstan in support of its counterterrorist operations in Afghanistan as pretexts for an actual strategy to surround and destabilize the PRC. The tacit US defense commitment to Taiwan has historically been the most salient PRC grievance. [15]

China's growing dissatisfaction with US defense architecture in the Asia-Pacific is not limited to Taiwan, however. The hub-and-spokes alliance system that provides the mainstay of Australian extended deterrence has attracted increasingly critical Chinese attention, as articulated fairly clearly since the late 1990s in its new security concept and more recent Asian security concept. China, for several years, has expressed its discomfort with the pentagonal alliance system in general and with ANZUS (the Australia, New Zealand, United States Security Treaty) in particular. Supportive of the alliance during the Sino-Soviet dispute, China, since the Obama state visit in 2011 and the agreement to rotate up to five thousand marines through Darwin, has become increasingly disenchanted. [16] In March 2005, senior Chinese diplomat He Yafei publicly suggested that Canberra review its military alliance with Washington. [17] In a March 2017 address to the Australian parliament, Li Keqiang told parliamentarians that China did not want to see countries "taking sides, as happened during the cold war." [18] China's position on ANZUS is that it, like the other four US-Asian bilateral mutual defense treaties, is a relic of the Cold War that needlessly aggravates relations, and more to the point that such pacts are part of a grand strategy to encircle and contain China and impede its rise.

The other related source of Chinese discontent with ANZUS has to do with its South China Seas claims and specifically with the Malacca dilemma (i.e., China fears its supply of oil passing through the Strait of Malacca might be cut off in the event of hostilities). Beijing has hence assigned the People's Liberation Army (PLA) Navy to prepare to secure China's sea lanes of communication (SLOCs). According to recent reports, China's maritime sensitivities have led the National People's Congress (NPC) to consider legislation to bar foreign warships from the South China Sea and allow friendly passage only to commercial vessels, in effect transferring responsibility for the security of all Northeast Asian SLOCs to China. [19] In 2005, Beijing sought to bar Canberra's participation in the East Asia Summit, unsuccessfully proposing a core membership of ASEAN Plus Three while relegating Australia, New Zealand, and India to an affiliate membership. Australia has no claim on the South China Sea and is far from the Malacca Strait, but it has supported the US call for freedom of navigation and multilateral talks about maritime sovereignty issues, over Chinese objections. At the Shangri-La Dialogue in Singapore in 2017, Australia evoked democratic values and joined Japan and the United States in support of the 2016 Permanent Court of Arbitration (PCA) ruling, to the annoyance of the token Chinese delegation. Meanwhile, China's Asia policy is in a state of flux. Beginning the new century by revising the terms "peacefully rise" to "peaceful development" because the former was too provocative, Beijing ended its first decade with firm assertions and strategies for the enforcement of previously tabled territorial claims.

The reasons for Australia's enhanced national insecurity complex are not exclusively China focused—Australians have also been victims in the war on terror, for instance. There has also been some friction with Australia's closest neighbor, Indonesia, particularly during the latter's Konfrontasi with Malaysia in 1964–66 and during the civil war over the secession of East Timor (now Timor-Leste), which Australia supported over Jakarta's objections. Relations with the Southeast Asian neighbors, however, have always been diplomatically negotiable, in contrast to China's sovereignty claims in the South China Sea. Although the ADF has cooperated most frequently with Japan or India, there have also been some confidence-building measures with China—in October 2014, soldiers from the PLA participated for the first time in a trilateral military exercise (Exercise Kowari) with ADF and US forces in northern Australia.

IMPLICATIONS

The boom in Sino-Australian trade has come to be viewed as a risky anomaly, in that the nation's strategic interests may conflict with its economic livelihood. Clearly China offers great economic opportunity to Australia, and even amid a slowdown of the economic miracle future prospects seem bright. Yet although Australia has no territorial claims in the dispute, it does have a stake in Southeast Asian stability and in the rules-based global economic order. And it has a mutual defense alliance with a country whose relations with China have stumbled over this issue. This perceived dissonance between Australia's strategic and economic interests has inspired various attempts to realign the two. On the one hand are those who extrapolate the booming economic relationship with China into the indefinite future and conclude that the country should fundamentally rethink its strategic orientation. To avoid being dragged by the United States into a war with China that would not be in Australia's interest, some Australian leaders have already sought to extricate their country from affiliated US treaty commitments to Asian allies such as Taiwan, or even Japan.[20] After the United States unilaterally withdrew from the Trans-Pacific Partnership (TPP) in January 2017, Malcolm Turnbull suggested that China be invited to take its place. Defense intellectual Hugh White has led in this effort, placing the onus, however, not on Australia but on the United States. In Hugh White's view, "given these inevitable [growth] trends, America has three options for responding to China's rise. It can withdraw from Asia, share power with China, or compete with it for primacy."[21] White deems the third option unfeasible in the long run, the first as unlikely, and the second as conducive to regional stability. It would be advisable, he counsels, for the United States to strike a deal now while it still enjoys strategic dominance rather than later when the tables have turned.

But this will not be easy, not only because of the perceived conflict of interest over China's ill-defined maritime territorial ambitions but also in view of the lack of strategic trust between the two.[22] For the United States must share power with China "as an equal" while "surrendering primacy and all that goes with it."[23] What if the United States proves unwilling to take White's advice? And what precisely should be understood by "all that goes with it"? The Chinese leadership has expressed its preference for the United States to leave Asia to the Asians. Should the United States take that advice, where would that leave Australia? Australia would logically need to consider abrogating the alliance and a shift to a more nonaligned position, as Li Keqiang has advocated. A neutral position would imply that Australia must either become more accommodative to China's core interests (including presumably Taiwan, and sovereignty over the East and South China Seas) or that it must acquire sufficient power to resist them—which would be costly.

But not all agree with this vision of inevitably destabilizing conflict among rising powers, even among realists. Kenneth Waltz, for example, considers a multilateral system the least stable, and a bipolar system the most stable.[24] Classic balance-of-power realists, too, generally deem a bipolar balance (as existed during the forty-year Cold War) high stakes but relatively stable.[25] White's prognosis, however, coincides in this respect with that of offensive realist John Mearsheimer.[26] Based implicitly on power transition theory, both foresee escalating Sino-US polarization that will ultimately force a painful choice on Australia.[27] Such a choice will be difficult, but White's preference for China appeasement is one many Australian politicians and defense intellectuals have been hesitant to embrace. Shifting from realism to idealism, some advocate resolving the discrepancy by aligning more forthrightly with liberal democracies, as in the quadripartite alliance proposed in 2007 by Japanese prime minister Abe Shinzo, to include Australia, the United States, Japan, and India. Like the late TPP, this would have left China out—and China objected strenuously to what it perceived to be part of a containment strategy. The plan was soon abandoned, though there has been growing military cooperation among the same nations at an informal level. China has been extraordinarily effective at diplomatic intervention to prevent the formation of external balancing coalitions deemed inimical to its interests, partly by scolding the would-be balancers for fantasizing a chimerical China threat and scheming to encircle and contain its rise, and partly by using charm campaigns and statecraft to court and divide opponents. And there are of course powerful vested interests on the other side in favor of sustaining the economic synergy.

The debate over the role of security and economics in Australia's China policy continues. Meanwhile, Australia's pragmatic response to these two in different ways attractive partners has been to try to cultivate both. China has been a lucrative customer and trade partner, and the United States has been a strong and reliable strategic supporter. Australia, given its bifurcated economic and security needs, has sought to balance between the two, to play the pivot role. But as the weakest member of the triangle, this is a difficult position for Australia to play, because it lacks sufficient resources either to intimidate or reward the other actors and both attempt to force Australia to take sides. Still, at the present relatively low level of tension, balancing is probably Australia's best option. To the Chinese, Australia has refreshingly few hegemonic pretensions of a responsibility to police the world or to proselytize universal values that might involve Australian interference in Chinese internal affairs. Canberra has attempted to cultivate China's goodwill diplomatically while maintaining substantive security alliance commitments with the United States. The alliance with the United States is deemed second only to Commonwealth ties to Great Britain (and the related Five Power Defence Arrangements with the UK, Malaysia, Singapore, and New Zealand) as Australia's oldest and most essential foreign commitment. In triangular terms, it may be to Australia's advantage that relations between the United States and the PRC have been running into headwinds, potentially incentivizing each to more eagerly solicit Australia's support. In sum, these relationships both serve Australia's national interests and, to some extent, offset each other. Tensions have arisen between the two, and these tension points may eventually impel Canberra to make a choice. Canberra's response has been to "hedge,"[28] mollifying Washington with arms purchases, joint exercises, and use of Australian defense facilities while reassuring Beijing that its alliance commitments shall not conflict with China's security interests.

POLITICAL GEOMETRY

From a triangular perspective, the current configuration might at first blush be deemed a ménage: despite their disagreements and strains, all three actors derive such profit from the status quo that none should risk the adverse repercussions of a miscarried attempt to change it. But upon closer examination, we see that it is not a ménage at all. Australia and the United States have a formal defense alliance, time tested and still very much in force. No, the current triangle is a marriage, as Beijing is quite aware. While Beijing maintains cordial relations with both allies it can contain its enthusiasm for an alliance it suspects is directed against itself. In terms of positional advantage, the triangle is hierarchical with the two spouses holding leverage over the pariah. There is also a hierarchy of strategic capabilities, with the actor having greatest capabilities serving as the natural pivot, with whom each wing would prefer to bandwagon to reduce defense costs and boost capabilities. From either positional or strategic perspective, Beijing is currently hierarchically disadvantaged and hence has the greatest incentive to challenge the status quo by seducing either Canberra or Washington or by driving a wedge between the two.

Albeit hierarchically at a disadvantage, China has one major intangible asset: growth. China is growing faster than either the United States or Australia, its real GDP having doubled between 2004 and 2014. China long ago surpassed the United States as Australia's largest trade partner, and because it is growing faster than either and because China has a larger proportion of Australia's total trade than Australia's proportion of China's trade there is asymmetric dependency in the trade relationship. As is the case with Australia's Southeast Asian neighbors to the north, the China factor has loomed increasingly large in terms of diplomatic and even symbolically sensitive domestic policy options by dint of the threat of its possible withdrawal of market access. As trade and inbound investment continues to thrive, this asymmetric dependency will grow. To what extent does economic dependency imply a threat to Australian security? Australia's import dependence on China is negligible (and has been falling), but it is highly export dependent. If China were to withhold market access, it could seriously damage Australia's export-dependent economy. China has been Australia's most important export market since 2009 and, in recent years, has been central to overall export performance. In 2013–14, China accounted for almost 80 percent of all Australian export growth in value terms; the scale of China's contribution to overall export growth dwarfs all other export recipients—roughly ten times that from Japan or the United States, for example. Even aside from the threat of cutting imports for political reasons, China's growth has been decelerating, and it has been in the process of shifting from an export-dependent growth model to one based on domestic demand. This is a central pillar of the reform proposal Xi Jinping presented at the Third Plenum of the Eighteenth Party Congress in December 2013 and reaffirmed at the Nineteenth Party Congress in October 2017 but not yet successfully implemented. Were he to do so, however, this would entail diminution of the overcapacity heavy industrial sector on which Australia relies for export demand.

In terms of direct military threat, China's military capability has grown disproportionately in correlation with its more rapid economic growth. China has given a sustained high priority to defense modernization for the past three decades and has made impressive advances, including recent acquisition of its first aircraft carrier, nuclear submarines capable of carrying submarine-launched ballistic missiles (SLBMs), space-based weaponry, multiple independently targeted reentry vehicles (MIRVs), stealth jet fighters, hypersonic glide vehicles, and antiship ballistic missiles (ASBMs). But given the alliance, the relevant comparison is not bilateral but between China and Australia plus the United States, equilibrating the balance. China did not start prioritizing military modernization until a decade after the inauguration of reform, and there remains by most assessments a wider strategic gap between the PLA and the US military than the GDP gap between the two economies. In other words, according to most projections China will overtake the United States in terms of aggregate GDP sooner than it will surpass it in military power. Such a strategic lag is not unusual. While the United States surpassed the UK in terms of GDP by the end of the nineteenth century, Britannia continued to rule the waves (naval power at the time being the most decisive expression of force-projection capability) in total tonnage well into the twentieth century, essentially until World War II. Moreover, strategic capability is not necessarily equivalent to threat, which involves a combination of capability plus intention. Intentions are of course more opaque than capabilities, accounting for their tendency to fall out of the equation. But there is as yet no evidence of a conflict of strategic intentions between China and Australia sufficient to anticipate conflict. A Sino-US conflict drawing in Australia is another story.

Responsible political leadership requires planning not only for today but for tomorrow, and at the heart of White's argument is a speculative glimpse into the extrapolated future when China will have surpassed the United States not only in terms of aggregate GDP but in military technology and force-projection capability. It is no doubt fair to say that the United States suffers from overstretch, as it struggles to retain its hegemonic stabilizer role while its relative superiority in GDP diminishes. Yet the decline and fall of the United States has oft been prematurely announced. No one knows the future, and this may turn out to be just another premature epitaph. But as White points out, China is by far the most formidable adversary the United States has faced in terms of population size and quality, resource base, and other national assets. Not only that, based on an extrapolation of its growth rate (noting here the repeated failure of predictions of China's collapse), China in the foreseeable future will overtake the United States and become the looming Asian hegemon. At this point, Australia, again based on a projection of trade statistics, will become even more economically dependent on China than it is now. Assuming projections of recent trends are accurate, the future will present the following challenge: In triangular terms, China will become the natural pivot, and both Australia and the United States will become increasingly solicitous of, even dependent upon, Beijing's favor for any plausible Asian initiative. Though humbling, this is not necessarily fatal to Australia's existential security. Two additional contingencies must be present. First, the relationship between the United States and China becomes increasingly competitive, possibly over China's ambition to command the first and second island chains and the regional seas beyond versus a contending US struggle to retain continuing control of the regional commons. Second, in this increasingly competitive context, both China and the United States exert increasing pressure on Australia (and other small and medium Asian powers, particularly US alliance partners) to choose sides.

What are Australia's options in such a scenario? Canberra can escape this dilemma, White argues, only by persuading the United States to compromise and form a "concert" with the PRC. In other words, the essential problem is not Australia's but that of its patron. Washington should be blamed for its stubborn refusal to yield gracefully to the inevitable shift in the balance of power. Once it does so, China will be satisfied and all will be well. This presupposes that China's ambitions are limited to those limited territorial adjustments (Taiwan, the South China Sea) currently at issue (although Whyte has been shy about which of these he would readily concede). The presumption is that China does not wish to be regional hegemon, an ambition it has frequently disavowed, but only to be fully accredited as a major power and as a "pole" in a concert of equals including, say, Russia, Japan, India, and the United States. But does not such a concert already exist, in which China is fully included? China is an active member of the UN Security Council, International Monetary Fund (IMF), World Bank, Asian Development Bank (ADB), the ASEAN Regional Forum (ARF), Asia-Pacific Economic Cooperation (APEC), and most other existing international and regional organizations, and has even started to introduce new ones, such as the SCO and the Asian Infrastructure Investment Bank (AIIB).

In any event, the concert of powers is a normative ideal that has not necessarily functioned well in practice. The concert of powers as it played out in, say, Europe between the Congress of Vienna and World War I was not at the time viewed as a stable or peaceful system (cf. the 1848 revolutions, the Franco-Prussian and Crimean wars, and growing polarization between the Triple Alliance and the Triple Entente), and whether a concert could integrate a diverse array of actors and constrain them to "play in tune" seems questionable. Where does the concert leave ASEAN, the former center of East Asian integration efforts? It is on the whole credible that China does not currently wish to challenge the United States for regional primacy. But recent experience in the wake of China's surpassing Japan suggests that China's ambitions are dynamic, and may grow in correlation with its power. And China's growing identification with its imperial legacy may lead it to prefer the more hierarchical tributary ideal, modernized to include sovereignty over adjacent waters. What if China does not agree to a concert—or, more likely, publicly agrees but continues to strive for a hierarchical regional order excluding the United States, Japan, Australia, and other likely troublemakers (as in its preferred early vision of the EAS)? The "concert" will have become no more than a euphemistic gloss on the same old Darwinian struggle—leaving Australia's dilemma intact.

So again, Australia, *quo vadis*? In classic balance-of-power realism, the expected response to a formidable threat is a strengthened alliance with another threatened state, as each ally needs the other to defend against the greater threat. The increased capability of the threatened vis-à-vis the threat creates a security dilemma, polarization, and arms racing. Having reinforced its sole bilateral alliance, Australia has begun reaching out to India and Japan to augment its external balancing coalition. If the two sides are reasonably balanced this may (according to classic realism) constitute a reasonably stable deterrent. This, however, would be implausible in triangular logic, according to which change gives rise to uncertainty and danger as new configurations become realistically possible. As China approaches the tipping point of surpassing the US level of GDP and comprehensive national power, we should anticipate enhanced tension levels and higher probabilities of hegemonic war. Australia, given its bifurcated economic and security needs, has sought to balance between China and the United States, to play the role of pivot. But as noted, it is difficult for Australia to play pivot, because it lacks sufficient resources either to intimidate or reward the other two actors, and both will try to force Australia to take sides. Australia may be forced to choose.

There are two dissenting arguments against this bleak prognosis. The first is the power of path dependency, or inertia: Growth is on the side of the challenger, but inertia (prudence, alliance loyalty, economic regime type, traditional values, soft power) supports the status quo. True, inertia cannot really be considered a causal factor but more a drag on causes, but it can be quite powerful. Second, the hard logic of the triangle points to some escape options. As the capability gap between challenger and hegemon narrows, the former becomes at once a more attractive partner and a more formidable foe. When (and if) China acquires truly hegemonic power it becomes the natural pivot of the triangle. Each member of the alliance will hence logically be tempted to defect to the pivot while preventing the other member from defecting first. China will wish to encourage such defection, preferably from the weaker partner—but doing so will not be easy. To become a successful pivot, China must strike a delicate balance between powerful disciplinarian and generous patron and protector of the regional commons. To be powerful but merely efficiently self-interested risks being pigeonholed as "China threat" from which nothing can be gained without undue risk, an epithet China has cannily sought to avoid. Since the late 1990s, China has been acutely sensitive to the need to strike this balance, to lubricate hard with soft power. However, Beijing's international behavior since the global financial crisis and its rise to number two appears to have deviated from this template for success, driving Australia as well as many of its regional neighbors, back into the protective US embrace. And the domestic China model's determined movement toward greater top-down power and sustained growth under tight-ened authoritarian discipline makes it appealing only to other dictatorships. In the past, Beijing has launched charm campaigns and temporarily paused when its policies aroused pushback, but it has tended to do so less and less as it has become more powerful. The calculation seems to be that size and power alone will make Beijing's offers irresistible. Bandwagoning with a formidably superior power may be the most rational choice, but it will take more than a cool and rational comparison of strategic options to dislodge a nation from the powerful inertia of cultural path dependency.

CONCLUSIONS

Australia has ridden the shifting post–Cold War international economic and political waves like a champion surfer, but it has become increasingly nervous about a perceived incongruence between its booming economic relationship with China and its alliance commitment to the United States. The incongruence is not yet urgent, as relations between China and the United States remain cordial and Australia maintains good relations with each, fostering smooth business relations with China while maintaining close military and political ties with the United States. But there have been warnings that the future will be marked by an inevitable increase in tensions between China and its neighbors as the former overtakes and surpasses the United States in aggregate GDP and in its regional military deterrent capability. Not only China's territorial expansiveness but also its more assertive recent role in regional and international organizations signal this. [29] Since the 1990s, Australia has contributed to the construction of regional collective security organizations, but these have proved unable to resolve the contradiction. [30] This combination of shared bilateral tensions, and concomitant pressures from each side for Australia's support, could force Canberra into an awkward dilemma: renounce its booming economic relationship to side with an economically moribund West, or betray old alliance commitments in pursuit of a lucrative relationship with a rising but ideologically alien new hegemon.

All three actors in the Australian triangle have a short-term interest in playing down the disequilibrating impact of China's rise and its sometimes divergent economic and security interests and maintaining the current mutually beneficial ménage for as long as possible. But if economic growth rates continue to diverge, the incongruence is apt to make itself felt in various ways. China will become more confident in its demands, more conspicuously generous in rewarding loyalty, more skilled in using its economic clout to discipline noncompliance. If maintaining compliance with continuing US strategic primacy in the region becomes untenable, China may force Australia to choose. Hugh White has it this dilemma can be avoided by placating China with a position in a regional concert of powers—in triangular terms, a ménage. But what if one of the smaller powers awarded to China in White's concert—Vietnam, say, or Taiwan—prefers to fight rather than switch? Does the United States stand aside while the PRC crushes the dissident? And what if China does not agree to join another concert? For one thing, a ménage implies formal equality among the actors, which, however consistent with Westphalian rules, may seem unrealistic to the strongest.

If a ménage becomes no longer sustainable, either because US foreign policy becomes too impotent or distracted to protect its allies' core interests or because China becomes too big and too powerful or too dissatisfied to put up with the status quo, Australia (and/or other states in the region) may indeed choose to cast their lot with Beijing as the new regional hegemonic stabilizer. In that case, the incumbent superpower will find it increasingly difficult to keep allies in line, any one of which will be weaker and more economically dependent on the PRC. The PRC will at this point prudently attempt to narrow the scope of conflict to encourage defections among those not directly affected. If bilateral Sino-US tensions reach a breaking point over say, Japan or Taiwan, Australia, like the Philippines, may opt to defect in order to avoid estranging its increasingly powerful economic partner to the north and getting trapped in an irrelevant and costly conflict.

This contingency is foreseen in the logic of the strategic triangle. But unless the United States commits a regional foreign policy blunder comparable in magnitude to the Iraq invasion, or a hegemonic war occurs from which China emerges victorious, it will not be easy for China to seize regional primacy, even if and when it becomes regional growth locomotive with the world's largest economy and mightiest military. China's increase in soft power has not kept pace with its growing hard power. And inertial loyalties and shared ideological legacies may exert considerable drag on the transition. For Beijing to achieve a cheap and peaceful power transition, the trick will be twofold. First, China must demonstrate dominant strategic capabilities without posing a perceived threat to the actors it hopes to lead (at least not to all at the same time). Second, China must sustain its own inspiring growth rate in a way that also opens win-win opportunities for the aspirations of neighboring countries to achieve their own wealth and power. That will be difficult.

NOTES

1. See Hugh White, "The Limits to Optimism: Australia and the Rise of China," *Australian Journal of International Affairs* 39, no. 4 (December 2005): 469–80; and Hugh White, "Why War in Asia Remains Thinkable," *Survival* 50, no. 6 (December 2008–January 2009): 85–104, inter alia.

2. The ANZUS alliance between the United States, Australia, and New Zealand was negotiated in 1951 and came into effect the following year and remains in full effect, though New Zealand exited the alliance in 1987 based on its opposition to nuclear weapons and the US refusal to vouchsafe their absence from ships transiting New Zealand ports.

3. *China Commerce Yearbook Editorial Committee*, 2009, p. 423; as cited in Chang Sen Yu and Jory Xiong, "The Dilemma of Interdependence: Current Features and Trends in Sino-Australian Relations," *Australian Journal of International Affairs* 66, no. 5 (November 2012): 579–91.

4. Clyde Russell, "Australia Avoids Commodity 'Dutch Disease,' for Now: Russell," Reuters, August 28, 2014, http://www.reuters.com/article/us-column-russell-australia-commodities-idUSKBN0GS1DU20140828.

5. For example, during the 2010 fishing boat incident and the subsequent flare-up of the Senkaku/Diaoyu issue China temporarily embargoed the export of rare earth elements to Japan, and in dudgeon at the Philippines' appeal to the International Court of Justice in 2013, there was a spontaneous Chinese boycott of Philippine bananas. After Liu Xiaobo was awarded a Nobel Peace Prize in 2010, China stopped buying Norwegian salmon (and broke diplomatic ties with Oslo for the next six years).

6. Australian Government Department of Foreign Affairs and Trade, "Australia and Foreign Investment," 2016, http://dfat.gov.au/trade/topics/investment/Pages/which-countries-invest-in-australia.aspx. According to the Australian Bureau of Statistics, Chinese FDI at the end of 2016 amounted to $41.9 billion. This compares with US investment of $195 billion, Japanese investment of $90.9 billion, British investment of $67.9 billion, and the Netherlands of $50.4 billion.

7. While China, based on strategic criteria, has had limited incoming FDI since 2006, Australia's avowed principle for screening foreign investment is not resource nationalism but resource liberalism, which purportedly "places the processes involved in the development of natural resources squarely 'in the international market' rather than under some form of state-mandated political control." Jeffrey D. Wilson, "Resource Nationalism or Resource Liberalism? Explaining Australia's Approach to Chinese Investment in Its Mineral Sector," *Australian Journal of International Affairs* 65, no. 3 (June 2011): 286. Given the prominent role of SOEs in its outgoing foreign direct investment (OFDI), the Chinese see little practical difference.

8. See Jian Yang, "China in the South Pacific: Hegemon on the Horizon?" *Pacific Review* 22, no. 2 (May 2009): 139–58.

9. While Australia sent troops to Iraq and Afghanistan during the global war on terror, these commitments have aroused domestic controversy. See, for example, Mark Beeson, "Australia, the US and East Asia," *Pacific Affairs* 79, no. 4 (Winter 2006/7): 597–604; also see former prime minister Malcolm Fraser, "China's Defense Posture and Australian Interests," *East Asia Forum*, July 18, 2011, accessed July 25, 2011, http://www.eastasiaforum.org/2011/07/18/chinas-defence-posture-and-australian-interests/.

10. See Stephen Walt, "Alliances in a Unipolar World," *World Politics* 61, no. 1 (January 2009); also Glenn H. Snyder, "Alliance Theory: A Neorealist First Cut," *Journal of International Affairs* 44, no. 1 (Spring/Summer 1990): 103–24.

11. See Stephan Frühling, *A History of Australian Strategic Policy since 1945* (Canberra: Department of Defence, 2009), http://www.defence.gov.au/Publications/docs/StrategicBasis.pdf; and Paul Dibb, "The Importance of the Inner Arc to Australian Defence Policy and Planning," *Security Challenges* 8, no. 4 (Summer 2012): 14, https://www.regionalsecurity.org.au/Resources/Files/Vol8No4Dibb.pdf.

12. The planned multibillion-dollar military upgrade reportedly includes plans to buy up to one hundred F-35 jet fighters, air defense, destroyers, and amphibious assault ships. See also Jack McCaffrie and Chris Rahman, "Australia's 2009 Defence White Paper," *Naval War College Review* 63, no. 1 (Winter 2010): 61–74.

13. While in the 2013 White Paper, the phrase was used five times, in 2016, it was used forty-eight times, plus another three references to a "rules-based regional order." Cf. Commonwealth of Australia, *2013 Defence White Paper*, 2013, http://www.defence.gov.au/whitepaper/2013/; Commonwealth of Australia, *2016 Defence White Paper*, 2016, http://www.defence.gov.au/whitepaper/2016/.

14. Andrew Davies and Mark Thomson, "Australian Defense Policy in the Trump Era," *Asia Pacifica Bulletin* (East-West Center), no. 373 (February 27, 2017), http://www.eastwestcenter.org/system/tdf/private/apb373.pdf?file=1&type=node&id=36003.

15. James Manicom and Andrew O'Neil, "Accommodation, Realignment, or Business as Usual? Australia's Response to a Rising China," *Pacific Review* 23, no. 1 (March 2010): 34–36 (see section "Accommodation," 23–44).

16. In 2017, Australia hosts its sixth rotation of US marines in Darwin, including "the largest US aircraft contingent to Australia in peacetime history" and a full squadron of US F-22 Raptors. Cf. Elena Collinson and James Laurenceson, "Chinese Investment and Australian Sovereignty," *China Policy Institute: Analysis*, June 6, 2017, https://cpianalysis.org/2017/06/06/chinese-investment-and-australian-sovereignty/.

17. Mohan Malik, "Australia, America and Asia," *Pacific Affairs* 79, no. 4 (Winter 2006–7): 587–95.

18. Katharine Murphy, "Chinese Premier Warns Australia 'Taking Sides' Could Lead to New Cold War," *Manchester Guardian*, March 23, 2017, https://www.theguardian.com/world/2017/mar/23/chinese-premier-warns-australia-taking-sides-could-lead-to-new-cold-war.

19. This is not to my knowledge an official position, but based on my conversation with Chinese academics articulating their understanding of their government's preference.

20. Liberal foreign minister Alexander Downer in August 2004 said that in the event of hostilities across the Taiwan Strait, ANZUS would not apply, for which he was rebuked by Washington. Prime Minister John Howard responded with a clarification that Downer had "misspoken." Manicom and O'Neil, "Accommodation, Realignment, or Business as Usual?," 34–36. On a Japan contingency, see Benjamin Schreer, "Australia's 'Special Strategic Relationship' with Japan: Another 'China Choice'?" *Australian Journal of International Affairs* 70, no. 1 (2016): 37–49. However, during the 1995–96 Taiwan Strait crisis, Australia was the only country to support the US intercession.

21. Hugh White, "Our Role in Asia's Superpower Shuffle," Weekend *Australian*, September 4, 2010; Hugh White, "As China Rises, We Must Look beyond the U.S. Alliance," *Australian*, September 13, 2010; Hugh White, "China's Rise Calls for Shared Leadership," Australian *Financial Review*, September 23, 2010; Hugh White, "Wealth and Power: Coming to Terms with China," *ANU Reporter*, Autumn 2011, 29–30; and Hugh White, "Power Shift: Rethinking Australia's Place in the Asian Century," *Australian Journal of International Affairs* 65, no. 1 (February 2011): 81–93.

22. See Kenneth Lieberthal and Wang Jisi, *Addressing U.S.-China Strategic Distrust* (Washington, DC: Brookings, 2012), https://www.brookings.edu/wp-content/uploads/2016/06/0330_china_lieberthal.pdf.

23. Hugh White, "Power Shift: Rethinking Australia's Place in the Asian Century," *Australian Journal of International Affairs* 65, no. 1 (February 2011): 81–93.

24. Kenneth N. Waltz, *The Theory of International Politics* (Reading, MA: Addison-Wesley, 1979).

25. For example, Hans Morgenthau writes that "the balance of power and policies aiming at its preservation are not only inevitable but are an essential stabilizing factor in a society of sovereign nations." Hans Morgenthau, *Politics among Nations: The Struggle for Power and Peace* (New York: McGraw-Hill, 1985), 187–89.

26. John J. Mearsheimer, "The Gathering Storm: China's Challenge to US Power in Asia," *Chinese Journal of International Politics* 3 (2010): 381–96.

27. See A. F. K. Organski, *World Politics* (New York: Knopf, 1958); and Ronald L. Tammen et al., *Power Transitions: Strategies for the 21st Century* (New York: Chatham House, 2000).

28. White, "Limits to Optimism," 470.

29. See Sebastian Heilmann, Moritz Rudolf, Mikko Huotari, and Johannes Buckow, "China's Shadow Foreign Policy: Parallel Structures Challenge the Established International Order," *China Monitor* (Mercator Institute for China Studies), no. 18 (October 28, 2014).

30. Baogang He, "The Awkwardness of Australian Engagement with Asia: The Dilemmas of Australian Idea of Regionalism," *Japanese Journal of Political Science* 12, no. 2 (August 2011), 267–85.

Chapter Nine

Conclusions

This book holds that international relations in Asia since the Cold War can be usefully understood within a triangular framework embracing reciprocal relations between the three most powerful regional actors: the United States, the People's Republic of China (PRC), and the rest of Asia (ROA). "Triangularity" means that the three are all rational actors striving to maximize national interests by cultivating the most advantageous feasible relations with the other two, and that each bilateral relationship is premised on relations with the third. It is a simple schema, a set of roles that a variable cast of characters can play. But if they play, as they tend to do in this region, the possible configurations among them are logically limited to four configurations: unit-veto triangle, marriage, romantic triangle, and ménage à trois. This is clearly an oversimplification, but simplifications can sometimes be useful. If a complex, multifaceted problem can be broken down to its basic elements, those essentials can then be addressed more directly with greater economy of scale. While this is a realist framework, we must also take into account that realism is also an elective choice subject to definition and that each actor's definition of what is rational is formed from the perspective of that actor's national identity. The triangular framework is an ideal-typical construct that helps clarify the logic of rational decision making for each actor given that actor's position at any given time. The resulting shifts in triangular configurations—from marriage to romantic triangle, say—can be explained as an outcome of the fallible decisions of the three actors to escape from their current positions to a more advantageous or less threatening one.

At present, the triangle can be broadly characterized as a romantic triangle in which the rest of Asia (ROA) enjoys better relations with both China and the United States than the latter have with each other. This position was somewhat passively acquired, by dint of the delicate balance between the two great powers. But it is a positional advantage, and to keep it, the ROA must maneuver carefully between the two behemoths—friends to each, enemy to neither. The Sino-US relationship can be characterized not as an opposition so much as a rivalry between the two in which both are competing with a mix of hard and soft power for leadership of the ROA. Both naturally prefer to address the sensitive current state of affairs with somewhat more mellifluous rhetoric: to the United States, the question is the maintenance of a legal-rational, rules-based international order, while to the PRC the superior normative framework is an Asian security order based on international democracy divested of polarizing security alliances in which all sovereign nations form flexible win-win economic (and security) arrangements with one another. But these legitimating rationales are not faithfully adhered to by either party. The rivalry between them is in part bilateral and in part triangular, the latter being more structurally basic and complex, though the two are mutually reinforcing. The United States, as architect and pillar of the status quo, tends to be complacent, while the PRC, as challenger, tends to lapse into righteous indignation. The ROA is of course diverse in its preferences, all members, however, preferring both major powers to remain engaged in the region without either winning or losing completely. The intensity of the competition within this great romantic triangle varies with the temperature of specific hot spots intrinsically linked to the dissonant interests of the great powers, such as the North Korean nuclear issue, Kashmir, Taiwan, and various maritime and terrestrial border disputes.

How did this triangular configuration come into being? Asia is a vast panorama of change, and the triangle should not be reified at any particular point in time, as the configuration may be expected to change as disparate growth rates provide opportunities and risks to the various actors involved and they shift positions accordingly. In the beginning, upon dissolution of the ménage that defeated the Axis in World War II, the three most relevant actors on the Asian stage were the United States, the PRC, and the Union of Soviet Socialist Republics (USSR). The ROA was still in a confused and fragmented shambles, emerging from colonization and the devastation of war. The initial pattern was a Sino-Soviet marriage against the United States, based on shared ideological convictions, proposing to arouse the ROA to revolution against an oppressive imperialist regime controlled by Western capitalist states. Within months after marching into Beijing, Mao Zedong announced the decision to "lean to one side" (*yibian dao*)—that is, unreserved commitment to communist revolution as organized by the communist international movement. To Mao, this was a disjunctive choice; as he put it in a speech commemorating the twenty-eighth anniversary of the Chinese Communist Party (CCP) on June 30, 1949: "In the light of the experiences accumulated in these forty years and these 28 years, all Chinese without exception must lean either to the side of imperialism or to the side of socialism. Sitting on the fence will not do, nor is there a third road."[1]

For a while, this lips and teeth coalition functioned smoothly in tandem, but it fell apart at the end of a decade notwithstanding a formal mutual defense alliance, a consensual division of labor, and identical strategic global objectives. This was occasioned by a host of bilateral issues (led by Soviet rescission of its agreement to share nuclear technology), but triangular issues emerged during Nikita Khrushchev's visit to China following his tour of the United States. Here it emerged that China resented being left out of Soviet-US détente, the "spirit of Camp David" that briefly prevailed during Khrushchev's 1959 visit to the United States. As antagonism between the two poles diminished, friction between Beijing and Moscow intensified, culminating in the twenty-year Sino-Soviet dispute. The two Eurasian giants disagreed in principle both on how to deal with US imperialism and on how best tactically to mobilize the ROA against it. By the end of the 1960s, this internecine competition had become so fierce it became possible for the United States to play one side against the other, thereby introducing a romantic triangle in which the pivot maintained better relations against the two wings than they had with each other. While it is true that this intercommunist competition intensified efforts in pursuit of Third World revolution by both sides, the bilateral rivalry became so intense it frustrated their shared ideological objectives (as in Cambodia and Afghanistan).[2] Yet the US role as pivot not only played out to US relative advantage but also, arguably, functioned to mitigate the dangerously mounting tension between the two wings (e.g., by deterring a Soviet preemptive strike on China).

The Great Strategic Triangle featuring the PRC, the United States, and the USSR lasted until the dissolution of the Soviet empire at the end of the 1980s. The *Asian* cold war, however, ended some two decades earlier, with the Nixon rapprochement with China in 1971–72. During this triangular heyday, Sino-US relations blossomed for several years into a sort of tacit strategic alliance, while Soviet-US and Sino-Soviet relations both polarized around proxy wars and competitive arms buildups (the USSR at the time was perceived to be on the verge of strategic nuclear parity with the United States and in a position to knock out China's nascent nuclear capability), until finally the rise of Gorbachev resulted in an historic détente among the USSR and both the United States and the PRC. This somewhat ironically preceded the Soviet collapse in December 1991, which abruptly left the Sino-US rapprochement without a strategic raison d'être. Sino-US relations were nonetheless able to recover from the worldwide shock of the Tiananmen crackdown by shifting from a strategic to a commercial rationale. As for the ROA, Sino-US rapprochement and the Nixon Doctrine opened the way to intra-Asian rapprochement, with the so-called liberation of South Vietnam in 1975 and China's reform and opening to the outside world in late 1978. The negotiated end of Indochina proxy wars finally brought peace to Southeast Asia, where the organization and expansion of the Association of Southeast Asian Nations (ASEAN) offered a vague but uplifting example to the ROA. At the time, it seemed the major winner of the Asian cold war in the 1970s and 1980s was Japan, which in its last phase of high-speed growth began building a network of supply chains to Southeast Asia and China. Thus hypergrowth spread from Japan and the newly industrialized countries (NICs) to the Southeast Asian "small tigers" as footloose Japanese and Western capital flooded in.

In triangular terms, the end of the *global* Cold War in 1989–91 ushered in for the first time since 1945 a historic ménage à trois, though it was also a transition period lacking meaningful international structure. The Eastern European people's republics all divested themselves of Marxist-Leninist ideology, and the Soviet Union itself disintegrated in 1991, in effect dissolving the Soviet pole of the Great Strategic Triangle. Amid lofty US hopes of a new world order, this facilitated an economic integration of the capitalist and communist worlds. But Russia experienced a politically difficult and economically disappointing transition from centralized Leninism to capitalist democracy, ultimately resulting in a retreat to a more authoritarian order. The foreign policy implication was a sharp contraction of Russian international influence, felt especially deeply in the former Soviet periphery, where historical components of the Soviet and Russian empires, despite hosting sizable Russian minority populations, declared independence and distanced themselves from Moscow. Russian influence on the ROA, always narrowly based, also diminished, as Moscow came to be viewed in Asia as China's junior partner. The main beneficiary of the post–Cold War transition was China, which gained entry into the World Trade Organization (WTO) in 2001 and, after the suppression of aspirations for political reform at Tiananmen, refocused popular energies exclusively on rapid economic growth. The results were spectacularly successful, particularly in the export sector. The 1990s saw the bursting of the asset bubble and subsequent economic stagnation of Japan and the onset of a paradoxical combination of hot economic relations and cool politics as the two competed for Asian leadership. The Asian triangle accordingly dropped Russia and shifted membership to China, the United States, and the ROA. Until the Asian economic crisis, this was a period of strategic opportunity for ASEAN, which took advantage of the ménage among the powers to promote its own normative centrality in a spate of regionally inclusive multilateral institution building. The economies of Southeast Asia boomed during this period, with growth rates of 7–9 percent per annum. India, too, initiated market reform in the early 1990s, and while the Indian developmental model differed from the Chinese, growth also accelerated appreciably.

In the wake of the 2008 global financial crisis (GFC), China began to comport itself with growing self-confidence as the power balance shifted in its favor, graduating from active participation in existing multilateral organizations to a quest for regional and international leadership and, in loose coalition with Russia, increasingly refusing to yield to economic or political demands from the unipolar hegemon. Change was first discernible in Beijing's resistance to US demands to correct the trade imbalance via currency revaluation. Growing self-confidence could be seen in the contrast between Hu Jintao's agreement to drop the description of the South China Sea as an "issue of core national interest" during his visit to the United States in September 2010, and Xi Jinping's warning in January 2017 that China will never back down from its maritime territorial claims.

As the basis for strategic cooperation disappeared with the disintegration of the Soviet hegemon and China's territorial ambitions clashed with US vested strategic interests, the main avenue for continued cooperation became economic interdependence. The United States became the largest destination for Chinese exports while China became the largest source of US imports. American consumers enjoyed lower prices and an end to inflation, while millions of American workers lost their jobs because factories in the United States relocated their operations to China. We see an emerging romantic triangle in this period, in which the ROA finds itself sandwiched between a rising China still cooperating with while also challenging an established but relatively declining hegemon. While the pivot position offers the ROA the advantage of collecting competing benefits from each side, the pivot is weak relative to either wing and hence vulnerable to pressure to choose sides as competition intensifies. And if current trends continue, it will.

Since its withdrawal from Vietnam and the Philippine bases, the United States played a relatively passive role in the Asian Pacific while China moved into the vacuum. This was initially accompanied by a charm campaign invoking "peaceful rise" and "harmonious world" rhetoric that lasted until the GFC in 2008, which China seems to have read as the beginning of terminal US decline and a period of strategic opportunity. As we have noted, Beijing responded to calls to assume a more responsible international role befitting its economic arrival with a grasp for Asian leadership, joining and then leading in multilateral institution-building efforts, integrating into Asian supply chains, and rushing belatedly into the race to appropriate maritime resources. The United States under Barack Obama reacted to what it viewed as the more explicit China challenge to its geopolitical primacy by initiating the pivot or rebalance strategy. In retrospect, this initiative was boldly conceived but unconvincingly implemented. The United States declined to defend Scarborough Shoal in 2012 after having declared the South China Sea in the US national interest despite its mutual defense alliance with the Philippines, for example, and the Trans-Pacific Partnership (TPP) was left incomplete at the end of Obama's eight-year term. The Chinese, however, took the pivot quite seriously as a hostile encirclement strategy and reacted sharply against it, condemning US interference and launching an island-building and militarization campaign. Each side held frequent joint military exercises, attempting to intimidate each other and rally the ROA to its respective camp. Neither side wanted war in this protracted game of chicken, yet each was determined not to back down from the other.

Are the issues inherent or can they be resolved? We have divided the issues between the United States and China into two categories: bilateral and triangular. The bilateral tension may be divided into spiritual and material aspects. At the spiritual level, the essential contradiction is the gap between national identities. At early stages of the relationship, the identity gap appeared to be converging, as China disavowed ideological dogmatism and adopted a pragmatic, seemingly market-based economic model and opened up to the outside world. But as China has caught up in economic and political power it has turned to the past to deepen its national identity and moved away from the West, resulting in growing identity divergence.[3] This has been evident, on the one hand, in the retrieval of an "exceptional" national identity from the past after years of historical repression under Leninist ideological constraints, eclectically embracing legendary heroic figures from Confucius to Genghis Khan. On the other hand, we see the attempt to block Western spiritual contamination, as in the "seven perils" quietly mandated in 2013 as Central Document no. 9, or the "Great Firewall of China" erected to enforce Internet sovereignty. The domestic corollary is an intense crackdown on domestic dissent, which is generally linked to Western spiritual contamination. This identity gap germinated in the wake of the collapse of the USSR and Eastern European communism and the ensuing color revolutions and the Arab Spring, which alerted the CCP leadership to the risk of spiritual subversion by pluralist cultures and led to a patriotic education campaign in the post-Tiananmen era and to a subsequent upsurge of nationalism.

The growing focus on a unique national identity in a globalizing world threatening to dissolve national distinctions gives rise to a narrower focus on the national interest in the ideational superstructure guiding foreign policy as well. This tendency has spread since 2012 to the United Kingdom, the United States, and Turkey as well. The material dimension of the competition consists of friction over trade (chronically imbalanced) and investment. Both have intensified as China closes the technological gap and becomes more economically competitive and less dependent on foreign economic inputs. The identity gap has also infected economic relations in that while US economists tend to uphold market rationality is a universal panacea and judge Chinese reform in that light, the PRC since the mid-1990s has embraced a hybrid form of capitalism in which the party-state continues to reign supreme over the economy (and can outbid any Western corporation at will). In foreign economic policy, it is clearly the state that decides, not markets or multinational corporations. In the security realm, the overriding concern in the United States is China catching up. China has acquired the weaponry to defend its near waters, break through the island chains, and challenge US defense of Asian allies and strategic dominance of the Western Pacific. All this friction has taken place in the delicate context of China's spectacular political and economic rise and the relative US decline since the GFC.

In chapter 2, we concluded that bilateral tension is sensitive essentially because it evokes the neuralgic prospect of power transition: the rise of the PRC at the expense of the relative decline of the United States. Overtaking the United States has long been a conscious goal of the PRC, though it would prefer to do so without a hegemonic war. What are its chances? After thirty years of breakneck growth, they would seem to be quite good, although it is also true that China since the GFC has experienced a major increment of debt and consequent growth slowdown. Yet the leadership remains competent and determined, and the populace has relatively low per capita incomes and hence a strong incentive to raise them. We thus estimate that there is a good likelihood (though by no means a certainty) that if current trends continue, China will indeed overtake the United States in nominal GDP in the foreseeable future and in military capability a decade or so later. As sensitive as this prospect is, power transition is not a casus belli *in itself*, popular construals of Thucydides to the contrary notwithstanding. A peaceful power transition will require the conscious or tacit cooperation of both powers, which is difficult but not impossible. After all, the United States and the USSR never faced one another in battle, despite four decades of tense bipolarity. For a peaceful transition to be possible, three conditions must be present: First, the challenger must not infringe on the incumbent's core interests. Second, the incumbent hegemon must be willing to yield gracefully to the challenger's reasonable demands. Third, both must share a determination not to let their differences become kinetic. Thus far, only the third condition is clearly present. Yet it may be enough, given the mutually assured capability of both powers to inflict unacceptable devastation on each other, a capability that will survive any transition in comprehensive national power for some time (cf. Russia). But the ultimate outcome of the contest will be decided by the stakes.

The triangular issue involves the ROA, which is at once an interested audience to the bilateral rivalry and the stakes of the game. This multilateral competition is more complex and sensitive than bilateral opposition for two reasons. First, it involves the military. Aggravating as they are, there are no strictly bilateral issues that would bring China and the United States to the brink of war: China is far away, there are no territorial disputes between them, and economic and spiritual differences are not generally recognized as a casus belli. China since the end of the Cold War has sought to proselytize its ideology or model, but without noteworthy success in the United States.

But the United States is formally committed to the defense of its allies, and China has declared that it has core interests it is willing to fight for. These commitments unfortunately overlap, and the military in both countries is strongly committed to them. Second, while bilateral issues involve only Washington and Beijing, triangular interests involve the national interests and aspirations of the various Asian states. That means that each Asian state must decide how to adapt to the competition and putative power transition between China and the United States. This sets up a trilateral competition between China and the United States for the allegiance of the ROA, which plays out in the demonstration and strategic application of force, in economic statecraft, in diplomatic maneuvers and the mobilization of soft power, and in the organization and manipulation of multilateral fora. Let us briefly review and assess the state of play in each realm.

1. The Asian consensus is that the United States remains supreme in sheer military power, though China is narrowing the gap, particularly in its near waters. As challenger to the status quo, China has taken the initiative in its territorial claims as well as its actions to realize these claims but, sensitive to continuing US strategic superiority as well as the Asian aversion to hegemonism, has been careful to portray its actions as defensive reactions to unjustified provocations. The last remaining terrestrial border dispute (with India) remains bilateral, focused on China's claim to what it calls Southern Tibet and India calls Arunachal Pradesh (though India also still claims the China-occupied Aksai Chin). Since the rise of Xi Jinping, there have been two nonlethal border confrontations (2014 and 2017) fitting the same pattern: India reports a Chinese "incursion" across the Line of Actual Control (LAC), often in connection with a road-building operation, and mobilizes troops; China denies any incursion and countermobilizes troops; after a few weeks' negotiations, an informal truce is reached. American support for India's nuclear weaponization brings this bilateral rivalry into the triangular strategic game. A conspicuous example of China's peaceful expansion tactics could be seen in the uproar that followed the Japanese governmental purchase of three of the five Senkaku/Diaoyu islets in September 2012 from the family from whom it had previously leased them. This precipitated riots in over a hundred Chinese cities, an unofficial boycott in the sale of rare earth elements, and implementation of a "new normal" involving routine Chinese patrols of Japanese territorial waters. Another Chinese tactic has been gradual expansion under misleading pretexts, often using apparently civilian fishing fleets to claim dominance, or proclaiming a fishing moratorium to protect the environment. The cumulative result of this salami-slicing approach has been a steady, incremental expansion of

the domain of China's air and naval control despite resistance. In the East China Sea, the Diaoyu/Senkaku claim remains suspended in crisis, but China has begun to exploit subsurface oil deposits in territorial waters as it defines them (e.g., Chengxiao) and has unilaterally proclaimed an air defense identification zone (ADIZ) including the disputed territory. In the Paracels, China has achieved de facto uncontested control over land features after defeating Vietnam in 1974 and 1988 sea battles. In the Spratly Islands, the upshot has been Chinese occupation and reclamation of seven previously unoccupied islands, three of which have been equipped with airstrips, aircraft hangars, ports, radar, anti-aircraft missiles, and small service communities. China has been good at the game of "chicken," gradually advancing its claims and then drawing red lines around them and threatening war should anyone dare to cross them. The US response has been a symbolic challenge to China's red lines by disputing their legality and sailing ships into claimed territorial waters, but freedom of navigation operations (FONOPs) have not been able to push them back or halt their continuing fortification. Yet seven years on, the results of this clever campaign have been fairly modest, in effect freezing exploitation of subsurface hydrocarbon resources by the ROA rather than a sweeping proliferation of Chinese offshore oil rigs.

2. Economic statecraft is inherently ambiguous because it consists of trade and investment that can normally be deemed perfectly innocuous but, if shrewdly employed, can also be used to political advantage. China's economic expansion into its periphery since the turn of the millennium has been very rapid on all sides, particularly Central and Southeast Asia, with more outgoing foreign direct investment (OFDI) since 2015 than incoming FDI. The Belt and Road Initiative (BRI), or One Belt, One Road (OBOR), has lent visionary coherence to this expansion, knitting together disparate ongoing projects and some new ones. It is not always clear from the closely held financial terms of these projects to what extent China's motives are realist and to what extent they are mercantilist: in other words, is China out to make money, or to expand political influence? It appears so far that Chinese exports exceed imports in most places (excepting Taiwan and Japan), that loans exceed investments, and that investments exceed aid, which would fit a mercantilist paradigm. Yet BRI may do both. If China makes megaloans to a client with inadequate resources to service the debt, long-term political dependency may ensue, in which (depending on the terms of the deal) émigré microcommunities may be permanently ensconced to manage ports, farms, or other infrastructure facilities. This is an emergent propensity in Sri Lanka, Cambodia, Laos, Myanmar, and Pakistan. The majority of the most eager participants

are relatively poor and underdeveloped states that will have difficulty repaying Chinese loans. In a premature diagnosis, OBOR has been an outstanding public relations success that, if consistently pursued, may reorient China's surplus capacity to its underdeveloped periphery, thereby also institutionalizing an enduring political-economic sphere of influence. The risk is that the more controversial aspects of the Chinese model will also be included in the package: economically unsustainable infrastructure megaprojects, heightened inequality, corruption, and lasting foreign policy dependency.

3. China's diplomacy has been energetic and hands on, with a fully engaged leadership: Xi Jinping, for example, made twenty-two overseas trips to forty-six countries in five continents from 2013 through 2016, and Premier Li Keqiang and Foreign Minister Wang Yi have also been busy. China has established eighty Confucius Institutes in Asia (as of 2017) and has active exchange programs, particularly with the more advanced Asian countries. Among China's Asian neighbors, there is now widespread acknowledgment of China's increasingly dominant political and economic influence in the region.[4] According to public opinion polls in the region, China is now likely to overtake and surpass the United States in economic capacity in the near future or has already done so.[5] The United States, though viewed as having waning influence, does retain a more *positive* image in the region. Yet this may well be slipping as well.

4. Both China and the United States have actively participated in multilateral as well as bilateral diplomacy, joining Asia-Pacific Economic Cooperation (APEC), the ASEAN Regional Forum (ARF), the "noodle bowl" of free trade agreements (FTAs), and the EAS. China's active engagement in such regional forums as the ARF has been influential but self-interested, blocking any attempt to thwart its nationalist ambitions. The United States became particularly active during the Obama era, signing the Treaty of Amity and Cooperation (TAC) and actively engaging in the ARF and the EAS. Trump's withdrawal from the TPP in early 2017 (to which Clinton was also committed) is generally regarded in ROA as a diplomatic mistake, as it cedes the multilateral FTA field to China. And China has shown avid interest in filling the perceived leadership void left by the United States. In January 2017, a senior Chinese diplomat volunteered that "if it is necessary for China to play a leadership role, then China must take on this responsibility. China is prepared to take the helm of the global economy if the Western countries choose to abdicate their leadership role."[6] The US withdrawal was premised on Trump's assumption that better trade deals can be struck bilaterally than multilaterally by taking advantage of asymmetry (a premise shared by China with regard to the

South China Sea). Thus far the Trump administration has seen no strategic utility in multilateral free trade agreements, assessing them solely from a mercantilist perspective.

We now turn to those countries over which the rivalry is being contested, the ROA. From a triangular perspective, these are the clear winners in the current configuration, playing the pivot role in a romantic triangle in which they enjoy better relations with the two competing wings than the latter have with each other. Southeast and South Asia play the United States against the PRC, while Central Asia plays Russia against China. A frequent pattern is increasing economic dependence on China while relying on the United States (or Russia, in Central Asia) for security. And as China continues to grow faster than most other large economies, this economic dependency will increase. But whether economic dependency results in political realignment into China's orbit, even upon falling into a debt trap, remains unclear. There are some forty sovereign nations in Asia, and each has its own national interest and independent foreign policy. While all the ROA can be characterized as being in play between the two great powers in the triangle, their interests and concerns are otherwise quite diverse. Some are large and powerful, and some are small and relatively weak; each has its own distinct mix of cultural, ethnolinguistic, and political-economic aspirations, and threat perceptions. As sovereign actors, they can make these choices individually or try to make them en bloc, as part of a multilateral association. The reasons these countries choose one future course or another are complex and inconsistent.

Can the triangle tell us anything about the most plausible future options of the medium and smaller countries? It can tell us that there are three choices for these countries: join one or other of the two great powers, resist encroachment by self-strengthening and seeking external support, or try to navigate between the two. As competition intensifies and polarizes, pressure on the ROA will ratchet up to take sides. The options will be identical for all of the ROA, but not all will make the same choices. Responses will differ based on ideological/identity values, geoeconomic conditions (proximity to China, resource base, export or import dependence), national size and power, historic patronage ties, alliance commitments, and even the character of the leadership. These various factors may point in contrary directions, necessitating a difficult choice. The United States has its pentagonal network of mutual security alliances (Japan, South Korea, Thailand, the Philippines, and Australia), while China has an alliance with North Korea, a strategic partnership with Russia, and an all-weather friendship with Pakistan. These are assumed to be reasonably path dependent if not necessarily binding contracts. But conditions change, and alliances are subject to interpretation, as China has indicated regarding its alliance with the Democratic Republic of Korea (DPRK). Australia has been a loyal US ally for over a century, but Australia's dominant trade partner and export market is now the PRC, which has asked it to take a more neutral position. Trade and investment patterns seem apt to pull many Asian countries into China's orbit, but the cases of Japan and Taiwan, both of which are heavily economically dependent on the PRC, show that politics does not necessarily follow the money. Leadership matters, as most recently demonstrated by the 2016 presidential elections in the Philippines and in the United States. In October 2016, Rodrigo Duterte made his first non-ASEAN state visit to China, never mentioning his country's successful Permanent Court of Arbitration (PCA) case, whereupon he announced his country's supposed separation from the United States, brought home some $24 billion in investment promises, and personally welcomed a Russian warship to Manila Bay. Trump, during his presidential campaign, disparaged US alliances as a bad deal economically, opened the door to nuclear proliferation in Japan and South Korea, and seemed willing to sell protection to the highest bidder. In both cases, institutionalized interests have since pulled both back to a somewhat more path-dependent foreign policy. Ideology qua national identity also plays a role, as states, like people, generally prefer to affiliate with the like minded. The United States prefers to associate with other democracies (and tries to encourage democratization), while China has particularly cordial relations with other autocracies. The balance of power will tempt smaller and weaker states to bandwagon with a powerful patron; China has thus attracted political support from Myanmar, Laos, Pakistan, and Cambodia, all beneficiaries of munificent PRC investment and aid. More powerful and advanced political economies seem more likely to balance politically (e.g., Japan and Taiwan) even as they enjoy robust trade ties with China.

Only a few of the ROA states have decided on the first or second option, while most have sought to avoid a clear choice and to maneuver between the two, avoiding offense and maximizing benefits from each. Indonesia, Malaysia, Myanmar, Vietnam, Singapore, Thailand, and the Philippines all seek to balance between wings, sometimes tilting one way or the other. While the United States and China have competed for the allegiance of these countries, using both economic inducements and diplomatic pressure, most have remained artfully equivocal. China has tried to expand its realm of control by moving into apparently vacant or at least temporarily unguarded maritime areas surrounding these countries and trying to establish a permanent presence there. None of the islands it has paved over and militarized was physically occupied by another claimant.[7] The United States has found no reason to interfere directly in these advances, confining its use of force to military exercises and to continued FONOPs (navigation into areas over which China claims sovereignty). ROA members signal their patronage choices by joining the military exercises of one side or the other or by voicing opinions about the need to negotiate a binding Code of Conduct (COC), the proper legal jurisdiction of the Hague Tribunal, and the like. The Chinese response has been to decry US meddling and talk ASEAN's dogged fifteen-year pursuit of a binding COC to a standstill. The competition for the allegiance of these states is likely to continue. Meanwhile, Chinese economic statecraft, particularly as exercised through OBOR, though much less coordinated than it looks, has been a highly effective magnet for the ROA that the United States with its economic and political doldrums has found no way to match.

While any one of these inducements may be decisive for a given state at any given time, as a basis for sustainable commitments the ROA is likely to rely on two relatively invariant criteria: power asymmetry and economic necessity. Power is gradated in a hierarchy, not a triangle. As Yang Jiechi pointed out in 2010, gazing directly at the Singapore delegate, "China is a big country and other countries are small countries, and that is just a fact."[8] While the Treaty of Westphalia unrealistically declared that each state (no matter how large or small) is equal in international law, Yang's implication was that smaller states must defer to larger ones. But if a powerful state wants something from a weaker one, it must dispense ample incentives to induce compliance. Because it is big and powerful, it can offer (or withhold) protection and investment and other advantages unavailable to smaller states. As the first- or second-biggest trading partner to the ROA, China in recent years has made clear that these lucrative economic ties entail an implicit political price. Yet whether it will be paid is by no means certain. In domestic politics, China has ample power to coerce compliance if resistance emerges, but in international politics, if a smaller state opts to resist hierarchical logic, the more powerful state must then use the necessary force to enforce its will, or climb down. Yet using force even against an inferior opponent incurs open-ended costs. If China finally decides to invade Taiwan, say, it may have to destroy the island's value to prevail, gambling with the prospect of an international blockade and a postinvasion insurgency. And if China suddenly refuses to buy Australian coal or Malaysian palm oil, there are alternative customers in the international market. So neither stick nor carrot may compel in a given case: China ignores US requests to negotiate the South China Sea dispute, and Taiwan is not engaging in reunification talks with the mainland.

Despite such caveats, in the final analysis China is now stronger than any neighboring Asian state or combination of states, trade balances are generally in its favor, it still has massive financial reserves, and it is determined to maintain a growth rate compounding that asymmetry going forward. Except for Taiwan and in more complex ways Korea, the ROA is not threatened by physical destruction or annexation by China's mounting ambitions, so if the United States continues its decline while China continues its rise, why not bandwagon with the new hegemon? Certainly that is one option, but the cautious still hedge their bets. There are at least three reasons for this. First, it is not yet certain that China will indeed overtake the United States; recent trends are not necessarily a reliable indicator of future performance. China's growth has been decelerating since 2010 and may slow still further, what with demographic aging, rising wages, declining export demand, environmental despoliation, stalled political reform, and an unsustainable combination of overcapacity and peak debt load. The US economy, progressing at a snail's pace since the GFC, may yet regain momentum. Second, whether a weak state bandwagons with a more powerful one depends not only on relative power but also on whether the larger one poses a perceived threat. From 1990 to 2010, China accompanied its rise with a discourse of reassurance well designed to assuage such fears: peaceful rise/development, harmonious world, and win-win solutions. This rhetoric has continued, but meanwhile, a more militant rhetoric in defense of core interests and sovereign rights has begun to appear, accompanied by increasingly muscular actions to enforce China's claims.[9] Third, despite its budgetary and organizational focus on enhancing its soft power, results so far have not been convincing. The importance of soft power, which is not easily fungible, has often been exaggerated, but it can function as a multiplier of economic or military power, other things being equal.

Economic need is the other basic factor that may determine future choices. Is there an economic triangle? Not necessarily, but there are economic hierarchies, and those at the top may be expected to claim the most advantageous position in the triangle, *caeteris paribus*. But there are actually at least two economic hierarchies, one a hierarchy of aggregate and per capita GDP, the other a hierarchy of technological development, and they do not necessarily coincide. China now has the largest nominal GDP in the region and second largest in the world (the largest, calculated in purchasing power parity [PPP]), and it has had one of the world's fastest growth rates for the past four decades. Per capita GDP, however, has lagged aggregate GDP, ranking seventy-second in the world according to the World Bank (seventy-fourth according to the International Monetary Fund [IMF]). In terms of technological advancement, China still lags Japan, South Korea, Singapore, Hong Kong, Russia, and the United States. Aggregate GDP is arguably more relevant for the enhancement of foreign policy power, as it provides the wherewithal for a large trade and investment network and to fund foreign aid and arms budgets. China's booming economy and its opening to the outside world have already made it the central hub for Asian supply chains; hence it is the economic locomotive of the region. The role of regional hegemon to which China now aspires entails the provision of public goods, and it has begun to avail itself of its huge cache of foreign exchange reserves to provide such public goods as the Asian Infrastructure Investment Bank (AIIB), the China Development Bank (CDB), the OBOR fund, and so on. All this will naturally be conducive to economic harmony on terms favorable to China in that states do not normally like to interfere with a mutually profitable trade and investment regime. China has learned to securitize its economic clout, using informal consumer boycotts against France, Norway, Japan, the Philippines, and most recently South Korea for its installation of the terminal high-altitude area defense (THAAD) antimissile system. In the second hierarchy of technological advancement and popular living standards, China does not yet rank as high as it does in trade or aggregate GDP, despite its astounding progress. This will temporarily modulate the power the hegemon can safely wield against smaller but more advanced states because the former still needs something from the latter that they can withhold. This may also explain China's failure to take Taiwan.

China's achievement of its two centenary goals in 2021 and 2049 is no sure thing.[10] Still, given its large and still relatively rapidly growing economic base, China may reasonably expect to overtake the United States and take its place as Asian hegemon on schedule. Perhaps in view of the recent slowdown, China has not been content to rely exclusively on economic growth and diplomatic charm to bring this to pass, but has mobilized its military and paramilitary forces to implement a subtle coercive strategy to seize key vantage points in its near seas. After Tiananmen, China reached a decision that it could not rise like Japan as a mere trading state but that it must also have a powerful military to defend its interests; since that time, it has spent generously to build a powerful security apparatus. At the important Conference on Peripheral Diplomacy held in October 2013, the CCP leadership resolved to make a clear distinction between friends and enemies, to dispense positive reinforcements to the former and negative to the latter, and to use appropriate strategies to achieve global leadership. There is no question China's greater military strength has helped it to achieve a stronger position in its near seas and beyond. Yet this is a double-edged sword. To the extent that China's neighbors come to see China as a threat to their vital interests, they may opt to balance rather than bandwagon (Manila has recently opted both ways). This is still a safe option, as China has approached the brink but avoided war. Invoking the famous nine-dash line was in retrospect perhaps a tactical mistake, particularly as interpreted to claim the waters as well as the land features. China could have achieved its expansive ends more easily had it not claimed ownership of such a vast and distant maritime expanse.

Thanks to core leader Xi Jinping's visionary nationalist rhetoric and tough actions backing it up, contemporary China has come to view the rise of Xi as a tipping point in its realization of the China Dream. This, combined with the protracted economic slump in the United States and Europe, has inspired an ambitious new vision of China's role in the post-GFC world as an alternative to the failed Washington consensus. What will China's new order look like? This vision consists of both a normative model of international conduct and a set of goals to further China's national interest. Beijing tends to conflate the two, to believe that what is good for China is good for the world. There are three general principles in this vision.

First is a commitment to global economic development with the developing world receiving greater support from the developed world. Since 2013, the focus is more on the Asian neighborhood, but China has also greatly expanded its economic interests in Africa and Latin America. This is premised on the assumption that the developing world, like China during its century of humiliation, has been oppressed and exploited by the First World and deserves compensation. This entails a reformed international economic order, reducing the hegemonic role of the United States as holder of the predominant global reserve currency and principal stakeholder in international financial institutions. If the First World fails to reform to meet these just demands, China will rise to the occasion by creating new and more serviceable institutions.

Second is international political relativism—all regimes are equally legitimate, their sovereignty is sacred, and there should be no interference in internal affairs for humanitarian or any other reason. China admittedly has human rights failings, but then so does the United States, while China has pulled some seven hundred million people out of poverty and thus made a major contribution to international peace and prosperity. International value relativism coexists uneasily with domestic political absolutism, but it has been a central pillar of Chinese foreign policy since Zhou Enlai and Jawaharlal Nehru formulated the Five Principles of Peaceful Coexistence in the early 1950s. The core of the five principles is noninterference in the internal affairs of other countries, or "global democracy."

Third is a commitment to multilateralism underpinned by the central role of the United Nations (UN) as the guarantor of global security. Beginning in the 1990s, China overcame its previous suspicion of international organizations as puppets of the superpowers and became a joiner. China won UN admission over unsuccessful US resistance with the support of the developing world, and it has conscientiously cultivated its support ever since. China sees itself as the natural leader of this group, as the biggest, the most successful, the only one with a permanent seat on the UN Security Council and the only nuclear weapon state among them. China's identity as a developing country has resulted in a PRC voting record on UN General Assembly roll-call votes concurring with the developing world majority 60–80 percent of the time, far more than any other permanent member of the Security Council. China has also been a recent but avid joiner of FTAs, the most recent being with the ten-nation ASEAN (ASEAN-China FTA, or ACFTA), which took full effect in January 2010. Even runaway province Taiwan has been integrated into a trade deal, the Economic Cooperation Framework Agreement, though the island is not yet interested in accepting China's standing invitation to negotiate a peace treaty or national reunification.

CONCLUSIONS

The evidence and arguments presented in this chapter lead us to conclude that China is likely to get much of what it wants, as currently defined. China will probably overtake the United States and expand its lead over Japan and Russia. If currently extrapolated growth rates continue, it will soon have the military power to make the East and South China Seas into Chinese lakes. China will do its best to legitimize this via soft power. Certainly there are no guarantees. China faces a high debt load, a ruined environment, over-stretched banks, industrial overcapacity, a housing bubble, and a lot of other difficulties. Still, odds are good China is likely to become the leading state in East Asia and a global "pole." It has convinced relevant constituencies of the inherent justice of this narrative, and many in Asia are of the opinion the great surpassing has already occurred. The US decline, according to many, has been accelerated by the rise of Donald Trump. That may be so, but US withdrawal from the TPP and the collapse of the rebalance antedated the election, and the stunning electoral outcome also demonstrated that, to many, the US decline was already well under way.

But one question few have asked is this: What next? In the early 1980s, the late Soviet Union, according to the judgment of many Soviet and US defense analysts at the time, had finally achieved strategic parity with the United States. Forty years after being laid waste to by the Nazi invasion, the country had achieved record GDP growth rates, universal literacy, and the virtual elimination of poverty, launched the first satellite and intercontinental ballistic missile (ICBM), put the first man and woman in space, and still occupied half of Europe. But by the end of the decade, it was beginning to fall apart. What will China do when its nominal GDP surpasses that of the United States? Will China celebrate, as it did when Hong Kong returned to China in 1997? One expects it will be more discreet. But what will be China's next lodestar? Of course no one knows the future. But let us allow ourselves a few speculative guesses.

First, China's dazzling economic success story has been achieved at the cost of an intense discipline and focus in which the United States played a vital symbolic role as simultaneous bogeyman and ultimate goal. The United States may continue to be the focus of demonization (as Japan has been since its GDP was surpassed in 2010). But it will no longer function so effectively as a collective motivating symbol once that goal has been met and surpassed. There is a human tendency, after reaching a collective goal long diligently aspired to against insuperable odds, to think one can achieve all and have it all. Xi Jinping's anticorruption campaign may temper that tendency in the Chinese middle classes, but what about the elites? The BRI is a vast project that Chinese may expect to benefit from only in the distant future. Mean-while the sacrifices of lagging wages and per capita incomes and high pollution rates, inadequate health care and pensions, and the self-censorship and constraint on civil liberties that the Chinese people have willingly borne for the past several decades on behalf of the glorious socialist future will no longer seem so vitally necessary. Will there be increasingly insistent demands for governmental attention to deferred maintenance? Will the leadership incur the necessary public costs to satisfy such demands, or will it suppress them? Will it respond to added popular pressure to achieve the rebalance of the economy from exports and investment to consumption that has been promised since the twelfth five-year plan? Thus far, the Xi Jinping regime has quite dexterously blended collective nationalism and growing social demands, but this will become increasingly challenging as the population ages and growth declines.

Second, the United States is not going away. Nor is Japan, Russia, or India. The impact of China's rise on its Asian foreign policy thus far has been to increase Beijing's confidence, its generosity, and its assertiveness. Those countries that have enjoyed China's financial assistance and have supported China's foreign policies will expect that assistance to continue. The public goods China has so generously provided to the region will require China's continued support. The OBOR has been a great public-relations bonanza for China, but at a future cost that is still difficult to calculate. China may soon after rising face imperial overstretch. Contrariwise, those countries that see their interests adversely affected by China's assertiveness have grown apprehensive. The balance of power has shifted to China's advantage; everyone knows that and adjusts accordingly. Can Beijing persuade its neighbors of its benign intentions if it uses its military preponderance to get what it wants? The risk for Beijing is one of creating the very unfriendly encirclement that China has long decried.

Third, can Beijing sustain the economic performance legitimacy that has so far compensated for political reform? China's growth has slowed as the mounting incremental capital output ratio implies ever more investment is needed to sustain debt payments. As China catches up with First World technological levels, it can no longer grow by appropriating the innovations of the technological leaders because it will have reached the same level. Already China produces more steel, solar panels, coal-fired power plants, wind turbines, and many other products than it can consume or for which it can easily find international markets, and now it is moving into computers, IT, the internet of things, quantum mechanics, and biotech. Can China innovate for this new, higher value-added stage of development while insulating itself from Western cultural and ideational influences?

The purpose of this book has been to understand and to analyze the thrust of China's Asia policy since the Cold War and the implications it has had (and may continue to have) on China's neighbors. While the central event around which the regional changes of the past half century have reoriented themselves is the rise of China, our goal here is neither to celebrate nor to decry that rise, but simply to comprehend its implications. Nor is it our intent to determine what, if anything, ought to be done about it—by the Chinese, the Americans, or the rest of the Asians. What "is" can always be said to have a bearing on what "ought" to be done.[11] But that is beyond the scope of the present study. In politics, to draw on another lesson from Thucydides, such decisions are in fact most likely to be made by those with the power to make them.

NOTES

1. Mao Zedong, "On the People's Democratic Dictatorship," in *Selected Works of Mao Tse-tung* (Peking: Foreign Languages Press, 1969), 4:411–25, at p. 415.

2. Cf. Thomas Christensen, *Worse than a Monolith: Alliance Politics and Problems of Coercive Diplomacy in Asia* (Princeton, NJ: Princeton University Press, 2011).

3. Cf. Gilbert Rozman, ed., *National Identities and Bilateral Relations: Widening Gaps in East Asia and Chinese Demonization of the United States* (Stanford, CA: Stanford University Press, 2013), 1–15.

4. Richard C. Bush and Maeve Whelan-Wuest, "How Asians View America (and China)," Brookings, January 18, 2017, citing the Asian Barometer Survey, https://www.brookings.edu/blog/order-from-chaos/2017/01/18/how-asians-view-america-and-china/. These polls antedate the Trump election.

5. See Richard Wike and Bruce Stokes, "Chinese Public Sees More Powerful Role in World, Names U.S. as Top Threat," Pew Research Center, October 5, 2016, http://www.pewglobal.org/2016/10/05/chinese-public-sees-more-powerful-role-in-world-names-u-s-as-top-threat/; and Liu Kang and Chu Yun-han, eds., "China's Rise through World Public Opinion," special issue of *Contemporary Chinese Politics* 24, no. 92 (2015).

6. Josh Chin, "China Says Prepared to Lead the Global Economy If Necessary," *Wall Street Journal*, January 23, 2017, https://www.wsj.com/articles/china-says-prepared-to-lead-global-economy-if-necessary-1485178890.

7. Thus China's reclamation activities have stimulated other littoral claimants (notably the Philippines and Vietnam) to establish a physical or symbolic presence on the islands they currently control.

8. Geoff Dyer, "Beijing's Elevated Aspirations," *Financial Times*, November 14, 2010, https://www.ft.com/content/1cfa57c4-ed03-11df-9912-00144feab49a.

9. In March 2009, Rear Admiral Yang Yi of China's National Defense University argued that any discussions with claims in the South China Sea that overlapped China's "must be based on the premise that sovereignty belongs to China," and that China's desire for a favorable international image would not constrain its willingness to use force if necessary. Willy Lam, "PLA's Absolute Loyalty to the Party in Doubt," *China Brief* 9, no. 9 (April 30, 2009), http://jt.codingheads.com/program/plas-absolute-loyalty-to-the-party-in-doubt. In December 2010, Defense Minister Liang Guanglie said that "in the coming five years our military will push forward preparations for military conflict in every strategic direction. We may be living in peaceful times but we can never forget war." Peter Foster, "China Preparing for Armed Conflict 'in Every Direction,'" *The Telegraph*, December 29, 2010, http://www.telegraph.co.uk/news/worldnews/asia/china/8229789/China-preparing-for-armed-conflict-in-every-direction.html. General Luo Yuan of the PLA Academy of Military Science complained that Washington is a "deliberate spoiler" pursuing a containment policy toward China in Southeast Asia. Andrew Chubb, "Who Does Major-General Luo Yuan Speak For?" *Southseaconversations: China Comments on the South [China] Sea Disputes*, https://southseaconversations.wordpress.com/2012/04/27/who-does-major-general-luo-yuan-speak-for. Senior Colonel Liu Mingfu has (unofficially) proposed replacing "peaceful rise" with China's "military rise" (*junshi jueqi*) to

primacy in the "post-American era." Philip Saunders, "Will China's Dream Turn into America's Nightmare?" *China Brief* 10, no. 7 (April 1, 2010), https://jamestown.org/program/will-chinas-dream-turn-into-americas-nightmare.

10. China is aiming to have doubled its 2010 GDP and per capita incomes and completed the building of a moderately prosperous society by 2020. By the middle of this century, it should be a modern socialist country that is prosperous, strong, democratic, culturally advanced, and harmonious.

11. See John R. Searle, *Speech Acts: An Essay in the Philosophy of Language* (New York: Cambridge University Press, 1969), 131–36.

Selected Bibliography

Bajpai, Kanti, Huang Jing, and Kishore Mahbubani. *China-India Relations: Cooperation and Conflict*. New York: Routledge, 2016.

Bao Zonghe, and Yu-Shan Wu, eds. *Chong xin jian shi zheng bian zhong de liang an guan xi li lun* [Revisiting theories of cross-Strait relations]. Taibei Shi: Wu nan tu shu chu ban you xian gong si, 2012.

Bardhan, Pranab K. *Awakening Giants, Feet of Clay: Assessing the Economic Rise of China and India*. Princeton, NJ: Princeton University Press, 2010.

Bernstein, Thomas P., and Hua-yu Li, eds. *China Learns from the Soviet Union, 1949–Present*. Lanham, MD: Rowman & Littlefield, 2010.

Blackwill, Robert, and Jennifer Harris. *War by Other Means*. Cambridge, MA: Belknap Press, Harvard University, 2016.

Breslauer, George. *Gorbachev and Yeltsin as Leaders*. New York: Cambridge University Press, 2002.

Breslauer, George, and Victoria Bonnell. *Russia in the New Century: Stability or Disorder?* Boulder, CO: Westview Press, 2001.

Breslin, Shaun. *China and the Global Political Economy*. New York: Palgrave Macmillan, 2013.

Callahan, William A. *China Dreams: 20 Visions of the Future*. New York: Oxford University Press, 2013.

Chellaney, Brahma. *Asian Juggernaught: The Rise of China, India, and Japan*. New Delhi: HarperCollins, 2006.

Chen Jie. *Zhongguo min zhong zheng zhi zhi chi de ce liang yu fen xi* [Popular political support in urban China]. Guangzhou: Zhongshan da xue chu ban she, 2011.

Cheung, Tai Ming. *Fortifying China: The Struggle to Build a Modern Defense Economy*. Ithaca, NY: Cornell University Press, 2009.

Christensen, Thomas J. *The China Challenge: Shaping the Choices of a Rising Power*. New York: Norton, 2015.

———. *Worse than a Monolith: Alliance Politics and Problems of Coercive Diplomacy in Asia*. Princeton, NJ: Princeton University Press, 2011.

Chung, Chien-Peng. *Contentious Integration: Post–Cold War Japan-China Relations in the Asia-Pacific*. Farnham, UK: Ashgate, 2014.

Davin, Dalia, and Barbara Harris-White. *China-India: Pathways of Economic and Social Development*. Oxford: Oxford University Press, 2014.

Deng, Yong. *China's Struggle for Status: The Realignment of International Relations*. New York: Cambridge University Press, 2008.

Deng, Yong, and Feiling Wang. *China Rising*. Lanham, MD: Rowman & Littlefield, 2005.

Deng Xiaoping fang wen Xinjiapo san shi zhou nian ji nian lun tan [Deng Xiaoping's Singapore talks on the 30th anniversary of his visit]. Xinjiapo: Ba fang wen hua chuang zuo shi, 2009.

Denoon, David B. H. *The Economic and Strategic Rise of China and India: Asian Realignments after the 1997 Financial Crisis.* New York: Palgrave Macmillan, 2007.

Dittmer, Lowell. *Sino-Soviet Normalization and Its International Implications, 1945–1990.* Seattle: University of Washington Press, 1992.

Dittmer, Lowell, and Samuel S. Kim, eds. *China's Quest for National Identity.* Ithaca, NY: Cornell University Press, 1993.

Dittmer, Lowell, and George Yu, eds. *China, the Developing World, and the New Global Dynamic.* Boulder, CO: Rienner, 2010.

Eder, Thomas Stephan. *China-Russia Relations in Central Asia: Energy Policy, Beijing's New Assertiveness and 21st Century Geopolitics.* Wiesbaden: Springer Verlag, 2014.

Emmott, Bill. *Rivals: How the Power Struggle between China, India, and Japan Will Shape Our Next Decade.* New York: Houghton Mifflin Harcourt, 2008.

Fenby, Jonathan. *Will China Dominate the 21st Century?* Malden, MA: Polity Press, 2014.

Feng, Chongyi. *Zhong gong dang nei de zi you zhu yi: cong Chen Duxiu dao Li Shenzhi* [Pluralism within the Chinese Communist Party: From Chen Duxiu to Li Shenzhi]. Carle Place, NY: Ming Jing chubanshe, 2009.

Fingar, Thomas, ed. *The New Great Game: China and South and Central Asia in the Era of Reform.* Stanford, CA: Stanford University Press, 2016.

———, ed. *Uneasy Partnerships: China's Engagement with Japan, the Koreas, and Russia in the Era of Reform.* Stanford, CA: Stanford University Press, 2017.

Fogel, Joshua A., ed. *The Teleology of the Modern Nation-State: Japan and China.* Philadelphia: University of Pennsylvania Press, 2005.

Foot, Rosemary, ed. *Across the Divide: The Domestic and Global in Politics and Society.* New York: Oxford University Press, 2013.

Foot, Rosemary, and Andrew Walter. *China, the United States, and Global Order.* New York: Cambridge University Press, 2011.

Friedberg, Aaron. *A Contest for Supremacy.* New York: Norton, 2012.

Gao, Yu. *Nan er Xi Jinping* [Male, Xi Jinping]. Park, NY: Ming jing chu ban she, 2015.

Garver, John W. *Protracted Contest: Sino-Indian Rivalry in the Twentieth Century.* Seattle: University of Washington Press, 2001.

Genscher, Hans Dietrich. *Erinnerungen.* Berlin: Siedler Verlag, 1995.

Gilboy, George J., and Eric Heginbotham. *Chinese and Indian Strategic Behavior: Growing Power and Alarm.* New York: Cambridge University Press, 2012.

Godwin, Paul H. B., and Alice L. Miller. *China's Forbearance Has Limits: Chinese Threat and Retaliation Signaling and Its Implications for a Sino-American Military Confrontation.* Washington, DC: National Defense University Press, 2013.

Goldstein, Avery. *Deterrence and Security in the 21st Century: China, Britain, France, and the Enduring Legacy of the Nuclear Revolution.* Stanford, CA: Stanford University Press, 2000.

Goodman, David S. G., and Gerald Segal. *China Deconstructs: Politics, Trade and Regionalism.* New York: Routledge, 1994.

Gordon, Sandy. *India's Rise as an Asian Power: Nation, Neighborhood and Region.* Washington, DC: Georgetown University Press, 2014.

Gottlieb, Thomas M. *Chinese Foreign Policy Factionalism and the Origins of the Strategic Triangle.* Santa Monica, CA: Rand Corp., 1977.

Guo, Zhongjun. *Taiwan di qu min zhu zhuan xing zhong de min cui zhu yi: 1987–2008* [Populism in democratic transition in Taiwan]. Shanghai: Xue lin chu ban she, 2014.

Haggard, Stephan, and Marcus Noland. *Hard Target: Sanctions, Inducements and the Case of North Korea.* Stanford, CA: Stanford University Press, 2016.

Heinzig, Dieter. *Die Sowjetunion und das kommunistische China 1945–1950: Der beschwerliche Weg zum Buendnis.* Baden-Baden: Nomos Verlagsgesellschaft, 1998.

Henders, Susan J., ed. *Democratization and Identity: Regimes and Ethnicity in East and Southeast Asia.* Lanham, MD: Rowman & Littlefield, 2007.

Holslag, Jonathan. *China's Coming War with Asia.* Cambridge, MA: Polity Press, 2015.

Hook, Glenn D., and Hasegawa Harukiyo, eds. *The Political Economy of Japanese Globalization*. New York: Routledge, 2001.

Hu Angang, and Yan Yilong, eds. *Zhongguo guo qing yu fa zhan* [China's national essence and development]. Beijing: Zhongguo ren min da xue chu ban she, 2016.

Hughes, Christopher W. *Japan's Security Agenda: Military, Economic and Environmental Dimensions*. Boulder, CO: Rienner, 2004.

Hung, Ho-fung. *The China Boom: Why China Will Not Rule the World*. New York: Columbia University Press, 2016.

Hunt, Michael. *The Genesis of Chinese Communist Foreign Policy*. New York: Columbia University Press, 1996.

Ikenberry, G. John, and Takashi Inoguchi, eds. *Troubled Triangle*. New York: Palgrave Macmillan, 2013.

Ikenberry, G. John, and Michael Mastanduno, eds. *International Relations Theory and the Asia-Pacific*. New York: Columbia University Press, 2003.

Jian, Chen. *Mao's China and the Cold War*. Chapel Hill: University of North Carolina Press, 2001.

Johnston, Alastair Iain, and Robert S. Ross. *Engaging China: The Management of an Emerging Power*. New York: Routledge, 1999.

Jowitt, Ken. *New World Disorder: The Leninist Extinction*. Berkeley: University of California Press, 1992.

Katzenstein, Peter J., and Takashi Shiraishi, eds. *Beyond Japan: The Dynamics of East Asian Regionalism*. Ithaca, NY: Cornell University Press, 2006.

Kawashima, Yutaka. *Japanese Foreign Policy at the Crossroads: Challenges and Options for the 21st Century*. Washington, DC: Brookings, 2003.

Kim, Samuel S., ed. *China and the World: Chinese Foreign Policy Faces the New Millennium*. Boulder, CO: Westview Press, 1998.

———. *China In and Out of the Changing World Order*. Princeton, NJ: Center of International Studies, 1991.

———. *China, the United Nations, and World Order*. Princeton, NJ: Princeton University Press, 1979.

Kissinger, Henry. *On China*. New York: Penguin Books, 2012.

Lampton, David M. *The Making of China's Foreign and Security Policy in the Era of Reform*. Stanford, CA: Stanford University Press, 2000.

———. *Same Bed, Different Dreams: Managing US-China Relations, 1989–2000*. Berkeley: University of California Press, 2001.

Lanteigne, Marc. *Chinese Foreign Policy: An Introduction*. New York: Routledge, 2013.

Li, Peng, ed. *Tai hai an quan kao cha* [Looking at security in the Taiwan Strait]. Beijing: Jiu zhou chu ban she, 2005.

Li Xiuhua. *E luo si yu dong ya di qu di neng yuan he zuo* [Energy cooperation between Russia and East Asia]. Beijing: Beijing shifan daxue chubanshe, 2011.

Liu Junren. *Jiang jun da huo lin tou: Xi Jinping qing jun huan jiang xingdong* [General Catastrophe: Xi Jinping and the army]. Hong Kong [Xianggang]: Nei mu chu ban she, 2015.

Liu Mingfu. *The China Dream: Great Power Thinking and Strategic Posture in the Post-American Era*. New York: CN Times Books, 2015.

Lord, Carnes, and Andrew S. Erickson. *Rebalancing U.S. Forces: Basing and Forward Presence in the Asia-Pacific*. Annapolis, MD: Naval Institute Press, 2014.

Luethi, Lorenz M. *The Sino-Soviet Split: Cold War in the Communist World*. Princeton, NJ: Princeton University Press, 2008.

Lukin, Alexander. *The Bear Watches the Dragon: Russia's Perceptions of China and the Evolution of Russian-Chinese Relations since the 18th Century*. Armonk, NY: Sharpe, 2003.

McGiffert, Carola, ed. *Chinese Images of the United States*. Washington, DC: CSIS Press, 2005.

Mann, James. *About Face: A History of America's Curious Relationship with China from Nixon to Clinton*. New York: Alfred Knopf; distributed by Random House, 1999.

———. *The China Fantasy: How Our Leaders Explain Away Chinese Repression*. New York: Viking, 2007.

Nathan, Andrew J., and Andrew Scobell. *China's Search for Security*. New York: Columbia University Press, 2012.

Norris, William J. *Chinese Economic Statecraft: Commercial Actors, Grand Strategy, and State Control*. Ithaca, NY: Cornell University Press, 2016.

Olcott, Martha Brill. *Central Asia's Second Chance*. Washington, DC: Brookings, 2005.

Pei Minxin, ed. *Zhongnan hai de xuan ze* [The choice in the South China Sea]. Singapore: Ba fang wen hua qi ye gong si, 2004.

Percival, Bronson. *The Dragon Looks South: China and Southeast Asia in the New Century*. New York: Praeger, 2007.

Pomfret, Richard. *The Central Asian Economies since Independence*. Princeton, NJ: Princeton University Press, 2006.

Radchenko, Sergey. *Two Suns in the Heavens: The Sino-Soviet Struggle for Supremacy, 1962–1967*. Stanford, CA: Stanford University Press, 2009.

Reardon, Lawrence. *The Reluctant Dragon: Crisis Cycles in Chinese Foreign Economic Policy*. Hong Kong: Hong Kong University Press, 2012.

Reilly, James. *Strong Society, Smart State: The Rise of Public Opinion in China's Japan Policy*. New York: Columbia University Press, 2012.

Ross, Robert S., and Jo Inge Bekkevold. *China in the Era of Xi Jinping: Domestic and Foreign Policy Challenges*. Washington, DC: Georgetown University Press, 2016.

Rozman, Gilbert, ed. *China's Foreign Policy*. New York: Palgrave Macmilllan, 2013.

———. *Chinese Strategic Thought toward Asia*. New York: Palgrave Macmillan, 2010.

———. *The Sino-Russian Challenge to the World Order: National Identities, Bilateral Relations, and East versus West in the 2010s*. Stanford, CA: Stanford University Press, 2014.

Scobell, Andrew, and Larry M. Wortzel. *Shaping China's Security Environment: The Role of the People's Liberation Army*. Washington, DC: Strategic Studies Institute, 2006.

Shambaugh, David. *China Goes Global: The Partial Power*. New York: Oxford University Press, 2013.

———, ed. *Power Shift: China and Asia's New Dynamics*. Berkeley: University of California Press, 2005.

Shao Binhong, ed. *The World in 2020 according to China*. Leiden: Brill, 2014.

Shao, Kuo-kang. *Zhou Enlai and the Foundations of Chinese Foreign Policy*. New York: St. Martin's, 1996.

Shen, Simon. *Jie gou Zhongguo meng: Zhongguo min zu zhu yi yu Zhong Mei guan xi de hu dong (1999–2014)* [Deconstructing the Chinese dream: The dynamics of Chinese nationalism and Sino-American relations]. Hong Kong: Zhong wen da xue chu ban she, 2015.

Shi Weimin, et al. *Zhengzhi rentong yu weijing yanli* [Political identity and crisis pressure]. Beijing: Zhongguo shehui kexue chubanshe, 2014.

Shirk, Susan L. China: *Fragile Superpower*. Oxford; New York: Oxford University Press, 2007.

———. *How China Opened Its Door: The Political Success of the PRC's Foreign Trade and Investment Reforms*. Washington, DC: Brookings, 1994.

Slater, Dan. *Ordering Power: Contentious Politics and Authoritarian Leviathans in Southeast Asia*. New York: Cambridge University Press, 2010.

Steinberg, James, and Michael E. O'Hanlon. *Strategic Reassurance and Resolve: U.S.-China Relations in the Twenty-First Century*. Princeton, NJ: Princeton University Press, 2014.

Storey, Ian. *Southeast Asia and the Rise of China: The Search for Security*. New York: Routledge, 2011.

Sun, Xiyou. *Zhongguo "yi dai yi lu" zhan lüe de li lun shi ye* [New theory of China's "One Belt, One Road" strategy]. Beijing: Zhongguo she hui ke xue chu ban she, 2015.

Sutter, Robert. *Chinese Foreign Relations: Power and Politics since the Cold War*. Lanham, MD: Rowman & Littlefield, 2005.

———. *Foreign Relations of the PRC: The Legacies and Constraints of China's International Politics since 1949*. Lanham, MD: Rowman & Littlefield, 2013.

Swanstrom, Niklas. *Foreign Devils, Dictatorship, or Institutional Control: China's Foreign Policy towards Southeast Asia*. Uppsala, Sweden: Uppsala University, Department of Peace and Conflict Research, 2001.

Van Ness, Peter. *Revolution and Chinese Foreign Policy: Peking's Support for Wars of National Liberation.* Berkeley: University of California Press, 1970.

Vogel, Ezra F., Yuan Ming, and Tanaka Akihiko, eds. *The Golden Age of the U.S.-China-Japan Triangle, 1972–1989.* Cambridge, MA: Harvard University Press, 2002.

Voskkressenski, Alexei D. *Russia and China: A Theory of Inter-State Relations.* New York: Routledge Curzon, 2003.

Wan, Ming. *The Political Economy of East Asia: Striving for Wealth and Power.* Washington, DC: CQ Press, 2008.

———. *Understanding Japan-China Relations.* Singapore: World Scientific, 2016.

Wang, Dong. *The United States and China: A History from the 18th Century to the Present.* Lanham, MD: Rowman & Littlefield, 2013.

Wang Weiguang. *Makesizhuyi zhongguohua di cui xin chengguo: Xi Jinping zhi guoli zheng sixiang yanjiu* [The latest achievement of the Sinicization of Marxism: A study of Xi Jinping's political thought]. Beijing: Zhongguo she hui ke xue chu ban she, 2016.

Wang Weinan. *Zhong Mei guan xi zhong de Taiwan wen ti, 1948–1982* [Sino-American relations and the Taiwan issue, 1948–1982]. Jinan Shi: Shandong ren min chu ban she, 2007.

Weatherbee, Donald E. *International Relations in Southeast Asia: The Struggle for Autonomy.* 3rd ed. Lanham, MD: Rowman & Littlefield, 2015.

Weatherby, Robert. *Making China Strong: The Role of Nationalism in Chinese Thinking on Democracy and Human Rights.* New York: Palgrave Macmillan, 2014.

Womack, Brantly. *Asymmetry and International Relationships.* New York: Cambridge University Press, 2016.

———. *China among Unequals: Asymmetric Foreign Relationships in Asia.* Singapore: World Scientific, 2010.

Wu Wei. *Zhongguo bashi niandai zhengzhi gaige di qianmu hou* [On stage and backstage: China's political reform in the 1980s]. Hong Kong: Xin Shiji chubanshe, 2013.

Wu Yu-Shan. *Comparative Economic Transformations: Mainland China, Hungary, the Soviet Union, and Taiwan.* Stanford, CA: Stanford University Press, 1994.

Yan, Xuetong, ed. *Ancient Chinese Thought, Modern Chinese Power.* Princeton, NJ: Princeton University Press, 2011.

Yuzawa, Takeshi. *Japan's Security Policy and the ASEAN Regional Forum: The Search for Multilateral Security in the Asia-Pacific.* New York: Routledge, 2007.

Zhang Lihai, ed. *Dui Tai jun shi dou zheng zhun bei zheng zhi gong zuo yan jiu* [A political work report on preparations for the military struggle with Taiwan]. Xi'an: Xi'an zheng zhi xue yuan xun lian bu, 2002.

Zhao Dingxin. *She hui yu zheng zhi yun dong jiang yi* [Social and political movements discussed]. Beijing: She hui ke xue wen xian chu ban she, 2006.

Zheng Yongnian, and Liang Fook Lye, eds. *East Asia Developments and Challenges.* Singapore; Hackensack, NJ: World Scientific, 2013.

Zheng Yongnian, and Wang Gungwu, eds. *China and the New International Order.* New York: Routledge, 2010.

Index

Marxist-Leninist, 2, 260. *See also* Marxism-Leninism
Marxist-Leninist-Maoist thought, 21
McMahon Line, 203, 205
Meiji Restoration, 106
middle-income trap, 45
mini triangle, 147. *See also* Taiwan triangle
Modi, Narendra, 211, 216, 217, 218, 220
Mongols, 2, 60, 62
multilateral system, 246
multipolar balance, 94
multipolar world, 226. *See also* multilateral system; multipolar balance
mutual defense alliance, 50, 107, 242, 245, 259, 261

national identity, 18, 21, 47, 60; American, 19, 20; Chinese, 19, 20, 22, 43, 47; difference/gap, 26; Indian, 201
national liberation movement, 173, 176, 242
National Liberation War, 25
Nehru, Jawaharlal, 201, 203, 204, 205, 272; Nehruvian, 202
New Asian Security Concept, 37, 38
"New Normal," 264
New Thinking (*novo myshlenie*), 67
Next Steps in Strategic Partnership (NSSP), 220
Nine-dash line, 183, 187, 188, 189
1992 consensus, 148, 151, 154
Nixon Doctrine, 3, 65, 180, 190, 259
Nonaligned Movement, 170, 184, 188, 189, 204, 242, 271
Nordpolitik, 157, 161, 162, 163, 164
North-South Reconciliation/Reunification, 159, 161

Official Development Aid (ODA), 123, 180
One Belt, One Road (OBOR), 7, 22, 35, 116, 127, 191, 193, 194, 212, 213, 216, 217, 225, 265, 266, 269, 270, 274
"One China," 9, 112, 139, 143, 144, 148, 151, 154, 163
"one country, two systems," 144, 162, 163

path dependency, 251, 252

patron-client paradigm, 242
peaceful coexistence, 25, 26, 38, 63, 203, 272
peaceful development, 4, 5, 38, 39, 96, 116, 124, 186, 244, 270. *See also* peaceful rise
peaceful evolution (*heping yanbian*), 26, 29, 48, 73, 147
peaceful nuclear explosion, 207
peaceful rise, 38, 96, 124, 151, 211, 244, 261, 270
perestroika, 67
postcommunist liberal democracy, 68
power transition, 43, 44, 46, 47, 48, 51, 99, 263; peaceful transition, 51, 263
pseudo-Marxist idea, 29
Putin, Vladimir, 8, 73, 74, 77, 78, 79, 81, 85, 87, 90, 91, 92, 93, 94, 95, 97, 98, 99, 100, 106

quadrangle, 223, 228
quadripartite alliance, 246

reform and opening (*gaige kaifang*), 67, 223, 238
regional polarization, 40
rejuvenation (*fuxing*), 20; great rejuvenation of the Chinese nation, 44
responsible great power, 42, 225
responsible stakeholder, 42, 48. *See also* responsible great power
revival of China, 44. *See also* rejuvenation

San Francisco Peace Treaty, 108, 128, 129
second-strike capability, 190, 208
security dilemma, 28, 35, 39, 251; Sino-US, 35
Senkaku/Diaoyu islets, 9, 40, 117, 122, 128, 183, 264, 265; territorial disputes, 108
Shanghai Communiqué, 144
Shigeru, Yoshida, 107, 108, 122
Silk Road Economic Belt (SREB), 22, 85
Sino-American relations, 23, 27
Sino-Indian link, 223, 228. *See also* Sino-Indian relationship
Sino-Indian relationship, 202, 205, 214, 224, 225
Sino-Indian War, 212

About the Author

Lowell Dittmer is professor of political science at the University of California at Berkeley, where he teaches Chinese and Asian comparative politics, and editor of *Asian Survey*. He is currently working on an analysis of China's recent Asia policy. Recent works include *Sino-Soviet Normalization and Its International Implications* (1992), *China's Quest for National Identity* (with Samuel Kim, 1993), *China under Reform* (1994), *Liu Shaoqi and the Chinese Cultural Revolution* (revised edition, 1997), *Informal Politics in East Asia* (edited with Haruhiro Fukui and Peter N. S. Lee, 2000), *South Asia's Nuclear Security Dilemma: India, Pakistan, and China* (2005), *China's Deep Reform: Domestic Politics in Transition* (edited with Guoli Liu; Rowman & Littlefield, 2006), *China, the Developing World, and the New Global Dynamic* (2010), *Burma or Myanmar? The Struggle for National Identity* (2010), and many scholarly articles. His most recent book is *Routledge Handbook of Chinese Security* (edited with Maochun Yu, 2015).

ASIA IN WORLD POLITICS
Series Editor: Samuel S. Kim